D1564906

HISTORICAL DICTIONARIES
OF RELIGIONS, PHILOSOPHIES, AND MOVEMENTS
Jon Woronoff, Series Editor

Historical Dictionary of Schopenhauer's Philosophy

David E. Cartwright

Historical Dictionaries of Religions, Philosophies, and Movements, No. 55

The Scarecrow Press, Inc.
Lanham, Maryland • Toronto • Oxford
2005

SCARECROW PRESS, INC.

Published in the United States of America
by Scarecrow Press, Inc.
A wholly owned subsidiary of
The Rowman & Littlefield Publishing Group, Inc.
4501 Forbes Boulevard, Suite 200, Lanham, Maryland 20706
www.scarecrowpress.com

PO Box 317
Oxford
OX2 9RU, UK

British Library Cataloguing in Publication Information Available

Library of Congress Cataloging-in-Publication Data

Cartwright, David E.
  Historical dictionary of Schopenhauer's philosophy / David E. Cartwright.
      p. cm. — (Historical dictionaries of religions, philosophies, and movements ;
  no. 55)
    Includes bibliographical references (p.).
    ISBN 0-8108-5324-8 (hardcover : alk. paper)
    1. Schopenhauer, Arthur, 1788–1860—Dictionaries. I. Title. II. Series.

B3101.C37 2005
193—dc22

                                                                      2004015481

∞™ The paper used in this publication meets the minimum requirements of
American National Standard for Information Sciences—Permanence of Paper
for Printed Library Materials, ANSI/NISO Z39.48-1992.
Manufactured in the United States of America.

To those who have made, sustained, and will continue me:
Ernest and Audrey Cartwright,
Carol Lohry Cartwright, and
Elyse Lohry Cartwright

Schopenhauer daguerreotype, 3 September 1852. Used with permission from the Arthur Schopenhauer-Archiv, Stadt- und Universitätsbibliothek, Frankfurt am Main

Contents

Editor's Foreword

All philosophers, no matter how brilliant or varied their views, end up being summarized by a number of basic concepts and then marketed (or written off) with a label. Arthur Schopenhauer, like the others, could easily be summed up by terms (sometimes capitalized for effect), and in his case, those terms could be Will, Will to Life, representation, sufficient reason, the single thought, or forces of nature. This process of simplification might actually be easier in his case, since he wrote relatively little. But what he wrote was infinitely richer and covered a multitude of topics, some of which were ignored by philosophers before him and even during his time, and with several not really catching on until decades later, such as human sexuality—including homosexuality and love—respect for animals, interest in Eastern religions, science, but also suicide. His ethics looked closely at good and evil, considered compassion and philanthropy, and he excelled in his appreciation of the arts and aesthetics. All this still strikes a bell today and is worthwhile reading. What is less popular at present is the label pessimism, which has gone out of fashion. But even his intense concern—perhaps obsession—with death remains topical.

The content and range of Schopenhauer's thought has made him popular in some circles, and very unpopular in others, especially given his contempt for philosophers and philosophy professors who did not take their calling seriously. And some of his ideas will seem a bit dated and others may even be just wrong, who knows? But it is hard to tell without taking a good look at his life, his writings, his theories and concepts, and his terminology. This is greatly facilitated by the *Historical Dictionary of Schopenhauer's Philosophy*. A good overview of his life can be obtained in the chronology, and then again in a different form in the introduction, which also provides a gloss of his philosophy. The details are presented, explained, and otherwise conveyed by the numerous entries in the dictionary. But those who are truly interested will obviously not stop there, and they should consider further reading of Schopenhauer, either in the original or in translation, as well as other books and articles on specific areas or the whole of his philosophy as presented in the bibliography.

If you are going to devote your adult life to a philosopher, and spend countless years studying his works and then lecturing on them to successive classes of students, you should certainly know his works thoroughly, preferably in the original, and understand what he is trying to say. There is no requirement that you should agree with him, let alone find his ideas personally enriching, but that helps. At any rate, these qualifications apply to the author of this volume, David E. Cartwright. Professor Cartwright has been teaching philosophy, including Schopenhauer, at the University of Wisconsin–Whitewater since 1982. He has also published numerous articles and introductions to translations of several of Schopenhauer's works, along with a related translation, and he is presently writing an intellectual biography of Schopenhauer. He has long been active in the Schopenhauer Society. It is therefore not surprising that this volume not only relates what the philosopher said and sought to convey, but it gives us a feeling for the man and his passions.

Jon Woronoff
Series Editor

Acknowledgments

This book should be viewed as an expression of the act I have undertaken to relieve what I sense as a tremendous debt of gratitude. This debt is owed to a diverse group of individuals. Some of these people were my teachers; some were and continue to be my colleagues; and some I know only through their writings. In any case, I owe what is best about my understanding of Schopenhauer to these individuals, whereas, my own misunderstandings stem from my own limitations and inabilities to have learned better from them. My sense of this debt of gratitude may only be partially relieved, however, since some of my benefactors are dead and cannot receive my thanks. Still, I must thank John E. Atwell, Claudia Card, Patrick Gardiner, Georges Goedert, D. W. Hamlyn, Richard Howey, Angelika Hübscher, Arthur Hübscher, Christopher Janaway, Ludger Lütkehaus, Bryan Magee, Rudolf Malter, Jörg Salaquarda, Wolfgang Schirmacher, Ivan Soll, Richard Taylor, Julien Young, and Günter Zöller. In a broader sense, I must also thank my colleagues in the Schopenhauer-Gesellschaft and in its North American Division, especially Joachim Baer, Dale Jacquette, G. Steven Neeley, Dale Snow, and James Snow.

More obliquely, I must thank Friedrich Nietzsche. Some 25 years ago, I was first drawn to study Schopenhauer so I could understand Nietzsche more deeply. In this regard, I benefited substantially from Walter Kaufmann's translations of Nietzsche and E. F. J. Payne's translations of Schopenhauer. These talented translators enabled me to read both philosophers, and they stimulated me to learn German in order to read what they had not translated.

My colleagues in the Department of Philosophy and Religious Studies at the University of Wisconsin–Whitewater, Richard Brooks, Wade Dazey, Crista Lebens, Ann Luther, and Andrea Nye, also deserve my gratitude. They have supported my study of Schopenhauer, and they have patiently participated in many discussions of his thought.

Vickie L. Schmidt deserves special mention. She brought a keen mind to the production of this manuscript, and she improved my thought through her many queries and calls for clarification. Jacob Bare should be credited for much of the bibliography, and it would have been less thorough without his good work. For inviting me to write this book and for providing guidelines for its preparation, I must also thank the series editor, Jon Woronoff.

I must thank the Arthur Schopenhauer Archiv, Stadt- und Universitaetbibliothek, Frankfurt am Main, for permission to use the Ludwig Sigismund Ruhl portrait of Schopenhauer (1815) for the cover and the daguerreotype of Schopenhauer, 3 September 1852.

The order in which people are mentioned within the acknowledgment appears as if it were also an ordering of significance of these individuals for that which requires acknowledgment. But let me get to the thing in itself of this appearance by thanking Arthur Schopenhauer last. My study of Schopenhauer has transformed my life. He allowed me to understand what it means to say that the world is my representation, although I do not see the world as my will.

Reader's Note

Schopenhauer viewed his life as one thing and his philosophy as another, even though he believed that his philosophy was the purpose of his life. The merits of his philosophy stood alone, he thought, and to recognize its merits does not require knowledge of his life. In this regard, he was a man of his times. His philosophical hero, Immanuel Kant, held the same view, as did his later *bête noire*, Georg Wilhelm Friedrich Hegel. Although our age might have schooled us to reject this view, or at least to be deeply suspicious about it, I have given Schopenhauer his way in this introduction by providing separate glosses of his life and his philosophy. Certainly, there are overlapping points of contact in these glosses, since a major theme in Schopenhauer's life concerns how he came to his philosophy and how his faith in the truth of his views sustained him through the many years during which his thought was virtually ignored. He lived, he often claimed, for philosophy and for the truth, and in this way he thought he was unlike many of his contemporaries, whom he accused of living by philosophy, that is, of using philosophy as a means for advancing their own limited, self-serving ends.

The gloss of Schopenhauer's life presents a narrative that weaves the significant events of his life, which are given in the chronology, within the greater fabric of his life. It enables readers to better understand the highlights of his life by placing them in a context that grounds them in areas of less brightness. It also introduces a number of figures and concepts that are given separate entries within the dictionary. The gloss of Schopenhauer's philosophy serves the same purpose. It enables readers to place the various philosophical concepts and figures found in the dictionary within the general context of his entire philosophical thought. Of course, for those whose knowledge of Schopenhauer's life and philosophy is thin, the glosses should provide the necessary knowledge for a meaningful search for entries within the dictionary.

In the preface to the first edition of *The Two Fundamental Problems of Ethics*, Schopenhauer compared his philosophy to Thebes with a hundred gates. One can enter it from any direction and through any gate and arrive at the direct path to its center. It is my hope that any entry concerning Schopenhauer's key ideas, concepts, doctrines, or philosophical figures related to his thought, will open a gate that leads the reader to a basic understanding of his philosophy. Beginning with any particular entry, the reader will notice that there are some words in bold type, and there may also be at the conclusion of the entry a *see also*. Words in bold type indicate topics that have their own entries, and the *see also* refers to related entries that are not specifically mentioned in the text for that particular entry. By reading these additional entries, and the subsequent entries listed therein as bold words or under a *see also*, and by following this practice in each instance, readers will find that they have read virtually all of the entries in the dictionary.

For many of the entries concerning his philosophical ideas or doctrines, I have not provided specific reference to one of Schopenhauer's books. This generally indicates that an entry deals with a topic that is broadly discussed throughout his writings. When an entry does refer to one of his books, I cite the title and the relevant volume, chapter, section, or essay title. This mode of citation should enable readers to locate the relevant discussion in any edition of one of Schopenhauer's books. When I refer to one of Schopenhauer's letters, I always provide the name of its recipient and the date of the letter. This form of citation will allow readers to easily locate the letter in Arthur Hübscher's edition of *Arthur Schopenhauer: Gesammelte Briefe* (Bonn: Grundmann, 1987). My references to Schopenhauer's *Nachlass* are to the specific volume, sections or sections of specifically entitled essays in E. F. J. Payne's translation of *Arthur Schopenhauer: Manuscript Remains in Four Volumes* (Oxford: Berg, 1988–1989).

References to titles of Schopenhauer's books are from the translations provided by E. F. J. Payne, and I have also followed his translation for Schopenhauer's German, with three exceptions. He typically translated "*Erkenntnis*" as "knowledge," and I have used the broader term "cognition," reserving "knowledge" for Schopenhauer's use of "*Wissen*." Likewise, I have deviated from Payne by rendering "*Erscheinung*" as "appearance" and not as "phenomenon." Lastly, I have used "intuition" for "*Anschauung*," instead of "perception," a term I have reserved for Schopenhauer's use of the term "*Wahrnehmung*." In all cases, I have given the German in parentheses for each entry.

Chronology

1788   On February 22 Arthur Schopenhauer is born in the free city of Danzig (now Gdańsk, Poland) as the first child and only son of Heinrich Floris Schopenhauer, a successful merchant, and Johanna Schopenhauer (née Trosiener), later a popular writer and novelist.

1793   Schopenhauer's family moves to the free city of Hamburg prior to the Prussian annexation of Danzig.

1797   Schopenhauer's only sibling, a sister, Louise Adelaide (Adele) is born on 12 June. In July Schopenhauer travels to France with his father, and he remains in Le Havre to live for two years with the family of a friend of his father.

1799   Schopenhauer returns to Hamburg from France. In August he is enrolled in Dr. Johann Heinrich Christian Runge's private school, an institution geared to educating future merchants.

1803   In May Schopenhauer begins a tour with his family of Holland, England, France, Switzerland, and Austria. The tour is a reward for Schopenhauer's agreement to undergo training as a merchant instead of pursuing an education for an academic career. To learn English, Schopenhauer lives for six months in England.

1804   In August Schopenhauer returns to Hamburg. From September until December he is apprenticed to a merchant in Danzig.

1805   In January Schopenhauer begins service as an apprentice to a merchant in Hamburg. On 20 April Schopenhauer's father dies. His father's death is likely a suicide.

1806 Schopenhauer's mother and sister move to Weimar after selling the family business.

1807 In June Schopenhauer abandons his training as a merchant and he prepares for a university education by enrolling in the gymnasium at Gotha. Schopenhauer quits school in reaction to being penalized for writing a lampoon of one of his teachers. He moves to Weimar, living separately from his mother and sister, and he enrolls in the gymnasium at Weimar in December.

1809 Upon reaching the age of majority Schopenhauer gains control of his inheritance from his father's estate (19,000 talers). In October he matriculates as a student of medicine at the University of Göttingen.

1810 Schopenhauer studies philosophy under Gottlob Ernst Schulze, whose recommendation of Plato and Immanuel Kant introduces Schopenhauer to the two philosophers he would esteem the most.

1811 In the fall Schopenhauer transfers to the University of Berlin to study philosophy, where he would attend lectures by Johann Gottlieb Fichte and Friedrich Ernst Daniel Schleiermacher.

1813 In May Schopenhauer leaves Berlin, because of a possible attack by Napoleon, and he moves to Rudolstadt, where from June to September he writes his dissertation, *On the Fourfold Root of the Principle of Sufficient Reason*. In October Schopenhauer's dissertation earns him a doctorate of philosophy, *in absentia*, from the University of Jena. Schopenhauer's dissertation is published in a printing of 500 copies. In the winter Schopenhauer meets Johann Wolfgang von Goethe at his mother's salon in Weimar, and Goethe invites Schopenhauer to study color theory with him.

1814–1818 Schopenhauer lives in Dresden.

1816 Schopenhauer's *On Vision and Colors* is published.

1818 In December Schopenhauer's *The World as Will and Representation* is published, bearing a publication date of 1819. Schopenhauer begins a tour of Italy.

1819 In the spring a daughter is born out of wedlock to Schopenhauer, and she dies in the late summer. Schopenhauer concludes his Italian tour in August and returns to Dresden.

1820–1822 Schopenhauer is an unsalaried lecturer (*Privatdozent*) at the University of Berlin. Schopenhauer fails to attract students due, in part, to his insistence on scheduling his lectures at the same time as Georg Wilhelm Friedrich Hegel's lectures.

1821 In August Schopenhauer allegedly beats and injures a neighboring seamstress, Caroline Marquet, for failing to stop visiting with her friends in the anteroom of his apartment. After five years of hearings, Schopenhauer is required to pay Marquet damages for the remaining 20 years of her life.

1822–1823 Schopenhauer takes a second tour of Italy and returns to Munich in May 1823.

1824–1825 Schopenhauer lives in Bad Gastein (Switzerland), Mannheim, and Dresden. He returns to Berlin in April 1825.

1826–1831 Schopenhauer's name appears in the prospectus of lecturers (*Vorlesungsverzeichnis*) at the University of Berlin, but he never enrolls a course.

1830 An abbreviated Latin version of Schopenhauer's *On Vision and Color*, "*Commentatio undecima exponens Theoriam Colorum Physiologicam eandemque primariam*," appears in the third volume of *Scriptores Ophthalmologici minores*.

1831 Schopenhauer flees Berlin to Frankfurt am Main to escape the cholera epidemic.

1832 Schopenhauer moves to Mannheim. He translates into German Gracián's *Oráculo manual y arte de prudencia,* which is published posthumously in 1862.

1833 Schopenhauer returns to Frankfurt am Main, where he would live for the remainder of his life.

1836 Schopenhauer's *On the Will in Nature* is published.

1838 Schopenhauer's mother dies on April 17.

1839 Schopenhauer's essay *On the Freedom of the Human Will* receives the gold medal in an essay contest sponsored by the Royal Norwegian Society of Sciences.

1840 Despite being the only entry, Schopenhauer's "On the Foundation of Morality" is not awarded the prize in an essay contest sponsored by the Royal Danish Society of Scientific Studies.

1841 Schopenhauer's two "prize" essays are published as *The Two Fundamental Problems of Ethics.*

1844 A second edition of *The World as Will and Representation* is published. He adds a second volume containing 50 essays that supplement his original work.

1847 A second revised and expanded edition of *On the Fourfold Root of Sufficient Reason* is published.

1849 Schopenhauer's sister, Adele, dies from cancer in Bonn on 25 August.

1851 Schopenhauer's two volume *Parerga and Paralipomena* is published.

1853 The start of Schopenhauer's fame begins with the April publication of John Oxford's essay on Schopenhauer's philosophy, "Iconoclasm in German Philosophy" in the British *Westminster Review* and its subsequent German translation in the *Vossische Zeitung* in June.

1854 Second editions of *On the Will in Nature* and *On Vision and Colors* are published.

1856 The University of Leipzig sponsors an essay contest on the exegesis and critique of the Schopenhauerian Philosophy.

1857 The first lectures on Schopenhauer are delivered at the Universities of Bonn and Breslau.

1859 A third edition of *The World as Will and Representation* is published.

1860 The second edition of *The Two Fundamental Problems of Ethics* is published. Schopenhauer dies on 21 September in Frankfurt am Main after a brief illness.

Introduction

SCHOPENHAUER'S LIFE

Arthur Schopenhauer was born 35 years too early. Had he been born in 1823, by the time he would have written his philosophical masterpiece, Europe also would have been more receptive to his thought. But had he had any choice about his birth, it is likely he would have preferred to be like Gotthold Ephraim Lessing's son, a figure whose wisdom he mentioned several times in his writings, noting that he departed this world immediately after birth. Schopenhauer also was not born in England, much to his father's chagrin, since he had traveled with his pregnant wife to England so his first child, and hoped for son, would enjoy British citizenship and the benefits this would confer on a future merchant. But Schopenhauer's father submitted to his own insecurities and the longing of his homesick wife, and the family returned home before his son's birth. He did have the pleasure, however, of naming his son "Arthur," a cosmopolitan name he thought fitting for a merchant. And, although his father would never know it, England would play a significant role in his son's future success, but not in success as a merchant.

Thus Arthur Schopenhauer was born on 22 February 1788, in the Hanseatic free city of Danzig (now Gdańsk, Poland). His father, Heinrich Floris Schopenhauer was a successful merchant and one of Danzig's leading citizens. When Prussia was on the verge of annexing Danzig in March 1793, the liberty-loving Heinrich Floris moved his family to the free city of Hamburg, a move that would cost the family one-tenth of its fortune in taxes. His mother, Johanna (neé Trosiener), who also was descended from a family of merchants, was 18 years old when she married the 38-year-old Heinrich Floris. She was fluent in French and English, like her husband, and as her son would become. Johanna Schopenhauer would later become a popular writer, and her collected works, consisting of 24 volumes, would be published in 1831. It would be in her literary salon in Weimar where Arthur would associate with the poet C. M. Wieland, the Kantian philosopher Carl Leonhard Reinhold, the brothers Grimm and Schlegel, and the illustrious Johann Wolfgang von Goethe.

Although Schopenhauer's father possessed a somewhat cultured, cosmopolitan sensibility, he was also a very practical man who thought the proper path for his son was to continue the family business. He also sought to duplicate in his young son the same sort of educational experiences he had enjoyed in England and France. So in 1797 he traveled with Schopenhauer to France, leaving his son to spend two years in Le Havre with the family of a business partner, M. Grégoire de Blésimaire. Also in that year, his only sibling, a sister, Louise Adelaide (Adele), was born. Schopenhauer became so used to French that when he returned home two years later, it was almost as if he had to relearn German. In his later years, Schopenhauer would regard his time in France as the happiest years of his childhood.

Upon Schopenhauer's return to Hamburg in 1799, his father enrolled him in Dr. Johann Heinrich Christian Runge's private school, which was highly regarded as a training institution for future merchants. Schopenhauer was enrolled in Runge's School for four years, during which time he studied geography, arithmetic, algebra, bookkeeping, ethics, history, natural history, French, German, English and Latin. Instead of developing a taste and excitement about becoming a merchant, however, Schopenhauer longed to attend a gymnasium, and he began to loathe the life his father desired for him. The father recognized his son's despair and to draw him back to his proper life path, Heinrich Floris dangled a lure that would make it difficult for his 15-year-old son not to bite. Arthur was offered a choice. He could enroll in a gymnasium and prepare for a university education and the life of a scholar, or he could join his family for a lengthy tour of Europe and a later apprenticeship with a merchant. This choice was really no choice at all for the son of parents who had already instilled in him a love for travel.

During this tour, the Schopenhauers spent six months in England, three of which Arthur spent in the Reverend Thomas Lancaster's boarding school in Wimbledon, where he would perfect his English and develop a strong distaste for the narrow religiosity required of the students. Although he would share his father's Anglophilia his entire life, he would never forget the "infamous bigotry" he also associated with religion in England. The Schopenhauers' tour continued on through England, Holland, France, and Switzerland and it deeply affected the young man, who was shocked by the dreadful social conditions he frequently encountered. Later, he would compare his experiences on this tour to the Buddha's life-transforming experiences of sickness, old age, pain, and death. Schopenhauer's experiences moved him to no longer think of this world as the creation of an all-bountiful, good being; it appeared instead to be the work of a devil who created its creatures in order to gloat over their agony and misery.

At the close of the tour, Schopenhauer's father would return to Hamburg, while mother and son returned to Danzig, where Arthur was confirmed and where he would be apprenticed to the merchant Jacob Kabrum from September through mid-December of 1804. Soon after his return to Hamburg in January 1805, young Schopenhauer received a new master when he started his apprenticeship with the merchant Martin Jenish, a placement for which Schopenhauer showed no inclination or interest. Later he would complain that no one had a lesser devotion to business than he. The year 1805, however, was one of the most crucial in his life, and it was likely the saddest. On 20 April, his father died. It was probably a suicide. At least, that is what Arthur thought. Years later, he would blame his father's death, unfairly as it were, on his mother.

It is highly unlikely that Schopenhauer would have become a philosopher without the death of his father. However, due both to his sense of duty and to the inertia of his grief, Schopenhauer continued his apprenticeship with Jenish. It was at this point that Schopenhauer's mother played a significant role in liberating him from his bondage. Shortly after the death of her husband, Johanna sold the family business, and being drawn to the excitement of its cultural life, she and Adele moved to Weimar. The sale of the business relieved Schopenhauer's sense of obligation, since there was no family firm to run. Still, the future philosopher remained in Hamburg, sending letters complaining of his unhappy life. Schopenhauer's mother ultimately encouraged her son to follow his own lights and pursue a life consistent with his nature. Schopenhauer resigned his apprenticeship, and in 1807, he enrolled at the gymnasium at Gotha. Although Schopenhauer proved to be a bright and ready student, he felt it necessary to leave Gotha, after being penalized for writing a lampoon of one of his teachers.

After Johanna arranged for Schopenhauer to attend a gymnasium in nearby Altenberg, Schopenhauer moved to Weimar. At his mother's insistence, however, he would be living in separate quarters. She wrote to him saying that while she desired his happiness, she did not feel a need to observe it. Johanna had found her son's personality to be irritating and overbearing. His melancholy attitude, coupled with his argumentative and critical temperament, often smacked of arrogance. Johanna anticipated that if her son were to live with her, they would clash violently. For his part, Schopenhauer viewed Johanna as an inadequate wife to his father and an unloving mother to her son. He found her to be superficial and extravagant. He feared that she would squander his father's fortune and his inheritance. Worse, he feared, she might remarry. After Arthur agreed to a schedule for visiting her and for attending her parties, his mother arranged a comfortable home for him, but under a separate roof.

On 22 February 1809, Schopenhauer reached the age of majority and received 19,000 talers, one-third of his father's estate. Schopenhauer would later regard his inheritance as a consecrated treasure, a sacred trust, given to him for the purpose of solving a problem that he viewed as having been given to him by his nature. This problem was that which his philosophy would strive to solve. Schopenhauer would provide an explanation for the all-pervasive nature of suffering and death in the world, and his philosophy would seek to ascertain the meaning of living in such a world. His inheritance also would enable him to live, as he put it, for philosophy and not live, as he accused his contemporaries, by philosophy. Others may put bread, family, social status, religion, and the state ahead of philosophy, Schopenhauer believed, but he would seek the truth, even if it entailed not saying that which would please others or that would serve some other selfish aim.

Schopenhauer matriculated as a student of medicine at the University of Göttingen in the fall of 1809. His classes in natural history, physics, botany, comparative anatomy and physiology helped develop Schopenhauer's life-long interest in the natural sciences, and they would lead him to contend that anything worthy of calling itself philosophy must recognize the best findings of science. In 1810 Schopenhauer studied philosophy with the skeptical philosopher, Gottlob Ernst Schulze, who encouraged him to study Plato and Immanuel Kant. These two would become the philosophers Schopenhauer esteemed the most. Schulze moved Schopenhauer to switch his allegiance from medicine to philosophy. Before he made this move, the poet Christoph Martin Wieland warned Schopenhauer about impractical studies like philosophy. Schopenhauer told him, however, that life was an unpleasant business, and he would use his life to reflect on it.

Drawn primarily by the lure of the idealistic philosopher Johann Gottlieb Fichte, Schopenhauer transferred to the recently founded University of Berlin in the fall of 1811. Fichte was the first elected president of the University, and he enjoyed the reputation of being the philosophical heir to Kant. Schopenhauer hoped that in Fichte he would become acquainted with a great philosopher. He attended Fichte's series of lectures on the facts of consciousness and the doctrine of science, and he was soon to regard Fichte as a sham. One can read Schopenhauer's notes on these lectures and find his increasing dissatisfaction with Fichte. Instead of presenting a "doctrine of science [*Wissenschaftslehre*]," Schopenhauer found an "emptiness of science [*Wissenschaftsleere*]." At one point in his lecture notes, Schopenhauer expressed his desire to put a pistol to Fichte's chest, and before shooting him, ask him whether there might be any clear meaning behind the jumble of words he presented, or was it his point simply to make fools of his students? Like Hegel and Schelling, Fichte would become for Schopenhauer one of the three great sophists who had spoiled the rare insights articulated by the great Kant and whose obscure writings had stupefied the German public. It was also during his Berlin period that Schopenhauer would privately and more intensively study Kant. Later, he would compare Fichte's relationship to Kant with the relationships of characters in a German puppet show, where a buffoon was attached to a king or hero. Kant, of course, would play the role of king or hero, and Fichte the buffoon.

Schopenhauer did not receive his degree from Berlin, however. He fled Berlin in May 1813 because he feared an attack by Napoleon. He went to Dresden and then to his mother's house in Weimar. He decided to go to nearby Rudolstadt shortly after arriving at Weimar, where he retired to a small country inn from June to November to work on his dissertation, *On the Fourfold Root of the Principle of Sufficient Reason.* Schopenhauer considered submitting his work to Berlin, but he feared that the war would not allow its safe passage. So instead, he sent it to the University of Jena. He was granted his doctorate *in absentia* by Jena, being passed *magnum cum laude*. Overjoyed, the freshly minted Doctor of Philosophy arranged to have 500 copies of his dissertation published, and he sent a copies of it to Johann Wolfgang von Goethe, whom he had met at his mother's house, but upon whom he had not yet made any effect; Friedrich Schleiermacher, with whom he had studied the history of philosophy at Berlin; the Kantian philosopher, Carl Leopold Reinhold, whom he had also met at his mother's salon; and Schulze, his first philosophy professor.

As would be the case with all of his publications, Schopenhauer anticipated a warm reception of his thought and the recognition of his genius. Neither was forthcoming. Yet his published dissertation did have at least one significant effect; it allowed him to circulate closer within the orbit of Goethe. In November 1813, Goethe approached Schopenhauer during one of his mother's parties, shaking his hand as he congratulated the young Schopenhauer on his dissertation and thanking him for sending it to him as a gift. Goethe's recognition of Schopenhauer, whom he had virtually ignored in the past, probably was motivated by Goethe's sense of an affinity between their ways of thinking. Schopenhauer shared Goethe's mistrust of the purely conceptual and rational, and in his dissertation, Schopenhauer argued that geometrical proofs required a visual representation, a requirement which Goethe had also set for optical proofs in his theory of colors. Goethe also sensed in Schopenhauer a proselyte for his color theory, which had failed miserably in 1810 when Goethe published his massive *On the Theory of Colors*. Oddly enough, Goethe regarded his work on color theory more highly than his poetry, a judgment that the German public did not share. Schopenhauer, he thought, might be able to help reverse the fortunes of his color theory.

Schopenhauer met frequently with Goethe during the winter of 1813–1814, discussing philosophy generally, color theory specifically, and conducting experiments on color. The fruit of these labors appeared in 1816 with the publication of a small treatise, *On Vision and Colors*. Before he published it, however, Schopenhauer sought Goethe's blessings. Yet the inspiring source for Schopenhauer's color theory would not endorse it. Goethe, of course, had good reasons for not doing so. A review of their exchanges of letters is revealing. Schopenhauer is bold, self-confident about his views, and demanding. While he always expressed a sense of awe of Goethe, Schopenhauer's letters, as well as his essay, contained a number of assertions at which Goethe could have taken offense. Goethe's replies to Schopenhauer were, however, good-natured, marked by restraint, and they tended to ultimately master the situation. Finally, after being told by Schopenhauer that he (and not Goethe!) had produced the first true theory of color in the history of science, and that he did this work on color theory as a secondary concern when compared to other ideas he was entertaining, Goethe wrote to Schopenhauer that it would be a vain effort for them to reach an understanding. Thus Schopenhauer published his work without Goethe's endorsement, and he sent a copy to Goethe, remarking that he did not expect Goethe's comments. Later, when a friend asked Goethe what he thought about *On Vision and Colors*, Goethe said that while Doctor Schopenhauer was a significant thinker, and even though he started from his perspective, Schopenhauer had become his opponent.

It is likely that Schopenhauer would not have even written *On Vision and Colors* without the force of Goethe's personality. Already in 1813, Schopenhauer felt growing within him a philosophy that would become metaphysics and ethics in one. This philosophy unifying metaphysics and ethics had been the other ideas he told Goethe he had been entertaining while working on his color theory. They were finally expressed in what would become his "main work," *The World as Will and Representation*, which appeared in December 1818, bearing a publication date of 1819. Schopenhauer had been working on this book in Dresden since 1814, and he would view the Dresden years of 1814 to 1818 as his most productive. While this is not true concerning the volume of his work, this observation is true in the sense that *The World as Will and Representation* presented the fundamental ideas and concepts of his thought. Schopenhauer would regard the next 40 years of his philosophizing as simply clarifying, augmenting, and extending his original thought to new domains of inquiry. He would later claim that he did not change any of his fundamental ideas during his lengthy philosophical career.

The World as Will and Representation repeated a pattern already established in *On Vision and Colors*. Schopenhauer considered Goethe to be one of the two greatest minds that Germany had ever produced. He esteemed his association with Goethe, and he never lost respect for Goethe's greatness. Still, he argued that his own writings on color had taken Goethe's work and moved it to the august level of theory. This entailed, of course, that he had advanced color theory beyond the views of the great Goethe. The other of his "greatest German minds," was Kant, and he would take great pride in the Kantian roots of his philosophy, never losing his great appreciation for Kant. Yet *The World as Will and Representation* included a lengthy appendix in which he criticized Kant. He also claimed that he had taken Kantian insights, and by correcting Kant's mistakes, he had developed a philosophy that advanced beyond that of his philosophical hero. Although he never said it, the implication is clear that he believed he had trumped the two greatest minds ever produced in Germany. Schopenhauer prefaced *The World as Will and Representation* with a quote from Goethe, "Might not nature yet finally reveal itself?" He sent a copy to Goethe. For Schopenhauer, nature had revealed itself. It revealed itself as will.

In *The World as Will and Representation*, Schopenhauer argued that he had discovered what Kant claimed could not be discovered. Schopenhauer claimed he discovered the thing in itself. This had been the great unknown of Kant's philosophy, whose transcendental idealism told us that we could only know things as they appear and not things in themselves, which were beyond the bounds of all possible experiences. Schopenhauer denoted things as they appear to be representations, but unlike Kant, he viewed the will, an unconscious, goalless, ceaseless, striving to be, as the thing in itself. From the standpoint of our consciousness of other things, the world is representation, and from our self-consciousness, Schopenhauer argued, we discover that the world is will. Schopenhauer maintained that everything in the world, the world as representation, is an objectification of the will, which is the essence or content of all representations. Through these means, Schopenhauer saw the will as metaphysically primary. The will is also primary in human conduct. Intellect and reason are secondary in human behavior. They are merely instrumental, since they serve the will. Through his metaphysics, he argued that suffering is essential to life, and suffering is evil. This entails that life itself is evil, and so Schopenhauer believed his metaphysics demonstrated the moral significance of the world. Thus he claimed that his philosophy avoided what he regarded the greatest and most pernicious error, which faith had personified as "antichrist," the belief that the world has only a physical and no moral significance. Later, Friedrich Nietzsche, whose philosophy owed important debts to Schopenhauer's, would recall Schopenhauer's words and characterize his own amoral worldview as "antichrist."

Schopenhauer's metaphysics of the will was a metaphysics of misery. He attempted to account for the ubiquity of evil, suffering, and death in the world. The world is wretched, he concluded, because it is the expression of the will. He also attempted to articulate the meaning of living in the world. The meaning is to move beyond the misery of the world by denying that which gives existence its miserable form. Schopenhauer claimed that this is possible by denying the will, by repudiating that which gives existence its horrid tone. In *The World as Will and Representation*, it is as if he had discovered the means to provide a philosophical explanation for what he had sensed when he was just 17 and on his European tour. At that time he had posited the devil as the source of the wretchedness and misery of the world. This devil became the will in his philosophy, and salvation follows by denying not the devil, but by denying the will.

Those four years Schopenhauer spent in Dresden writing *The World as Will and Representation* are curious. He seemed not to have cultivated any deep friendships, and he spent much of his time writing and attending the theater and the opera. He gained a reputation as an eccentric, as someone given to rough jokes and sarcasm. He was outspoken about philosophical and literary matters, and he did not tolerate fools gladly. He found, however, that Dresden was full of fools, and he delighted in getting into quarrels with members of Dresden's various literary cliques, who came to fear his erudition and sarcasm. Depending on which side a person stood in relation to Schopenhauer's barbs, you either despised him and feared him, or you admired him and feared him.

Schopenhauer left Dresden for a tour of Italy in the fall of 1818, before the appearance of *The World as Will and Representation*. While in Rome, he received a copy of his book, and learned from his sister that Goethe was reading it with delight. But while he was vacationing in Italy, things were unraveling on the home front. In Dresden, Schopenhauer had engaged in a number of relatively meaningless affairs, one of which bore unexpected results. A maid gave birth to his daughter in the spring of 1819. It appears that Schopenhauer admitted paternity and was willing to support the child financially. But the unfortunate child died that summer, an event that did not seem to affect Schopenhauer deeply. He was affected, however, by another affair. The Danzig banker with whom Schopenhauer had entrusted one-third of his estate and with whom his mother and sister had invested all of their money, had suspended payments in May 1819, and he sought a settlement with his creditors to avoid bankruptcy. Despite the pleas of his sister, Schopenhauer refused to settle, advising his sister not to do so also.

His mother and sister, however, refused his advice, and they lost almost three-quarters of their fortune in their settlement. A year later, when the banker again became solvent, Schopenhauer would collect his entire investment. He did not seem to be bothered by the fact that his success was fueled partially by the losses of his mother and sister.

Both the publication of *The World as Will and Representation* and the subsequent financial difficulties of 1819 moved Schopenhauer to seek a new direction in his life. Schopenhauer had worked on his philosophy with a deep sense of mission, and the subsequent birth of his philosophy occasioned a form of postpartum depression, since he felt he had completed his life's mission with the publication of *The World as Will and Representation*. But it had become increasingly clear to Schopenhauer that the world was not ready to recognize the philosopher who solved the problem of existence. His book received little notice, and the few scholarly reviews that it did receive were dismissive. He was viewed as an epigone of idealism, as an author who had simply reiterated insights expressed more fully by Fichte and Schelling. Thus his critics claimed that he had made no contribution to the body of philosophical knowledge. His reviewers also charged that his philosophy was paradoxical, inconsistent, and contradictory, a theme that continues today in the secondary literature. Schopenhauer would view the lack of reception of his thought as a conspiracy of silence by his contemporaries. While there was silence, he was mistaken about there being a conspiracy. His contemporaries did not need to conspire against him. They had no reason to take Schopenhauer that seriously. He posed no threat. Yet Schopenhauer would claim that this conspiracy of silence against him was the product of the prevailing "Hegel*gloria*" of his time. Hegel sat on the philosophical throne, and no one recognized that the King had no clothes. Hegel's philosophy had so befogged and corrupted the German mind that it was incapable of understanding the truth, Schopenhauer thought.

Thus Schopenhauer's new direction in life would be to seek an academic appointment. This would provide income and it would also provide the opportunity to battle on the home turf of his enemies while promoting his philosophy. After pursuing leads about an academic post at the Universities of Göttingen and Heidelberg, Schopenhauer applied for the rights to do his habilitation and to lecture at the University of Berlin. Perversely, he also requested that he have his lecture scheduled at the same time as Hegel's principal course. The arrogance of Schopenhauer's request was not lost on the dean of the faculty or on the faculty itself. Schopenhauer read his test-lecture before the philosophy faculty on 23 March 1820. The topic was the traditional concepts of the four causes. During the course of the examination, Schopenhauer and Hegel engaged in a brief exchange. Hegel asked Schopenhauer what motivates a horse to lie down on the road. After receiving Schopenhauer's reply, Hegel asked him whether he considered animal functions, such as heartbeat and the circulation of the blood, to be reasons. Schopenhauer corrected Hegel, replying that only conscious motions of the body are animal functions. Hegel continued his objection until Martin Lichtenstein, a doctor of medicine and a friend of Schopenhauer's mother, interrupted the debate and supported Schopenhauer's use of the term "animal functions." Schopenhauer was given a passing grade on his lecture, even from Hegel, who also knew about Schopenhauer's odd request concerning his lecture time. Thus Schopenhauer became a private teacher, an unsalaried lecturer (*Privatdozent*) at Berlin.

Schopenhauer was granted his wish to schedule his lecture at the same time as Hegel's. His topic was universal philosophy, the essence of the world and of the human spirit. Students flocked to Hegel and ignored Schopenhauer. While Hegel enrolled around two hundred of Berlin's approximately eleven hundred students, Schopenhauer enrolled only five. Although Schopenhauer's name would be listed in the prospectus of lectures from 1820–1822 and 1826–1831, he never enrolled and completed a course. His academic career was a disaster.

Troubles with his academic career were coupled with troubles with women during this stage in Schopenhauer's life. In 1821, he met the 19-year-old Caroline Richter, later "Medon," a minor actress and chorus girl. Schopenhauer probably loved Richter as much as he could any woman, and he engaged in an on-again, off-again affair with her that lasted around 10 years. He even contemplated marrying Richter on more than one occasion, but his mistrust of her motives and suspicions about her health prevented a union. Consequently, despite his belief that a marriage would ground him more deeply within society and his career, Schopenhauer would never marry. On 12 August 1821, as Schopenhauer waited for a visit from Richter, a second Caroline unpleasantly intruded into his life. Caroline Marquet, a 47-year-old seamstress, was visiting with two friends in the antechamber to Schopenhauer's apartment.

Schopenhauer told the women to leave. Marquet refused to leave, and Schopenhauer dragged her out of the room and tossed her belongings out the door. Marquet claimed that Schopenhauer beat and kicked her. She sued Schopenhauer for injuries, and after a series of lawsuits lasting five years, and during which her injuries seemed to get worse, Schopenhauer had to pay her 60 talers a year for as long as Marquet's injuries persisted. This turned out to be for the remaining 20 years of her life. Schopenhauer would later write on her death certificate, the Latin phrase "*Obit anus, abit onus* [the old woman dies, the burden departs]."

Schopenhauer's experiences with the two Carolines and his failure as a teacher moved him to take a second Italian tour in May 1822. We know relatively little about this tour. He returned to Munich in the spring of 1823, where he spent a miserable year, suffering from gout, hemorrhoids and depression. He also lost hearing in one ear. After spending this hellish year in Munich, he traveled to Bad Gastein, Switzerland, in May of 1824, but the baths brought him no consolation. During this time Richter bore another man's son. Still, Schopenhauer ultimately would recognize her in his will.

Also during this time, Schopenhauer adopted a new strategy for gaining some acknowledgment. He sought recognition as a translator. He proposed translating into German David Hume's *Natural History of Religion* and *Dialogues Concerning Natural Religion*; he also proposed to F. A. Brockhaus, the publisher of *The World as Will and Representation*, a German translation of one of Schopenhauer's favorite novels, Laurence Sterne's *Tristram Shandy*; and he proposed to a British publisher an English translation of Kant's *Critique of Pure Reason*, *Prolegomena to Any Future Metaphysics*, and *Critique of Judgment*. There were no takers. Brockhaus even passed on his offer of a German translation of the Spanish treatise by Baltasar Gracián, *Oráculo manual y arte de prudencia*, which would appear in 1862, two years after Schopenhauer's death. Schopenhauer's only success during this period would be his Latin revision of *On Vision and Colors*, which appeared in 1830.

Schopenhauer had returned to Berlin in 1825, where he would remain until 1831, when Berlin was threatened by a cholera epidemic, during which Hegel died. He dreamed of a second edition of *The World as Will and Representation*, but he was informed by its publisher that the world still was not ready for his thought, and he had much of its first edition turned into scrap. Schopenhauer fled Berlin by going to Frankfurt for the winter of 1831–1832, and then he struck out for Mannheim in July 1832, where he once again battled serious illness and depression. Mannheim would not ultimately suit his spirit, and after doing a cost-benefit analysis of Mannheim and Frankfurt, he decided to move to Frankfurt in 1833. He appeared to be won over to Frankfurt because of the excitement and comforts offered by a larger city, the presence of "more Englishmen," good, healthy weather, able dentists, and "less bad physicians." As a major trading center, he probably also felt comfortable, to some degree, living among its many merchants and bankers. Although Schopenhauer would remain in Frankfurt until his death, he remained a citizen of Prussia, foregoing Frankfurt citizenship.

Schopenhauer would not, however, abandon his plan to publish a second edition of *The World as Will and Representation*. He realized also that he would have to cultivate an audience for his philosophy before he could achieve his goal. So Schopenhauer collected his observations on science and the philosophy of nature and published them in 1836 as *On the Will in Nature*. The subtitle of this book, "A Discussion of the Corroborations from the Empirical Sciences That the Author's Philosophy Has Received since Its First Appearance," is somewhat misleading. It is not that he simply used the natural sciences to support his ideas in *The World as Will and Representation*; rather, he attempted to show how the best findings of science would receive a more thorough grounding explanation through his metaphysics of will. This work included the chapter "Physical Astronomy," which Schopenhauer believed was crucial to his philosophy, because it contained the most important step of his philosophy, namely the transition from appearance to the thing in itself. This step, he said, is stated there with more clarity than in any other of his writings.

Schopenhauer had offered *On the Will in Nature* to Brockhaus, but he declined it. He managed to have it published by a firm in Frankfurt, but only after he waived the author's honorarium. This book received less attention than Schopenhauer's main work. It initially received one negative notice in which the reviewer would correctly predict that it would fail to draw readers to his philosophy. Five years later, it received a second negative review. At that point, it had only sold 125 copies of the original printing of 500.

Despite the failure of *On the Will in Nature*, Schopenhauer began to experience some minor successes. Around 1826 Schopenhauer discovered the first edition of Kant's *Critique of Pure Reason*. Prior to this, he had only read its later editions. This led him to embark on a serious study of the differences between the first and later editions of Kant's masterpiece. When he learned in 1837 that a new edition of Kant's collected works was being prepared by two Königsberg professors, Karl Rosenkranz and Friedrich Schubert, he sent a letter to Kant's editors in which he pleaded with them that they publish the *Critique of Pure Reason* according to its first edition. He argued that this was the most important work ever written in Europe, and it should appear in its pure and genuine form. Kant had falsified and spoiled his masterpiece with the second edition, Schopenhauer charged, and he had moved away from his original commitment to idealism and the radicalism of the first edition because of external pressures and the weakness of old age. The result, he continued, was that the book is contradictory and obscures Kant's original insights. Later, Schopenhauer sent a letter to Rosenkranz in which he gave a collation of altered passages and omitted pages, as well as a list of various printer's errors in others of Kant's books. Rosenkranz and Schubert followed Schopenhauer's recommendations. Later, when Rosenkranz called Schopenhauer "an eremite of this [Kant's] philosophy" and he published extracts from Schopenhauer's letters within the final volume of the collected edition, Schopenhauer was delighted. And, although Rosenkranz published kind words about the fourth book of *The World as Will and Representation*, he would later become an opponent of Schopenhauer.

Schopenhauer tasted another minor success in January 1839, when the Royal Norwegian Society of Science awarded his "On the Freedom of the Human Will" the prize in its essay contest. Schopenhauer's essay was written in response to the question, "Can the freedom of the will be proven from self-consciousness?" To simplify his answer, he argued "no." At best, self-consciousness can reveal what he called "physical freedom," the ability to do what we will. The deeper question, he argued, is whether we are free to will what we will. His answer to this question was also "no." All human behavior, he claimed, is subject to strict necessity, being a function of a person's character and circumstances. Yet he also argued that the strict necessity of human actions was compatible with the idea that our essence, our will, is free, and this freedom, he claimed, was implied by our sense of being responsible for our actions and of being the doers of our deeds. Freedom, he then argued, is transcendental. It belongs to the world as will, which is outside the scope of all necessity. Although Schopenhauer followed Kant concerning our freedom from natural necessity, he did not attempt, as Kant, to view freedom as some alternative type of causality other than that which prevails in the world. Our freedom, he argued, is a mystery.

As he was working on his essay for the Royal Norwegian Society, Schopenhauer learned of another essay contest sponsored by the Royal Danish Society of Scientific Studies. This time the question was, "Are the source and foundations of morals to be looked for in an idea of morality lying immediately in consciousness (or conscience) and in the analysis of other fundamental moral concepts springing from that idea, or are they to be looked for in a different ground of knowledge?" Despite being the only entry to the contest, Schopenhauer's "On the Basis of Morality" was not awarded the prize. In their verdict, the Royal Danish Society claimed that Schopenhauer relegated to an appendix that which should have been central to his essay, a discussion of the connection between metaphysics and ethics; that he failed to prove that compassion was the basis of morality and an adequate foundation of morality; and that he had offended the society by his treatment of several distinguished philosophers of recent times. Schopenhauer, of course, was enraged by the verdict, since he was absolutely confident that his essay would be crowned. He had virtually told the society this when he submitted his essay. He also informed them that he planned to publish both of his prize essays in a work to be called *The Two Fundamental Problems of Ethics*. This book appeared, as planned, in 1841. It included a lengthy, vitriolic preface in which he furiously berated the Royal Danish Society's verdict and in which he heaped abuse on Fichte and Hegel, whom he identified as the Society's "distinguished philosophers." It is likely that the Society was also offended by his treatment of Kant in this essay, but Schopenhauer seemed oblivious to this possibility. *The Two Fundamental Problems of Ethics* did nothing to raise Schopenhauer's stock in the philosophical world.

On 16 April 1838, while Schopenhauer was busy answering essay questions, his mother died. Johanna Schopenhauer's death did not seem to have any remarkable effect on her son. In a letter to a childhood friend, he confided that his mother was a good writer of novels and a bad mother. He also believed she had been a poor wife to his father, and he even blamed her for his father's "suicide." The last time Schopenhauer had even seen his mother, however, had been in May 1814. They had had a violent quarrel, and after that time, with the exception of a few letters, any communications between son and mother were mediated by his sister. His mother disinherited Schopenhauer in her will—in both senses of that term.

After years of persistent inquiry, Schopenhauer was finally able to convince Brockhaus in 1843 to publish a second edition of *The World as Will and Representation*, which appeared in 1844. Schopenhauer, however, had to waive his honorarium. He also assured his publisher that he would be able to recoup his publishing expenses through the sale of his masterpiece. A few years later, Schopenhauer would ask Brockhaus about the sale of his book, to which Brockhaus would reply that he had made a bad deal with it and he did not want to go into details.

It is likely that Schopenhauer was able to entice Brockhaus to take another gamble with his book because of his description of its second edition. He told Brockhaus that the first edition was like a sketch of his philosophy, but the second was like a finished painting. The "paint" for his "sketch" consisted of a second volume of essays, arranged in an order that mirrored the four books into which the original edition was divided. These essays were designed to clarify, extend, and augment his original ideas. What had been the original edition became the first of a two-volume work. Schopenhauer only made some minor additions to the first edition, primarily by adding references drawn from Eastern thought. He did, however, substantially revise the appendix, his "Criticisms of the Kantian Philosophy." Within the essays of the new, second volume, Schopenhauer made numerous references to *On the Will in Nature* and *The Two Fundamental Problems of Ethics*. These two works, he would claim, also supplemented his original ideas, and since he did not wish to repeat himself, he recommended to his readers that they should also consider these books. Later, he would claim that anyone who wished to understand his philosophy must read every line he wrote.

The second edition of *The World as Will and Representation* was no more successful than the first. Two negative reviews appeared in journals published by Brockhaus. One was written by a former student of Johann Herbart, who had himself given a bad review of the first edition; the other was written by a student of Friedrich Jacobi, a figure Schopenhauer bashed almost with the same furiosity as he bashed Hegel, Fichte, and Schelling. A third review, generally positive, also appeared, but it failed to draw readers to the book. Despite the failure of Schopen-

hauer's philosophy to excite either professors of philosophy or the educated public, in the mid-1840s he started to gain a cadre of early followers of his philosophy. These individuals were professional men,
many of whom were lawyers. Schopenhauer referred to members of this
group as either "apostles" or "evangelists," depending on how active
they were in promoting his philosophy. These early adherents served
Schopenhauer in a number of ways. They kept watch for any references
to him in print; some wrote tracts advocating his philosophy; some
wrote apologetics. Schopenhauer's interaction with these followers, and
especially his classification of them as apostles or evangelists, depicted
Schopenhauer's messianic sense of mission. Schopenhauer's exchange
of letters with two of these men, Julius Frauenstädt, who would be the
future editor of Schopenhauer's collected works and his literary executor, and Johann Becker, a lawyer, provide some insight into Schopenhauer's metaphysics and ethics.

In 1844, Schopenhauer was 56 years old, and he started to fear the loss
of his intellectual capacities. He also sensed his own mortality. The lack of
reception of the second edition of *The World as Will and Representation*
would lead Schopenhauer to a new strategy for drawing a readership to his
philosophy. He hoped to issue a third edition, but he also knew he had to
have readers to convince Brockhaus of the need for this work. In 1850, he
approached Brockhaus once again, but he did so with a new work, the two-
volume *Parerga and Paralipomena*. The first volume was comprised of his
reflections on a variety of subjects that were not systematically related to
his philosophy. The second volume consisted of 14 essays that were supplements to his philosophy, along with 17 essays containing his miscella-
neous observations on a variety of subjects. In his attempt to sell this book
to Brockhaus, Schopenhauer argued that this book would break the silent
opposition to his philosophy by the "guild of professors of philosophy,"
because he had written a "philosophy for the world," which would draw a
broad audience that would become eager to read his other books. Brockhaus, having been burned twice by Schopenhauer, was unimpressed by
Schopenhauer's argument, and he declined the offer. Not to be deterred,
and largely through the efforts of one of his "arch evangelists," Julius
Frauenstädt, Schopenhauer saw his *Parerga and Paralipomena* published
in 1851 through the Berlin publisher, A. W. Hayn.

While Schopenhauer had worked on *Parerga and Paralipomena*,
he faced the revolutionary year of 1848 with apprehension about his

philosophical fate, about his money, and about the unstable political conditions of that time. On 18 September 1848, Frankfurt was in an uproar. The streets were barricaded, and rifle fire pierced the air. Schopenhauer observed a large crowd of "rabble" from the window in his apartment. He heard a loud rapping on his door, so he barred it, fearing it was the crowd. He soon discovered, however, that it was a group of soldiers who wished to fire their rifles down at the revolutionaries. But a neighbor's apartment offered a better vantage point, so the soldiers soon vacated his apartment. To aid them, Schopenhauer sent over his double opera glasses. Afterwards, in *Parerga and Paralipomena* he would argue that because humans are largely egoistical, unjust, deceitful, and unintelligent, we need a Hobbesian sort of state to curb our aggressiveness toward one another and to obtain security. Although Schopenhauer was sensitive to the wretched social conditions that drove some of the revolutionaries, he considered the mob to have been misled by the intellectuals, many of whom were young Hegelians, whose delusions about the reforming capacity of the state had fueled an empty optimism. Later, in his will, the main heirs to his estate would be the Prussian soldiers who had become disabled in 1848, and those left behind by the soldiers who lost their lives in the fight. This may in part be attributed to the fact that he had no heirs. Adele, his sister, had died in 1849. Never married, Adele suffered greatly as an intermediary between Schopenhauer and his mother, who had preceded her in death by only nine years. Poor Adele had the misfortune of being crushed between two dominant and forceful personalities.

Parerga and Paralipomena received a wider reading than any of Schopenhauer's books. His early followers also spread his name. Yet the watershed event that provided him with a greater readership, and which initiated the beginning of his fame, occurred in England, the place that Schopenhauer's father had dreamed would be the catalyst for his son's successful future. In April 1853, the British journal, *The Westminster Review,* published John Oxenford's essay "Iconoclasm in German Philosophy," which was published one month later in a German translation in the *Vossische Zeitung*. Oxenford's article promoted Schopenhauer's philosophy. People soon began traveling to Frankfurt, and he almost became a minor tourist attraction. Lectures were given in Bonn and Breslau on his philosophy, and in 1856, the University of Leipzig sponsored a prize contest for the best exposition and critique of Schopenhauer's philosophy (although he was personally displeased with the winning entry). From exile in Switzerland, Richard Wagner, who came to understand his own works through the lens of Schopenhauer's philosophy, invited Schopenhauer to visit him. Schopenhauer declined the offer, and instead received from Wagner a handsomely bound copy of the libretto for the *Ring of the Nibelung*, with a dedication "from respect and gratitude." Schopenhauer conveyed his thanks to Wagner through a meeting with a member of Wagner's circle, but he also included the advice that Wagner should stop writing music and simply pursue his genius as a poet. Schopenhauer's loyalties remained with Mozart and Rossini.

Schopenhauer's fame enabled him to publish new editions of all of his works, with the exception of *Parerga and Paralipomena*. The hoped for third edition of *The World as Will and Representation* was published in 1859. In August 1860, Schopenhauer managed a second edition of *The Two Fundamental Problems of Ethics*, despite the fact that since April of that year he had suffered some heart palpitations, which required him to rest and shorten his daily vigorous walks. On 18 September, Schopenhauer suffered another episode of fainting. He was visited that day by Wilhelm Gwinner, the executor of his will and later biographer. Gwinner found Schopenhauer in a peaceful and reflective mood. Gwinner reported that Schopenhauer's impending death did not alarm the philosopher, nor did the thought that worms would soon be consuming his body. However, Schopenhauer said that the prospect of what professors of philosophy would do to his "spirit," his philosophy, was another matter. As Gwinner left, Schopenhauer told him he had a clear intellectual conscience and it would be a blessing to vanish into absolute nothingness, but he doubted that death offered him that prospect. Three days later, on 21 September, his maid found Schopenhauer slumped over in the corner of his sofa, dead. He was buried in Frankfurt on 26 September 1860, underneath a flat, black granite stone, inscribed only with his name. There was no edifying or ironic epitaph, and not even the dates of his birth and death. He had given the world his philosophy; that was enough.

SCHOPENHAUER'S PHILOSOPHY

Schopenhauer is notorious for his metaphysics of the will and his pessimism. He developed a voluntaristic metaphysics in which the will, described as a blind, goalless, ceaseless, striving to be, is said to be the inner content and essence of everything that appears in the world. This meant for him that everything, as a manifestation or objectification of the will, expresses the same restless nature as the will; everything is as it is because of the will. Although Schopenhauer never formally described his philosophy as "pessimistic," the pessimistic tone of his philosophy is expressed by his claim, which he stated in self-conscious opposition to Gottfried Wilhelm Leibniz, that this is the worst of all possible worlds. What gives the world its horrid cast is the will. All the conflict and strife, pain and suffering, destruction and death permeating this world follow from the essence of all, the will. This led Schopenhauer to formulate his most important truth; that it would be better for humans not to exist than to exist. He did not advocate suicide, however, since he regarded it as a willful act and, therefore, an affirmation of the will. To escape the inevitable evils necessarily embodied in the world requires the denial of that which gives the world all of its ills, the will. The denial of the will constitutes human redemption or salvation, Schopenhauer argued, and he closed the first volume of his main work, *The World as Will and Representation*, by stating that, for those who have overcome the world, that is, denied the will, this very real world of ours, with all of its suns and galaxies, is nothing.

While Schopenhauer's metaphysics and pessimism made his philosophy notorious, other dimensions of his thought are also historically and philosophically significant. If one accepts the argument that Friedrich Wilhelm Joseph Schelling's *System of Transcendental Idealism* (1800) and Georg Wilhelm Friedrich Hegel's *Encyclopedia of the Philosophical Sciences in Outline* (1818) are just sketches for a system of philosophy, then Schopenhauer's *The World as Will and Representation*, which appeared in late 1818 with a publication date of 1819, was the first system of philosophy to appear in Germany after Kant. He was also the first important Western philosopher whose work was both informed and shaped by Eastern thought. When he first published his main work, Schopenhauer's knowledge of Eastern thought was rather thin, but he still recommended knowledge of the *Vedas* as a means for his reader to be prepared to understand him, and he used concepts drawn from Hinduism and Buddhism to help express his ideas. Schopenhauer read indological and sinological materials throughout his life, and this literature helped shape his later writings. Unlike his more Eurocentric contemporaries, Schopenhauer believed that Eastern thought articulated important insights that were lacking in the writings of Europeans. It was not without considerable pride that Schopenhauer would indicate that his philosophy agreed with Eastern thought on a number of issues, and he took consolation in the belief that many dimensions of his philosophy found problematic by Europeans would be seen as orthodox by Eastern peoples.

Schopenhauer also wrote well, and when compared to his philosophical contemporaries, he wrote wonderfully. He hated obscurantism of any kind, and he viewed the torturous styles of Fichte, Schelling, and Hegel as showing a poverty of thought that they attempted to hide by their incomprehensible language and ponderous sentence structures. Schopenhauer strove to express his ideas directly and clearly, and his writing style seems more akin to the British empiricists John Locke and David Hume than it is to other German philosophers. Schopenhauer wrote with passion and style, irony and wit, polemically and straightforwardly. His writing style would become one of the reasons for his being read by a general audience. The clarity of his writing also makes it relatively easy to spot difficulties with his thought, since they are not hidden by a dense terminology embodied in unwieldy sentences. His writing comes alive through his use of real life examples, as well as through his many references and quotations from great philosophers, writers, poets, religious figures and scientists.

Schopenhauer also explored deeply almost all facets of human life, which may account for why his philosophy has exercised multifold effects among intellectuals and artists. Among philosophers, his influence can be detected in the writings of Eduard von Hartmann, Friedrich Nietzsche, Henri Bergson, Max Horkheimer, Max Scheler, and Ludwig Wittgenstein. The reception of his philosophy, however, followed a common pattern. There is an assimilation of some of his views, a modification and an extension, but a rejection of the totality of his thought. The two most important philosophers he affected, moreover, tend either to downgrade the ultimate significance of his thought (Nietzsche) or to express indifference toward mentioning the precursors of his own views (Wittgenstein). And if it makes sense to speak of schools of philosophy, for example, Hegelian or Marxist, there was no school of Schopenhauerians.

Schopenhauer's philosophy also found resonance in the works of such diverse figures as Jacob Burckhardt, Émile Durkheim, Albert Einstein, Sigmund Freud, Karl Jung, Erwin Schrödinger, Georg Simmel, and Wilhelm Wundt. Both Richard Wagner and Arnold Schönberg were influenced by Schopenhauer's philosophy, especially by his aesthetics, and a strong case could be made for the claim that few philosophers have had Schopenhauer's influence on writers. His darkly compelling world view and depiction of the vanity of human existence affected the works of Samuel Beckett, Jorge Luis Borges, Joseph Conrad, George Eliot, Gustave Flaubert, Theodor Fontane, André Gide, Thomas Hardy, Herman Hesse, Franz Kafka, Thomas Mann, Guy de Maupassant, Marcel Proust, Leo Tolstoy, Ivan Turgenev, Virginia Woolf, and Émile Zola.

Along with its far-reaching effects, Schopenhauer's philosophy is also marked by a singularity in both his philosophical project and his thought. He philosophized with a deep sense of mission. His task was to solve what he called the "ever-disquieting puzzle of existence," which Schopenhauer believed could be solved by explaining why suffering and death were ubiquitous features of the world and by determining the meaning or significance of living in a world permeated by these evils. Schopenhauer thought he was born to solve this puzzle of existence, and he believed that by examining the world itself, the key to solving it could be found. When *The World as Will and Representation* (second edition 1844; third edition 1859) first appeared in late 1818, he thought he had accomplished this task with a book whose thousands of sentences were said to communicate a single thought. Fate was unkind to Schopenhauer's masterpiece, however, and it fell from the press almost as stillborn as Hume's *Treatise of Human Nature*. The failure of *The World as Will and Representation* moved Schopenhauer to seek an audience for his philosophy, and he spent over 40 years trying to clarify, augment, substantiate, and extend into new subjects of inquiry the basic ideas found in his main work. Schopenhauer's singularity in purpose and thought is relatively rare in philosophy, as is also his claim to have never changed the basic ideas of his philosophy.

THE ANIMAL METAPHYSICUM

Schopenhauer's philosophical mission to solve the problem of existence received expression in his account of the human need for metaphysics.

He agreed with Plato and Aristotle that philosophy begins in wonder. But unlike Plato and Aristotle, he did not think that philosophical astonishment arises from a simple confrontation with an unknown world. Rather, he argued that the wonder that prompts philosophical speculation about the world is grounded in the recognition of the all-pervasive distribution of suffering and death in the world. Humans, the metaphysical animal, want to know why conflict and strife, pain and suffering, destruction and death, are omnipresent features of the world. Schopenhauer so intimately connected the recognition of the evils of the world with the drive to philosophize that he thought we would not wonder about the world at all in the absence of these "evils." Instead we would simply flow along with the course of nature. We want to know why suffering and death are ubiquitous, and we desire to know the meaning of living in a world in which the vanity and fruitlessness of all our efforts follow from the miserable and ephemeral form of our existence.

Schopenhauer also saw a deep kinship between philosophy and religion, since he believed that religious speculation about the world results from the same type of wonder that stimulates philosophical speculation. Yet he noted a significant difference between religion and philosophy. Religion expresses its truths figuratively, masked in myths, fables, and allegories. It is a "metaphysics of the people," serving the metaphysical needs of the masses. Philosophy must, he thought, express its truths in a strict and proper sense; it must demonstrate its truths. Although Schopenhauer would attempt to draw support for his views by claiming that his philosophy articulated truths expressed allegorically by world religions, he thought he had established the truth of his views by independent means.

To gain an overview of Schopenhauer's philosophy, and to appreciate the scope of his thought, following the general themes of the four books of the first edition of *The World as Will and Representation* presents a natural path.

EPISTEMOLOGY

It was with considerable pride that Schopenhauer called himself a Kantian. He claimed also to be Kant's only legitimate heir. Like Immanuel

Kant, he ascribed to transcendental idealism. Yet his allegiance to transcendental idealism resided in the importance Schopenhauer saw in the distinction between things as they appear, which he called "representations," and things in themselves. Kant argued that we could only know things as they appear and that we could never know things in themselves, which stand beyond the bounds of possible experiences. Here, of course, Schopenhauer would not follow Kant, since he viewed the will as the thing in itself. Instead of considering his philosophy to be antithetical to Kant's concerning our knowledge of the thing in itself, he claimed that he had only thought out Kant's philosophy to its proper conclusion. Whenever Kant had managed to bring the thing in itself closest to light, Schopenhauer argued, it appeared as the will. The problem with Kant, he thought, was that he was unable to grasp his own insights. Schopenhauer's direct work in epistemology is found in his dissertation, *On the Fourfold Root of the Principle of Sufficient Reason* (first edition 1813; revised second edition 1847); the first chapter of *On Vision and Colors* (first edition 1816; Latin summary 1830; second edition 1854); and the first book of the first volume of *The World as Will and Representation* and in the second volume, chapters 1–22.

While Schopenhauer's theory of knowledge followed many of the general contours of Kant's, it also deviated significantly from that of his mentor. Schopenhauer was dismissive of the transcendental arguments Kant employed to establish the necessary conditions for the possibility of experience, and he did not accept Kant's attempts to justify synthetic *a priori* propositions, statements that were informative about the world, but which were also universal and necessarily true. Schopenhauer thought Kant's method was too abstract and conceptual, and he employed a more directly phenomenological analysis of the contents of cognition. Schopenhauer's method proceeds from what he called the facts of consciousness, the objects of extrospective and introspective experience. In this way, his method shows an affinity to that of the British empiricists, John Locke, George Berkeley, and David Hume. Comparing his method to Kant's, he claimed that Kant is like a man trying to measure the size of a tower by its shadow, whereas, his method is to measure the tower itself. Yet, despite their differences, Schopenhauer viewed his philosophy as continuing a coherently consistent train of thought, originating in Locke, but modified and given more depth by Kant.

Schopenhauer agreed with the Kantian view that human cognition structures our experiences of things. Everything we experience is, for this reason, called a representation or an appearance. He strove, however, to simplify the highly complex and sophisticated account of human cognition presented by Kant, which recognized two *a priori* forms of sensibility, time and space, the 12 pure categories of the understanding (Schopenhauer would claim that the understanding involved only the non-conceptual employment of causality), the transcendental unity of apperception, and so much more. Schopenhauer attempted to account for all human cognition and knowledge through one basic principle, the principle of sufficient reason. He argued that this principle was the basis of all proof or demonstration, and it was something that could not be proven, because it was the ultimate principle of all demonstration. To demand a proof for this principle, he thought, was absurd since this was akin to demanding a proof for the right to demand a proof. This principle, moreover, allows us to ask why something is so, and it is the form of all necessity and determination.

The most general *a priori* form for all possible and conceivable experience, Schopenhauer argued, is the subject/object distinction. There is no experience without a subject of experience and an experienced object. Schopenhauer's slogan, "no object without a subject, and no subject without an object," is often referred to as the correlativity thesis, a thesis he would use to chide realism and some forms of idealism. The former forgets, he thought, the subject, while the later ignores the object. The correlativity thesis is echoed in the opening line from *The World as Will and Representation*, which states, "The world is my representation." This is a truth, he argued, whose recognition marks the dawn of philosophical discernment. Although he was critical of some forms of idealism, particularly the subjective idealism of Johann Gottlieb Fichte, he thought the standpoint of philosophy must be idealistic, because what we take as the world is an object for a subject, and the world, as such, is conditioned by the subject, through impositions of our own cognition on experience.

Schopenhauer used a statement by Christian Wolff to articulate the principle of sufficient reason, namely, "*Nihil est sine rationale cur posit sit quam no sit* [nothing is without a reason why it is rather than is not]." He made clear, however, that this principle was only an abstraction and it must be analyzed into four different forms or "roots" to understand how it functions in human cognition. The four roots correspond to four different faculties of the human mind, and they apply to four distinct classes of objects of cognition. The "four roots" of this principle are: 1) the principle of sufficient reason of becoming, which is a function of the understanding and whose objects are intuitive representations of the world; 2) the principle of sufficient reason of knowing, which is a function of human reason and whose objects are concepts or abstract representations; 3) the principle of sufficient reason of being, which is a function of pure sensibility and whose objects are the *a priori* intuitions of space and time; and 4) the principle of sufficient reason of acting, which is a function of self-consciousness and whose object is the will. Schopenhauer argued that the principle of sufficient reason is the source of all necessity or determination, and he associated, respectively, the following types of necessity revealed in the four roots: physical, logical, mathematical, and motivational.

The key for understanding Schopenhauer's move from his epistemology to his metaphysics can be found in his claim that perception is intellectual, a function of the understanding, which he attributes to both humans and other animals. His account of perception, which is included in his analysis of the principle of sufficient reason of becoming, and which was first detailed in the first chapter of *On Vision and Colors*, figures dominantly in the first book of *The World as Will and Representation*, whose topic is the world as representation, which is subject to the principle of sufficient reason. In his main work, he again emphasizes the correlativity of the subject/object, arguing that no objects exist outside their being cognized. Our perceptions of things or objects in the world are again seen as being conditioned or structured by our cognition, so that we perceive things in the world as spatial, temporal objects standing in causal relations to other things.

Thus far, Schopenhauer agreed with Kant. Schopenhauer read Kant as claiming that the perception of an object requires the application of categories or concepts to intuitions. Schopenhauer thought that perception presents us with an object without any element of judgment or the application of a concept to some sensuous presented given. For one thing, he held that animals perceive objects, yet they are incapable of conceptual and discursive thought. For another, he thought that concepts are abstracted from the perception of objects, something that entails the priority of perceptions or intuitions over concepts. Schopenhauer's account of perception entails that our perception of an object proceeds from felt changes in our body, sensations of "things beneath the skin," which function as the raw materials upon which the understanding automatically takes as the effect of some cause located in space and time. It is as if the understanding immediately creates objects of perception out of data furnished by the senses.

METAPHYSICS

While Schopenhauer's epistemology deviated significantly from Kant's, his conception of metaphysics is squarely at odds with Kant's, although it is, once again, faithful to a number of Kantian commitments. Kant argued that metaphysics seeks a form of knowledge that goes beyond the possibility of experience and we cannot gain knowledge that transcends the bounds of experience. Thus he claimed that metaphysics seeks the impossible, and Kant thought his critical philosophy had sounded the death knell for speculative metaphysics. Schopenhauer accepted Kant's claims that knowledge that transcends the bounds of all possible experience is impossible, and speculative metaphysics is vacuous. Schopenhauer also embraced the Kantian thesis that philosophy must always remain immanent, confined to principles falling within the bounds of possible experience. To remain faithful to these Kantian insights, Schopenhauer conceived of metaphysics as providing the correct explanation of experience as a whole. For this reason, Schopenhauer claimed that metaphysics must have an empirical basis, and it must draw all of its concepts ultimately from the whole of experience. Metaphysics and its concepts must stem from the outer experience of things that seem to stand independent from the perceiver, that is, the experience of spatial-temporal objects that are in causal relationships to other objects of the same kind, and also from inner experiences, whose only form is time, and which includes the experience of the whole range of the cognizer's affective inner life, including feelings of pleasure and pain, desires, wishes, hopes, longings, and passions. The whole of experience presents itself like a cryptograph, Schopenhauer argued, and his metaphysics attempts to decipher this puzzle. The correctness of metaphysics is found, he thought, in its ability to provide the best possible explanation of experience as a whole. This can only be done, he argued, when the philosopher is able to explain the connection between inner and outer experiences. Schopenhauer would claim that the key to solving the puzzle of experience is found in the inner experience of willing. Schopenhauer's direct work in metaphysics is located in the second book of the first volume of *The World as Will and Representation* and in chapters 18–28 of its second volume; in *On the Will in Nature* (first edition 1836; second edition 1859); and in *Parerga and Paralipomena* (1851), with his essays "Sketch of a History of the Doctrine of the Ideal and Real," and "Transcendental Speculation on the Apparent Deliberateness in the Fate of the Individual" from the first volume, and essays 4, 10, and 14 of the second volume.

In the second book of *The World as Will and Representation*, Schopenhauer was led to develop his metaphysics of the will by considering a problem that emerges from the first book. There he considered the world of outer experiences, revealed in intuitive perception, which he argued is conditioned by the principle of sufficient reason. More specifically, he claimed that normal perceptions of objects are conditioned by the cognizing subject through space, time, and causality. Moreover, his account of the intellectual nature of perception entails that the understanding automatically works sensations into the perception of an object by viewing it as the effect of some cause located in space and time. This leads him to wonder whether the world is only representation and something akin to a dream or an illusion produced by the subject. Is there something more to the world than representations?

Schopenhauer claims that if there is something more than representations, it cannot be discovered in the experience of representations governed by the principle of sufficient reason. Our experiences of the world as representations, of spatial-temporal objects in causal relationships, present themselves exactly as they appear. Consequently, the problem remains. Direct scrutiny of these types of representations fails, and even more general modes like mathematics and the findings of natural science provide no more hope. Mathematics is governed by the principle of sufficient reason of being, and it only describes representations as they occupy time and space. The natural sciences, which he classified into two main branches, only deal with the description of the recurring forms of natural objects (morphology) or with the explanation or changes in the world (etiology) by formulating laws of nature which describe regularly occurring changes in the world. Moreover, in etiological descriptions of the world, science employs the notion of natural forces, such as gravity, weight, impenetrability and the like, which are necessary features of its explanations, yet are not scientifically explainable. Schopenhauer, who held the sensible view that any good philosophy must acknowledge the best findings of science, held that his metaphysics would complete the scientific account of the world by explaining that which is necessary in scientific descriptions of the world, but which science cannot explain.

To discover whether the experiences we have of the world as representation are something more than an empty, dreamlike illusion, Schopenhauer shifted his consciousness from outer experiences to experiences revealed in self-consciousness. Each of us, he argued, is aware of our bodies in a twofold fashion. We perceive our body as an object of outer experience, viewing it as an object in space and time, standing in a causal nexus with other objects. When I attend to my hand that is writing this sentence, I perceive it at a particular place, at a specific time. I see it move and interact with my pen, creating marks on the page. I notice its shape, size, and color. Thus my hand appears like any other object of my perception. Yet, if I shift the focus of my consciousness and attend to the inner experience of my body, I become aware of the resistance of the pen on my hand and the pressure felt as it moves up and down on the paper as my thoughts are expressed in the symbols appearing on the page. So I experience my hand as no other representation; I discover, as it were, the interior of my body as an active agent. I discover my body as will. Schopenhauer viewed the identity of one's will with one's body as the philosophical truth *par excellence*, distinguishing this truth from any other. Thus he claimed that the representation of perception we call our body is also our will when we experience it as an item of inner or self-conscious experience. The action of one's body, he argued, is nothing other than an act of will objectifying itself, that is, becoming an object of perception.

In this way, Schopenhauer made one's body, or better yet, the experience of one's body, the key to metaphysics. For this reason, some scholars have emphasized that Schopenhauer is the philosopher of the body. By doing this, Schopenhauer put into play what he called his "revolutionary principle," the principle that we are to understand nature from ourselves, and not ourselves from nature. Since Schopenhauer regarded the knowledge we have of our body to be the most intimately known, he thought that it should be the basis of understanding all of nature, that which is not known. If we regard our body as microcosm, then ultimately the world, the macrocosm, is understood by Schopenhauer as macranthropos. Viewed in these terms, Schopenhauer's metaphysics reverses the modernistic tendency to subordinate human to nonhuman studies, to reduce *Geisteswissenschaften* to *Naturwissenschaften*.

Schopenhauer's claim that the will is that which is objectified or expressed in our experiences of the world, that the will is the interior of all representations, rejects a view he called "theoretical egoism," the view that I am the only real individual in the world, because I am the only being that I experience as both will and representation. Schopenhauer never took any form of skepticism too seriously, and while he admitted that theoretical egoism or solipsism could not be refuted by proofs, he viewed this stance as a doctrine no one outside a madhouse could take seriously. Once inside it, however, the egoist did not need a refutation, but rather a cure. With the rejection of theoretical egoism, Schopenhauer then mounted an argument from analogy, whereby he concluded that the will is also the interior of all other representations of the world standing at the same level as this representation of the body. In this way, the self-conscious experience of one's will becomes the key for Schopenhauer's metaphysics, where the will as the thing in itself is the essence of all representations of the world. Schopenhauer's argument from analogy, however, is not the only argument Schopenhauer used to support his thesis that everything in the world is an objectification of the will. He also thought that the phenomena of compassion, sexual love, magic, magnetism, musical genius, and mysticism also provide support for his view.

Schopenhauer's apparent identification of the will with the thing in itself has received considerable critical commentary. According to Kant, the thing in itself is something beyond all *a priori* forms of cognition. This meant for both Kant and Schopenhauer that it was something to which neither the principle of sufficient reason nor the subject/object division applied. Yet if we have knowledge of the will, and the will is discovered through the inner sense or self-consciousness, then the will is object for a subject and our self-conscious experience of the will is within the *a priori* form of time. Thus Schopenhauer's critics have argued that the will cannot be the thing in itself, and that the proper conclusion for Schopenhauer should be a form of Kantian agnosticism regarding the thing in itself. The will cannot be the thing in itself.

Schopenhauer was sensitive to this problem, and his later writings and correspondence suggest to some scholars that he developed two senses of the thing in itself. The will as thing in itself, he said, is only the thing in itself relative to other appearances, since it is the least conditioned experience, falling within the correlation of subject and object and having only one *a priori* form, time. As such, the will is the essence or content of all representations, and he thought that he was justified in making this claim, because it enables him to provide an explanation of the totality of experiences. Schopenhauer also seemed to retain another notion of the thing in itself that corresponds to Kant's conception of the thing in itself as something beyond the subject/object distinction and all *a priori* forms of cognition. Here he claimed that the thing in itself appears under the lightest of veils as will, but is itself never an object for a subject. This second sense of the thing in itself retains its Kantian definition, and he appears to believe that it is revealed to the mystic as an ineffable state. It should be noted, however, that Schopenhauer never clearly employed these two different senses of the thing in itself. One reason for this concerns the structure of his publications. He would add materials to new editions of his books, so that his later thoughts stand close to earlier formulations, and where later distinctions are not drawn. So the presentation of his writings obscures his distinction between the two senses of the thing in itself.

It is also in the second book of *The World as Will and Representation* that Schopenhauer introduced his doctrine of Platonic Ideas. As we have seen, Schopenhauer viewed everything to be the expression or objectification of the will. He came to have a hierarchical ontology of the world as representation that is based on the degree to which the will manifests itself. His hierarchy ranges from the least clear and most universally expressed dimensions of the will, the forces of nature, such as gravity, fluidity, elasticity, electricity, and so forth, and then to plants, then to animals, and ultimately to human beings, who most clearly express the will. Schopenhauer introduced the notion of Platonic Ideas to provide a philosophical account of natural forces and natural kinds in order to explain the ultimate findings of etiology and morphology. Schopenhauer claimed that all natural kinds of things into which we classify numerous discrete, particularized individuals have Platonic Ideas. Paralleling his hierarchical ontology, Platonic Ideas represent his ontology of the objectivity of the will. Platonic Ideas are representations, for Schopenhauer, objects for a subject, but they are not cognized within the principle of sufficient reason; however, their many particularized, individual things are cognized within the subject/object division and the principle of sufficient reason. Platonic Ideas will be discussed further in the next segment, where they play a central role in Schopenhauer's aesthetics.

AESTHETICS

Schopenhauer's parents strove to develop the aesthetic sensibilities of their young son. They succeeded in this quest, since he passionately enjoyed the arts throughout his entire life. As a child, and through the middle years of his life, Schopenhauer visited the most beautiful cities in Europe, where he enjoyed their architecture, theaters, art galleries, museums, and gardens. He consumed the literature in his father's library and studied the classics in school. Schopenhauer's philosophy abounds with allusions to great works of art and with quotations from literature and poetry. He referred to Johann Wolfgang Goethe almost as often as he did to Immanuel Kant, and both men represented to him the highest expression of genius. For significant stretches of his life, he would also attend plays, concerts, and operas on a daily basis. Schopenhauer took especial solace in music, and it was his custom for many years of his life to play the flute daily, for an hour before lunch and after he spent three hours writing. He loved the music of Mozart and Rossini, and he purchased all of Rossini's works arranged for flute. Given Schopenhauer's love of the arts, it is no wonder that he wrote his aesthetics from a deep appreciation and experience of the arts. When he compared his aesthetics to Kant's, to which his aesthetics owed some significant debts, he pointed out with considerable pride that his aesthetics stems directly from the experience of the beautiful, unlike Kant who worked theoretically from judgments about the beautiful. It is not surprising that Schopenhauer's love of art would translate into his philosophy, where he presented a more detailed analysis of aesthetic experience and the arts than is generally found in most philosophers. He thought that others had failed to appreciate the significance of art, the "flower of existence," and he resolved that he would not make the same mistake.

Schopenhauer's direct writings on aesthetics are found in the third book of the first volume of *The World as Will and Representation*, and in chapters 19–29 of the second volume, as well as the essay "On the Metaphysics of the Beautiful and Aesthetics," in the second volume of *Parerga and Paralipomena*. His initial treatment of aesthetics in the third book of *The World as Will and Representation* followed his first analysis of the world as representation (Book 1) and the world as will (Book 2). His aesthetics returns to a consideration of the world as representation, but this time he considers representations which are not governed by the principle of sufficient reason, although they are still structured by the subject/object division. Schopenhauer's aesthetics could only have followed his first examination of the world as will, since it is in the second book where he claimed that the thing in itself is the will; that the ubiquity of strife, conflict, destruction, suffering, and death in the world is due to the world being an expression of the will, and it was within the context of his metaphysics that he introduced his doctrine of Platonic Ideas, which would play a central role in his explanation of the aesthetic contemplation of great works of art, his theory of genius, and his discussions of the individual arts.

Schopenhauer viewed aesthetic experience, the contemplation of a great work of art, as a rare and extraordinarily revealing experience. In the ordinary course of our lives, we perceive many individual things that stand in various relationships to other things. Even more fundamentally, we perceive things in an interested fashion, that is, as possible means for satisfying or thwarting our desires, goals, and aspirations. In aesthetic experience it is as if we are suddenly torn out of our everyday way of perceiving things. It is as if we lose ourselves, our individuality, and we become absorbed in our perceptions. Our worries and woes seem to disappear, time seems to stand still, and calm and tranquility prevail. It is as if our consciousness becomes one with its object, and our eye seems to be a pure mirror reflecting the item of our experience, which no longer appears as a mundane thing. Well, this is what Schopenhauer thought.

To explain this extraordinary experience, Schopenhauer argued that aesthetic experience involves a radical transformation in both the subject and object of cognition. The subject becomes a pure, will-less, timeless, painless subject of knowledge, and the object of cognition becomes a Platonic Idea. This experience entails a form of cognition, Schopenhauer thought, that abandons the principle of sufficient reason and the perceiver's stance as willing subject. It also entails that the object is no longer an individual thing. Instead it is the universal and essential instantiated in numerous examples of its kind, but which is never perfectly exemplified in any tokens of its type. This object of the experience of aesthetic contemplation is a Platonic Idea, an object of cognition that is not perceived as an individual thing, which could satisfy desire. Aesthetic experience, therefore, represents for Schopenhauer a liberation from the will, and as such, a liberation from suffering. It also represents an experience that possesses a higher cognitive value than is even given by science, since its objects, Platonic Ideas, possess a greater degree of reality than the objects of both normal perception and scientific explanation.

Great art reveals metaphysical truth, according to Schopenhauer. The visual and verbal arts communicate Platonic Ideas, and he viewed music as presenting a copy of the will. Great artists repeat in their creations the world cognized objectively or disinterestedly. A great work of art is the product of genius, a term Schopenhauer reserved almost exclusively for great artists and philosophers. He viewed artists as possessing an overabundance of intellect, compared to the ordinary person, and as having the ability to see what other people cannot. This wealth of intellect allows artists to perceive things objectively, without reference to their wills, and to perceive things outside the scope of the principle of sufficient reason, to cognize not simply individual things, but Platonic Ideas. A great artist could view a stone, plant, animal, or human, and cognize the universal instantiated in the particular, the Platonic Idea expressed by the particular object. This capacity also entails for Schopenhauer that artists possess a high degree of imaginative ability, since individual things never perfectly express a Platonic Idea, and the artist has to creatively remove unnecessary and inessential features of a thing to perceive the Idea. Lastly, the artist has to have the technical ability to convey the Platonic Idea in a work of art. A great work of art allows the ordinary person, provided he or she has some degree of aesthetic sensibility, to experience what the artistic genius has experienced. Schopenhauer believed such genius to be innate, and aesthetic rules prescribing good art cannot guide a person in producing a great work of art.

Schopenhauer's account of artistic genius and his discussion of the individual arts entail that everything in nature is beautiful. Everything can be perceived objectively, that is, without a reference to an agent's desires, and the artistic genius is said to be able to cognize a Platonic Idea expressed by any individual, particularized thing, and all individual natural things are instances of Platonic Ideas. While Schopenhauer did not think there were Ideas for manufactured items, such as tables and chairs, he argued that these types of things could also be beautiful, provided the materials used to create them revealed Ideas. Any object of aesthetic experience is beautiful. Hence, Schopenhauer held that any object whose cognition involves the spectator's transformation into a pure, will-less subject of cognition is beautiful. Yet he also noted that some objects are experienced as more beautiful than others. Schopenhauer accounted for this by appealing to the type of Platonic Idea revealed in the aesthetic experience and its effects on the observer. His general view was that the cognition of the higher Platonic Ideas, those which show a higher level or grade of the will's objectification, are more beautiful than those which are of lower Platonic Ideas, those which show less clearly the nature of the will.

Although all aesthetic experiences presuppose the subject and object correlation, his analysis of the aesthetic enjoyment of the beautiful emphasizes one side or the other of this correlation to explain aesthetic enjoyment. When the object of aesthetic experience is an Idea of one of the lower grades or levels of the will's objectification, say those associated with the inorganic world and plant life, Schopenhauer emphasized the tranquil and peaceful countenance of the pure subject as the aesthetic effect. When the Idea expresses a higher grade of the will's objectification, say one associated with animal or human life, he emphasized the nature of the object of experience, such that the revealed Idea connotes something terrible or hostile to the human body, and the aesthetic effect is a state of exaltation reached by the contemplation of those terrible objects. Therefore Schopenhauer's distinction between the beautiful and the sublime concerns the object of aesthetic experience. If the Idea reveals more of the terrible nature of the will, then the feeling of the sublime involves the exaltation of the subject beyond the hostility of the object to the will. If no such exaltation takes place, and the transformation into pure subject occurs smoothly and effortlessly, then the contemplator has the feeling of the beautiful. In both the feelings of the beautiful and the sublime, the aesthetic observer becomes a pure subject of cognition, and he or she no longer perceives individual, particularized objects as the means to satisfy or thwart desires and needs.

Schopenhauer's account of the individual arts mirrors the various levels or grades of his hierarchical ontology, and it includes his discussion of aesthetic enjoyment in greater detail. Art reveals metaphysical truth. Yet some arts are more revelatory than others. This depends on the ontological status of what it reveals. Although Schopenhauer viewed everything in the world as representation as being coequal expressions of the will, he also viewed items in the world as representation as expressing different grades or levels of the objectification of the will, that is, different degrees of the nature of the will. The scale he used to develop his hierarchical ontology was based on the degree to which the nature of the will is revealed. The lowest levels of the will's objectification are found in inorganic nature. The next level is plant life, which is followed by animal life. Human life, for Schopenhauer, reveals in the greatest clarity the nature of the will, and so human life represents the highest level and most complete expression of the nature of the will. With the exception of music, Schopenhauer ranked the various arts on the basis of the positions in which the Platonic Ideas communicated by particular arts rank in his hierarchical ontology. In other words, if the Idea falls in inorganic nature, the art that communicates it is ranked at the lowest end of the scale, and if it communicates the Idea of human life, it ranks in the highest level of his aesthetic scale.

Schopenhauer ranked architecture as the lowest of the fine arts, since he believed that it brings to clear perception the lowest grades of the objectification of the will. Unlike the other arts, which present Ideas in their media, the artistic architect uses stone (Schopenhauer rejected wood as the medium for beautiful buildings), the material itself, to bring to cognition the Ideas of gravity, rigidity, and light. The beauty of a building is found in the suitability and stability of its structure, where the conflict between gravity, which would pull everything down into a single mass, and rigidity, which resists this impulse, are resolved by the stability of the building. So, in a beautiful building, its position, size, and form have a necessary relationship to its stability, such that, if any part of the building were removed, the building would collapse. A fine work of architecture also reveals the Idea of light as it is intercepted, impeded, and reflected through its mass. The beauty of a building leads, almost without effort, to a calming effect on the perceiver.

The artistic arrangement of water, hydraulics, is next on Schopenhauer's hierarchy of the arts. Tumbling waterfalls, water dashing and foaming over rocks, springs gushing upward as columns of water, and clear reflecting ponds and lakes reveal the Idea of fluidity and its resolution with gravity. Artistic horticulture, since it deals with plant life, is more revelatory of the nature of the will than is architecture and hydraulics. Yet Schopenhauer viewed the beauty of a created landscape to be a lesser artistic accomplishment than those of architecture and hydraulics, since the beauty of a landscape is more a product of nature itself. The artistic horticulturalist does little more than clearly separate or distinctly arrange plants in a fitting association and succession, something that exists at the whim of nature, whose inclemency can easily destroy the landscape. However, since the plant world itself more readily offers itself for aesthetic enjoyment without any mediation by the artist, landscape painting, Schopenhauer thought, is more suitable for the artistic depiction of plants, and he saw in the still life, and paintings of architecture, ruins, and church interiors, a revelation of the lower grades of the will's objectivity than is found in landscape painting, in which a higher grade is expressed. In painting and sculpture of animal life, however, still higher grades of the will are expressed. Schopenhauer claimed that the restlessness, striving, and conflict embodied in animal life suggest the same sorts of conflicts found in more vehement form in human life.

But it is art concerned with the human form that constitutes the highest of the visual arts for Schopenhauer, because humans represent the highest or most adequate expression of the will. But the visual arts, he argued, are limited by their media, being unable to present the complexity of human life due to their static nature. This is even true of historic painting, in which the depiction of an event in human life presents more of the mien and countenance of a person, and thus, of an individual's character.

The verbal arts, all of which he referred to as "poetry," are the most capable of expressing human life and the Idea of humanity, according to Schopenhauer. Curiously neglecting the novel, Schopenhauer divided the verbal arts into three kinds: lyrical, epic, and dramatic poetry. He viewed lyrical poetry as the most subjective form of poetry, since it highlights the emotive and passionate side of human life, whereas epic and dramatic poetry are capable of depicting more of the complexity of human life. Epic poetry is capable of bringing to greater clarity than lyrical poetry the essence of life by narrating the struggles of individuals to survive, face obstacles, and obtain goals. Yet it is tragedy or tragic drama that stands on the summit of the pictorial and verbal arts for

Schopenhauer, since it reveals the terrible side of human existence, depicting the wretchedness and misery of human existence, the suffering of the just and innocent, and the painful blows of chance. These connote the antagonism of the will with itself in the greatest clarity, Schopenhauer thought. In great tragedy, through the tragic hero's struggles and ultimate fall, Schopenhauer thought that the denial of the will is expressed. He claimed that the atonement for the hero's sin signifies atonement of the will for "original sin," the guilt of existence itself. The experience of great tragedy is the experience of the highest expression of the sublime, he held, since it presents to the spectator the world as the battleground of the will, and it counsels resignation from the world, the denial of the will. In this way, great tragedy expresses Schopenhauer's most important truth, that nonexistence is preferable to existence, since it depicts and recommends the denial of the will by showing the terrible price that is paid by the affirmation of the will.

Unlike the visual and verbal arts, Schopenhauer did not view great music as communicating Platonic Ideas. Rather, he claimed that music has the capacity to copy the will itself without depicting anything within the world as representation. Playing off a remark by Gottfried Wilhelm Leibniz about music and arithmetic, Schopenhauer said that music is an unconscious exercise in metaphysics in which the mind does not know that it is philosophizing. Just as Schopenhauer argued that the world as representation is objectified willing, he argued that the world as representation could be viewed as objectified music. He also emphasized a direct kinship between philosophy and music, believing that if one could state verbally what is expressed in music, you would have philosophy, or if one would express in tones what is stated in philosophy, you would have music. Both express the inner nature of the world. Although Schopenhauer had the deepest respect for music, he was also aware that his metaphysics of music was fraught with difficulties, since it suggests that music provides a copy of an original that cannot be copied, a representation in tones of that which cannot be represented. Schopenhauer, therefore, left it to the discretion of his readers to accept or reject his views on music, but only after they can both understand the single thought that is expressed in his philosophy and experience the effect produced by great music.

ETHICS

A strong case can be made that ethics is the *leitmotif* of Schopenhauer's philosophy. In 1813, when he started to think about the philosophy that would be expressed in *The World as Will and Representation*, he envisioned a philosophy that would be metaphysics and ethics in one. Later, in *On the Will in Nature*, he would claim that he was more justified than Baruch Spinoza to call his metaphysics "ethics." Finally, in his last book, *Parerga and Paralipomena*, he described his philosophy as culminating in a metaphysical-ethical standpoint. Schopenhauer also wrote with a broader sense of moral philosophy than is usually the case with most contemporary work in ethics. In fact, he recognized two dimensions in his moral philosophy. There is his higher metaphysical-ethical standpoint in which he used his metaphysics of the will to explain the moral significance of the world, claiming that salvation or redemption is possible only through the denial of the will. It is also within this context that he would discuss death, eternal justice, the metaphysics of sexual love, asceticism, and mysticism. The second dimension of his moral philosophy, which he referred to as morality in the narrower sense of the term, concentrates on human conduct from a moral point of view. Within this context, he discussed freedom and determinism, moral responsibility, the philosophy of right, moral virtues and vices, moral psychology and character types, and he argued that compassion is the source of all actions possessing genuine moral worth. Ultimately, Schopenhauer would provide a metaphysical explanation for his analysis of moral behavior that would connect the two dimensions of his moral philosophy.

Schopenhauer wrote more directly on ethics than he did on epistemology, metaphysics, or aesthetics. His direct writings on ethics are found in the fourth book of the first volume of *The World as Will and Representation*, and in chapters 40–50 of the second volume; the chapter "Reference to Ethics" in *On the Will in Nature*, and also in *The Two Fundamental Problems of Ethics* (first edition 1841; second edition 1860); and in chapters 8 and 9 of the second volume of *Parerga and Paralipomena*, whose first volume contains the well known "Aphorisms on the Wisdom of Life," his attempt to provide instructions for living a happy life, one whose existence is preferable to its nonexistence. Schopenhauer noted in this essay that his "eudemonology" requires the suspension of his higher metaphysical-ethical standpoint, which concludes that nonexistence is preferable to existence. *The Two Fundamental Problems of Ethics* has never been published in English translation under this title. The two essays that comprise this book, both of which were written for prize essay contests, have appeared in English as *Prize Essay on the Freedom of the Will* and as *On the Basis of Morality*.

Schopenhauer's ethics is not prescriptive, that is, he does not attempt to articulate rules stating what we morally ought or ought not do. Virtue, he thought, is as little taught as genius, and since he believed that willing cannot be taught, and ethics has to do with what a person wills, he held that ethics cannot be taught. Ultimately, and fundamentally, the moral quality of a person's conduct followed, he thought, from a person's character, and since he believed that one's character is innate and unchangeable, he thought that the moral quality of a person's conduct cannot be changed. He argued that at its best, moral philosophy could only provide knowledge that would enable a person to act more consistently with his or her character. That is, it could aid someone with a good character to act more consistently with his or her desires, but moral knowledge itself is insufficient to make an evil person good. Freedom, for Schopenhauer, is not found in anything expressed in the world as representation, which, of course, is within the principle of sufficient reason. He thought that everything we do is necessary; that we could not have done otherwise than we have done. Yet he claimed that we are still morally responsible for our actions since what we do follows from what we are. This doctrine, which is sometimes referred to as actualism, embodies a very different notion of moral responsibility than that advocated by many moral philosophers, who typically hold that moral responsibility requires the ability to act differently than one has acted.

While Schopenhauer took great pride in the Kantian roots of his theoretical philosophy, and he viewed his own epistemology and metaphysics as retaining fidelity to Kant, despite their deviations, he viewed Kant's ethics as an intellectual catastrophe. Thus he wrote his ethics in diametrical opposition to Kant's practical or moral philosophy. Schopenhauer rejected the Kantian claims that moral behavior is rational behavior and that pure reason is the source for discovering moral laws. He also rejected Kant's ethics of duty, which employed the categorical imperative, the principle that morally right actions or duties are actions whose maxims could become a universal law valid for all rational beings, as the means for discovering moral laws. Thus, he rejected also the idea that moral laws constitute categorical rules for conduct, rules that are unconditionally binding on all people regardless of their interests.

Schopenhauer argued that Kant's ethics began with a claim that needs justification, namely, that there are nonempirical moral laws prescribing what people ought to do, and he claimed that Kant's ethics took its form from theological ethics. The problem, as he saw it, is that Kant had correctly argued for the independence of ethics from theology, but had unwittingly borrowed concepts from theology in framing his ethics. Thus he claimed that Kant's central moral ideas were meaningless, since they required a theological context to make sense, a context in which there is a lawgiver who issues commands (God), and who has the capacity to reward compliance with the law or punish disobedience. Schopenhauer thought that the logic of Kant's moral concepts and his unconscious theological yearnings were revealed in his moral theology, where it becomes reasonable to believe that there is a God, that we have an immortal soul, that our actions are free, and that the virtuous will be happy. While Kant argued that his moral theology was based on his ethics, Schopenhauer argued that it simply articulated the presuppositions of his ethics. Thus Schopenhauer claimed that Kant's ethics was a version of a theological ethics, and since he believed, like Kant, that a theologically based ethics is self-interested, and that self-interest can never be the basis for actions possessing moral worth, he claimed that Kant's ethics is self-interested and that its followers would perform actions that lack moral worth.

In contrast to Kant's nonempirical, rational, and prescriptive ethics of duty, Schopenhauer developed an empirical and descriptive virtue ethics in which passion and desire (the will) are viewed as primary in human behavior. Schopenhauer's ethics attempted to explain and trace to their ultimate sources human behavior from a moral point of view. Consequently, he held that there is no other way to discover the foundation of morality than an empirical one. He would brag that his ethics contained no *a priori* construction, no absolute moral legislation for all rational beings; that it employed no theological or transcended hypotheses; and that he showed that the ethical significance of human conduct is metaphysical.

Schopenhauer's ethical methodology is a specific instance of his overall philosophical method. Just as he conceived that the task of the philosopher is to provide a comprehensive explanation of the totality of human experiences, his ethics attempts to provide a unified explanation of moral experience. He claimed that all human behavior can be classified into three classes of actions. Some actions possess moral worth, such as actions expressing voluntary justice and pure philanthropy; others are morally reprehensible, such as acts of pure cruelty and maliciousness; while others are morally indifferent, being neither morally reprehensible nor worthwhile, which constitute the majority of our actions. Schopenhauer defined his moral value terms by focusing on the affective responses toward an action by both the agent of the action and by an impartial witness. Actions possessing moral worth draw the approbation of an impartial witness as well as the approbation of the agent's conscience; actions that are morally reprehensible evoke both the disapprobation of the witness and the agent's feeling of disapprobation, or the "sting of conscience"; and those that are morally indifferent evoke neither approbation nor disapprobation by either the doer of the deed or the uninvolved spectator, because there is no affective response, either positive or negative.

Schopenhauer was then led to ask why humans perform actions bearing different moral values, and he explored the various incentives or motives for these actions. Schopenhauer detailed four basic incentives for all human conduct. He argued that all human conduct is intentional, having as its ultimate aim something that is in agreement with or contrary to the will. Ends that are in agreement with the will are identified as aiming for someone's weal or well-being, and those contrary to a person's will have as their aims someone's woe or misfortune. Thus he contended that all actions have as their ultimate end someone's well-being or woe. Since an action is aimed at either a person's own well-being or misfortune, or that of another, Schopenhauer recognized four ultimate or basic incentives for a human action. His four incentives are egoism, which desires one's own well-being; compassion, which desires another's well-being; malice, which desires another's woe; and an unnamed incentive, which desires one's own woe. Schopenhauer provided little description of this last incentive, and he claimed in a letter that it does not possess moral value, but its value is ascetic. Like egoism, he also claimed that this unnamed incentive only concerns actors themselves, so it is also a nonmoral incentive. In other words, he believed that actions possessing either a positive or negative moral value concern a person's desires regarding another's weal or woe, and never for a person's own.

Schopenhauer argued that egoism is the incentive for morally indifferent actions, malice for morally reprehensible actions, and compassion for actions possessing moral worth. He did this through an argument by elimination, claiming that neither egoism nor malice could be the incentive for voluntary justice and pure philanthropy. He supplemented this argument by contending that compassion is the source of the cardinal virtues of justice and philanthropy, virtues from which, he thought, all other virtues are derived. Schopenhauer used his analysis of the fundamental incentives to discuss the moral characters of individuals. He thought that the degree to which a person is motivated by these incentives accounts for the moral quality of a person's character. An evil character is one disposed to being highly malicious, whereas a good character is disposed to being highly compassionate. While Schopenhauer rejected Kant's categorical imperative, he did propose a moral principle, namely, "Injure no one; rather help everyone as much as you can." Instead of prescribing right conduct, Schopenhauer claimed that his principle simply summarizes the line of conduct to which he attributed moral worth. The first clause of his principle, "Injure no one," summarizes his conception of justice, whereas the second, "Help everyone as much as you can," summarizes his conception of philanthropy or loving-kindness.

Schopenhauer regarded egoism as exemplifying the natural standpoint of humans and nonhuman animals, since both strive to secure their survival and well-being. However, he viewed self-interested behavior as being the hallmark of human behavior because only humans possess reason, the capacity to think conceptually and discursively. Therefore, unlike nonhuman animals, he saw humans as capable of thoughtfully and methodologically pursuing their own well-being. Because Schopenhauer emphasized self-interest as the dominant and natural incentive for human conduct, when he analyzed compassion, he had to explain how it overcomes our deeply egoistic tendencies. He argued that compassion is always directed toward another's distress, and in compassionating another's woe, the agent is led to treat the other's suffering as one's own, that is, one is moved to prevent or eliminate it. Schopenhauer claimed that the compassionate agent literally experiences the suffering of another just as one's own, but in the other's body. He thought that this phenomenon could not be explained psychologically and that the phenomenon of compassion is deeply mysterious, the "great mystery of ethics," requiring a metaphysical explanation. The possibility of compassion, he held, is due ultimately to the metaphysical unity of all beings. He claimed that compassionate or good people view others in a manner that is captured by the Vedic formula "*Tat twam asi* (that thou art)." Borrowing another phrase from Hinduism, he held that good people see behind the "veil of *māyā*" by treating others as themselves. Evil people, individuals whose lives are dominated by extreme egoism and malice, view others as non-egos, and thereby, live entangled in a delusion. In contrast to these types of people, the behavior of compassionate people expresses the standpoint of the unity of all beings. Schopenhauer said that the behavior of good people toward other living things is a form of "practical mysticism," since their conduct expresses what the mystic realizes—the unity of being. Good people thus exhibit a mode of life that is consistently metaphysically warranted.

Schopenhauer connected his analysis of moral goodness and nobility of character to his theory of salvation by arguing that both spring from the same source, a cognition that penetrates beyond the *principium individuationis*, space and time. The difference between a good person and a saint concerns how clearly one recognizes metaphysical truth. The good person, he thought, only dimly recognizes that other sentient creatures, humans and nonhuman animals, are an "I once more." The saint, however, more clearly recognizes that everything is an expression of the will and all suffering in the world is due to its being an expression of the will. This cognition shows suffering is essential to life, since all living, cognitive beings necessarily suffer. So he concluded that the problem of suffering cannot be solved by loving others as oneself. This knowledge, he thought, leads the saint to develop a strong aversion to the inner nature of the world, the will or the will to life, the cause of all suffering, and the saint denies the will, resigns, and becomes completely indifferent to everything. This phenomenon, Schopenhauer thought, is shown in the lives of saints and great souls among Christians, Hindus, Buddhists, and followers of other religions.

Schopenhauer also recognized a second path to salvation and denial of the will that is distinct from the knowledge of the metaphysical basis of all suffering. He also thought this is the most frequent way in which people are led to deny the will. Some individuals are led to renounce everything they formally desired, and instead of hungrily longing for the objects of their desires, they develop a deep aversion to everything in the world, because of extreme personal suffering. Like the saint, who is led to resign from life, these individuals also deny the will and come to experience an inviolable peace and calm. Schopenhauer saw the story of Gretchen's suffering in Goethe's *Faust* as the best depiction of this phenomenon in literature, but he also believed that it can be found in numerous stories of people who have had very adventurous lives, yet resigned from life to become hermits and monks. As an example, he cited the story of the love-drunk *bon vivant* Raymond Lull, who saw hell in the cancer ravished breast of the woman he so desperately desired. This horrid experience led Lull to renounce worldly life and flee into the wilderness to do penance.

Schopenhauer believed there is no causal explanation for the denial of the will. He saw the denial of the will as embodying a contradiction to the world as representation, in which everything is causally determined, since it represents the appearance of freedom in the world. He did not believe that either knowledge of suffering or suffering itself produced denial of the will as the effect of a cause. Rather, he saw it as something that happens, coming as it were, from the outside, proceeding as an "effect of grace," using a term he borrowed from Christian theology. The denial of the will, the appearance of freedom in a world in which everything is determined, occasions a transcendental change in its subject, one in which there is no will, no world, and no representation. This is not to say that for the denier of the will there is some absorption into nothingness. The state obtained by the overcomer of the world is a relative nothing, Schopenhauer argued, the negation of everything in the world. This phenomenon suggests, Schopenhauer thought, that behind our existence is something that only becomes accessible by shaking off the world, but whatever this state is, it is something about which nothing can be meaningfully said.

Thus ended Schopenhauer's philosophy, which he claimed only ranged from the affirmation to the denial of the world, from willing to not willing, from an account of the world to the denial of the world.

The Dictionary

– A –

ABSOLUTE, THE (*DAS ABSOLUTUM*). Schopenhauer categorically rejected the idea of an absolute and any term that purported to refer to some ultimate, infinite, unconditioned, necessary, or primordial being, as well as any term used to denote something that serves as the first ground of the world. To put it simply, he absolutely rejected the absolute. In particular, he decried the use of this term by post-Kantian, German philosophers and theologians, and he especially condemned the use of the idea of the absolute by **Johann Gottlieb Fichte, Friedrich Wilhelm Joseph von Schelling**, and **Georg Wilhelm Friedrich Hegel**. He argued that an absolute and unconditioned being could not be thought, since he held that anything thought must be an object for a subject, which entails that such a being is conditioned. Moreover, he argued that the absolute is something unknown and the unknown cannot be used to explain the known, the world. He therefore prided his own philosophy as always using the better known to explain the lesser known, and he based his **metaphysics** on what he regarded as the most intimately known, the **will**.

Schopenhauer, moreover, argued that the idea of the absolute has been used by post-Kantian, German philosophers to serve as a proxy for the idea of **God** found in the type of speculative metaphysics that had been crushed by **Immanuel Kant**. By re-baptizing God as the "Absolute," these philosophers were mounting a rearguard action against Kant through duplicitous means. The word "Absolute," he said, sounds so serious and carries such a foreign, decent, and aristocratic connotation that it makes it seem like something stands behind it. Closer examination reveals that any claim about the existence of

1

an absolute, he said, is the conclusion of an enthymeme, whose un-stated premises, when recognized, would show it to be the cosmo-logical argument for the existence of some self-caused, first cause of all things. Kant, he said, had demolished this argument, and so its ad-vocates had to hide it behind tortuous narratives. To make what was bad even worse, these "philosophers" had to invent fantastic concepts of the faculty of **reason** as the means to cognize their ultimates. Thus he claimed that Schelling's **intellectual intuition** was akin to the sixth sense of bats, and Hegel's conception of reason as the capacity to reconcile the contradictory concepts of the understanding was an expression of the want of understanding. Fichte, he said, treated the **principle of sufficient reason** beyond its scope of application as he tried to deduce everything from the absolute ego. Schopenhauer, in contrast, viewed the faculty of reason as the capacity to develop **con-cepts**, which must ultimately be drawn from experience to have any significance, and which can never serve to refer to anything beyond experience. *See also* PRINCIPLE OF SUFFICIENT REASON OF BECOMING.

AENESIDEMUS. *See* G. E. SCHULZE.

AESTHETICS (*AESTHETIK*). Schopenhauer passionately enjoyed the arts throughout his entire life. Consequently, it is not surprising that he would write thoroughly and personally about aesthetics or the philosophy of **art**. His first systematic treatment of aesthetics ap-peared in the third book of *The World as Will and Representation* (1818), which he supplemented by chapters 19–29 in the second vol-ume of his *magnum opus* (1844). His last major statement of his aes-thetics appeared in the essay, "On the Metaphysics of the Beautiful and Aesthetics," from the second volume of *Parerga and Paralipom-ena* (1851). *See also* BEAUTIFUL; CONTEMPLATION; GENIUS; HISTORY; MUSIC; PLATONIC IDEAS; SUBLIME; TRAGEDY.

ANIMALS (*TIERE*). Schopenhauer viewed the difference between humans and nonhuman animals as a difference in degree and not kind. His metaphysics details the essence of both as the **will**, although he also believed that human life expresses the nature of the will more clearly and more vehemently than animal life. The kinship between humans and animals is also shown, he thought, through the study of comparative anatomy and zoology. He claimed that it is the possession of the faculty of **reason** that distinguishes humans from nonhumans, but for both, he also thought that the will is primary in their behavior. Thus he attributed **egoism**, the craving for continued existence and individual well-being, as the dominant incentive for both human and animal behavior. Only humans, he said, are capable of self-interested behavior, since only humans are capable of abstract, conceptual, and discursive thought. Therefore, he held that only humans are capable of reflectivity and the systematic pursuit of their own well-being. Still, Schopenhauer maintained that both human and animal behavior is causally determined by the will's response to a particular **motive**. The only differences between humans and animals are the types of motives to which they are susceptible. Animals, he wrote, are only moved by immediate, intuitive **representations**, since they lack the faculty of reason; whereas, humans can be motivated by abstract, conceptual thought. Since Schopenhauer saw reason as the source of wonder that prompts philosophical speculation about the world, as well as the faculty that produces philosophy, he called humans the *animal metaphysicum*, a designation that emphasizes a kinship and difference between humans and other animals.

While viewing reason as that which distinguishes humans from animals does not separate Schopenhauer from the dominant view in Western philosophical thought, he rejected the traditional claim that rationality is the essence of humanity. Reason was viewed by him as secondary in human behavior, serving instrumentally the will. Nor did he believe that the possession of reason is a morally significant difference between humans and animals. Thus he took **Immanuel Kant** harshly to task for viewing the possession of reason as definitive of moral standing, and he viewed as barbaric Kant's claim that we have no direct moral duties to animals. By viewing animals as things and as having no moral standing, he claimed Kant had simply assumed a prejudice embodied in Judeo-Christian theology. Thus Schopenhauer argued, with considerable pride, that his morality, based on **compassion**, finds animals to be morally significant for they, like humans, suffer. He also claimed that some of the higher animals exhibit good characters, suggesting that some animals are capable of compassion. Naturally, he praised **Hinduism** and **Buddhism** for their enlightened views of animals, and he saw his views on the moral status of nonhumans as a strong point of contact between his philosophy and Eastern thought. *See also* CHARACTER; PHILOSOPHY; VOLUNTARISM.

APPEARANCE (*ERSCHEINUNG*). Schopenhauer took this term and its contrast, "**thing in itself**," from **Immanuel Kant**. He regarded this distinction as one of the greatest of Kant's insights, and he decried the post-Kantian idealists, **Johann Gottlieb Fichte**, **Friedrich Wilhelm Joseph von Schelling**, and **Georg Wilhelm Friedrich Hegel**, for abandoning Kant's profound distinction between appearances and the thing in itself. Schopenhauer tended to view the term "appearance" as equivalent to "**representation**," and in particular, as referring to anything given in sensory experience or perception. Like Kant, he argued that our sensory experiences of things are of appearances and are not of the thing in itself, since sensory experiences are structured by *a priori* forms of space, time, and causality.

　　E. F. J. Payne tended to translate "*Erscheinung*" and its derivatives as "phenomenon," a term that naturally invites its contrast "noumenon." Schopenhauer read this as a contrast between the perceivable (phenomenal) and the conceivable (noumenal), and he censured Kant's use of these terms. He, thus, refrained from employing them within his own philosophy. *See also* TRANSCENDENTAL IDEALISM; WILL.

ARISTOTLE (384–322 B.C.E.). Schopenhauer's first philosophy professor, **G. E. Schulze**, recommended that he not read Aristotle and **Baruch Spinoza** until he had mastered **Plato** and **Immanuel Kant**. Schulze's advice subordinated Aristotle to Plato and Kant, and Schopenhauer concurred with his teacher's judgment. He called Aristotle the "organizer of philosophy" and the "father of logic," designations that highlighted Aristotle's deft abilities for enumerating an infinite number of things and classifying them under higher genera. Consequently, he praised Aristotle's power of observation, sagacity, and versatility. Aristotle's thought, he said, expressed great range, but compared to Plato, it lacked depth. Thus he viewed Aristotle's observations as reasonable and as expressing the type of thought that dominates practical life and science, which remains within the scope of the **principle of sufficient reason**. Plato, however, was deep, and Schopenhauer said his thought was that of **genius** and was akin to **art**. This judgment was reflected in a focused form when Schopenhauer asserted that Aristotle's metaphysics was shallow and that where Aristotle was the most hostile to Plato over his theory of **Platonic Ideas**, Plato was correct.

Schopenhauer praised Aristotle's empirical frame of mind, but he also diagnosed this as the source of his lack of philosophical depth. Aristotle's observations were only based on a **consciousness of other things**, he argued, and he ignored the resources revealed in **self-consciousness**. This resulted, he said, in Aristotle working with data too poor to truly get to the essence of things, since only self-consciousness provides the key for truly understanding the world. Schopenhauer also charged that Aristotle was not a consistent and methodical empiricist, which was something clearly revealed in his cosmology, where he employed a number of *a priori* theses and generated a number of profound errors that were only corrected by Francis Bacon, Nicolaus Copernicus, Galileo Galilei, Johanes Kepler and Isaac Newton. Despite these errors, however, Schopenhauer believed that Aristotle's writings were "immortal" and that he was still profitable to read. But he also added to this observation that reading Plato was profitable to the "highest degree."

ART (*KUNST*). Schopenhauer referred to art as the "flower of existence," because he found the aesthetic **contemplation** of a great work of art to be a transforming experience, one that lifts a person beyond the many concerns, pressures, and aggravations of everyday life, and indeed, beyond the wretchedness of existence itself. In this regard, he saw the enjoyment of art as presenting a foretaste and hint of that which is realized by the **denial of the will**. Due to the great significance he attributed to art, it would have been interesting to draw some deep inner connection between his **aesthetics** and the fact that his dear friends called him "Art," rather than "Arthur." But Schopenhauer personally was no "flower"; he was much more a thorn, and it is difficult to imagine that he had friends so dear that he would have accepted such a familiar form of address. It is also tempting to say, in a Nietzschean sense, that his life was a work of art, but it even fails on Schopenhauer's own criterion for a great work of art—its contemplation does not bring consolation. It was not a **tragedy**. It may be better to think of his philosophy as his life, for in that case, an analogy could be drawn between art and Arthur, since Schopenhauer believed that **music**, the pinnacle of the arts, expressed in tones that which is said in words by philosophy.

Schopenhauer's exaltation of art is something that may have made his parents proud, since they made sure he was exposed to the various arts during his formative years, and they sought to develop his aesthetic sensibilities. From his childhood through his middle years, Schopenhauer experienced the great cities of Europe, and he enjoyed their great architecture, art galleries, theaters, museums, and gardens. He studied the classics in school, and he was a voracious consumer of literature and poetry. His philosophy, moreover, is peppered with allusions to great works of art and quotations from literature and poetry. It is not too distant from the truth to observe, moreover, that he enjoyed literature and some artistic presentation, some play, concert, or opera almost everyday of his adult life. He also had all of the music of his beloved Rossini arranged for the flute, and he was said to play the flute daily, an activity that, among others, led **Friedrich Nietzsche** to wonder whether he was truly a **pessimist**.

Schopenhauer's deep involvement in the arts is clearly reflected in his aesthetics, which is articulated and motivated by his personal observations and experiences. His exaltation of art can be found, moreover, in his assessment that art was more metaphysically revealing than the **natural sciences**, a thesis that made his philosophy attractive to artists. The same can also be said about his use of the term "**genius**," which he reserved almost exclusively for the great artist. One could well imagine that had he not been a philosopher, he probably would have liked to have been an artist, given the deep kinship he found between art and philosophy. *See also* BEAUTIFUL; PLATONIC IDEAS; SUBLIME; WAGNER, RICHARD.

ASCETICISM (*ASKESIS*). It is common for Schopenhauer to use the terms "asceticism" and "**denial of the will**" as synonyms. Still, he recognized other salvific disciplines, such as **quietism** and **mysticism**, as also expressing the denial of the will. Thus he discussed a "narrower sense" of asceticism in which he referred to traditional religious practices expressed by the saints and great souls found in

Christianity, **Hinduism**, and **Buddhism**. In this sense, the ascetic attempts to deliberately break the will by refusing the agreeable things of life (those things that satisfy the will, i.e., **good** things); by seeking the disagreeable things of life (those things that are contrary to the will, i.e., **bad** things); and by constantly mortifying the will through penance and self-chastisement. In particular, since he viewed the **body** as the objectification of the will, he tied his narrower notion of asceticism directly to the mortification of the body. Ultimately, asceticism led him to recognize a desire for one's own **woe** as a basic or fundamental **incentive** for human behavior, and he thereby placed it at par with **egoism**, **malice**, and **compassion**. (In a letter to **Johann August Becker**, dated 10 December 1844, he said that this incentive possesses ascetic rather than moral value.)

Consequently, he claimed that ascetics ate little and neglected their health, gave away their possessions to alleviate the suffering of others, accepted all harm inflicted by others and embraced their suffering, practiced chastity and denied the sexual impulse, the strongest **affirmation of the will** and the means by which the will to life constantly renews itself. He claimed, moreover, that the most extreme form of asceticism was a voluntarily chosen death by starvation, and he argued that this was the only form of **suicide** that is immune to moral criticism.

Like all cases of the denial of the will, Schopenhauer argued that ascetic practices do not cause this denial, since it is the free act of the **will**. Moreover, like all cases of the denial of the will, it is a constant struggle to maintain this condition as long as a person is alive. Consequently, he wrote that ascetic practices are often used by individuals who have denied the will to return to this state. For this reason, he drew a close connection between asceticism, quietism, and mysticism, and he argued that whoever professes one is led to the other.

ASEITY (*AESITÄT*). Schopenhauer took this term from theology, where it is used to describe the being of **God**. It is derived from the Latin *a se*, "from oneself," and it is used to refer to the self-derived or self-originated nature of God and his absolute independence from anything else. On this view, everything in creation is *ab alio*, dependent on God for its existence. Schopenhauer preserved these basic notions by claiming that the **will** has aseity. The will is self-derived and self-determining, independent from anything else, and everything in the world is dependent on the will. Everything in the world is as it is due to the will, and everything is as the will is.

Schopenhauer conceived of everything in the world to be an objectification of the will, and he held that the will is the essence of the world. The will, he argued, is free, that is, it is beyond the scope of the **principle of sufficient reason**, which is the source of all necessity. Everything that happens in the world happens necessarily, he held, since everything within the world is subject to the principle of sufficient reason. By viewing the will as the essence of everything in the world, as that which is expressed in everything in nature, he argued that he had shown that **freedom** is compatible with necessity. In other words, while all events in the world, including human actions, are necessary, the essence of all these events is free. He captured this notion by the Latin slogan, *operari sequitur esse*, "acting follows being," that is, everything that happens in the world, all actions, follow from the being or essence of things and, he held, this essence is free.

Schopenhauer argued that the freedom of the will is **transcendental**; something presupposed by our deep feelings of being both the doers of our deeds and for being responsible or accountable for them. Thus he claimed in the chapter "Reference to Ethics," in *On the Will in Nature* that the twin pillars of all ethics, freedom and **responsibility**, are "inconceivable without the assumption of the will's aseity." Although all of our actions follow necessarily from a **motive**, since he held that what makes a motive a sufficient motive is ultimately a person's intelligible **character** and that this character is a person's essence and the will, what originates the actions is free. For this reason, he claimed, we are responsible for our character, which is the independent source for all that we do, and all guilt or merit for a person's conduct attaches to his or her will. He held the same view concerning all events in the world; they are as they are due to the will, and all the guilt or merit found in the world has a metaphysical basis. Since he also believed that he had shown that the wretchedness of the world is due to its being the objectification of the will, he argued that all the **evils** in the world, all of the guilt, fell back to that responsible for it, the will.

Thus Schopenhauer distanced himself from theologists who ascribed aseity to God and tried to maintain that God is not responsible for the evils in the world, since God endowed his creatures with a *liberum arbitrium*, a free choice of the will, which is the basis of evil. This idea of a free will is vacuous, Schopenhauer argued, and he prided his philosophy as honestly recognizing that the evils of the world follow from the will and that which possesses aseity. *See also* THEISM.

ASHER, DAVID (1818–1890). Asher was a scholar and teacher of English at a commercial school in Leipzig. Schopenhauer tried several times, but without success, to induce Asher to translate his philosophical writings into English. Asher published several works about Schopenhauer and his philosophy, most notably *Arthur Schopenhauer: The Latest of and on Him* (*Arthur Schopenhauer. Neues von ihm und über ihn*. Berlin 1876).

– B –

BAD (*SCHLECHT*). Schopenhauer defined as "bad" any inanimate or nonconscious thing that is contrary to an individual's desires or **will**. Consequently, "bad" weather is weather that prevents a person from gardening. *See also* EVIL; GOOD.

BAD, MORALLY. *See* REPREHENSIBLE, MORALLY.

BASIS OF MORALITY, ON THE (*ÜBER DIE GRUNDLAGE DER MORAL*). In 1837, the Royal Danish Society for Scientific Studies sponsored an essay contest. The question posed by the Society was: "Are the source and foundation of morals to be looked for in an idea of morality lying immediately in consciousness (or conscience) and in the analysis of the other fundamental moral concepts springing from that idea, or are they to be looked for in a different ground of knowledge?" Schopenhauer responded in 1839 with this essay, whose original title was "On the Foundation of Morality [*Über das Fundament der Moral*]." Despite being the only entry in the contest, the Society declined to award the prize to Schopenhauer. Within their judgment on Schopenhauer's essay, the Society claimed that he had failed to answer the question, since he had relegated to an "appendix" that which is central to the question, a discussion of the relationship between metaphysics and **ethics**. They also claimed that Schopenhauer had failed to demonstrate that **compassion** is the basis of morality or that it is an adequate foundation for morality. Lastly, the Society noted that they took grave offense at Schopenhauer's abusive treatment of "several distinguished philosophers of recent times." The Society published its negative verdict on 17 January 1840, in Denmark, and also in two German journals nine months later.

Schopenhauer was enraged by the society's judgment. He fully expected that this essay would have the same success as his **"On the Freedom of the Human Will,"** which won the prize for a contest sponsored by the Norwegian Scientific Studies in 1839. Schopenhauer was so confident of another victory that when he sent his essay to the Danish Society, he told them he would publish both of his "crowned" essays in a future work entitled *The Two Fundamental Problems of Ethics*, a book that would contain a complete outline of ethics. His book on ethics appeared in 1841, but with the notation that "On the Basis of Morality" was not awarded a prize. He also added a lengthy preface in which he spent almost as much energy abusing **Georg Wilhelm Friedrich Hegel**, whom he recognized, along with **Johann Gottlieb Fichte**, as one of the Society's "abused," distinguished philosophers of recent times, as he did criticizing the substantive objections raised by the Society against his work.

It is odd, however, that it never occurred to Schopenhauer that the Society was probably also offended by his treatment of **Immanuel Kant**. Schopenhauer spent over one third of the essay harshly criticizing Kant's ethics, claiming to be doing so to clear the grounds for a new foundation for morality and also because opposites illustrate each other. Thus he claimed that his foundation for morality was diametrically opposed to Kant's, which he viewed as an intellectual catastrophe, occasioned by Kant's increasing philosophical reputation and the numbing effects of old age. In contrast to Kant's non-empirical, rational ethics of **duty**, Schopenhauer presented an empirical and descriptive virtue ethics, which concentrated on moral character and moral psychology, offered a unified theory of the virtues and vices, drew on affinities to Eastern thought, and presented a metaphysical basis for ethics that affords moral status to nonhuman **animals**.

The structure of the essay is straightforward. In Part I, "Introduction," Schopenhauer analyzed the question posed by the Royal Danish Society, previewed his intent, and briefly considered earlier attempts to ground morality. In Part II, "Criticism of the Basis Given Ethics by Kant," he attempted to demolish the foundations of Kant's practical or moral philosophy in order to clear the grounds for a new basis for morality. Part III, "The Foundation of Ethics," presented a new groundwork for ethics, and the concluding part, Part IV, "On the Metaphysical Explanation of the Primary Ethical Phenomenon," provided a metaphysical basis for his ethics.

Schopenhauer initiated his assault on Kant's ethics in Part II by first noting some of the meritorious dimensions of his moral philosophy in section 3. Schopenhauer referred to virtually all of Kant's writings on ethics within the essay, but he concentrated primarily on Kant's *Groundwork of the Metaphysics of Morals* (*Grundlegung zur Metaphysik der Sitten*), whose theme Schopenhauer claimed was the same as the subject of the prize essay contest. He then proceeded to criticize the imperative form of Kant's ethics (section 4), his views of duties to oneself (section 5), the basis of Kant's ethics (section 6), the categorical imperative (section 7), alternative statements of the categorical imperative (section 8), and Kant's theory of **conscience** (section 9). In section 10, Schopenhauer praised Kant's doctrine of the coexistence of **freedom** and determinism, which he called Kant's "most brilliant merit in the service of ethics" and "the greatest of all achievements of the human mind." Naturally, he used Kant's ideas on this issue to advance his own very un-Kantian views of freedom and **moral responsibility**. Section 11 concluded Part II, and in it he used the ethics of "Kant's buffoon," Fichte, to magnify the problems inherent in Kant's ethics.

In Part III, Schopenhauer developed his foundation for ethics by arguing that the basis of morality could not be found in the stilted maxims of Kantian ethics, but must be found in the reality of things (section 12). He then argued against moral skepticism, which he identified with the claim that all human actions are motivated by **egoism**, and he claimed that the purpose of ethics is to explain and trace the varied behavior of humans from a moral point of view, which requires an empirical basis for ethics. By uncovering the **motives** or **incentives** for actions possessing different moral values, and by explaining human susceptibility for these motives, Schopenhauer asserted that the ultimate grounds of morality are discovered (Section

13). He considers the "anti-moral incentives" of egoism, a desire for one's own **weal**, and **malice**, a desire for another's **woe**, in section 14, and argues that, given the prevalence of these motives in human conduct, it is difficult to uncover a motive for actions of pure **justice** and real **philanthropy**. Thus he proposed that the criterion for actions possessing moral worth is that the action is not motivated by egoism or malice (section 15). He concluded in section 16 that the only possible motive for actions possessing **moral worth**, actions that aim to prevent or relieve the suffering of another, is compassion, a desire for another's weal. To supplement his argument, he attempted to prove that the virtue of justice follows from compassion (section 17), as does the virtue of loving kindness or philanthropy (section 18). Since Schopenhauer believed that justice and philanthropy are the cardinal virtues, the virtues from which all other virtues are derived, he claimed that all virtues are derived from compassion. Section 19 offers more confirmation for Schopenhauer's claim that compassion is the motive for all actions possessing moral worth, and it is thus the basis of morality, by exploring nine different examples of reflections about moral conduct. Part III concludes with Schopenhauer's argument that the ethical differences of human **character**, the differences regarding the types of motives to which a person is susceptible, are innate and unchangeable, and so he concludes that no system of ethics can alter the moral quality of a person's character. Yet everyone is morally **responsible** for his or her actions, he argued, since what we do follows from what we are.

Schopenhauer believed he had answered the question posed by the Royal Danish Society by the end of Part III. He had shown, he thought, that egoism is the incentive for **morally indifferent** or neutral behavior, malice for **morally reprehensible** behavior, and that only compassion is the incentive for all actions possessing moral worth. Employing a term he took from **Johann Wolfgang von Goethe**, he called these incentives primary phenomena, and in Part IV he provided a metaphysical explanation of the primary ethical phenomena. Thus in section 21 he justified his metaphysical explanation of these phenomena by appealing to the intellectual desire to have a comprehensive account of primary phenomena, since he thought that both philosophy and religion hold that the ultimate meaning of existence is ethical. In section 22, the final section,

Schopenhauer presented his sketch for a metaphysical grounding of ethics. He argued that morally good people treat others as themselves, and that their behavior expresses in action the ultimate metaphysical identity of all beings. Thus, he thought that compassionate conduct is metaphysically warranted. Morally bad people, individuals who are motivated by either extreme egoism or malice, treat others as absolute non-egos. Their behavior is unwarranted, he argued, and contrary to the metaphysical unity of all beings.

BEAUTIFUL, THE (*DAS SCHÖNE*). To call any object "beautiful" implies that it is an object of aesthetic **contemplation**, and Schopenhauer argued that natural objects as well as works of **art** could become objects of aesthetic contemplation. The experience of the beautiful entails two inseparable constituent parts: the object of experience, which is a **Platonic Idea** and not a particular thing, and the **subject of cognition**, a pure, will-less, painless, timeless subject of cognition. The transition from normal cognition, cognition in the service of the **will**, in which objects are viewed as the means for satisfying or thwarting desire, to a pure **subject of knowledge** is due to the nature of the object of cognition. This transition, contrary to the feeling of the **sublime**, which he viewed as involving a struggle, happens automatically and without any resistance or struggle. The aesthetic pleasure or enjoyment of the beautiful, the serenity and tranquility he associated with the experience of the beautiful, results, he claimed, from the release or liberation from willing, from the normal, willful **consciousness of other things**. *See also* AESTHETICS.

BECKER, JOHANN AUGUST (1803–1881). Becker was an attorney in Mainz, and from 1836 to 1850, he lived in Alzey, returning to Mainz in 1850 as a district judge, and later to a seat on the High Court of Appeal in 1873. In 1854 Becker introduced himself to Schopenhauer with a letter in which he expressed some "doubts" about elements of Schopenhauer's philosophy. Becker so impressed Schopenhauer with his understanding of his philosophy that Schopenhauer's reply initiated an exchange of thought and friendship that would last until Schopenhauer's death in 1860. Schopenhauer considered Becker as possessing the best understanding of his philosophy among all of his early followers, and he said that their correspondence contained the best ideas found in all of his letters. Becker pressed Schopenhauer with questions concerning both his metaphysics and **ethics**, and Schopenhauer's letters to Becker in 1844 from 23 August, 21 September, and 10 December help clarify a number of Schopenhauer's basic doctrines. Occasionally, Becker helped provide Schopenhauer with legal advice, and in an almost unheard of fashion, Schopenhauer would even visit Becker, when Becker moved to neighboring Mainz in 1850. Perhaps the only way Becker disappointed Schopenhauer was that he did not become active in writing to promote Schopenhauer's philosophy. Thus he remained, as Schopenhauer said, an "apostle," and he never became a "writing evangelist" for Schopenhauer.

BERKELEY, GEORGE (1684–1753). Schopenhauer opened the first section of *The World as Will and Representation* with the claim that "the world is my **representation**." This is not a new truth, he said in its first edition, since Berkeley was the first to articulate it. In Schopenhauer's second edition, he wrote that Berkeley was the first to do so positively, since **René Descartes** had done so negatively through his "skeptical reflections." By enunciating this truth, he continued, Berkeley "rendered an immortal service to philosophy, although the remainder of his doctrines cannot endure." These brief remarks summarize Schopenhauer's assessment of Berkeley's philosophy. He praised Berkeley as the father of **idealism** and credited him with the great insight that there could be no object without a subject. These were high words of praise on Schopenhauer's part. Moreover, he argued that philosophy is necessarily idealistic and that even the great **Immanuel Kant** had failed to appreciate the significant implications of Berkeley's insight that the **subject and object** distinction is the most basic form of all possible experience. Still, he did not find much value in Berkeley's philosophy, and he diagnosed his theistic commitments and his clerical and Episcopal positions as the source of his failures. (Berkeley would ultimately become Bishop of Cloyne in Ireland.) The problem was, as Schopenhauer saw it, Berkeley's theism confined his thought within a narrow circle of ideas that he could never challenge. Thus he was never able to develop the basic insights of his philosophy, Schopenhauer argued, and he could not provide a cogent account of the object of experience by claiming that our experiences of things are caused by **God**. *See also* HUME, DAVID; LOCKE, JOHN.

BODY, THE (*DER LEIB*). Few major philosophers have placed as much weight as Schopenhauer on the body as the source of philosophical insight. Due to this emphasis, a number of his commentators have called him "the philosopher of the body." It is only because we are our bodies that we are connected to the world, and it is only because we are our bodies that we possess the key for understanding the meaning and content of the world. Against dualistic positions, which view humans as composites of thinking and extended substances, and reductivist views, which make the mind the body or the body the mind, Schopenhauer viewed a person's body as one thing that is given to each person in a twofold way. We experience ourselves as a physical body, as an item in **space** and **time** that stands in causal relationships with other like objects. Thus, like our **consciousness of other things**, that is, as objects of our external sense, we have an intuitive perception of our body just like we do for all other objects in the natural world. We can see and touch our body as we can all other external objects. Thus I see my hand holding a pen just as I see the paper and the letters appearing in sequence on its surface. My hand is a **representation** just like all others in my visual field. But unlike other representations, which appear as surface phenomena, I have a unique experience of my hand, as well as any representation of what I identify as my body, since I also experience it from the inside, as it were. I experience the same phenomenon as an object of **self-consciousness** in which I recognize it as **will**. Without this experience, I would have no sense of anything that I perceive as my body, and my hand would appear simply like the pen, letters, and paper. It would not even be "my" hand. All would appear as items in my visual field—all surface, floating before me and to which I have no connection. According to Schopenhauer, if this were the case, the world would appear as if it were a dream whose meaning I could never ascertain. It would be as if the very words I write have no meaning. I would not even have the sense that I am writing them.

Yet I experience my hand not just as I do other representations. The pressure I feel of the pen in my hand, the resistance I sense as the pen touches and moves on the page, the meaning I strive to express through the words appearing behind my moving hand that holds the pen, and the pain I suffer when my hand clumsily slides across the edge of the paper, resulting in a paper cut, make me conscious of the representation of my hand in a way, Schopenhauer claimed, that is *toto genere* different than my experience of other representations. My body, my hand in this case, is an objectification or visualization of my will. They are identical, Schopenhauer argued, one and the same, and just as my body is an objectification of my will, the world itself is the objectification of the will. To deny this claim would be to embrace **theoretical egoism**, the view that one is fundamentally unique from and different than all representations other than that of one's body. While Schopenhauer believed that theoretical egoism is immune from refutation by philosophical proof, he also held that its serious advocate could only be encountered in a madhouse, where a cure rather than a refutation is the proper course of treatment.

By employing our twofold consciousness of our body as will and representation to attribute the will to all representations that constitute the natural world, Schopenhauer employed what he called his "revolutionary principle," in a note from 1816—that from yourself you will understand nature, not yourself from nature (*Arthur Schopenhauer: Manuscript Remains*, vol 1, para 621). Later, in his chief work, *The World as Will and Representation*, he would call the world "*macranthropos*," the great human being, because of the central role the experience of the human body plays in his philosophy. To be sure, he recognized that our self-conscious experience of our will is not the experience of the will as a unity, but only as acts of will which entail that they are objects for the subject and are within the *a priori* form of time. Yet, in chapter 18 of the first volume of his chief work, he claimed that the proposition, "My body and will are one," is a distinct kind of truth, the "philosophical truth *par excellence*" and as such, it differs from all truths recognized by the **principle of sufficient reason**, since it is a judgment of the relation of a perceptual representation (one's body) to something that is not a representation (the will).

Schopenhauer's identification of the body and will, his identification of acts of will or volitions with actions of the body, led him to break with the long-standing philosophical tradition that viewed volitions as the causes of actions. There is no causal relationship between volition and action in his view; rather, a volition is an action and an action is a volition. Again, they are one thing viewed from two different perspectives. The identification of the body and will also figure into his analysis of aspects of our body in terms of will or desire. Thus he claimed, for example, that the teeth, gullet, and intestinal canal are objectified hunger and that the **genitals** objectify sexual impulse. Indeed, he also argued that one's body, the outer person, is a graphic reproduction of the inner person (one's will or character). Therefore, he said that if one possesses a penetrating eye for physiognomy, one could take in a person's inner character in a glance. And if we were to return to the words left by my hand, Schopenhauer would claim that my writing style is the physiognomy of my mind.

BROCKHAUS, F. A. The publishing house of F. A. Brockhaus was established in Amsterdam in 1805 by Friedrich Arnold Brockhaus (1772–1823). In 1811 it relocated to Altenburg and in 1817–1818 it moved to Leipzig. After World War II, it moved to Wiesbaden, and in 1984 it merged with Bibliographisches Institut AG. Brockhaus continues to publish and it still offers the descendent of the first collected edition of Schopenhauer's works.

As Schopenhauer was approaching the completion of *The World as Will and Representation* early in 1818, he sought a publisher. Through an inquiry from a friend, Baron Ferdinand L. K. von Biedenfeld, he learned that Brockhaus was interested in his work. Brockhaus accepted Schopenhauer's book, sight unseen, after Schopenhauer promised that his work was a new philosophy, "new in the fullest sense of the word." It probably also helped that Brockhaus was publishing **Johanna Schopenhauer**'s *Reise durch England und Schottland* (*Travels through England and Scotland*). Later, Brockhaus would publish the 24-volume edition of her collected works. Schopenhauer was as eager to see his book published by Michaelmas 1818 as he was to receive his honorarium. During the book's printing, which was behind schedule, the nervous Schopenhauer managed to alienate Brockhaus by demanding prompt payment of his honorarium. He told him that he had heard that Brockhaus had a reputation for not paying or for paying honoraria slowly. Brockhaus challenged Schopenhauer to verify his accusation by noting one case in which he had failed to compensate his authors. Schopenhauer ignored this challenge and did not retract his charge.

Brockhaus responded by writing Schopenhauer that he would not accept any of his letters. Schopenhauer did receive timely payment of his honorarium on 18 September 1818, but his book did not appear until December of that year, bearing a publication date of 1819.

After the death of the elder Brockhaus in 1823, the business was run by his two eldest sons, Friedrich and Heinrich, whom Schopenhauer approached in 1825 with a proposal to translate into German **Lawrence Sterne**'s *Tristram Shandy*. Brockhaus declined the offer. Later, Schopenhauer approached Brockhaus once again in 1828. This time he sought a second edition of *The World as Will and Representation*. Brockhaus was not interested, and Schopenhauer discovered that 150 copies of the original printing of 750 of his book remained in stock, even after many copies had been sold for scrap. In 1829 he once again approached Brockhaus with a proposal for a translation into German of **Baltasar Gracián**'s *Oráculo manual y arte de prudencia*. Once again, Brockhaus declined. After publishing *On the Will in Nature* with another firm in 1836, he wrote to Brockhaus, predicting that this book would create a demand for a second edition of his chief work. His prediction, however, did not come true. Finally, after agreeing to waive his honorarium, Brockhaus published the second edition of *The World as Will and Representation* in 1844. However, it did even worse than the first edition. Consequently, it should not have come as a surprise to Schopenhauer that Brockhaus had no interest in 1850 in publishing his *Parerga and Paralipomena*, and that he would have to find another publisher.

Brockhaus would ultimately profit by its association with Schopenhauer. After 1853, which began the period that marked the rise of Schopenhauer's popularity, Brockhaus published new editions of all of Schopenhauer's works, including a third edition of *The World as Will and Representation* in 1859, and his translation of Gracián in 1862. In 1873 and 1874, it published in six volumes *Arthur Schopenhauer's sämmtliche Werke*, edited by **Julius Frauenstädt**, which is the ancestor of **Arthur Hübscher**'s historical and critical edition of *Arthur Schopenhauer: Sämtliche Werke*, whose fourth edition was published by Brockhaus in 1988.

BUDDHISM. Schopenhauer wrote in the chapter "Sinology" from *On the Will in Nature* that Buddhism was the most distinguished religion in the world because of its intrinsic excellence, truth, and large number of followers. In the well-known 17th chapter in the second volume of his main work, *The World as Will and Representation*, he states that if the results of his philosophy were to become the standard of truth, then Buddhism would rank the highest of all religions for articulating the **truth**. He also mentioned that the points of agreement between his philosophy and Buddhism pleased him, since he developed his views independently from its influence. To support this claim, he cited the fact that his main work appeared in 1818, a time during which there was little accurate and complete literature on Buddhism, and what was available was confined almost exclusively to the British journal *Asiatick Researches*.

Schopenhauer's commentators have generally accepted his claim about the lack of formative influences of Eastern thought on his philosophy, as they have also embraced his assertion that he did not change his mind about any of his central ideas throughout his lengthy philosophical career. Both of these claims have been subject to increasing scrutiny by contemporary scholars, however. This recent challenge to the received view about Schopenhauer's philosophy greatly complicates the discussion of the relationships between Buddhism and Schopenhauer, as does the recognition that Buddhism is not a monolithic religion, but one that is diverse historically and culturally, especially when it is examined in its Indian, Chinese, Tibetan and Japanese forms. The questions of the possible influence of Buddhism are further complicated by Schopenhauer's reading of religions as expressing their truths allegorically. Already in his early notes on Buddhism, Schopenhauer read Buddhism as presenting myths that express some of his doctrines.

It is clear, however, that Schopenhauer's interest in Buddhism was developed early in his philosophical career and that his enthusiasm for Buddhism intensified throughout his life. His study of Buddhism kept pace with the ever-increasing literature on Buddhism in the 1830s, 1840s, and 1850s. While Schopenhauer never made a detailed philosophical comparison between his ideas and Buddhism, he would often add reference to it in new editions of his books. He did, moreover, refer to himself as a "Buddhist," and in the early 1830s he would compare his experiences of the misery and wretchedness of life during his tour of Europe in 1803–1804 to those of the Buddha's youthful years. In addition to the plaster-of-Paris bust of Immanuel Kant, which sat on his desk, he had a gilded bronze statue of Buddha displayed prominently in his apartment in Frankfurt am Main. There is little doubt that Schopenhauer's praise of Buddhism inspired many Europeans to study it and that his understanding of Buddhism influenced the thought of many of its students.

It appears that Schopenhauer became aware of the *Asiatick Researches* and the *Asiatische Magazin* by his attendance at lectures offered on ethnography given by the Göttingen historian Arnold Heeren (1760–1842) in the summer of 1811. His meeting with the indologist Freidrich Majer (1772–1818) in the winter of 1813–1814 at his mother's house in Weimar also stimulated Schopenhauer's interest in Eastern thought, and he borrowed two volumes of *Asiatische Magazin* from the Anna-Amalia Library in Weimar when he was developing his philosophy from 1813–1818 in Dresden. Schopenhauer carefully studied articles from various volumes of the *Asiatik Researches*, and in 1815–1816 he befriended the German philosopher Karl Christian Friedrich Krause (1781–1832), who lodged in the same house as Schopenhauer and who was consumed by all things Eastern. (Krause, unlike Schopenhauer, read Sanskrit.) Already during this early stage in Schopenhauer's philosophy, and prior to the publication of his main work in 1818, he had drawn connections between the Buddhist notion of *nirvāna* and the **denial of the will**, and he recognized the significance of the morality behind this atheistic religion. As he continued to develop and extend his philosophical ideas after the publication of *The World as Will and Representation*, Schopenhauer's knowledge of Buddhism increased, as did his references to it in his writings. It is likely that shifts in his claims concerning the knowability of the **thing in itself** and the denial of the will were motivated, in part, by his deeper understanding of Buddhism. It also appears that Schopenhauer became acquainted first with Theravada Buddhism, then Mahayana Buddhism, and lastly with the Theravada Pali Buddhism of Ceylon. In 1858 he would write in a note that "Buddha, [Meister] Eckhart, and I teach essentially the same thing."

But what is it that Buddha and Schopenhauer teach essentially the same? Perhaps to begin to come close to an adequate answer, it is best to highlight the points of contact Schopenhauer saw between his philosophy and themes common to Buddhist thought. Although this approach ignores the various schools of Buddhism and assumes that Schopenhauer understood Buddhism as we do today, the points of agreement are worth drawing, even though they overlook specific affinities of Schopenhauer's philosophy and particular expressions of Buddhism, as well as the points of difference. Two features of Buddhism that Schopenhauer consistently praised were its atheism and its **pessimism**. He thought the belief that the world is the creation of a perfect **God** is absurd, given its wretched nature. He found this insight shared by Buddhism, and he connected it with the pessimism that he saw expressed in Buddhist thought, which he found in its recognition that the world is not praiseworthy and good, but it is something that ought not to be. With the Buddhist notion of *samsāra*, the world of change and transmigratory existence, Schopenhauer saw a parallel to the world as **representation**, the affirmation of the will, the world of individuality, change, and destruction, the world of "illusion." Schopenhauer also claimed that Buddhism shared his view that the world is permeated by sorrow, suffering, and misery, and that the basis of this misery is desire or striving. Likewise, he understood Buddhism as recognizing that the cessation of suffering is the cessation of this desiring or striving, and that this follows from enlightenment or knowledge. The salvific state, which the Buddhists recognize as *nirvāna*, is parallel to the state of his overcomer of the world, the denier of the will, and he thought this accomplishment could only be described negatively. In addition, he favored the less extreme form of asceticism in the Buddhist "Middle Way," celibacy, voluntary poverty, humility, obedience, and abstinence from animal food, to the more extreme forms of self-castigation found in some forms of **Hinduism**. In his moral philosophy, Schopenhauer saw his morality of **compassion** echoing Buddhist thought, and he claimed that his **ethics** addressed all sentient creatures, humans and **animals**, just as in Buddhist ethics.

BURCKHARDT, JACOB (1818–1897). Burckhardt was a student of the historian Leopold Ranke, who along with Johann Gustav Droysen, was a key figure of the Historical School, and later he was to become a Professor of History at the University of Basel. He is best known for his *Die Cultur der Renaissance in Italien* (*The Civilization of the Renaissance in Italy*, 1860) and his posthumously published lectures from 1868–1871, *Weltgeschichtliche Betrachtungen* (*Reflections on World History*, 1905). It has been said that his *Reflections on World History* represents the first philosophy of **history** from a Schopenhaurian perspective. At first, this remark may appear ironic, since a major aspect of the *Reflections* was a rejection of the philosophy of history and the promotion of history as a consideration of the intellectual world through observations that cut cross-sections through events, from as many directions as possible, which are then coordinated. A "philosophy of history," he said, using one of Schopenhauer's favorite terms of dismissal, was a "*contradictio in adjecto*," in other words, it was an oxymoron. Like Schopenhauer, he thought that history was not **philosophy**; it was not capable of understanding human existence as deeply as philosophy or poetry.

Yet Burckhardt's rejection of the philosophy of history was a rejection of **Georg Wilhelm Friedrich Hegel**'s speculative philosophy of history. Schopenhauer's imprint on Burckhardt's work can be seen in the means by which he rejected Hegelian approaches to history and by his understanding of the domain of historical inquiry, as well as the methodological and practical values expressed by his treatment of the objects of history. In his opposition to the philosophy of history, he employed a number of Schopenhauer's claims found in "On History," the 38th chapter of the second volume of *The World as Will and Representation*. Schopenhauer had argued that history is not a science since it lacks the hallmarks of science, the subordination of the particular under universal or generic **concepts**. Instead, it takes particular and individual events and coordinates them within a narrative. Burckhardt took Schopenhauer's distinction between subordination and coordination to argue both that history is not philosophy and that coordination is history's task. A Hegelian approach to history, he argued, approached history with preconceived ideas that shape its subject. These ideas are not discovered in history; moreover, they are imposed by historians on its subject. Siding with Schopenhauer, Burckhardt also rejected the view that reason rules history, that it is necessarily progressive and teleological, a movement through time of the world spirit. In agreement with Schopenhauer, he held that the object of philosophy is the suffering, striving, and acting of humans as they are, ever were, and always will be. The wretched, fallen state of humans is historically ever the same. In this fashion, Schopenhauer's **pessimism** found deep resonance in Burckhardt's thought.

Burckhardt's admiration of Schopenhauer's philosophy is perhaps best illustrated in his letters from the 1870s where he was more inclined to be philosophical than he was in his historical works. It was not uncommon for him to refer to Schopenhauer as "the" or "our" philosopher. He delighted in learning from his correspondents about the ever-increasing familiarity within the intellectual world of Schopenhauer's thoughts, and he wrote about Schopenhauer's special mission for his age. **Friedrich Nietzsche**, who was a younger colleague of Burckhardt at the University of Basel from 1869 to 1879, and who probably attended some of his lectures, was drawn to Burckhardt, in part, by their mutual enthusiasm for Schopenhauer.

– C –

CALDERÓN DE LA BARCA, PEDRO (1600–1681). Calderón is one of Spain's most esteemed playwrights, and he was, with Lope de Vega, the dominant figure in Spain's Golden Age of theater. Schopenhauer first became aware of Calderón on Easter 1811 in Weimar, when he attended a performance of his play *El príncipe constante* (*The Constant Prince*), which was based on a German translation of the play, *Der standhafte Prinz*, by A. W. Schlegel. The play was directed by **Johann Wolfgang Goethe**, who also owned its German performance rights. In *The Philosophy of Schopenhauer in Its Intellectual Context*, **Arthur Hübscher** claimed that Schopenhauer's experience of this play contributed significantly to his intellectual development. In *The Constant Prince*, a martyr of the faith stoically bears his life-long imprisonment and obtains a state of indifference to life's pleasures and woe, until his death frees him from death itself. Hübscher claims that this play helped to ingrain the themes of the transitory nature of human existence, death as the goal of life, and death itself as connoting the eternal, which are enduring features of the philosopher's worldview.

Already in the first edition of *The World as Will and Representation*, Schopenhauer quoted from Calderón's best known play, *La vida es sueño* (*Life is a Dream*), and after its second edition, he would use three times the following lines:

> Pues el delito mayor
> Del hombre es haber nacido
>
> (For his greatest offense
> Is that man has been born).

The first time Schopenhauer cited these lines was within his analysis of **tragedy**, where he claimed they illustrate the true significance of the fall of the tragic hero, which represents not the sins of an individual, but rather, the guilt of existence of itself. The next two involve the assertion that these lines express the idea of original sin, an allegorically expressed truth that his philosophy demonstrates philosophically. "Original sin" becomes the **affirmation of the will** for Schopenhauer, the source of the misery of our existence and for which we are guilty, since we are will.

When Schopenhauer started to learn Spanish in 1825, he did so to read his beloved Calderón in the original. Ultimately, he would refer to six of his plays within the corpus of his philosophy. These references, moreover, were always used in a way that supported his own views. Later, in *Parerga and Paralipomena* (1851), he claimed that Shakespeare and Calderón were the greatest dramatic poets of modern time.

CAUSALITY, LAW OF (*GESETZ DER KAUSALITÄT*). Schopenhauer viewed the law of causality as one of the specific forms or roots of the **principle of sufficient reason** that shapes the experience of any being possessing intellect or the faculty of **understanding**. He called the law of causality the most universal and essential form of the understanding because by its means alone is the **intuition** or **perception** of the real external world brought about. Like **Immanuel Kant**, he held that the law of causality is known *a priori* and that it is a necessary law as regards the possibility of all experience. As such, it governs all perceptions or conceptions of the physical world, and he held that nothing in experience happens without a **cause** and that everything in the world as **representation** happens necessarily. *See also* PRINCIPLE OF SUFFICIENT REASON OF BECOMING.

CAUSE (*URSACHE*). All changes in the world as **representation**, Schopenhauer claimed, follow from a sufficient reason or cause. When he used the term "cause" in what he said was its "narrowest sense," he referred to changes in nonliving or inorganic bodies. Thus he recognized specific causal relationships between chemical, mechanical, and physical causes and their specific effects on inorganic bodies. For example, in the case of one billiard ball striking another, the struck ball receives as much motion as the striking ball loses. The general hallmarks of causal relations within the inorganic realm, Schopenhauer thought, are that the cause tends to undergo a reaction proportionate to its action and that there is a general uniformity between the intensity of the cause and that of the effect. He further identified the determination by causes only of this kind to be the essential characteristic of inorganic bodies. *See also* MOTIVE; STIMULUS.

CHARACTER (*DER CHARAKTER*). Schopenhauer distinguished between two factors that causally operate in empirical objects: a force inherent in an item upon which some causal influence is exercised and a **cause** that occasions the manifestation of a force. Although he tended to restrict the term "character" to refer to the force associated with **animals**, including humans, he also employed the term broadly to refer to the force found in plants and inorganic nature. Following the lead of **Immanuel Kant**, he also distinguished between the intelligible and empirical characters, and he viewed the empirical character as the appearance of the intelligible character. The former, he argued, is within the scope of the **principle of sufficient reason** and it is, as such, causally determined. Since he claimed that the latter is beyond the scope of the principle of sufficient reason, he argued that the intelligible character is neither causally determined nor subject to any form of necessity. Consequently, he attributed **freedom** to the intelligible character.

Schopenhauer's account of character in regard to animals concentrates on the **will** as the specific force manifest in animal life, while he claimed that the character of nonhuman animals or nonrational animals varies among species, and he held that the behavior of members of a particular species manifests uniformly the character of the species. He distinguished between species by focusing on the specific quality of the will to respond to the same **motive** in different ways.

Thus a mongoose pounces on a snake and a mouse flees. Schopenhauer did attribute a modicum of individuality to the behavior of the members of the higher species of nonhuman animals, especially to his beloved **poodles**. He emphasized the individuality or uniqueness of the human character, which he found in the phenomenon whereby different humans react differently to the same motive. Schopenhauer also correlated the intelligible characters of all empirical objects with **Platonic Ideas**, and due to the individuality of the human character, he suggested that each human being could be regarded as the objectification of a unique Idea.

In addition to being individual, Schopenhauer also claimed that human character is empirical, constant, and inborn. It is empirical, he argued, since it is only known through experience, by observing what a person does over a long period of time. It is constant, because it is unchangeable and unalterable, he said, and it is innate, because it is fully formed at birth and is not the product of natural and cultural influences, nor is it something produced by the person. At the very best, a person can develop what Schopenhauer referred to as the acquired character, the ability to rationally and deliberately live a course of life in tune with the fundamental dispositions of his or her intelligible character. This requires, he argued, a precise knowledge of one's empirical character and **knowledge** of the world. Although a person can acquire character, Schopenhauer also argued that the moral quality of a person's character cannot be changed. So he held that a wicked man is born with his wickedness as much as a serpent is with its fangs, and he is as little able to change his character as the serpent his fangs. Consequently, Schopenhauer argued that **ethics** cannot be taught, that is, knowledge cannot make an **evil** person **good**, since the moral quality of a person's character is constant and inborn.

CHRISTIANITY. When measured against the various denominations and Christian churches, Schopenhauer's attitude toward Christianity was ambivalent. He emphasized the kinship between his philosophy and "original and genuine Christianity." And insofar as a church or denomination deviated from his conception of true Christianity, he found problems with it. He argued that the New Testament contains important ideas of Indian origin, and that it expresses insights found in **Hinduism** and **Buddhism**, but that it only teaches what the whole of Asia knew better before it. Schopenhauer conjectured that Jesus was educated by Egyptian priests, whose religion was of Indian genesis, and that he accepted important elements of Indian ethics and the idea of an *avatar*, an earthly manifestation of the divine. These Indian elements, he continued, were adapted by Jesus to the Jewish dogmas of his native land. The Jewish dogmas, which he identified as the claims that there is a creator **God**, distinct from creation, who created humans out of nothing, in his image, and thereby made humans radically distinct from all other living creatures, distanced Christianity from its Asian ancestors and introduced flaws within its worldview. Consequently, he argued that it is logically absurd to think that something could be created out of nothing; that humans bear **moral responsibility** when their will is the product of another will; and that humans are not intimately related to other living creatures, a view that spoiled Christian morality because it viewed **animals** as things. One could use as a rule of thumb concerning Schopenhauer's analysis of Christianity that the more a denomination or church promoted what he regarded as "Jewish dogma," the more he emphasized its problems and flaws, and the closer he saw it expressing ideas he identified as of Indian origin, the more insightful and true he found its ideas.

Schopenhauer argued that **religion** expresses true ideas allegorically and that the fundamental difference between religions is whether they are **optimistic** or **pessimistic**. He claimed that genuine Christianity is pessimistic and promotes **asceticism**. Thus he claimed that true Christianity teaches that the deep guilt of the human race is its very existence and that salvation entails the heaviest sacrifice, the denial of the self. He found the concept of original sin to be a figurative expression of his idea of the affirmation of the will, and he saw the cross, an instrument of torture, as suggesting his claim that suffering is a means for salvation. Christian ethics, he thought, teaches selflessness by emphasizing boundless love for one's neighbors, including one's enemies. The asceticism he saw in genuine Christianity concerns its recognition that we ought not love the world, since it is ruled by the devil, and so we must overcome the world to obtain salvation. This entails, he thought, the denial of that which attaches us to the world, so it advocates celibacy, humility, poverty, and self-denial, the ideals expressed by Jesus' life and by the compelling image of the crucified savior. He considered Protestantism as a degenerate form of Christianity because it abandons the ascetic character of true Christianity, especially celibacy. It thereby becomes, he thought, a shallow religion for comfortable, married, and civilized persons. *See also* JUDAISM.

COGNITION (*ERKENNTNIS*). A cognition is an item of awareness, and the faculty of cognition, according to Schopenhauer, is the capacity to have **representations**. All **animals**, human and nonhuman, have nonrational cognitions of the external world, Schopenhauer argued, but only humans have the faculty of **reason**, and thus, he held that only humans have the capacity to have abstract representations or **concepts**. Consequently, he held that only humans are capable of rational, discursive thought while nonhuman animals are capable of only **perception**.

Although Schopenhauer generally restricted cognition to the **principle of sufficient reason**, he also recognized cognitions outside the scope of this principle, such as the cognition of **Platonic Ideas**. However, all cognition is within the **subject and object** division. *See also* KNOWLEDGE; PRINCIPLE OF SUFFICIENT REASON OF BECOMING; PRINCIPLE OF SUFFICIENT REASON OF KNOWING; UNDERSTANDING.

COLOR (*FARBE*). Arthur Schopenhauer maintained a lively interest in color theory throughout virtually his entire philosophical career. His personal acquaintance and work on color theory with **Johann Wolfgang von Goethe** inspired his second publication, *On Vision and Colors* (1816), an essay that received a Latin version (1830) and a second edition (1854). Between its Latin version and second edition, he also published the essay "On the Theory of Color," in the second volume of *Parerga and Paralipomena* (1851). Schopenhauer had, however, an ambivalent attitude toward his work on color theory. While he never doubted its **truth**, he viewed his theory as broadly "scientific" in nature, and so he considered it as lacking the deeper universal significance of his **philosophy** proper. This ambivalence is expressed in the preface to the second edition of *On Vision and Colors*, where he wrote that its philosophical value is that it would move philosophically inclined readers to a deeper comprehension of the subjective nature of all **cognition** by showing them the likewise subjective nature of colors.

Like Goethe, his mentor, Schopenhauer viewed white light as homogenous, and he also rejected Isaac Newton's claim that white light contains the seven-color spectrum. Goethe argued that color is produced by the interplay of light and darkness and that it is something cloudy or shadowlike. While Schopenhauer embraced Goethe's thesis that color is shadowlike and that it contains darkness, he rejected Goethe's claim that light and darkness, or white and black, are primary phenomena, basic phenomena incapable of further explanation. Goethe, he said, made the same mistake as Newton by concentrating on the **cause** of color and not its effect. By moving to the analysis of the effect of color, to physiological color, Schopenhauer sought to explain Goethe's primary phenomena by focusing on the "seeing eye," the subject perceiving color. Light or white, he argued, is the full activity of the retina and darkness or black is the inactivity of the retina. Color, he claimed, is the qualitatively divided activity of the retina. Schopenhauer's subjective account of color also retained allegiance to his mentor's view that color necessarily contains an element of darkness. Still, he drew Goethe's reproach by conceding that Newton was correct by claiming that color is a divisional process. Schopenhauer's subsequent claim that color is a divisional process of the retina and that it is not, as Newton claimed, a divisional process of light, did nothing to relieve Goethe's sense of betrayal. Worse, from Goethe's perspective, was that Schopenhauer agreed with Newton that white light could be produced by colored lights. To be sure, Schopenhauer had also agreed with Goethe that there are six primary colors and not seven as Newton claimed, and he even suggested that Newton's theory itself had misled Goethe about the production of white from colors, but this did nothing to alleviate Goethe's sense that Schopenhauer's theory was in opposition to his own.

Schopenhauer took especial pride in his description of colors in terms of definite numerical functions. By viewing color as the qualitatively divided activity of the retina, with black or the inactivity of the retina equaling zero and white or the full activity of the retina equaling one, Schopenhauer believed that he could describe each of the six primary colors in definite numerical fractions and that he could show that one of the primary colors and its complementary color could be shown to equal one, or white, the full activity of the retina. Thus he claimed that violet was ¼ of the full activity of the retina; that blue was ⅓; that green was ½; that red was ½; that orange was ⅔; and that yellow was ¾. (Technically, Schopenhauer recognized that colors shaded imperceptibly into one another, as seen in a color sphere, and that this entails an infinite number of colors. He was not troubled by this, however, since he also held that the activity of the retina is likewise infinitely divisible. His six primary colors, he argued, took pride in place in his color theory because they are recognized distinctly by all people at all times and each receives the same general name, names that are used to refer to other colors that resemble them. For example, we speak of yellow and resembling colors as greenish yellow or orangish yellow.) When one considers the three pairs of complementary colors, Schopenhauer claimed that it is easy to show that the sum of each set of complementary colors is 1, white, or the full activity of the retina. Thus, the complements yellow and violet are, respectively, ¾ and ¼; orange and blue ⅔ and ⅓; and red and green ½ and ½.

Schopenhauer was keen to have his work in color theory translated into English. So in a letter from 1840, addressed to Charles Lock Eastlake, a British painter who had translated most of Goethe's massive *Zur Farbenlehre* (1810) into English as *On the Theory of Colours* (1840), Schopenhauer sent an edited version of his *Über das Sehn und die Farben*, and he practically begged Eastlake to publish either an English translation or extract of it, but Eastlake declined Schopenhauer's request.

COMPASSION (*MITLEID*). A strong case could be made for the claim that Schopenhauer developed the most comprehensive analysis of the nature and the moral significance of compassion within the Western philosophical tradition. He also saw a deep connection between his philosophy and **Buddhism** because of their mutual emphasis on the fundamental role of compassion within human moral life. His most extensive discussion of compassion is found in *On the Basis of Morality*, a work that he could have simply called *On Compassion*, since he argued that compassion is the basis of morality, the source of all actions possessing **moral worth** and the *leitmotif* of people possessing morally good **characters**. Ultimately, he explained compassion by grounding it in his **metaphysics** of the **will**.

Schopenhauer held that compassion is an ultimate or basic human **incentive**. As such, he claimed that practically everyone is susceptible to it to some degree, and he found that it is expressed throughout a range of conduct in which individuals do something to promote another's **weal**. These actions may be as simple as restraining oneself from doing something that would cause another's **woe**, or they may be those actions that would require the sacrifice of one's time, energy, resources or even one's own life, to secure another's well-being. Consequently, he defined compassion as the desire for another's weal, and he emphasized that compassionate agents identify with others by treating others' weal as their own. To explain the dynamics of compassion and how it leads agents to seek another's well-being, he claimed that compassion involves an extraordinary experience of another's woe. This experience of another's suffering, he maintained, leads individuals to treat that suffering of another just as they would treat their own. In other words, compassionate people seek to prevent or relieve another's suffering just as they would normally their own. This is done, he held, because in compassionating another, a person experiences the other's suffering like his or her own and the compassionate person experiences this suffering in the other's **body**. This extraordinary experience cannot be explained psychologically, he said, and it is the primary phenomenon (*Urphänomen*) of morally worthwhile behavior, or that which explains all actions possessing moral worth and which itself is unexplained by any such actions. Because of the primary role of compassion in his explanation of morally worthwhile conduct, he called it "the great mystery of **ethics**," and he held that it requires a metaphysical explanation.

Schopenhauer employed a number of strategies to prove that compassion is the basis of morality. These strategies included formal argumentation, appeals to earlier philosophical and religious views, and appeals to his readers' sensibilities. Two of his more noteworthy arguments were an argument by elimination and an argument purporting to show that the cardinal virtues of **justice** and **philanthropy** spring from compassion. In the former, he argued that **egoism**, **malice** and an unnamed incentive, or a desire for one's own woe, could not be the source of morally worthwhile behavior. Thus by eliminating three out of four of the ultimate human incentives as the source of actions that possess moral worth, he concluded that these types of actions follow from compassion. In the latter, he argued that since the virtues of justice and philanthropy follow from compassion, and these virtues are the virtues from which all other virtues are derived, he concluded that compassion is the source of all virtuous conduct. Moreover, Schopenhauer took especial pride in his view, since he thought he had shown that compassion defeated egoism. This was something he argued that **Immanuel Kant**'s ethics failed to do, and he asserted that this is necessary for any adequate account of ethics, since the absence of egoistic motivation is a necessary condition for any action possessing genuine moral worth.

Schopenhauer grounded his analysis of compassion in his metaphysics of the will. He explained the "great mystery" of compassion, the cognition of another's suffering in the other's body, by arguing that the distinction between individuals is only apparent and that metaphysically everything is an expression of the will. Compassionate individuals, those who possess a good character, treat others as an "I once more," and he employed a Vedic formula, "*tat tvam asi* [that thou art]," to express the form of cognition revealed in the conduct of **good** people. Their behavior makes less of a distinction between themselves and others; unlike other people, who act as if there is an absolute separation between people and who treat others as non-egos, good people treat others as themselves. The dispositions and form of life expressed by compassionate people, he contended, are metaphysically warranted. By living as if others are identical with themselves, good characters practically express that which is theoretically demonstrated in his philosophy, namely, individuality is a delusion; everything is one. For this reason, Schopenhauer referred to the conduct of good people as "practical **mysticism**," since he attributed the root of such behavior to the same source of all mysticism, a cognition that penetrates the *principium individuationis*, a recognition of the unity of all being. He held that the possibility of compassion, the capacity to suffer with another, which is the literal meaning of *Mitleid*, and the subsequent disposition to treat another's woe just like one's own, is due to the metaphysical unity of being.

CONCEPTS (*BEGRIFFE*). Schopenhauer thought of concepts as "**representations** of representations" or abstract representations. Both of these designations reflect the secondary status of concepts in his **epistemology** and metaphysics. By calling concepts "representations of representations," he emphasized their dependency on intuitive or perceptual representations. The capacity to formulate these second order representations constitutes the primary function of the faculty of **reason**, according to Schopenhauer. Concepts are developed, he said, through abstraction, that is, by abstracting them from perceptual representations, which involves the elimination of everything inessential to a number of intuitively perceived particular things in order to recognize what is common among them. He also tagged the abstract nature of concepts in a number of different ways. Unlike perceptual representations, concepts lack concreteness, that is, you cannot get your hands around the concept of a "beer bottle" like you can a bottle of beer. Moreover, concepts are not imagistic or pictorial in any sense, even for concepts he referred to figuratively as "*concreta*," those that appear to be grounded directly in the world of perception, such as "man," "stone," and "horse," compared to concepts like "virtue," "investigation," and "relation," which he called "*abstracta*." In this regard, he saw his views agreeing with **George Berkeley**'s and **David Hume**'s critique of **John Locke**'s analysis of general ideas. Concepts are fixed by words, and he regarded words as sensible signs for concepts and the basis of communication.

Concepts are also general, he thought, since they refer to numerous individual things, but he also claimed that this is not an essential feature of a concept, since you can have concepts that refer to one thing. For example, he said that you could have a concept of a definite town, say "Frankfurt am Main," which refers to one town, but because of the generality of a concept, it can also refer to other towns that only differ from Frankfurt am Main in a few details. Thus he said that the generality of concepts is not because they are abstracted from several particulars, but because they apply to more than one thing. Hence he claimed that the "non-determination of the particular" is the essence of the concept. This, however, is the basis for his claim that concepts, even when they are rigidly and sharply delineated, are not capable of capturing the richness of detail and content found in **perception**. For this reason, Schopenhauer held that all genuine **art**, virtue, holiness and original pieces of **knowledge** proceed from **intuition**.

Because concepts are abstracted from perceptual representations, Schopenhauer maintained that they are empirical, that they have their meaning and content only in reference to perceptual representations. Consequently, he denied that we have *a priori* concepts or concepts inherent to consciousness. Moreover, this entailed for him that meaningful concepts are tied to experience, to **appearances** of things and not to the **thing in itself**. Since the formation of concepts is the primary function of the faculty of reason, and concepts are unified to formulate judgments, concepts ultimately deal with **truth** and fall within the domain of the **principle of sufficient reason of knowing**. *See also* PHILOSOPHY.

CONSCIENCE (*GEWISSEN*). A person's conscience provides an individual with an acquaintance with the moral quality of his or her unalterable or intelligible **character**. This acquaintance is made possible only through reflection and on one's deeds, the entire set of which Schopenhauer referred to as the empirical character. Schopenhauer held that an actor feels some pain in the performance of a **bad** action, whether it is a form of injustice arising out of **egoism** or a wicked action born from **malice**. He called this pain, depending on its duration, the sting of conscience or the pangs of conscience. Conversely, he viewed the **good** conscience as the opposite of the sting of conscience, which is the feeling of satisfaction that the actor experiences after the performance of an action possessing **moral worth**. Schopenhauer employed the phenomena of the approbation of an individual's conscience or its disapprobation as one of the bases for the moral evaluations of actions. *See also* INDIFFERENT, MORALLY; REPREHENSIBLE, MORALLY.

CONSCIOUSNESS OF OTHER THINGS (*BEWUβTSEIN ANDERER DINGE*). Schopenhauer distinguished between two types of consciousness, **self-consciousness** and the consciousness of other things, things not identified immediately with the **will**. The consciousness of other things is the awareness of the external world, populated by individualized, spatial-temporal objects standing within causal relationship. These things include material objects, other people, and one's own body as intuitive **representations**. He also included the universal and *a priori* conditions, **space**, **time**, and **causality**, as belonging to our consciousness of other things and not jointly to self-consciousness. Schopenhauer thought that consciousness of other things constitutes the dominant mode of our awareness.

CONTEMPLATION (*KONTEMPLATION*). Schopenhauer reserved the term "contemplation" or "pure contemplation" (*reine Kontemplation*) to refer almost exclusively to a cognitive state in which the object of cognition is a **Platonic Idea**, and the **subject** of cognition is a pure will-less, painless, timeless **subject of cognition**. In contemplation, the individual has no sense of being distinct from the object of cognition, and Schopenhauer claimed that the cognizer becomes a pure mirror of the object of cognition. Unlike in the subjective or the normal cognition of individual things, which is governed by the **principle of sufficient reason** and colored by the consideration of things as the means for satisfying or thwarting a person's desires, contemplation was considered by Schopenhauer to be objective, beyond the principle of sufficient reason and interested or will-colored cognition. He believed that any natural object could prompt contemplation, since all natural objects express Platonic Ideas. Still, he argued that contemplation is the preeminent ability of the **genius**, who cognizes the essential and abiding element in the phenomena of the world. This cognition is a matter of **intuition** and it is something available to the non-genius through a great work of **art**, which Schopenhauer always recognized as the work of genius. *See also* BEAUTIFUL, THE.

CORRELATIVITY THESIS. *See* SUBJECT AND OBJECT.

– D –

DEATH (*TOD*). Schopenhauer took death seriously, but he did not somberly anticipate his own death. During a visit three days prior to his death, he told **Wilhelm Gwinner** that he was not distressed by the fact that worms would soon be gnawing at his body, but he did dread that his "spirit," that is, his **philosophy**, would be butchered by philosophy professors. Still, he said, it would be a kindness if death were an absolute nothingness, but he doubted that it offered that prospect. Schopenhauer's tranquil attitude toward his own death was well prepared by his analysis of the nature and meaning of death. Few philosophers before him, and not many after him, have made death such an intimate aspect of their philosophical reflections. His books contain numerous remarks about death, and the 41st chapter of the second volume of *The World as Will and Representation*, "On Death and Its Relationship to the Indestructibility of Our Inner Nature," is the lengthiest section in his main work, with the exception of its appendix, "Criticisms of the Kantian Philosophy." Seven years later, in 1851, he supplemented that discussion with the essay "On the Doctrine of the Indestructibility of Our True Nature by Death," from the second volume of *Parerga and Paralipomena*. Schopenhauer ultimately would argue that death would end his **consciousness** and that which individuated him, but he also held that it would not annihilate his essence, which is the **will**.

It is not surprising that Schopenhauer would make the topic of death a central theme of his philosophy and that he would face the prospect of his own death well. He claimed that death is the inspiring genius of philosophy, and he accepted **Plato**'s remark from the *Phaedo* that philosophy is a preparation for death. Unlike Plato, he did not believe that philosophy was a dying away from the senses and the **body** as a preparation for enlightenment, nor did he believe that we have an immortal psyche. Still, like Plato, he held that what we are, our essence, is indestructible and not touched by death. This last claim, he thought, brings consolation about death, something that he thought is implicit in the deep human need for metaphysics. Like Plato, he held that philosophy is based on wonder, but the basis of Schopenhauer's wonder was deeply existential, born from the recognition of the ubiquity of suffering and death in the world. In fact, he held that this existential astonishment is the prompt for both religious and philosophical speculations about the world, both of which seek to explain the wretchedness of existence in a way that consoles us about our fate. Yet the philosopher serves a higher standard than the theologist, Schopenhauer held, since the philosopher must demonstrate the truth of his or her claims. Consolation about death is not sufficient to meet the philosopher's need for metaphysics: the philosopher's need is only sated by the **truth** itself. Ultimately, Schopenhauer argued that death is not evil; the fear of death is irrational; and death does not destroy our "inner nature."

Schopenhauer believed that Eastern people had a more enlightened view of death than Europeans. He attributed this to the influence of **Hinduism** and **Buddhism**, both of which taught that perishing individuals are, in reality, the original being for whom all coming to be and perishing are foreign. By identifying themselves with this eternal being, Eastern people, he argued, face death more calmly than Europeans, who, under the influence of **Judaism** and inauthentic forms of **Christianity**, believe that they were created out of nothing by a **God**, who is distinct from creation; that their existence began at birth; and that they have a soul that expresses their individual personalities forever. Most Europeans accept these beliefs, Schopenhauer argued, because they were inculcated in their early childhood, and because they lack the intelligence necessary to ascertain their falsehood. Consequently, their beliefs serve the metaphysical needs of these people, and console them with their deaths. The story is different with Europeans with "mature minds," he claimed, and these people are able to see how these Judeo-Christian beliefs are untenable. But since they are unable to formulate better ideas, they are led to view death as their absolute annihilation, and they adopt a completely physical or **materialistic** viewpoint. To sate their metaphysical needs, they are moved to adopt the attitude that they should eat, drink, and be merry, since after death there is no joy. This attitude, Schopenhauer claimed, can be described as bestiality, and he attributed this view to socialists in England and young Hegelians in Germany.

Schopenhauer found the two dominant European viewpoints on death to be highly problematic. Those consoled by Western religious beliefs ought not to be consoled, and those who maintain the physical standpoint need consolation. Ultimately, he judged that both perspectives are based on false beliefs. There is no personal immortality and death is not our absolute annihilation. On the nature and meaning of death, he claimed that Eastern trumps Western thought. He claimed that it professes a higher standpoint. Thus he delighted in noting affinities between his thanatopsis and that which he perceived in Hinduism and Buddhism. Still, he also recognized that, at best, **religion** only expresses its truths allegorically. The philosopher, he thought, had to literally demonstrate the truths of a higher standpoint.

In his most important and concentrated discussion of the nature and meaning of death, which is found in chapter 41 of the second volume of *The World as Will and Representation*, Schopenhauer employed two general lines of argumentation to articulate his higher standpoint. At times, however, these lines intersect and he used elements of one line to explain the other. Nevertheless, he appealed first to an entirely empirical or naturalistic point of view and then to a metaphysical viewpoint, one that serves to ground the empirical, without becoming **transcendent**, that is, one that does not go beyond the bounds of possible experience. Within these lines of argumentation, Schopenhauer considered a robust set of data that he drew from multiple sources, including observations drawn from religion, poetry, literature, science, and philosophy. Ultimately, he drew freely on claims that he believed he had already proven either earlier in his main work or in his other philosophical writing.

Schopenhauer argued that from an entirely empirical point of view, it is clear that all **animals** fear death. In nonhuman animals, this fear is expressed by their striving to avoid pain and destruction and their efforts to live as long as they can. Human behavior expresses the same fear of death, but unlike nonhuman animals, we possess the faculty of **reason** and we know that we will die. Indeed, the recognition of our death is one of the ways by which we can suffer more profoundly than animals. We view our death, he claimed, as the greatest of **evils**, and our greatest anxiety is anxiety about our own death. Our natural recognition of death as an evil is so great, he said, that not only is our greatest fear the fear of our death, we even lament and become anxious about the death of friends and family members. This is not due to **egoism**, he argued, or because we see another's death as our loss. Rather, our **compassion** is due to our perception that the other's death is a great misfortune for that person.

Schopenhauer argued that neither the fear of death nor the judgment that it is evil have a rational foundation. All they show is how naturally and strongly we are attached to life. The fear of death implies that death deprives us of something of value, but he thought that the value of life is uncertain, if not doubtful. Indeed, he held that mature reflection reveals that nonexistence is preferable to existence. If we were to awaken the dead from their graves and offer them life, he said they would decline the offer. He then cited **Socrates** and Voltaire as agreeing with his view. If we were to think of nonexistence as terrible, to disengage us from this foolish thought, Schopenhauer appealed to death like states of life, dreamless sleep or fainting spells, to indicate that these states are far from terrible. All they entail is the loss of consciousness, the very condition necessary to experience anything terrible and evil. Often our thought that death is terrible is due to confusion over events in life, which are terrible, but which cease with death. For example, he thought we often associate the painful destruction of our body by sickness and old age with what follows, death. Yet that which is terrible and evil is the suffering, and it is death that ends this woe. Death, he reminds us, is not an event in life, something that we experience. Consequently, he quoted with approval the observation of Epicurus that when we are, death is not, and when death is, we are not. Further, he recommends thinking of the time prior to our existence. We find, he claims, that we do not regard that time as terrible, and he recommends the same attitude toward the time after our death.

From considerations like those given above, and from many more of like kind, Schopenhauer concluded that there are no rational grounds for fearing death and regarding it as an evil. Because of the way these attitudes toward death are irrational, he attributes them to the **will to life**, which is a blind craving for existence; reason enables us to know the wretchedness of life. From a higher empirical standpoint, by observing how nature itself operates, we can also come to know that what perishes in death is not our true nature. Thus he notes that nature favors the species at the expense of the countless, transitory individuals it grinds through its mills. He also observes that all **forces of nature**, including the vital force, neither come into being nor perish, and he appeals to his doctrine of **Platonic Ideas** to show what is universal and untouched by any coming to be and all perishing. Through these sorts of appeals, Schopenhauer argued that death does not touch the true and real inner being of things, including our own. In fact, he held that only small and narrow minds fear death as their annihilation, because they are unable to transcend the particular.

Ultimately, Schopenhauer's metaphysics of the will provides the answer to the question concerning our continued existence after death. Our coming to be and perishing is a feature of the world as representation, whose most basic *a priori* form is **time**. Everything within the world as representation is temporal. **Immanuel Kant**, he observed, demonstrated the ideality of time; it applies to the **appearances** of things and not to the **thing in itself**. Unlike Kant, however, Schopenhauer argued that we can know the will as thing in itself, although we do not have an exhaustive knowledge of its nature. Still, he claimed that he demonstrated that our essence, the essence of the world of representation, is the will. The will, moreover, is not temporal and not in time, which is necessary for any coming to be or perishing. Consequently, he argued that death is our end, but we must be eternal and imperishable. We are perishable as representations, but eternal as will. Death is the end of consciousness, of the intellect, but not the will. Our essential nature, therefore, is indestructible, but this entails that what is eternal about us is not individual and conscious. To ask what it is to be this, he claimed, is a transcendent question for which there is no answer.

DESCARTES, RENÉ (1596–1650). Descartes has been traditionally recognized as the central figure in the development of modern philosophical thought. Schopenhauer concurred with this judgment, and he called him the "father" of modern **philosophy**. In particular, he applauded Descartes for rejecting authority, especially the authority of the Bible and **Aristotle**, as the means for solving philosophical problems, and he praised his advocacy of **reason** as the source of truth. As Schopenhauer put it, he taught the faculty of reason to stand on its own two feet. Still, he viewed Descartes' philosophy as an example of the type of speculative metaphysics that **Immanuel Kant** had so thoroughly pulverized, and he claimed that there is not a word of truth in his doctrines. In fact, he held that Descartes' independence from theological doctrines was only apparent and that his skepticism about the existence of **God** and the soul was lacking in true earnestness, since it was only a temporary means used to endorse more firmly the ideas of his age. Thus he found Descartes to be like all modern philosophers down to Kant. They all failed to truly emancipate thought from the fetters of theology, and thus, they did not truly usher in a new period of impartial and original investigation. For a 19th century philosopher to follow Descartes, he said, would be like someone following Ptolemy in astronomy. Schopenhauer particularly censured his dualism, that is, Descartes' recognition of two fundamentally different substances, minds or thinking things and bodies or extended things, and his reduction of the **will** to a function of the **understanding**. About the latter, Schopenhauer claimed that to a certain extent his entire philosophy consisted in the refutation of that fundamental error.

Nevertheless, Schopenhauer viewed Descartes as a great man, because he was a pioneer. Thus he credited him with bringing to modern philosophical consciousness the question of the relationship between the ideal and the real, between what is subjective and what is objective, that is, the relationship between how things appear to us and things in themselves. This, he said, was the axis on which the whole of modern philosophy turns, and the question concerning the real and the ideal, along with the question of the **freedom** of the will, were the two most profound and difficult problems of modern philosophy. (Naturally, Schopenhauer also claimed to have solved these problems.) He also paid a backhanded compliment to Descartes in the opening section to *The World as Will and Representation* by claiming that his assertion that "The world is my **representation**," the very first proposition of his main work, was by no means new, but could be found in the skeptical reflections from which Descartes started. Descartes, however, was a **realist**, so immediately after making this remark, he noted that **George Berkeley**, an **idealist**, was the first to enunciate it positively.

DEUSSEN, PAUL (1845–1919). Deussen was a German philosopher, indologist, and professor of philosophy at the University of Kiel. He was also a life-long friend of **Friedrich Nietzsche**, who encouraged Deussen to study Schopenhauer. Deussen is often regarded as the first Western philosopher to include Eastern thought within the general history of philosophy in a systematic fashion. His chief work was *Universal History of Philosophy* (*Allgemeine Geschichte der Philosophie*, 1884–1917). He also translated a number of classical Hindu texts from Sanskrit into German, as well as publishing commentaries and analyses of these texts. In 1911 he founded the Schopenhauer-Gesellschaft, and in 1912 he established the *Schopenhauer-Jahrbuch*, both of which continue today. In addition, he served as the Schopenhauer-Gesellschaft's first president and the first editor of the *Jahrbuch*. He held both of these positions until his death. He also edited a collected edition of Schopenhauer's writings in 1911. Perhaps the best statement of Deussen's high estimation of the value of Schopenhauer's philosophy is found in his chief work, where he argued that Schopenhauer's philosophy presented a unified doctrine that was grounded in experience and based on the clarification of insights drawn from **Immanuel Kant**, **Plato**, Vedanta, and **Christianity**. Deussen held that Schopenhauer's philosophy would become the foundation for all future systematic and religious thought.

DORGUTH, FRIEDRICH LUDWIG ANDREAS (1776–1854). Dorguth was a judge in the Court of Appeal in Magdeburg and the author of a number of philosophical tracts. He was the first member of a group of early devotees of Schopenhauer's philosophy. He discovered Schopenhauer in the late 1830s and he became totally infatuated with his philosophy, claiming in 1843 that Schopenhauer was the first real systematic thinker in the history of literature. Schopenhauer once called Dorguth a "troglodyte of philosophy," and he read Dorguth's tracts out of a sense of duty engendered by Dorguth's undying enthusiasm for Schopenhauer's work, and not because of his philosophical competence. In the preface to the second edition of *On the Will in Nature* (1854), Schopenhauer used Dorguth's remark that Schopenhauer was the Casper Hauser (a German foundling youth of controversial origins, who claimed to have spent most of his life in solitary confinement) of the philosophy professors. He announced that, after 40 years of being ignored by them, their Casper Hauser had escaped into the world and that some imagined him a prince.

DOSS, ADAM LUDWIG VON (1820–1873). Doss was a lawyer in Munich when he read the second edition of *The World as Will and Representation*. This reading moved Doss to journey to Frankfurt to meet his philosophical hero. Doss' enthusiasm for Schopenhauer's philosophy delighted the philosopher considerably, and it led to Schopenhauer referring to Doss as "John the Apostle." Doss wrote numerous letters advocating Schopenhauer's philosophy, even to people he did not know. Schopenhauer enjoyed receiving letters from Doss, and he once remarked that the zeal of this "fanatic" defied description.

DUTIES TO OURSELVES (*PFLICHTEN GEGEN UNS SELBST*). Schopenhauer rejected the Kantian conception of duties to ourselves. A **duty**, he argued, is based on a free agreement with another by which the duty-holder assumes a liability or debt to another in exchange for a right. In this sense, a person cannot have a duty to oneself, since there is no second party who confers a right and to whom one has a debt. Moreover, since he argued that the failure to discharge a duty constitutes a **wrong**, something contrary to the **will** of another, a person could never wrong him or herself, because everything a person does is what he or she wills. Consequently, all actions are in conformity with and not contrary to a person's own will. For this reason, he concluded that it is logically impossible to have duties to oneself.

DUTY (*PFLICHT*). Schopenhauer conceived of a duty as a voluntarily assumed liability or debt that a person enters into in exchange for some **good**. Consequently, he viewed an expressed and mutually agreed upon contract as the basis of a duty. For example, in exchange for wages an employee has a duty to the employer to perform work of some type. The failure to discharge a duty constitutes an injury to the person to whom the duty is owed. Since he identified an injury to another as a **wrong**, he defined a duty as referring to an action the omission of which constitutes a wrong done to another. The only exception to this is the duty of parents to support their children, which he claimed is instituted by an act (having a child) and not by an agreement. This duty, however, confers a right to the parents, the obedience of the child, who has a duty to obey his or her parents. *See also* DUTIES TO OURSELVES.

– E –

EGOISM (*EGOISMUS*). Schopenhauer claimed that egoism, the craving for existence and one's own **weal**, is the chief and fundamental **incentive** for all **animal** behavior. He argued, however, that only humans exhibit self-interested behavior, because only humans possess the faculty of **reason**, and thus, he claimed that only humans have the capacity to deliberately and systematically plan the means to secure their own enjoyment and well-being. In any case, because of the dominance of egoism in human conduct, he advised that as a rule, we should always first attempt to explain any given action as proceeding from egoism. Naturally, Schopenhauer followed his own rule, and he was deft in unmasking the ways in which we try to hide this motive from both ourselves and others.

Schopenhauer held that egoism expresses the natural standpoint of humans in two ways. Egoism represents the **affirmation of the will**, and so he tied it directly to his metaphysics. He also saw it as a stance inherent in **consciousness**. Thus he argued that everyone is given to him or herself directly and everything else indirectly as a **representation** for the subject and as something dependent on the subject, such that, it appears as if when one dies, the world itself ends. For this reason, Schopenhauer claimed that the conduct of egoistic individuals expresses in deed **theoretical egoism**, the view that the individual is the only real being in the world. It is, perhaps, ironic to note that he believed that a theoretical egoist could only be found in a madhouse, whereas he believed that its practical correlate, egoism, is commonplace, ordinary, and the fundamental incentive for all cognitive beings. Instead of believing that one is the only real being, like the theoretical egoist, the egoist, he argued, acts like he or she is the only being whose existence and well-being matters. In pursuing his or her own self-interests, the egoist acts as if there is no other being whose interests matter.

Due to the lack of recognition that others have interests that matter, Schopenhauer emphasized the ways egoism leads to various sorts of **wrongs**. Still, he held that actions motivated by egoism are morally indifferent, that is, they are neither **morally reprehensible**, like those springing from **malice**, nor possessive of **moral worth**, like those resulting from **compassion**. The basis for Schopenhauer's ascription of moral indifference to egoistically based behavior was his belief that the moral value of an action concerns whether the end or aim of an action is another's **weal** or **woe**; whether the action ultimately aims at advancing another's well-being or causing another's misery. Since the ultimate aim of an egoist's action is his or her own well-being, its effect on another is purely secondary, Schopenhauer argued; it depends on how others are related to this end. Sometimes others may be benefited by an egoistic action, he claimed, and sometimes they may be harmed. In either case, the egoist is indifferent to the other. Hence, Schopenhauer's view of egoism highlighted the lack of any logical connection between the aim of an egoist's behavior and its effect on others. Sometimes others may be helped and at other times, harmed; it simply depends on how others stand in relation to what the egoist is trying to accomplish.

Like all incentives, Schopenhauer viewed egoism as having a range of expression. Consequently, he distinguished between egoism and extreme egoism (*äusserster Egoism*) and between egoists, people for whom the desire for their own self-interest is relatively mild and restrained, and extreme egoists, people for whom the desire for their own well-being is intense and extreme. From egoism, he deduced specific vices, such as greed, intemperance, lust, selfishness, avarice, covetousness, injustice, hardness of heart, and arrogance, the character traits that tend to emphasize the brutal nature of egoistic **characters**. The maxim, the principle that describes the line of conduct exhibited by extreme egoists, he said, is *"Neminem juva, imo omnes, si forte conducit, laede* [Help no one; on the contrary, injure all people if it brings you any advantage]," a maxim that makes it clear why extreme egoism precludes the virtues of **justice**, not harming others, and **philanthropy**, helping others.

EGOISM, THEORETICAL (*THEORETISCHER EGOISMUS*). In the 19th chapter of the first volume of *The World as Will and Representation*, Schopenhauer used the unique experience of one's own **body** as **will** and **representation** to mount the claim that all perceptual representations are also will. To deny this conclusion, Schopenhauer argued, one must assume that one's own body is the only **appearance** of the will, that is, one is the only real individual in the world and all other perceptual representations are phantoms or mere representations. He identified this view as theoretical **egoism**, and he saw this as the denial of the reality of the external world. He held that theoretical egoism could never be conclusively refuted by philosophical proof, but he also believed that it expresses a perspective that is simply a "skeptical sophism." It could only be found as a serious conviction by someone in a madhouse, he said, where its advocate needs not so much a refutation as a cure. It is curious to note, however, that even though he did not believe that theoretical egoism could be maintained by a sane person, he also held that most people live as if they are the only real beings in the world, since they act as if they are the one being whose interests count. He called this view "practical egoism."

EPISTEMOLOGY (*ERKENNTNISLEHRE*). Schopenhauer's direct writings on epistemic issues are found in *On the Fourfold Root of the Principle of Sufficient Reason*; chapter one of *On Vision and Colors*; the first book of the first volume of *The World as Will and Representation* and chapters one through 22 of the second volume. *See also* COGNITION; CONCEPTS; CONSCIOUSNESS OF OTHER

THINGS; INTELLECT; INTUITION; KNOWLEDGE; PERCEPTION; PRINCIPLE OF SUFFICIENT REASON; REASON; SELF-CONSCIOUSNESS; SENSIBILITY; SUBJECT AND OBJECT; SUBJECT OF COGNITION; TRUTH; UNDERSTANDING.

ETERNAL JUSTICE (*EWIGE GERECHTIGKEIT*). Unlike temporal **justice**, which Schopenhauer viewed as having its seat in the state, and thus a phenomenon in the world as **representation**, he analyzed eternal justice as a feature of the world itself. Like his account of temporal justice, Schopenhauer's discussion of eternal justice focuses on what could be called retributive justice, the fair treatment of wrongdoers. Whereas temporal justice needs to be effected by human institutions to insure that wrongdoers are punished in order to deter others from committing like wrongs and to prevent these wrongs in the future, eternal justice functions immediately and perfectly in the world, independent from human institutions. Schopenhauer argued that the world expresses eternal justice, that independent from the state, all wrongs or offenses are identical to a perfectly retributive and certain punishment. Schopenhauer grounded this claim by appealing to his metaphysics of the **will**. All the wretchedness of life, all the **evils** and wrongs, and all suffering and **death** in the world are the case because the will so wills. The will is responsible for all the evils in the world, but it is also, at the same time, the sufferer of these evils. Thus Schopenhauer argued that the world itself is the tribunal of the world. If one could place all the misery of the world in one pan of the scales of justice and all the guilt in the other, the scales would balance. In other words, from a metaphysical perspective, the world is perfectly retributive. The severity of the wrong is proportional to the severity of the punishment. It is as if all the misery caused by the will is suffered by the will, and they are both self-generated. From this perspective, the tormentor (the will) is the tormented (the will).

The idea of eternal justice is withdrawn from any perspective following the **principle of sufficient reason**, Schopenhauer argued, and its realization involves seeing through the *principium individuationis*, **space** and **time**, which are the conditions for the possibility of plurality. Since he held that this glance beyond the *principium individuationis* is inaccessible to the majority of humans, it appears to most people in this world that one person is the tormentor and another the tormented and that all miseries of life are undeserved, but in reality, the opposite is the case.

ETHICS (*ETHIK*). Schopenhauer wrote more on topics directly related to ethics than he did on topics in **aesthetics**, **epistemology**, or metaphysics. His specific writings that focus on ethics are the fourth book of the first volume of *The World as Will and Representation* and chapters 40 through 50 of the second volume; the chapter "Reference to Ethics" in *On the Will in Nature*; *The Two Fundamental Problems of Ethics*; and chapters eight through 15 in the second volume of *Parerga and Paralipomena. See also* BAD; COMPASSION; DUTIES TO OURSELVES; DUTY; EGOISM; ETERNAL JUSTICE; EUDAEMONISM; EVIL; FREEDOM; FREEDOM, MORAL; GOOD; INDIFFERENCE, MORALLY; JUSTICE; LOVE; PESSIMISM; PHILANTHROPY; PHILOSOPHY; OPTIMISM; OUGHT; REPREHENSIBLE, MORALLY; RESPONSIBILITY; SALVATION; SCHADENFREUDE; SUICIDE; TAT TVAM ASI; TEMPORAL JUSTICE; WEAL; WOE; WORTH, MORAL.

ETHICS, THE PRINCIPLE OF (*DAS PRINCIP EINER ETHIK*). In section six of *On the Basis of Morality*, Schopenhauer described the principle or fundamental proposition of an ethical system as the most concise expression for the lines of conduct prescribed by it, or as summarizing the lines of conduct to which it attributes genuine moral worth. Schopenhauer rejected, however, any prescriptive ethical theory. Consequently, his principle of **ethics** is merely descriptive of the lines of conduct to which he attributed **moral worth**. His principle is "*Neminem laede; imo omnes, quantum potes, juva*, [Injure no one; on the contrary, help everyone as much as you can]." He maintained that all teachers of ethics were really in agreement with this principle, although they often expressed it in different terms. He also thought that the justification of this principle was the constant endeavor of all moral philosophies. With his characteristic lack of modesty, Schopenhauer claimed that he was the first to do so; that he was the first to provide the foundation of ethics.

Schopenhauer's strategy for showing the basis or foundation of morality is straightforward. The first clause of his principle of ethics, "injure no one," represents the virtue of **justice**, and the second, "help everyone as much as you can," signifies the virtue of **philanthropy**

Since he held that justice and philanthropy are the cardinal virtues, the virtues from which all other virtues are derived, by showing that these cardinal virtues are based on **compassion**, he held that he had shown the basis or foundation for all virtues and for all actions to which we attribute moral worth. Compassion, he thusly held, is the basis or foundation of morality.

EUDAEMONISM. Schopenhauer identified as eudaemonistic any view that tries to prove that virtue and happiness are identical or that maintains that happiness is the consequence of virtue. He regarded the **ethics** of most ancient Greek philosophers, with the exception of **Plato**, as eudaemonistic, and although he praised **Immanuel Kant** for purging eudaemonism from ethics, he also claimed that he did so more in appearance than in reality, since Kant's doctrine of the highest **good** or *summum bonum* reintroduces the notion that the virtuous will be happy. Schopenhauer rejected eudaemonism from ethics because he thought that any promise of happiness for moral conduct leads to self-interested or egoistical behavior, behavior that lacks **moral worth**.

EVIL (*BÖSE*). Any conscious being that thwarts a person's desires or willful efforts was judged as "evil" by Schopenhauer. For example, a man who prevents me from leaving my room by locking the door is "evil," whereas, a rock that blocks my doorway is "bad." *See also* GOOD.

– F –

FEELING (*GEFÜHL*). Schopenhauer contrasted **knowledge** (*Wissen*) with feeling. The concept "feeling," he argued, has a negative content or intension, since it denotes something present to consciousness or **cognition** that is not a **concept**, not the abstract cognition of **reason**. Given the broad range of application or the extension of this concept, he claimed that numerous heterogeneous things are feelings, such as feelings of sexual pleasure, feelings of physical pain, feelings of the **sublime** and the **beautiful**, and even the *a priori* forms of the pure **sensibility** and the pure **understanding**. Given this broad conception of "feeling," Schopenhauer held that **philosophy** (which is rational and conceptual) seeks to provide knowledge of what is expressed concretely as a feeling.

FICHTE, JOHANN GOTTLIEB (1762–1814). Along with **Friedrich Wilhelm Joseph von Schelling** and **Georg Wilhelm Friedrich Hegel**, Schopenhauer viewed Fichte as a sophist whose pseudo-philosophy abandoned **Immanuel Kant**'s great insights and corrupted German philosophy and literature. He condemned Fichte's cumbersome and convoluted writing style, and he saw it as serving as the model for philosophical writing made even worse by Schelling and "perfected" by Hegel. Schopenhauer despised Hegel more than he did Fichte, but he disliked Fichte more than he did Schelling. Consequently, he called Hegel Schelling's buffoon and Fichte was Kant's, and he said that, compared to Hegel, Fichte was a "man of talent." Given Schopenhauer's low regard for Hegel's abilities, however, this was not much of a compliment. He had such a low regard for Fichte's philosophical judgment that in the first preface to *The Two Fundamental Problems of Ethics*, Schopenhauer used his remark that **John Locke** was the worst of all philosophers to praise Locke. Indeed, he did not even regard Fichte as a genuine philosopher, since he believed that true philosophers are prompted to their task by a deep astonishment about the world and that they are committed to the **truth**. Fichte, he said, was moved to philosophy by his puzzlement about Kant's philosophy, especially by Kant's idea of the **thing in itself**. Instead of living for philosophy, he saw Fichte living by philosophy and serving his own interests rather than the truth. He also loathed any reference to a Kantian-Fichtean philosophy, and he was particularly offended by any suggestion that Fichte had surpassed Kant. Naturally, Schopenhauer delighted in discovering that the Old Kant became angry whenever he heard Fichte's name.

Schopenhauer, however, did not always disdain Fichte. Although Fichte's philosophical reputation was waning when Schopenhauer left the University of Göttingen to enroll in the University of Berlin in the fall of 1811, he was drawn to Berlin to attend Fichte's lectures. In Fichte, he thought, he would be exposed to a great philosophical mind. He attended Fichte's introductory lecture in his lecture cycle, and he enrolled in the cycle, "The Facts of Consciousness and On the

Doctrine of Science," in the winter semester of 1811–1812. He also borrowed a student's notes for Fichte's lectures on jurisprudence and morals from the winter semester of 1812–1813, and he started to study Fichte on his own, beginning in 1812. His lecture notes and his notes to his self-study show that he read Fichte very seriously and intensely. They also reveal, however, as Schopenhauer would later remark, how his "*a priori* veneration" for Fichte turned into contempt and derision. These notes show his increasing dissatisfaction with Fichte's obscure mode of expression and increasing skepticism concerning the content, or better yet, the lack of content to Fichte's thought. His "doctrine of science [*Wissenschaftslehre*]," he said, was "empty of science [*Wissenschaftsleere*]." Yet, his study of Fichte served him well, since it also moved him to study Kant even more intensely.

Although Schopenhauer went to some lengths to distance himself from Fichte, and he was highly displeased when reviewers claimed to sense Fichte's spurs in *The World as Will and Representation*, it is not surprising that they would do so. Like Fichte, Schopenhauer held that the ultimate in the world is an active force whose free act, one outside the bounds of the **principle of sufficient reason**, is the world. They both, moreover, subordinated the intellect to a secondary role in human activity and viewed the intellect as serving this ultimate. In addition, they viewed the moral significance of the world as following from its being the expression of the ultimate. Moreover, both rejected **realism**, the claim that objects exist independently of **consciousness**, for the reason that it cannot account for the conscious subject. Schopenhauer, however, claimed that any points of contact with Fichte's philosophy follow simply from the fact that they have a common point of departure for their views, Kant's philosophy.

Still, in spite of some points of contact, Schopenhauer arrived at his conclusions through a fundamentally different method than that of Fichte, and he did so by maintaining allegiance to Kant's distinction between the thing in itself and **appearances**. While Schopenhauer held that Kant failed to provide a strict deduction of the thing in itself and that he had employed the law of **causality** transcendentally by claiming that it is the cause of appearances, he chided Fichte for rejecting Kant's distinction. Fichte viewed the external world as being derived from the ego or subject. He argued that this absolute ego or subject posits or asserts (*setzt*) the non-ego. Schopenhauer rejected Fichte's subjective **idealism** and his attempt to, as he put it, make "the non-ego result from the ego as the web from the spider." Fichte merely duplicated Kant's error, Schopenhauer argued, by making the ego the ground of the non-ego, a move that also showed that Fichte treated the principle of sufficient reason as a *veritas aeterna*, as having an unconditional validity. Of course, Schopenhauer held that this principle was nothing but the general form of the non-ego or object and had no validity outside the object. In fact, Schopenhauer accused Fichte of expressing the opposite view of the realist. Just as the realist cannot account for the subject by making the object primary, he claimed that Fichte, by making the subject primary, could not account for the non-ego or object. (He also claimed that the only thing interesting about Fichte was his opposition to realism.) By starting from the **representation**, the first fact of consciousness, Schopenhauer contended that his **philosophy** was a form of idealism and his method was *toto genere* different from both Fichte's and the realist's, since he recognized that the **subject and object** division is the essential and most basic form of all experience. Moreover, by subsequently recognizing the principle of sufficient reason as only applicable to the object, as the form of the object for a subject, he claimed to have placed this principle in its proper place. By demonstrating these claims, Schopenhauer argued that he had also shown the complete and universal relativity of the world as representation, something that suggests that the inner nature of the world is entirely different from the representation. Thus, he found his philosophy capable of accommodating the idea of the thing in itself, something that cannot be discovered from the **consciousness of other things**, but only through **self-consciousness**.

Schopenhauer took Fichte's practical philosophy far less seriously than his theoretical. While he actually took some time to argue against the latter, he viewed the former to be absurd and not worthy of refutation. In section 11 of *On the Basis of Morality* he used Fichte's *System of Moral Philosophy* (*System der Sittenlehre*) and *The Doctrine of Science Presented in General Outline* (*Die Wissenschaftslehre in ihrem allgemeinen Umrisse dargestellt*) to show the worthlessness of Kant's foundation of ethics. Fichte's ethics, he claimed, serves as a mirror for magnifying Kant's errors. While

Schopenhauer admitted that Fichte's ethics was a caricature of Kant's, one that at times, he said, bordered on the comic, his treatment of Fichte once again implies that Fichte was attracted only to the defects of Kant and not to his insights. Fichte takes, he observed, Kant's moral pedantry to its absurd ends by claiming that not only are **compassion**, sympathy, and **philanthropy** non-moral, but also they are contrary to morality. And although Schopenhauer attributed moral significance to the world, since it is the free expression of the ultimate, he found it sufficient to simply quote Fichte's expression of this idea to show that Fichte's **ethics** was the articulation of ultimate nonsense, since it took the unproven imperative form of Kant's ethics to make the external world the stage for the ego for doing its duty and perceiving itself as "the absolute **ought**," thereby reducing human beings to mere tools of the moral law.

FORCES OF NATURE (*NATURKRÄFTE*). Schopenhauer identified two factors necessary for the causal explanation of natural occurrences, that is, changes among spatiotemporal objects. He therefore distinguished between some original force intrinsic to an object upon which some causal influence is exerted and a determining **cause** that makes the force manifest, in order to ultimately explain some change or effect. He called those forces that prevail among inorganic bodies "forces of nature" or "natural forces," having in mind forces like gravity, electricity, and magnetism, and he argued that it is from these forces, which are neither caused nor causing, that effects proceed, with such effects being occasioned by the causes. He held that in scientific explanations of changes in the natural world, the scientist ultimately has to appeal to natural forces and the scientist can only describe the invariable constancy of the appearance of a natural force under specific conditions, formulating thereby laws of nature. He argued, moreover, that these laws, which have to appeal to forces of nature, only state the constancy of the manifestation of the forces, but say nothing about these forces themselves. They remain, therefore, *qualities occulta*, occult qualities, necessary but scientifically inexplicable elements of scientific explanations of the world.

Schopenhauer argued that natural forces represent the lowest grades of the objectification of the **will**, and "life force" is the general force expressed in living beings, and he claimed that the intelligible character or will is the force expressed in human life, which expresses the highest grade of the will's objectification. By attributing a **Platonic Idea** to natural forces, and by resolving Platonic Ideas as the will as **thing in itself**, Schopenhauer claimed that his **philosophy** completes the scientific picture of the world by providing a philosophical explanation for what was presupposed and unexplained by science. *See also* NATURAL SCIENCES.

FOURFOLD ROOT OF THE PRINCIPLE OF SUFFICIENT REASON, ON THE (*ÜBER DIE VIERFACHE WURZEL DES SATZES VOM ZUREICHENDEN GRUNDE*). This book was originally Schopenhauer's dissertation, which he submitted to the University of Jena in October 1813. Jena passed Schopenhauer's dissertation, with the distinction of *magna cum laude*, and awarded him a doctorate in philosophy *in abstentia*. In late 1813, Schopenhauer paid to have 500 copies of it published by the Commission der Hof-Buch-und Kunsthandlung, in Rudolstadt. Schopenhauer's first book failed to bring him any philosophical notoriety. The three reviews it initially drew were not positive, even though one was written by Schopenhauer's first philosophy professor, **G. E. Schulze**. Schopenhauer prepared a second, revised and expanded edition of his dissertation, which was published in 1847 by the Johann Christian Hermann'sche Buchhandlung F. E. Suchsland, in Frankfurt. It drew no reviews. The tone and style of the second edition is very different from the first, which, as a dissertation, had a somewhat dry and pedantic style, compared to the more fiery and lively style found in his later writings. The second edition also provided more of a metaphysical dimension to his earlier work, and it included an elaborate account of his arguments on the *a priori* nature of causality. Schopenhauer regarded this book as the "introduction" to *The World as Will and Representation*, especially to the first book of his main work. This book is usually read in its second edition, and it is generally recognized that the alterations between the two editions are significant.

The preface to the work was written for the second edition. Schopenhauer discussed in it the differences between the two editions, which he saw as primarily a variation in the tone and style of expression found in the first edition, which expressed a young man's belief that philosophers are interested solely in the **truth**, and the later material, which expressed the harsh and indignant voice of an old man, who recognized the self-serving ends of professional philosophers. The difference in the expressions of materials, Schopenhauer claimed, would make it obvious to the reader when the 26 year old was speaking and when it was the voice of the 60 year old. Consequently, Schopenhauer did not indicate within the text what material belonged to the first edition and what was the new material in the second. Like all of Schopenhauer's later prefaces, he also used the preface to abuse **Georg Wilhelm Friedrich Hegel**.

In the first chapter, the "Introduction," Schopenhauer articulates the two methodological principles that guided his study, principles he attributed to his two favorite philosophers, **Plato** and **Immanuel Kant**. He referred to these principles as the law of **homogeneity** and the law of **specification**. The former, he observed, requires the observation of similarities and agreements between things, uniting them into species, and then into genera, until one comes to the highest concept that embraces everything. Conversely, he noted, the latter requires that one clearly distinguish between all species united under a genera, and between the higher and lower kinds of things united under a species. When it came to the very principle of all **knowledge**, the **principle of sufficient reason**, he claimed previous philosophers had neglected the law of specification, since they had neglected to draw distinctions between different applications of the principle and thereby they treated it as if it were a single principle. Schopenhauer contended that the principle of sufficient reason, which he stated by using a formation employed by Christian Wolff, "Nothing is without a reason why it is rather than is not," does not follow from one kind of fundamental knowledge, but instead it is an abstraction from different kinds of knowledge, which are inherent within human **cognition**, and as such, are *a priori* and serve as the basis of all necessity. By clearly distinguishing between the various forms or "roots" of the principle of sufficient reason, Schopenhauer claimed that philosophers would be better able to express their thought with greater lucidity and precision, and thus avoid the ambiguity and errors of sloppy thinking, as well as be spared the deception occasioned by sham philosophers who try to conceal the paucity of their ideas by the incomprehensibility of their language.

In the second chapter, Schopenhauer provided a historical overview of the use of the principle of sufficient reason by philosophers ranging from Plato to adherents and critics of Kant. In addition to chiding many of these philosophers for their failure to distinguish between various forms of the principle, he also argued that the principle of sufficient reason, the basis for all proof, has no proof itself. He noted that it is absurd to demand a proof for this principle, since this demand itself assumes allegiance to the principle, which is found in the demand for a proof for the right to demand a proof. In the third chapter, Schopenhauer argues that the two forms of the principle of sufficient reason that were gradually recognized by previous philosophers, namely that any change in real objects must have a **cause** and that any true judgment must have a reason for its truth, failed to account for all specifications of the principle of sufficient reason. Schopenhauer proposed that four species of the principle of sufficient reason could be ascertained by exploring the four classes of objects into which all of our **representations** can be divided, and within which the principle of sufficient reason appears in a different form. The next four chapters were devoted to Schopenhauer's analysis of the four specifications of the principle of sufficient reason.

The fourth chapter, which runs close to 100 pages, or almost 40 percent of the second edition, contains Schopenhauer's analysis of the principle of sufficient reason in relationship to the cognition of intuitive **perceptions**, the recognition of natural objects standing in causal relations to other spatial and temporal objects. He called this "root" the **principle of sufficient reason of becoming** or the **law of causality**, which states that if a change of one or more real objects appears, another change must have preceded it upon which the new change follows regularly as often as the first change exists. Schopenhauer claimed that the perception of natural objects is intellectual, the product of the **understanding**, which creates the perception of the objective, external world through the transformation of raw sensations, things which are, so to speak, "underneath the skin," and which, as provided by **sensibility**, have the *a priori* forms of **space** and **time**. This entailed for Schopenhauer that sensation is not perception, since it is the function of the understanding to construe sensed-bodily-changes as the effects of objects beyond the **body** in space and time. Section 21, which was added to the second edition, continues Schopenhauer's physiological arguments for the *a priori* nature of the law of causality, which are viewed by many commentators as his strongest arguments for **idealism**, and section 23 contained his critique of Kant's proofs for the *a priori* nature of the law of causality.

The fifth chapter presents Schopenhauer's analysis of the **principle of sufficient reason of knowing**, whose class of objects is **concepts** or abstract representations. Schopenhauer viewed judgments as a function of the combination of concepts in which the mind draws inferences from a ground or consequence, and he viewed the faculty of **reason**, the cognitive ability to formulate concepts derived from intuitive representation, as that which separates humans from other **animals**. Schopenhauer expressed the principle of sufficient reason of knowing as the statement that any knowledge claim or judgment must have a sufficient reason by virtue of which it is true. He distinguishes between four types of truths or judgments. If the ground for a judgment is another judgment, its truth is purely logical or formal. If the ground for a judgment is experience and the judgment is informative about the world, it is an empirical truth. If the ground of a judgment is one of the *a priori* forms for the possibility of experience, it is a **transcendental** truth. Lastly, if its ground or reason is a formal condition for all thought, then it states a metalogical truth. Schopenhauer closed the chapter with section 34, in which he employed his analysis of the faculty of reason to criticize the metaphysical pretensions of reason found in the philosophies of Friedrich Heinrich Jacobi, **Friedrich Wilhelm Joseph von Schelling**, and Hegel.

The subject of the sixth chapter is the **principle of sufficient reason of being**, whose class of objects contains two objects, the *a priori* forms of space and time considered purely formally and not as they are sensuously perceived. Schopenhauer argued that all parts of space and time stand in a mutual relation, such that all parts are determined and conditioned by another, with the relation in space constituting position, in time succession. According to Schopenhauer, space provides the basis of geometry, and time is the basis of arithmetic. Section 39 contains Schopenhauer's argument that geometrical proofs require a visual representation, a view that helped to dispose **Johann Wolfgang von Goethe** to perceive an affinity in their thoughts.

The seventh chapter presents the last of the fourfold roots, the **principle of sufficient reason of acting**, whose class of objects contains only one member, an individual's own **will**. The application of the principle of sufficient reason as it applies to the individual's **self-conscious** experience of the will yields, Schopenhauer argued, the law of motivation, which states that for any action there is a **motive**, such that nothing but that particular action could have been performed by that agent at that time. In section 44, Schopenhauer described motivation as causality seen from within, parallel to the experience of causality as a feature of the perception of the external world.

Schopenhauer concludes the book with the eighth chapter, in which he made some general remarks about the structure of his exposition of the principle of sufficient reason. He noted that his presentation of the principle was chosen for reasons of clarity rather than systematically. Had it been arranged systematically, he noted, he would have started with the principle of sufficient reason of being concerning its application to time, which is the simplest schema to which all other applications apply. He would then have discussed space, followed by the principle of sufficient reason of becoming, the law of causality, followed by the principle of sufficient reason of acting and the law of motivation. Lastly, he claimed, he would have discussed the principle of sufficient reason of knowing, which deals with concepts or representations of representations. In section 52, Schopenhauer stated the two main results of his work. The first is that the principle of sufficient reason and all of its roots are applicable only to the **appearances** of things and not to the **thing in itself**. The second, which Schopenhauer claimed is closely related to the first, is that the four laws of thought of our cognitive faculty apply to all objects of the **subject of cognition**, and any imagined fifth class of objects would also entail a new form of the principle. It would not entail, however, any justification for a claim about some absolute ground or reason in general for the world, which is simply an empty abstraction.

FRAUENSTÄDT, JULIUS (1813–1879). Frauenstädt was a Doctor of Philosophy, philosopher, and private scholar from Berlin. After a brief flirtation with **Georg Wilhelm Friedrich Hegel**, he became an admirer of the German philosopher Ludwig Feuerbach until, in 1836, he ran across, quite accidentally, a reference to Schopenhauer in an article on **idealism** in an encyclopedia. This led him to read *The World as Will and Representation*, and this experience changed the course of his life. He became Schopenhauer's "arch-evangelist," as Schopenhauer would later refer to Frauenstädt, and the most active member of a set of early adherents to Schopenhauer's philosophy. He wrote tracts promoting Schopenhauer's philosophy, apologetics, and he kept faithful watch for references to Schopenhauer in books and journals. Schopenhauer was inclined, however, to sometimes treat Frauenstädt harshly, especially for misunderstanding his philosophy. After Frauenstädt complained to Schopenhauer about his "yelling" at him in late 1856, Schopenhauer abruptly terminated correspondence with him, accusing Frauenstädt of maintaining a morality of **materialism**. The two men returned to good terms late in 1859, after Schopenhauer sent Frauenstädt a copy of the third edition of *The World as Will and Representation*. Despite this three-year period of silence, Schopenhauer's correspondence with Frauenstädt is the most extensive of all of the philosopher's letter exchanges. Due to his active support for his philosophy, Schopenhauer made Frauenstädt the heir of his philosophical writings and his handwritten manuscripts. After Schopenhauer's death, Frauenstädt continued to promote Schopenhauer's books and became the first editor of Schopenhauer's collected works in 1873.

FREEDOM (*FREIHEIT*). Schopenhauer's basic conception of freedom is negative. It connotes for him the absence of determination or necessity. Thus he argued that the **will** is free, since it is beyond the scope of the **principle of sufficient reason**, the basis of all necessity. On a more mundane level, Schopenhauer understood freedom as the absence of hindrances to the expression of some force. Thus a river is "free," if its natural course is not blocked by a dam.

FREEDOM OF THE HUMAN WILL, ON THE (*ÜBER DIE FREIHEIT DES MENSCHLICHEN WILLENS*). Schopenhauer wrote this essay in response to a prize essay contest sponsored by the Royal Norwegian Society of Sciences, which in April 1837 published the question, "Can the freedom of the will be proven from self-consciousness?" Schopenhauer sent this essay to the Royal Norwegian Society in April 1838, and it was awarded first place in the contest on 26 January 1839. It was published by the Society in 1840 in a Danish journal. Schopenhauer published it, together with the essay "On the Basis of Morality," in *The Two Fundamental Problems of Ethics*, 1841, second edition 1860.

Schopenhauer had to submit the essay anonymously. Consequently, he could not write it presupposing his own **philosophy**. Due to this, *On the Freedom of the Human Will* is relatively self-contained. It, as he would later say in the preface to the ***Two Fundamental Problems of Ethics***, does not presuppose his metaphysics or the **will**, but treats the issue of the freedom of the will in its own right. He also said that it leads, however, to his metaphysics. This essay is perhaps the clearest of all of his writings, which are generally known for their clarity.

The essay is divided into five sections: I, Definitions, in which Schopenhauer distinguishes between **physical freedom**, **intellectual freedom**, and **moral freedom**, and where he details his understanding of the term "**self-consciousness**"; II, The will before self-consciousness, where he argued that it is impossible to demonstrate the freedom of the will from self-consciousness; III, The will before the **consciousness of other things**, where he argued that it is not possible to prove the freedom of the will by our consciousness of other things; IV, Predecessors, where he considers "great thinkers," drawn from poetry, theology, and philosophy, who also denied the freedom of the will; and V, Conclusion and higher view, in which he analyzed the sense of our being the doers of our deeds, our sense of **moral responsibility** and accountability, to conclude that despite the fact that all of our actions are strictly determined, following from necessity, freedom lies in our essence, our intelligible **characters**, which are beyond the **principle of sufficient reason**, the scope of all necessity. Schopenhauer concluded the essay with an appendix, which supplements the first section, in which he provided more discussion of his conception of intellectual freedom and its relationship to **punishment**.

FREEDOM, INTELLECTUAL (*INTELLEKTUELLE FREIHEIT*).
Schopenhauer viewed intellectual **freedom** as the ability of agents to

do what they **will** because of the absence of some cognitive defect or error that would prevent them from doing what they want. In other words, when agents' intellects are capable of presenting a full range of **motives** for possible actions in a given situation, so that they are able to do what they want, the agents are intellectually free. Conversely, if agents are led to do something different than they imagine, due to some temporary or permanent defect in **cognition** or because of some overwhelming passion that precludes agents from entertaining some counter-motive that would prevent them from doing what they do, then agents in these conditions lack intellectual freedom. For example, if a landlord shot a servant entering his apartment late at night, because the servant was mistaken for a burglar, or if due to a powerful feeling of rage, a woman strikes her beloved crying baby, then in these cases, agents lack intellectual freedom. Schopenhauer also argued that legal and moral imputability for a deed presupposes intellectual freedom, the ability of a person to truly express his or her **character**.

FREEDOM, MORAL (*MORALISCHE FREIHEIT*). Schopenhauer believed that every action follows with strict necessity from the effect of a **motive** on a person's **will**. Therefore, he denied the concept of moral **freedom** that requires the possibility of a person to have acted differently than he or she had done under a specific set of circumstances or conditions. That is, if I consider going home after work or going to the library, and I go to the library, Schopenhauer would claim that it was necessary for me to go to the library; I could not have acted differently in the same set of circumstances. Although it is true to say that I went to the library because I wanted to, and had I wanted to go home, I would have gone home, Schopenhauer would argue that this is not sufficient to show that I could have acted differently. To show that, Schopenhauer claimed that one would have to prove that I could want what I want, that I could will what I will, and that this is impossible.

In his response to the prize essay contest sponsored by the Royal Norwegian Society of Sciences, *On the Freedom of the Human Will*, Schopenhauer argued that freedom cannot be proven from **self-consciousness**, which can only show us that we can do what we want. He denied, moreover, that humans possess a *liberum arbitrium* (free choice of the will) or *liberum arbitrium indifferentiae* (free choice of indifference), since both imply an absolutely undetermined willing, something denied by his thesis that all changes in the physical world have a sufficient reason or **cause**, including human behavior. In contrast to the spurious idea of moral freedom as the ability for a person to have acted differently, Schopenhauer recognized what he called true moral freedom, which is not attributed to human actions but to the essence of a person, the will. He captured this idea by the slogan *operari sequitur esse* (acting follows being), that is, what we do follows from what we are. This freedom is **transcendental**, he argued, because it does not occur in **appearance**. Instead, it is the freedom of the will or intelligible character, which is beyond the **principle of sufficient reason**.

FREEDOM, PHYSICAL (*PHYSISCHE FREIHEIT*). Schopenhauer conceived of physical **freedom** as the expression of some physical force, absent some material hindrance or barrier. Thus a stream is "free" when its flow is unimpeded by mountains or sluices, and an animal is free when it can roam the woods unrestricted by a cage, and a person is physically free when he or she can take the desired route home because the roadway is not blocked by an accident. He thought the idea of physical freedom was the original and popular sense of the term "**freedom**." He also saw political freedom as a form of physical freedom, which is realized when people are governed by laws of their own making.

FREUD, SIGMUND (1856–1939). It has long been recognized in the secondary literature on both Freud and Schopenhauer that there are striking affinities and parallels between their thoughts. Schopenhauer's concept of the **will** has been seen as pre-staging Freud's conceptions of the unconscious and Id; his account of the relationship between the will and **intellect** has been viewed as being mirrored in Freud's description of the relationship between the Id and **consciousness**; his explanation of **madness** as expressing the general contours of Freud's theory of repression and his first theory of the causality of neurosis; and his emphasis on the significance of early childhood for adult life has been said to have received a more complete articulation in Freud. Other points of contact have been found between Schopenhauer's philosophy and Freud's theory of free association, as well as Freud's recognition of the **death** instinct. Scholars have also highlighted their shared attitudes toward **ethics**, **aesthetics**, **women**, **religion**, and the human condition (a **pessimism**, tempered by the belief that intellect could overcome the will).

It is difficult to ascertain whether Schopenhauer influenced Freud, however. What makes the question of influence difficult is Freud's attitude toward Schopenhauer, which is probably best illustrated by a remark from Freud's "On the History of the Psycho-Analytic Movement" (1914). In this essay Freud said he had thought that his theory of repression was original and that he knew of no earlier work that guided him to his theory, until Otto Rank showed him a passage in Schopenhauer's account of insanity in *The World as Will and Representation*. Freud wrote "what he [Schopenhauer] states there concerning the striving against the acceptance of a painful piece of reality agrees so completely with the content of my theory of repression, that once again, I must be grateful to my not being well read, for the possibility of making a discovery." Others, he continued, have read his passage without making this discovery and perhaps the same would have happened to him, had he taken more pleasure in reading philosophers. In fact, he claimed, he even denied himself the pleasure of reading **Friedrich Nietzsche**, because he was worried about "preconceived ideas" shaping his psychoanalytic impressions. Although one can sense some resistance on Freud's part about recognizing his reading of Schopenhauer, he did retract his claim to the originality of this theory of repression: "I have, therefore, . . . to renounce all claim to priority in those many cases in which laborious psychoanalytic investigations can only confirm the insights intuitively won by the philosophers. The theory of repression is the pillar upon which the edifice of psychoanalysis rests."

Freud also claimed that he first read Schopenhauer when he was working on *Beyond the Pleasure Principle* (1920), so that he first read Schopenhauer late in life. In "Schopenhauer and Freud," Christopher Young and Andrew Brook suggest that Freud probably had "1915 or about then in mind" for his first reading of Schopenhauer, but they also found that he had referred to anecdotes about Schopenhauer in 1906 and 1909 and that in his *Interpretation of Dreams* (1900), he referred three times to the "Essay on Spirit Seeing and Everything Connected Therewith," (from the first volume of *Parerga and Paralipomena*), in which Schopenhauer presented his theory of dreams within the general framework of his philosophy and which contained references to *The World as Will and Representation* that, given Freud's interests, should have led him to consult that work. In addition to these citations, in *Totem and Taboo*, he remarked that whenever he had penetrated the mystery behind the obsessive acts of neurotics, "I have found that the expected disaster was death. Schopenhauer has said that the problem of death stands at the outset of every **philosophy**." He then draws a parallel finding: "We have already seen . . . that the origin of the belief in souls and demons, which is the essence of animism, goes back to the impression which is made upon man by death."

Young and Brook concluded, however, that there is no conclusive evidence that Freud read Schopenhauer before 1892 and before the publication of his own views. They also found that the pattern of his references to Schopenhauer is generally consistent with his claim that he read Schopenhauer after 1915. Nevertheless, they, like many scholars, find it astonishing to believe that he did not read Schopenhauer in the gymnasium and at the University of Vienna, since Schopenhauer was "virtually the official philosopher of the German-speaking world during those years." They also cite a student, who belonged to the same student study group as Freud, as claiming that **Richard Wagner**, Nietzsche, and Schopenhauer were regularly discussed, and they note that he was exposed to Schopenhauer through two of his professors, most noteworthy the philosopher Franz Brentano, and through his reading of **Eduard von Hartmann**'s *The Philosophy of the Unconscious* (1869). From these factors, plus his earlier than 1915 references to Schopenhauer, Young and Brook reason that "It is overwhelmingly probable that Freud had read some Schopenhauer before he formulated the ideas of psychoanalysis."

Still, from Freud's perspective, the commonalities and parallels between his views and Schopenhauer's were coincidental. In *New Introductory Lectures in Psychoanalysis* (1933), in anticipation of the claim that his work was "not science [*Naturwissenschaft*]" but Schopenhauerian philosophy, Freud replied, "But Ladies and Gentlemen, why should not a bold thinker have divined what is afterward confirmed by sober and laboriously detailed research?"

– G –

GENIUS, THE (*DAS GENIE*). A genius is a person capable of having an **intuition** of the universal in the particular, in contrast to ordinary people who, Schopenhauer claimed, are capable of only seeing particular things in a self-interested fashion, that is, as potential means for thwarting or satisfying their desires. The genius cognizes **Platonic Ideas**, according to Schopenhauer, and thereby sees things objectively and disinterestedly. He attributed this cognitive ability, possessed by a very few men (he thought **women**, while capable of great talent, were too subjective to possess genius), to be the result of a predominance of **intellect** over **will**, the reverse of this relationship seen among ordinary men and women. Schopenhauer reserved the term "genius" to refer only to creative artists and philosophers, with Mozart and **Johann Wolfgang von Goethe** representing the former, and **Plato** and **Immanuel Kant**, the latter.

GENITALS (*GENITALIEN*). From a personal and philosophical perspective, Schopenhauer did not think highly of the genitals. He viewed them as objectifications of the sexual impulse, which represent the most vehement form of willing. He found the brain to be the antithesis of the genitals, and while the genitals are the spatial and temporal objectification of the **will** to procreate, the brain objectifies the **intellect**, the will to know. Our genitals, therefore, put us in a double bind, according to him. They serve to continue life, thereby continuing the **affirmation of the will**, and they stimulate deeply interested **cognition**, which fetters **knowledge** and the **denial of the will**. **Sigmund Freud** observed in his *Civilization and Its Discontents* that the sight of the genitals is always exciting, but they are hardly ever judged to be beautiful. Schopenhauer concurred with this judgment. They seldom occasion the experience of the **beautiful**, which is always disinterested, and they typically stimulate the most willful interest. It is fortunate that he did not advocate total castration or genital mutilation as a means for overcoming sexual desire, but instead he found voluntary and complete chastity to be the means for overcoming one of the desires foremost in its ability to attach one to life, sexual desire. *See also* BODY; INTELLECT; LOVE, SEXUAL.

GOD (*GOTT*). In a note from 1843, Schopenhauer observed, "Whoever loves the truth hates the gods in the singular as well as the plural," (*Manuscript Remains*, Vol. IV, "Spicilegia," para. 104). While he professed love of the **truth**, Schopenhauer found no real object for his hatred, since he denied that the gods existed, either in the singular or the plural. Polytheism, he claimed, involves the personification of individual elements and **forces of nature**, and monotheism does the same with the whole of nature, at one stroke. Further, both conceive of their gods as distinct from nature. When Schopenhauer wrote of "God," however, he typically had in mind the concept of a single, all-perfect being, a being that summoned the world out of nothing, created everything in it, and sanctified creation by calling it "good." This is the basic conception of God found in the Western monotheistic religions, **Judaism**, **Christianity**, and Islam, he argued, and he claimed that this idea originated in Judaism.

Schopenhauer claimed that he rejected this idea of God based on his philosophical studies and his study of **Hinduism** and **Buddhism**. **David Hume** and **Immanuel Kant**, he maintained, destroyed all the classical proofs for the existence of God, and he argued that the idea that God created the world out of nothing is absurd, since it is logically impossible for something to come out of nothing. Moreover, he also held that the wretched nature of the world contradicts the idea that it is the product of an all-benevolent being. While he credited **Baruch Spinoza** with dispelling the absurdity of positing a creator God distinct from creation by calling nature or the world "God," he also claimed that naming nature "God" did nothing to explain the world, and he argued that Spinoza's deification of the world still stood in contradiction to its horrid nature. Because he thought that the idea of the **absolute**, employed by philosophers like **Johann Gottlieb Fichte**, **Friedrich Wilhelm Joseph von Schelling**, and **Georg Wilhelm Friedrich Hegel** descended, in part, from Spinoza, he viewed these philosophers as vainly trying to preserve the God of Western monotheism by hiding him behind a new name. *See also* OPTIMISM; PANTHEISM; RELIGION; THEISM.

GOETHE, JOHANN WOLFGANG VON (1749–1832). Schopenhauer quoted from Goethe more frequently than he did from any other figure, except for **Immanuel Kant**. This, however, should not be surprising, since he viewed Kant and Goethe as the two greatest minds that were ever produced in Germany. He also considered Goethe as providing an intellectual counterweight to Kant, whose critical philosophy boldly smashed so many deeply held metaphysical and theological beliefs. Schopenhauer cherished his personal acquaintance with Goethe, and on 21 December 1819, when he applied to the University of Berlin for the right to lecture, he said in his *curriculum vitea* that his interactions with Goethe were the most fortunate and joyful ones in his life. Goethe, moreover, almost seems to have served as the model for the artistic **genius** described in the third book of *The World as Will and Representation*.

Schopenhauer met Goethe through his mother's parties in Weimar. Unlike other members of Weimar's polite society, **Johanna Schopenhauer** accepted Christianne Vulpius' attendance at her parties, despite the fact that she was living openly and unmarried to Goethe. It appears that her acceptance of his unconventional living arrangement inclined Goethe to favor Johanna's parties. Goethe's presence, moreover, strongly inclined Arthur to attend these parties. At first, Goethe maintained a cool distance from the young Schopenhauer. This changed, however, in 1813 after Schopenhauer sent Goethe a handsomely bound, dedicated copy of his dissertation, *On the Fourfold Root of the Principle of Sufficient Reason*. In November of that year, Goethe approached Schopenhauer, thanked him for his gift, and congratulated him on receiving his doctorate. In this case, Goethe was probably being more than just polite; it is likely that he saw in the young philosopher a potential ally who would help promote his theory of **colors**, which was articulated in his massive work, *On the Theory of Colors* (1810). Goethe took especial pride in this work and viewed it as being more significant than his poetry, a judgment in which the intellectual world did not concur.

Schopenhauer met frequently with Goethe from the fall of 1813 through the spring of 1814, discussing philosophy generally and color theory specifically. They conducted experiments jointly, and Schopenhauer borrowed some of Goethe's equipment to run experiments on his own. Schopenhauer continued corresponding directly with Goethe for the next couple of years, and later he would do so indirectly through his sister, **Adele Schopenhauer**. In 1819, Schopenhauer sent Goethe a bound and dedicated copy of *The World as Will* *and Representation*, which originally had a quote from Goethe prefacing its second book. He was delighted, moreover, when he learned from his sister that Goethe was reading his book with enjoyment and that he had even underlined Schopenhauer's discussions of the anticipation of the **beautiful** and the acquired character. It is, however, unlikely that Goethe read all of the book.

Schopenhauer's work on color theory, *On Vision and Colors*, appeared in 1816. It is likely that he would not have published on this topic without the inspiration he received from his personal involvement with Goethe. Since 1814, Schopenhauer had been working on the key philosophical doctrines that would appear in *The World as Will and Representation*, and he even told Goethe that his work on color theory was a subordinate occupation to the greater theories he had in mind. Still, when he completed the manuscript for *On Vision and Colors*, he sought Goethe's blessing of his work, and he appealed for his aid in securing a publisher. He told Goethe, moreover, that his theory followed from Goethe's views "like fruit from the tree." But Goethe found strange fruit in Schopenhauer's manuscript, and he neither endorsed it nor helped him find a publisher. He even delayed in returning the manuscript to Schopenhauer, and Schopenhauer complained about this delay in the book's preface to its second edition 38 years later.

Schopenhauer attributed Goethe's coolness towards *On Vision and Colors* to the latter's demand that his work should express the "most unqualified agreement" with his own. In a letter to Goethe from 11 November 1815, he alerted Goethe to three ways in which his views "disharmonized" with Goethe's. They differed on whether white consisted of a mixture of colors and on the origin of the color violet. Moreover, Schopenhauer placed limits on Goethe's concept of polarity. Yet there were deeper reasons for the disharmony between Schopenhauer's and Goethe's views. The latter's **realism** was not compatible with Schopenhauer's **transcendental idealism**. According to Goethe, color is produced by the interplay of the polarities of lightness and darkness and is, thus, something shadowlike or cloudy. Goethe therefore regarded light and darkness as primary phenomena (*Urphänomene*), phenomena capable of no further explanation. But Schopenhauer found these phenomena to be secondary and objective, and he attempted to show that a deeper explanation for them was possible, one that highlights their subjective nature. Lightness or white, darkness or black, and colors, are all states or modifications of the eye. Sensation itself, he argued, is subjective. White is full activity of the retina, and black is inactivity of the retina, while color is the qualitatively divided activity of the retina. The *Urphänomen* is, for him, the polar activity of the retina. Color is an affection of the eye; it is independent of some object, Schopenhauer argued, and that object exists only when the understanding refers it back to some spatial and temporal object as its cause.

Even if Goethe did demand orthodoxy from his "proselyte's" theory, Goethe's aloofness toward Schopenhauer also had more personal grounds. Although there are no individuals for whom Schopenhauer had a higher regard than Kant and Goethe, he always strove to outreach his heroes. He took considerable pride in calling himself a Kantian, but he used Kant's philosophy as the basis to develop one that outstripped Kant's. He viewed himself as using Goethe's color theory for the same end. He said so both in *On Vision and Colors* and, more arrogantly, in their personal correspondence. In the former, he credits Goethe with supplying "abundant data" for a color theory, but he also claimed that Goethe failed to explain the essential nature of color and that he had raised Goethe's data to the august level of theory. In the latter, one can uncover any number of remarks from which Goethe could take umbrage. In a letter dated 11 November 1815, he told Goethe "I know with perfect certainty that I have produced the first theory of color, the first in the history of science." Later, after Goethe finally returned the manuscript to Schopenhauer, he pointed out how his views "disharmonized" with Goethe's, adding "it is not even possible for me to imagine that your excellence would not recognize the correctness of my theory; for the truth has spoken through me—in this small matter as in days to come it will in great ones." (23 January 1816). Not only did he tell Goethe that he had done what Goethe had not, he called this a small matter. (Color theory had been something Goethe had worked on, occasionally, for 20 years!) It is thus easy to understand why Goethe would write to Schopenhauer in a letter of 4 May 1816, "It would be a vain effort to wish for mutual understanding." Later, when a third party asked Goethe about Schopenhauer's book, he said, "Dr. Schopenhauer is a significant thinker whom I induced to take up my theory of colors . . . This young man, proceeding from my perspective, has become my opponent."

Goethe, however, had sensed Schopenhauer's character even before he published *On Vision and Colors*. Shortly after their last meeting in Weimar, he wrote the following verses in his epigram, "*Lahmung*":

> I would like to bear the teacher's burden still longer,
> If only the pupils did not at once become teacher.

Schopenhauer quoted this in the "Introduction" to *On Vision and Colors* as evidence simply of Goethe's demand for orthodoxy by his pupil. Still, Schopenhauer never lost his awe for Goethe, and his personal involvement with him was always regarded by Schopenhauer as one of the most significant experiences in his life. He also praised Goethe's work on color theory and he never ceased decrying its critics. When the city of Frankfurt celebrated the centennial of Goethe's birth in 1849, he wrote an entry into the *Frankfurt Goethe-Album* in which he took the intellectual world to task for failing to recognize the monumental significance of Goethe's color theory. Until this is done, he wrote, "no garlanded monuments, nor the firing of salutes, nor the ringing of bells, let alone banquets and speeches, can suffice to atone for the grievous and revolting injustice and wrong suffered by Goethe in connection with his *theory of colors*." (Schopenhauer's entry is also published in "On the Theory of Colors," in the second volume of *Parerga and Paralipomena*).

GOOD (*GUT*). Schopenhauer defined the term "good" as the fitness or suitableness of an object to any definite effort of the **will**. Consequently, he argued that everything agreeable to a person's desires, or anything serving the purposes of an individual's will, is good. He distinguished further between two subcategories of good, the agreeable and the useful. The former is that which immediately satisfies a person's desires, and the latter is that which is perceived as producing a satisfaction in the future. Since he recognized that individuals have different desires, something could be good for one person and the opposite for another. Consequently, Schopenhauer rejected the idea of an absolute good or a *summun bonum*, a highest good. *See also* BAD; EVIL.

GOOD, MORALLY. *See* WORTH, MORAL.

GRACIÁN, BALTASAR (1601–1658). Gracián was a Spanish Jesuit philosopher and writer, known for his satires, epigrams, and worldly wisdom. In a letter to Johann Georg Keil (16 April 1832), the editor of a collection of the plays of **Pedro de la Barca Calderón**, Schopenhauer referred to Gracián as his "favorite author" and said that his allegorical and pessimistic novel *El criticón* (*The Critic*), a work that caused Gracián some difficulties with Jesuit authority, was "his favorite book." It might be the case that Schopenhauer was inclined to exaggeration in this letter, since he was soliciting Keil's aid in securing a publisher for his translation of Gracián's *Oráculo manual y arte de prudencia* (*The Hand Oracle and the Art of Worldly Wisdom*), but the very fact that Schopenhauer selected Gracián to translate shows his high regard for him, especially when one recalls his attempts to translate **Lawrence Sterne**, **David Hume**, and **Immanuel Kant**. Moreover, in 1829 he had already approached his publisher, **F. A. Brockhaus**, with a proposal to translate the *Oráculo*. He had sent Brockhaus a manuscript in which he had translated 50 of its 300 aphorisms. Brockhaus declined the offer and returned the manuscript to Schopenhauer, who then entrusted it to a friend in Berlin. Schopenhauer fled Berlin in 1831, because of the cholera epidemic, and so when he approached Kiel in 1832, he had to retranslate his earlier work. Between the fall of 1831 and mid-April 1832, Schopenhauer completed his translation of the *Oráculo*. This redoubling of effort, naturally, shows both Schopenhauer's dedication to the project and the significance he attributed to Gracián's thought. It was not until 1862, two years after Schopenhauer's death, that his translation, *Gracians Handorakel und Kunst der Weltklugheit* would appear, due to the efforts of **Julius Frauenstädt**, and, ironically, it was published by Brockhaus. It is not uncommon for Schopenhauer's translation to be cited as a classical work of German translation.

Schopenhauer praised Gracián for his terse, concentrated, and aphoristic writing style. Whenever he referred to him in his published works, Schopenhauer used him to support one of his views or as a springboard to develop a point of his own. In particular, he endorsed Gracián's recommendation for a cautious approach to our relationships with others, his desultory views of **women**, and his recognition that we need to free ourselves from worldly illusions. Schopenhauer agreed with Gracián's view that worldly wisdom serves as the means for negotiating through the roughness and the vicissitudes of everyday life. He personally used Gracián to deal with the reception of his works by his contemporaries. A particularly good example of this is found in the preface to the first edition of *The Two Fundamental Problems of Ethics*, where Schopenhauer harshly criticized the Royal Danish Society's decision not to award the prize to his essay "On the Basis of Morality." Within their negative verdict, the Society noted his offensive treatment of "several distinguished philosophers of recent time," a remark Schopenhauer believed referred to his treatment of **Johann Gottlieb Fichte** and **Georg Wilhelm Friedrich Hegel**. To rebuke the Society for extolling the bad, he closed his preface with a lengthy quote from Gracián's *El criticón*.

GWINNER, WILHELM VON (1825–1917). Gwinner studied philosophy and law at Tübingen, became a lawyer and writer, served as the secretary of the courts of appeals, and later became a judge on the municipal court. Gwinner met Schopenhauer in 1847, but it was not until 1857 that he would become Schopenhauer's confidant. In 1858, when Schopenhauer's friend and legal advisor, Martin Emden, died, he became Schopenhauer's legal advisor. Schopenhauer appointed Gwinner as the executor of his will. He gave the funeral oration at Schopenhauer's burial on 26 September 1860 in Frankfurt.

In 1862, Gwinner published *Arthur Schopenhauer Depicted from a Personal Acquaintance* (*Arthur Schopenhauer aus persönlichem Umgang dargestellt*, Leipiz) a biography that received new editions in 1878 and 1910, and which was revised later by his granddaughter, Charlotte von Gwinner, in 1922 and 1963. Gwinner's biography caused a stir among Schopenhauer's followers, since it appeared that Gwinner had incorporated materials from a collection of personal and general observations that Schopenhauer recorded over a 30-year period. This collection of notes, amounting to some 30 loose leaves of paper, had been given by Schopenhauer a Greek title that translates as "About Myself." According to Gwinner, Schopenhauer had instructed him to destroy the manuscript after his death, since it contained personal observations about himself and others, which were unimportant and could, however, cause mischief if they fell into the wrong hands. Some of Schopenhauer's followers claimed that Schopenhauer had told them that he wanted this work published after his death, and others accused Gwinner of "plagiarism," because of the use of this material in his biography. In any case, it appears that Gwinner destroyed the work. It has, however, been reconstructed by **Arthur Hübscher** and can be found in his edition of Schopenhauer's *Handschriftlicher Nachlass*, Bd. 4, II, or **E. F. J. Payne**'s translation, *Manuscript Remains*, Vol. 4.

– H –

HARTMANN, EDUARD VON (1842–1906). Von Hartmann was a prolific author, who is best known for his three-volume *The Philosophy of the Unconscious: Speculative Results According to the Inductive Method of Physical Science* (1869). This book may have been the most popular philosophical book in the 1870s in Germany, and it won von Hartmann immediate and widespread fame. While he made his philosophical debts to Schopenhauer readily apparent, and it earned him a general reputation as a follower of Schopenhauer, it was also a reputation he disliked, since it belittled his originality. He took Schopenhauer's concept of the **will** to explain the dynamism of the world, but in a move that would have drawn Schopenhauer's scorn, he employed Hegelian notions to explain the emergence of **self-consciousness** from the unconscious, something that he claimed neither Schopenhauer nor **Georg Wilhelm Friedrich Hegel** could do themselves. This attempt to synthesize Schopenhauer and Hegel, which could also be found in attempts by lesser lights during this time, found expression in his claims that the unconscious will seized the Idea to create the world and that, by this means, the world obtained its purposiveness. Moreover, he also argued that the individual **will to life** could not deny itself through its own resources, but that this is done through a historic process. Although von Hartmann shared Schopenhauer's **pessimism** and agreed with him that it would be better if there were no world, which for von Hartmann was the end to which the world developed, he cited **Immanuel Kant** as the father of his pessimism. He also acknowledged his debt to **Friedrich Wilhelm Joseph von Schelling**'s conception of the unconscious as another formative influence on his view. Von Hartmann's work, nevertheless, contributed significantly to making Schopenhauer's concept of the will and his metaphysics of **sexual love** broadly known, and his *The Philosophy of the Unconscious* is often cited as a source of some of **Sigmund Freud**'s knowledge of Schopenhauer.

HEGEL, GEORG WILHELM FRIEDRICH (1770–1831). There is no other philosopher for whom Schopenhauer had a greater contempt than Hegel. His philosophy is peppered with harsh *ad hominems* directed against Hegel, his **philosophy**, and his influence on German philosophy. He regarded Hegel as a total charlatan and as a sophist who was devoted only to promoting his own self-interests rather than the **truth**, which is the aim of a genuine philosopher. In the introduction to *On the Will in Nature*, Schopenhauer referred to "Hegel's philosophy of absolute nonsense." He also claimed that it consisted of three-fourths cash and one-fourth crazy notions and that its jargon simply enabled people to talk for days on end, without saying anything. Schopenhauer's contempt for Hegel was also expressed in the most unrestrained terms in the vitriolic first preface to *The Two Fundamental Problems of Ethics*. In this case, his seething anger was provoked by his identification of Hegel as one of the "distinguished philosophers of recent times" whose treatment by him in *On the Basis of Morality* had led the Royal Danish Society for Scientific Studies to note their grave offense within their decision to deny him the prize in their essay contest. In this preface, he called Hegel a scribbler of nonsense unlike any person before him, and he said that anyone who read Hegel's *Phenomenology of Spirit* without feeling like he or she was in a madhouse would immediately qualify as an inmate for Bedlam. Hegel had, he also said, an extremely pernicious, stupefying influence on philosophy and German literature.

Schopenhauer's attitude toward Hegel was not a function of a cool assessment of his personal and philosophical merits. It signifies Schopenhauer's deep envy of the exalted status that Hegel achieved in the German intellectual world and his belief that the popularity of Hegel's philosophy played a significant role in the failure of his philosophy both to draw a readership and to be taken seriously by professors of philosophy. Thus, Schopenhauer complained to a friend that it was the prevailing "Hegel*gloria*" of the times that brought about the lack of attention that was paid to *The World as Will and Representation* and that it was the primary reason that he waited 17 years to publish his second book, *On the Will in Nature* (1836). *The World as Will and Representation* appeared in 1818, the very year in which Hegel ascended to the philosophical throne of Germany by taking the important chair in philosophy at the University of Berlin. Hegel would become the Rector of the University in 1829, and he remained at the University until his death in 1831. Schopenhauer applied for the rights to do his habilitation and to lecture at Berlin in 1819. In his letter to the Dean of the Faculty, Schopenhauer expressed his desire to offer his lectures at the same time as Hegel's principal course, a request that soon became well known to members of Berlin's faculty, including Hegel himself. Although Schopenhauer had a brief exchange with Hegel during his qualifying lecture, which Schopenhauer appeared to have won, Hegel voted to pass him, nevertheless. Schopenhauer was also granted his wish to schedule his lectures at the same time as Hegel's. Naturally, this was a self-defeating desire. Hegel drew 200 students to Schopenhauer's five. Schopenhauer would never enroll and complete a course at Berlin. His academic failure, of course, he also blamed on Hegel.

Schopenhauer's loathing of Hegel was grounded, however, on factors deeper than his envy of Hegel's status and his perception of Hegel's role in the failure of his main work and academic career. Philosophy was Schopenhauer's passion and he saw himself seriously engaged in the pursuit of truth. He sensed in Hegel a sham philosopher who sought personal advancement for which he employed obscure language and convoluted sentence structures to hide the poverty of his thought. Schopenhauer would later write that "style is the physiognomy of the mind," and Hegel's style demonstrated, he thought, the quality of his mind. Worse, he believed, he had succeeded in hoodwinking the learned world through his terrible style and, in the process, also ruined his readers' minds, rendering them unable to recognize clearly and directly stated truths. In as much as Schopenhauer personalized Hegel's philosophy, it appeared to him that attacking Hegel's character was an attack on the root of his philosophy. Moreover, Schopenhauer also wrote within a tradition in which it was not uncommon for philosophers to vent their hostile attitudes toward their rivals in ways that contemporary English-writing philosophers would regard as lacking the gentlemanly detachment of a scholar. To be sure, Schopenhauer tended to abuse his opponents more freely and repeatedly than his contemporaries, who usually did so in their correspondence or in exchanges with rivals. (**Friedrich Nietzsche** tended to follow Schopenhauer in this regard, even in his analysis of Schopenhauer.) In any case, his deep disgust for Hegel, and all things Hegelian, kept Schopenhauer oblivious to any points of contact between their thoughts. Indeed, he was always desperate to find support for **Johann Wolfgang von Goethe**'s color theory, and he never realized that Hegel championed Goethe and also wrote against Newton's views. Certainly, it does not make sense to seek any formative influences on Schopenhauer's thought, as it does with **Johann Gottlieb Fichte** and **Friedrich Wilhelm Joseph von Schelling**, both of whom he studied seriously prior to the publication of *The World as Will and Representation*. It was the failure of this work that brought Hegel into his orbit.

Schopenhauer's objections to Hegel's philosophy, however, were also based on less personal and emotional grounds. Hegel's absolute **idealism** conceived of everything as the Absolute Idea, and thus, of rational necessity, was antithetical to Schopenhauer's metaphysics. The real is the irrational and not the rational as Hegel would have it. Moreover, his interpretation of **history** as the Absolute Idea arriving at an awareness of itself as Absolute Spirit through its externalization in nature was something Schopenhauer rejected absolutely. Hegel's view connoted to Schopenhauer a deep betrayal of **Immanuel Kant** and a return to a pre-critical philosophical stance, since it failed to recognize that **time** is a form of the world as **representation** and that it is not constitutive of the **thing in itself** (abandoning the distinction between **appearances** and the thing in itself was a problem Schopenhauer also found in Fichte and Schelling). Moreover, although Hegel recognized the "slaughter bench of history," the wretchedness of life, Schopenhauer accused Hegel of expressing a "ruthless optimism" by viewing history as the gradual and inevitable progressive unfolding of the Absolute Spirit. Even if these things ultimately work out in the end, the realization of this end can never justify, Schopenhauer argued, the tremendous evils embodied in its realization. But, more deeply, Schopenhauer argued that there is no purpose or progress in history. It teaches that each time there is something different, whereas the essence of human life, as well as nature, exists in every present time. Philosophy teaches, he claimed, contrary to Hegel, that the same thing was, is, and always will be. Moreover, by making it seem as if the Absolute Spirit is **God**, and by having his social **ethics** culminate in the state, Schopenhauer claimed that Hegel was appeasing both **religion** and the state to advance his own academic career, moves no genuine philosopher would ever make.

HINDUISM. In a note from 1816, written as Schopenhauer was developing the **philosophy** articulated in his main work, *The World as Will and Representation*, he stated that his doctrines could not have originated without the *Upanishads*, **Plato**, and **Immanuel Kant** casting their rays of light simultaneously into the mind of a single person. When his main work appeared in late 1818, he wrote in the introduction that his thought required readers to be thoroughly acquainted with Kant's philosophy; that knowledge of Plato would make readers more susceptible to his views; and that readers who shared the benefits of the *Vedas*, whose access had been opened by the *Upanishads*, were best able to hear what he had to say, since it would not sound to them like he has spoken with a strange or even hostile tongue. It is not, he continued, that the **single thought** expressed through his main work could be found in the *Upanishads*, but everything in the *Upanishads* could be derived from this thought. Later, in the 17th chapter of the second volume of his main work, he wrote of the "almost superhuman conception" found in the *Upanishads*.

The *Vedas* are the basic scriptures of Hinduism, and the *Upanishads* is one of its four major divisions. The *Upanishads*, along with the *Bhagavad-Gītā* and the *Brahma Sutras*, constitute the basis of the Vedānta philosophy of which three schools exist: the Dualist, Qualified Non-dualist, and Non-dualist or Advaita Vedānta. In his writings, Schopenhauer did not distinguish between these schools, referring instead simply to Vedānta, but he usually had in mind Advaita Vedānta. That this was the case is not surprising, however, given the version of the *Upanishads* Schopenhauer cherished.

Schopenhauer appeared to be stimulated to read the *Upanishads* through a meeting with the Jena scholar and Orientalist, Friedrich Majer (1772–1818), that took place at his mother's house in Weimar in the winter of 1813–1814. In March 1814 he borrowed from the library in Weimar a two-volume translation of the *Upanishads* and later that year purchased his own copy. The title of this translation was *Oupenk'hat* (1801–1805), and it was the work of Abraham Hyacinthe Anquetil-Duperron (1731–1805) a Frenchman and one of the earliest Europeans drawn to India in pursuit of its wisdom. Duperron's translation was a curious work. It was a Latin translation of a Persian translation from the Sanskrit, made in the mid-17th century by the Sultan Mohammed Dara Shikoh and a group of Persian scholars. Unknown to Duperron and Schopenhauer, Prince Dara's translation was a collage of text and commentary by Śankara (c. 788–c. 820), the foremost exponent of Advaita Vedānta, whose views have been said to bear traces of the idealistic metaphysics of **Buddhism**. Duperron himself also drew parallels between Kant and the *Upanishads*. These features of the *Oupenk'hat* were likely to have been some of the bases by which Schopenhauer saw a deeper kinship between his thought and Hinduism than is found in the original texts. Schopenhauer read this work almost daily, and he said that it "has been the consolation of my life and will be that of my death" in the essay "Some Remarks on Sanskrit Literature," found in the second volume of *Parerga and Paralipomena*.

Schopenhauer's early reading of the *Upanishads* was supplemented by his study of Marie-Elisabeth de Polier's *Mythologie des Hindous* (1809), which he borrowed in 1814 from the Herzoglichen Library in Weimar, and also by his study of various volumes of *Asiatick Researches* in 1815–1816. From 1815–1817, Schopenhauer had the opportunity to discuss Eastern thought with his neighbor in Dresden, the obscure German philosopher Karl Christian Friedrich Krause (1781–1832) who, like Schopenhauer, also sought to synthesize Indian wisdom with his philosophy. Krause had an advantage over Schopenhauer, since he knew Sanskrit, and Krause was said to have introduced him to some basic techniques of meditation.

Schopenhauer would continue to read the secondary literature about Hinduism and translations of texts throughout the remainder of his life. Schopenhauer's reading and interpretation of Hinduism also stimulated much interest in it among Europeans, and his views highly influenced **Paul Deussen**'s understanding of Hinduism, something for which later scholars would criticize Deussen. When compared to contemporary understanding of Hinduism, Schopenhauer's interpretation seems superficial. He is far less sensitive to the diversity of phenomena that are referred to as "Hinduism"; he had far fewer reliable materials to study; and he seemed more interested in seeking confirmation of his doctrines than understanding Hinduism on its own terms. Certainly, he tended to read Vedānta philosophy as Hinduism *per se*, and he did not clearly distinguish between Vedānta and Buddhism, or the differences between those perspectives and his own. Yet Schopenhauer had an extraordinary openness to Eastern philosophy as well as to the possibility that it contained insights superior to Western philosophical and religious thought. Even though Schopenhauer's analysis of Eastern philosophy lacked interpretive accuracy, there can be little doubt that his understanding of Hinduism enabled him to rethink his original views as he sought to expand and clarify his philosophy throughout his philosophical career.

Schopenhauer claimed that there were a number of insights shared by his philosophy and Hinduism, which he frequently called "Brahmanism." Although some scholars have charged Schopenhauer with stigmatizing Hinduism by claiming that it was "**pessimistic**," he thought that it also taught that the world as it appears is something that it ought not to be, since it recognized that this world is the scene of rebirth, suffering, and **death**, and it advocated the overcoming of this world of suffering and death by overcoming ignorance and desire. He also thought Hinduism expresses a metaphysics akin to his own by pronouncing the phenomenal world, the transitory world of spatially-temporally individualized objects, insubstantial and impermanent, as that which is *māyā*, and by viewing ultimate reality, the sustainer of the world, *Brahman*, as that which is beyond all attributes. *Māyā* and *Brahman* were viewed by Schopenhauer as functional equivalents to his ideas of the world as **representation** and the world as **will**. In his analysis of the behavior of the morally good person, Schopenhauer used one of the great sayings of *Mahāvākya* of the *Upanishads*, "***tat tvam asi** (that thou art)*," the identity of the individual self or *ātman* with *Brahman*, to explain the behavior of these persons, who treat all others as an "I once more," and he appealed to the ultimate unity of all to provide a metaphysical explanation for **compassion**. Schopenhauer claimed that the **good** person glances through the "**veil of *māyā***" to cognize the unity of all, and Schopenhauer saw as being equivalent to the "veil of *māyā*" what he called the *principium individuationis*, **space** and **time**, the conditions for plurality. Unlike the **evil** person, who views all others as non-egos and is ensnared in the veil of *māyā*, he claimed that the good person's conduct is metaphysically warranted. Consequently, he called the behavior of the good person "practical mysticism," since it exhibits a line of conduct that expresses the same **knowledge** as the mystic. More deeply, he thought, the Hindu salvific goal, *mokṣa*, the overcoming of ignorance and desire, the end of suffering and rebirth, was equivalent to his salvific goal of the **denial of the will**. He read the goal of *mokṣa*, the release from worldly existence through knowledge of *Brahman*, to be a positive description of the salvific goal, but he said he preferred the Buddhist's idea of *nirvāna*, the negation of *samsāra*, because it is negative, and is, therefore, more akin to the denial of the will.

HISTORY (*GESCHICHTE*). In the well-known 38th chapter of the second volume of *The World as Will and Representation*, entitled "On History," Schopenhauer argued that history is not a science; that it is inferior to the **natural sciences**, **art**, and **philosophy** in knowing the true nature of humanity and existence; that the main purpose of philosophy is not the philosophy of history; and that the value of history is that it serves as the rational **self-consciousness** of the human race. While the power of **Georg Wilhelm Friedrich Hegel**'s speculative philosophy of history was waning when this essay appeared (1844), it helped figures like the Swiss historian **Jacob Burckhardt** further its decline, and it has been said that it also helped **Richard Wagner** turn away from historical opera.

Science, according to Schopenhauer, is an organized body of **knowledge** in which multiplicities of particular or individual items are subordinated under generic concepts, and these concepts themselves are separated by more specific ones. Within this conceptual framework, science makes possible the comprehension of numerous individuals without considering each by itself, as well as yielding knowledge of the relationship of the general to the particular. History, however, is tied to particular and individual facts and events that it seeks to coordinate through a narrative. Even when history seems to employ universal concepts by classifying its data in terms of periods of time or ages, the succession of kings, revolutions, wars, or peace treaties, Schopenhauer regarded these general frameworks as subjective, that is, without the objectivity found in science, which relates cases to rules, or events to **causal** laws. For example, science abstracts from the observation of numerous individuals the concept "mammal," and once this concept is formulated, we can know that any individual thing identified as a mammal will have a heart with double ventricles, seven cervical vertebrae, lungs, and other characteristics. Thus, by identifying the bat that you have just caught as a mammal, you know it has these characteristics without having to dissect it. Conversely, you can know in general that the Thirty Years War was a religious war waged in the 17th century, but this information does not tell you anything specific about the course of the war itself or its relationship to other events of this century. Yet it is the general knowledge that is most certain in history, whereas in science, since its universals are abstracted from the immediate apprehension of individuals, its generalizations are less certain than its original data, which can entail the modification of its **concepts** or laws based on new observations. In history, the particular events and their connections are less certain than its generalizations, but it is these particulars that are of more significance, he argued, and the deeper you go into historical detail, the more uncertain these generalizations become and the more history becomes like a work of fiction.

Because history concentrates on "what once was and was never again," and science focuses on the universal and constantly appearing, history is inferior to science as a source of knowledge. It, like science, he argued, is confined to the **principle of sufficient reason**, and although science moves past particular ephemeral items, it is still tied to the spatial-temporal world of items standing in causal relationships. Art, however, communicates **Platonic Ideas**, and the poet, he said, reveals the inner being of humankind, which represents the adequate objectivity of the **thing in itself** at its highest grade. History might teach us about human beings and their behavior toward one another, and from this we might obtain rules of conduct or maxims of worldly wisdom, but it is never capable of providing deep insight into the inner nature of humans. What history continuously shows, Schopenhauer argued, is really the same thing under different names and in a different cloak. Thus he recommended that the motto for history should be *eadem, sed aliter*, "the same but otherwise," and he claimed that, for a philosophical mind, reading Herodotus is enough history, since it contains everything the subsequent history of the world shows about human efforts, actions, suffering, and the fate of our earthly lives. Indeed, from a philosophical point of view, the essence of human life and nature exists in every present time, he said, and it only requires a depth of comprehension in order to be exhaustively known. In other words, Schopenhauer thought that the philosopher, who seeks to penetrate to the essence of things, could dispense with history.

The idea that philosophy could dispense with history led Schopenhauer to decry "Hegelians," who insisted that the purpose of philosophy was the philosophy of history. He rejected Hegel's view that history is teleological and represents the various stages of the development of Spirit (*Geist*) through time, to eventually culminate in spirit's consciousness of itself, a state of affairs identical with the world becoming congruent with itself. Since events in history march to this goal, Hegel argued that everything in history is necessary, justified, and good—the plan of Spirit. Against "Hegelians," Schopenhauer evoked his philosophical heroes **Plato** and **Immanuel Kant**, both of whom had shown that **time** is ideal and that the aim of philosophy is to grasp what exists; that which is today, was yesterday, and will be tomorrow. History is, thus, dispensable. There is no end or goal to history, he contended, and he accused "Hegelians" of being "glorifiers of history," and thereby of being realists, optimists, and "really bad Christians," since **Christianity**'s true spirit shows the vanity of all earthly happiness and the need to turn away from this life.

Although he viewed history as having less value than science, art and philosophy, Schopenhauer did not believe that it had no value. Thus he claimed that history is the rational **self-consciousness** of humanity, and he analogized that what the faculty of **reason** is to an individual person, history is to the human race. Reason enables humans to transcend **animal** consciousness, which is always restricted to the immediate and perceptually present, by formulating **concepts**, which make them capable of conceiving of the past and future. Without reason, humans would be ignorant and dull like animals. Analogous to this, a nation that does not know its own history is restricted to the present time of the current generation and so it cannot understand its present, because it is unable to refer its present to the past, nor can it anticipate its future. Only through history does a nation become completely conscious of itself, just as it is through reason that people become fully conscious of themselves. Every gap in history is like a gap in an individual's self-consciousness and it is, therefore, akin to a somnambulist who discovers in the morning what was done in sleep. The sleepwalker would find that what was done was strange and would not realize that he or she did it. Without history, humankind would be like this somnambulist. The pyramids of Egypt and the places of the Yucatan would appear strange to us, and we would stand senseless and stupid before them. History, he said, is the reflected consciousness of the human race; it provides unity to the consciousness of the human race, which is incessantly interrupted by the **death** of particular generations; and it allows ancestors to speak to descendants.

HOMOGENEITY, THE LAW OF (*DAS GESETZ DER HOMO-GENEITÄT*). In the introduction to *On the Fourfold Root of the Principle of Sufficient Reason*, Schopenhauer cited both **Plato** and **Immanuel Kant** as recommending two rules for the method of all philosophizing and all **knowledge** in general, namely the laws of **specification** and homogeneity. The latter instructs us to unite kinds of things into species, then into wider genera, and lastly into the highest unity that covers everything. Consequently, this law always seeks unity in diversity, or the one in the many. He claimed that this law is **transcendental** and essential to our faculty of **reason**. It presupposes, therefore, that nature is in harmony, he claimed, and it is an assumption expressed by the "old rule," the number of entities must not increase unnecessarily. In this work, Schopenhauer followed this law by claiming that the **principle of sufficient reason** is the single principle of all knowledge, and he claimed that its singular form, "nothing is without a ground or reason why it is," is the common expression of four specific instances of the principle, which detail the kinds of knowledge given *a priori*. Although he did not highlight this law in his subsequent books, it remained a constant principle of his philosophical method, which always strove to provide ever more comprehensive explanations of various experiences. *See also* PHILOSOPHY; SINGLE THOUGHT.

HOMOSEXUALITY. See PEDERASTY.

HÜBSCHER, ARTHUR (1897–1985). Hübscher is sometimes referred to as the "second Arthur" because of the significance of his life-long work with all things Schopenhauer. He produced the historical and critical editions of Schopenhauer's entire *oeuvre*; he wrote numerous books and articles concerning virtually all elements of Schopenhauer's life and thought; and he served for many years as the president of the Schopenhauer-Gesellschaft, the editor of the *Schopenhauer-Jahrbuch*, and the director of the Schopenhauer Archives. Consequently, he was buried next to Schopenhauer in the Frankfurter Hauptfriedhof, "Brother resting next to brother," as Rudolf Malter stated at his funeral—the scholar next to the philosopher.

Hübscher was born in Cologne and lived from 1902 to 1962 in Munich. He studied literature, germanistics, history, and philosophy, and he received his doctorate in philosophy in 1921 from the K. Ludwig-Maximilians University in Munich. He worked for a number of years as a journalist, editor, and critic, most notably for the *Suddeutsche Monatshefte*, until it was prohibited by the Nazis in 1936, and also from 1950–1962 as the cultural editor for the *Bayerische Staatszeitung*. Already in 1930, he had published articles on Schopenhauer in the *Suddeutsche Monatshefte*, and in 1933, he published *Schopenhauer's Conversations* (*Schopenhauers Gespräche*). In 1935, he commenced work on the historical and critical edition of *Schopenhauer's Collected Works* (*Arthur Schopenhauer: Sämtliche Werke*, 4th ed. 1988), which remains the authoritative source for the philosopher's books. In turn, he would produce the historical and critical editions of Schopenhauer's letters, handwritten *Nachlass*, and a revised edition of his conversations.

Hübscher became the president of the Schopenhauer-Gesellschaft and the editor of the *Schopenhauer-Jahrbuch* in 1936, positions he would hold until 1983. It is particularly noteworthy that he guided the Schopenhauer-Gesellschaft during the Nazi period without banishing a single one of its Jewish members. In 1965, Hübscher moved to Frankfurt am Main to become the director of the Schopenhauer Archives, which is still located there at the city and university library. He made Frankfurt the center for Schopenhauer research and the archives an international research center. He remained the director of the Archives until 1983, after which he was recognized as its honorary director. In 1966, he published his autobiography, *Life with Schopenhauer* (*Leben mit Schopenhauer*) and in 1973, he published his main work, *Thinker Against the Tide* (*Denker gegen den Strom*) 2nd edition 1982, 3rd 1982, and 4th 1988, which was edited by his wife, Angelika Hübscher, and translated as *The Philosophy of Schopenhauer in its Intellectual Context*, 1989). In this book Hübscher related the story of Schopenhauer's life to the genesis and development of his **philosophy** within, and against, the intellectual context of his time; his influence on later thinkers; and the implications of his thought for the future. In 1981 he published a comprehensive bibliography on the literature by and about Schopenhauer, *Schopenhauer-Bibliographie*. In addition to his publications on Schopenhauer, Hübscher also published separate works on topics in philosophy, literature, and cultural history.

Hübscher received numerous awards and recognitions. *Festschrifte* were published in honor of his 65th, 75th, and 85th birthdays. He was a member of the Royal Norwegian Society of Sciences, the Academy of the Plastic Arts of Nürnberg, and the Bavarian Academy of Sciences, which bestowed on him its medal "*Bene merenti*." The city of Frankfurt am Main also awarded him its Goethe-plakette, its Schopenhauer-medal, and its Ehrenplakette. In 1961 the Federal Republic of Germany honored him with its Great Distinguished Service Medal of the Order of Merit, and he was granted an honorary doctorate from the Johann Wolfgang Goethe University in 1977. He died in Frankfurt am Main on 10 April 1985.

HUME, DAVID (1711–1776). Schopenhauer first studied Hume briefly in 1816 and, more intensely, around 1824. In November of that year, Schopenhauer proposed to his publisher, **F. A. Brockhaus**, a translation into German of Hume's *Natural History of Religion* and *Dialogues Concerning Natural Religion*, under the title *David Hume's Religionsphilosophie*. Brockhaus, however, declined the offer. Nevertheless, Schopenhauer sketched a preface for this translation, which can be found in *Manuscript Remains*, vol. 3, section 108 of "*Brieftasche*." A reading of this preface is instructive, because it reflects his esteem for Hume, his contempt for his philosophical contemporaries, and his despair about the reception of his **philosophy**. He ironically contrasted Hume's work with contemporary German philosophy, and he said that if Hume had had the good fortune of sharing "the brilliant philosophical discovery of our day," he would have learned that the faculty of **reason** provides one with access to the supersensuous or the divine. Thus he could have abandoned his careful weighing of arguments and counter-arguments on religious issues; he could have given up reflection and rational investigation. Likewise, instead of writing in lucid, precise, vivid, and comprehensible prose, he would have striven to write in ponderous and endless sentences, employing strange and homemade words, so that he could cast a mysterious obscurity over everything he wrote. He also remarked that he called Hume's work "philosophy of **religion**," after current-day nomenclature, despite the fact that Hume made the effort to analyze the topic with reasoning and argumentation. Lastly, Schopenhauer said he was well qualified to translate Hume, since he was fluent in English, and he had the time. He was, he said, exempt from communicating his own ideas, since there were no readers among his contemporaries for his ideas.

Later, long after Schopenhauer had removed his self-imposed exemption from communicating his own ideas, he remarked that there was more to learn from a single page of Hume's writings than there was from the collected works of **Georg Wilhelm Friedrich Hegel**, Johann Friedrich Herbart, and Friedrich Ernst Daniel Schleiermacher combined. This remark, which he made in chapter 46 of the second volume of *The World as Will and Representation*, was certainly meant to praise Hume, but it also was made, more deeply, to denigrate his contemporaries. After all, he might have also claimed that there was absolutely nothing to learn from the three men he had cited. Consequently, his praise of Hume was not pitched as high as it might first appear. Indeed, Schopenhauer was, at best, ambivalent about the significance of the entire range of Hume's philosophy. He regarded highly Hume's "popular philosophy," his critical work on natural religion and his philosophy of religion, and he applauded his essay on **suicide**. In particular, he endorsed Hume's demonstrations of the inadequacies of various traditional proofs for the existence of **God**, his analyses of the origin of some religious beliefs from the fear of the unknown, and he praised what he saw as Hume's deep sense of the wretchedness of existence, which spoke against **optimism**. (Ironically, he noted, however, that Hume devastated "popular theology" and esteemed "speculative theology," while **Immanuel Kant** devastated "speculative theology" and esteemed "popular theology" by securing faith on moral feeling.) While Schopenhauer appreciated Hume's role in awakening Kant from what Kant described as his "dogmatic slumbers," he did not value Hume's "theoretical philosophy" and the skepticism of his empirical **epistemology**. In fact, he wrote of Hume's "palpably false skepticism" in regard to the **law of causality**, the very alarm that woke the slumbering Kant. Hume's skepticism left Schopenhauer cold, and nowhere did he praise Hume's attempt, as he put it in his masterpiece, *A Treatise of Human Understanding*, to apply the "experimental method of reason" to uncover the principle of human nature. He was also silent about Hume's work in **ethics**. Consequently, it is not surprising to discover that he made scant reference to Hume in his essays from the first volume of *Parerga and Paralipomena*, "Sketch of the History of the Ideal and the Real," and "Fragments for the History of Philosophy," both of which focus on metaphysics and epistemology, and in which Schopenhauer attempts to situate his philosophy within the Western philosophical tradition.

– I –

I (*ICH*). The word "I" refers to the identity of the **subject of cognition** and the **subject of willing**, which Schopenhauer said is the "knot of the world [*Weltknoten*]." This identity is inexplicable and outside the domain of the **principle of sufficient reason**, and because it is immediately given and inexplicable, he called it the "miracle *par excellence*."

IDEA. *See* REPRESENTATION.

IDEALISM (*IDEALISMUS*). Schopenhauer identified idealism with the thesis that the external world lying before us in **space** and **time** is **representations** of the **subject of cognition**. To put the claim in a slightly different way, he claimed that idealism views the material world of spatial and temporal objects standing in causal relations as merely the representation of the cognizing subject. He praised **George Berkeley** as the "Father of idealism," and he argued that philosophy itself is essentially idealistic, since it must begin with the facts of **consciousness**, which itself presupposes the correlation of the **subject and object**. He, therefore, rejected **Johann Gottlieb Fichte**'s idealism, because he attempted to derive the object from the subject. *See also* MATERIALISM; REALISM; SPIRITUALISM; and TRANSCENDENTAL IDEALISM.

IDEALISM, TRANSCENDENTAL. *See* TRANSCENDENTAL IDEALISM.

IMMANENT. Schopenhauer argued that his **philosophy** is immanent in the Kantian sense, that is, it makes no claims about anything beyond the possibility of experience; it provides an explanation and interpretation of what is given in the experiences of the external world and in **self-consciousness**. *See also* TRANSCENDENT.

INCENTIVES (*TRIEBFEDERN*). Schopenhauer held that all human actions follow from a sufficient **motive**, and all actions ultimately aim at some being's **weal** or **woe**. Thus he held that all motives ultimately refer to someone's weal or woe, the agent's own or that of another. On this basis, Schopenhauer claimed there were four ultimate or basic incentives for actions, although he also believed some actions follow from combinations of incentives. Schopenhauer's four basic incentives are: **egoism**, the desire for one's own weal; **malice**, the desire for another's woe; **compassion**, the desire for another's well-being; and an unnamed incentive, the desire for one's own woe. *See also* ASCETICISM; PRINCIPLE OF SUFFICIENT REASON OF WILLING.

INDIFFERENT, MORALLY (*MORALISCH INDIFFERENTE*). Schopenhauer's analysis of actions from a moral point of view determined the moral quality of an action by appealing to the affective responses toward the action by both the actor and an impartial or disinterested witness. Along with **morally reprehensible** actions and actions possessing **moral worth**, he recognized a third class of actions, which he called morally indifferent actions. This kind of action is one toward which the actor and witness experience neither a positive nor negative affective response. In other words, both are indifferent toward the action; neither experiences a feeling of approbation or disapprobation toward the action. Morally indifferent actions constitute the largest class of actions, and Schopenhauer argued that **egoism**, the desire for one's own **weal**, is the motive for actions of this kind. The main translator of Schopenhauer into English, **E. F. J. Payne**, translated "*moralisch indifferente*" as "neither **good** nor **bad**," which captured Schopenhauer's metaethics, where "good" means in conformity with a person's **will** and "bad" is contrary to a person's will, but it missed Schopenhauer's direct reference to the indifference of a person's will to this kind of action, as determining its moral quality.

INTELLECT (*INTELLEKT*). Any cognitive being, that is, any being that possesses **consciousness**, or the capacity to have **representations**, possesses intellect. Schopenhauer viewed this capacity as the hallmark of all **animal** life. He tended to identify the intellect with the faculty of **understanding**, and since he argued that this faculty makes it possible to have **intuitions**, **cognitions** of spatial, temporal objects that stand in causal relationships with other objects, he claimed that all **perception** is intellectual. He also identified the brain as the objective correlate of the intellect. Thus he claimed that intuitive perception is a function of the brain. *See also* VOLUNTARISM.

INTUITION (*ANSCHAUUNG*). In a broad sense, Schopenhauer used the term "intuition" to refer to any immediate and nondiscursive experience that could serve as the basis from which the faculty of **reason** abstracts **concepts**. More usually, however, he used this term to refer to our apprehension of empirical objects, that is, spatiotemporal particulars that stand in causal relations to other, like objects. A key thesis of Schopenhauer's philosophy is that all intuition is intellectual or, in other words, our experiences of natural objects, indeed, our experience of the objective, natural world, is a function of the **understanding**, which automatically and unconsciously refers bodily sensations to spatio-temporal causes. Thus, he claimed that the first, simplest, and ever-present manifestation of the understanding is the intuition of the actual world. Since the experience of the external world is a function of the understanding, and since he held that non-human **animals** also experience a spatio-temporal, causally organized world, he also attributed the faculty of understanding to other animals. And contrary to **Immanuel Kant**, whom he accused of confusing the intuition with abstract **cognition** and who held that the faculty of understanding is a faculty of judging, that is, of unifying a manifold of intuitions through **concepts**, Schopenhauer argued that intuition requires no thinking or discursive thought. **E. F. J. Payne** generally translated the term "*Anschauung*" as **perception** or as "intuitive perception."

INTUITION, INTELLECTUAL (*INTELLEKTUALE ANSCHAU- UNG*). Schopenhauer looked with contempt on anyone who held that humans have some cognitive faculty referred to as "intellectual intuition," a capacity for some immediate **cognition** of the ultimate or **absolute**. Consequently, he viewed the appeal to this capacity by German **idealists**, especially **Friedrich Wilhelm Joseph von Schelling**, as simply their playing fast and loose with the absolute and a sure sign that they had forgotten their **Kant**. Even if there were such a capacity, Schopenhauer argued, its contents could not be communicated, and thus, it would be like any mystical experience. In reality, however, he thought it was like the sixth sense of bats, and it was a lofty word used by those with low sentiments.

IRRATIONALISM (*IRRATIONALISMUS*). In his magisterial *Arthur Schopenhauer: Transzendentalphilosophic und Metaphysik des Willens*, footnote 4, (B) *Wissen und Gefühl*, Section 31 (*Arthur Schopenhauer: Transcendental Philosophy and Metaphysics of the Will*, 1991), Rudolf Malter observed that along with **voluntarism** and **pessimism**, irrationalism is the most frequently used term to describe Schopenhauer's philosophy. It is not, however, a term he employed to refer to his thought, nor is it a term that has received a precise philosophical definition. It is, moreover, often used as a term of derision, suggesting that any view that expresses irrationalism glorifies or praises the irrational at the expense of the rational. While it is not clear what it is to glorify or praise the irrational, it is clear that Schopenhauer's claim that the **will** is the essence of all things is made in the context in which the will is viewed as evil and as that which is to be denied. Marxist critics of Schopenhauer, like the Hungarian philosopher Georg Lukács (1885–1971) and the Russian philosopher Bernard Bykovsky (1901–1980), emphasized the flawed character of Schopenhauer's thought, which they said was not rationally justified, but was, instead, the irrational expression of a doomed bourgeois ideology and an indirect apologetics for capitalism. In *Die Zerstörung der Vernunft* (*The Destruction of Reason*, Chapter 5, 1955), Lukács spoke of the "bourgeois irrationalism" of Schopenhauer's philosophy. The great philosopher of science, Karl Popper (1902–1994), while sympathetic to Schopenhauer, called him the "father of modern irrationalism" in *Conjectures and Refutations* (1963). Malter himself argued in the earlier cited footnote that Schopenhauer's **philosophy** would be irrationalism had he ended *The World as Will and Representation* with the second book, his metaphysics of nature. However, he did not. The third book, his **aesthetics**, and the fourth, his **ethics**, depicted the ultimate victory of **cognition** over the irrational will, Malter argued. The victory of cognition to which Malter referred concerns Schopenhauer's account of **aesthetic contemplation** and the **denial of the will**.

In less partisan terms, Schopenhauer is often classified as an irrationalist due to the ways his philosophy reversed some of the main tendencies found in Western philosophy, especially as articulated by such figures as **Plato**, **René Descartes**, and **Georg Wilhelm Friedrich Hegel**. His metaphysics of the will found that the ultimate essence of the world is a non-rational striving that operates without a purpose or goal. Thus he denied that ultimate reality is spiritual or rational. In doing this, he also denied that the ultimate reality could be rendered transparent by reason. Since the will is also the essence of humans, he reversed a tradition that viewed **reason** as the essence of humans, as well as a subsequent identification of **consciousness** as the self. While Schopenhauer agreed that the faculty of reason is unique to humans, he argued that reason and the **intellect**, our capacities for cognition itself, are subservient to the will; that it is the will that determines the goals and ends of our actions. Consequently, he claimed that the ultimate ground of human motivation has a non-rational character, and he also emphasized the ways in which motivation escapes conscious recognition and can be masked from conscious thought, views that, if nothing else, presented a shift in perspective that helped prepare the grounds for **Sigmund Freud**. As the German philosopher Georg Simmel (1858–1918) put it in *Schopenhauer und Nietzsche* (1907), Schopenhauer's philosophy demoted the rational character of life.

– J –

JUDAISM. Schopenhauer tended to treat aggregating names for major
religions as if they implied the existence of a uniformity of beliefs
and practices among all adherents of a particular religion. While he
did recognize different denominations in **Christianity**, and as he became more familiar with **Hinduism** and **Buddhism**, he also recognized different schools in these religions, he treated Judaism as if
there were no divisions in it. He viewed Judaism in its early biblical
form, when it appeared to have no reward after **death** for the faithful.
Consequently, he believed that Judaism lacked a doctrine of immortality, which he viewed as an essential feature of a religion. Schopenhauer disdained Judaism, moreover, because he viewed it as expressing **realism** and **optimism**. Thus he argued that Judaism expresses a
false metaphysics and it maintains a pernicious attitude toward a
world steeped in suffering and **death**. In particular, Schopenhauer argued that the creation myth in Genesis is logically impossible, since
it posited a Creator **God**, distinct from Creation, as summoning the
universe out of nothing. God's pronouncement that creation is good
is contradicted by the dreadful nature of existence, Schopenhauer
also concluded. He claimed Judaism could not account for human
moral **responsibility** for their conduct by conceiving of human existence as proceeding from God's will. Moreover, he thought Judaism
radically separated humans from all other living creatures by viewing
humans as created in God's image. This stance, he argued, led Judaism to promote a morally repugnant view of **animals** as being
manufactured for human use. Schopenhauer said the only thing that
reconciled him to Judaism was the myth of the Fall, but he also
claimed that Judaism failed to appreciate how the myth suggested the
deep guilt of existence.

Schopenhauer's attitudes toward Judaism were colored by and
helped to engender anti-Semitic trends in German cultural and political life. He argued that it was a mistake to think of Jews as a religious group; they should be considered a homeless, nationalistic race,
whose monotheism was deeply ethnocentric. While he decried the
barbaric treatment of Jews in Europe, and while he argued they
should be granted civil rights and be allowed to marry Christians, he
also advocated that Jews should not be allowed to participate in the

governance of Christian countries and that intermarriage would diminish the number of Jews. Schopenhauer's contempt for Judaism and his harsh rhetoric concerning Jews, saying they lived "parasitically on other nations" and complaining that he could detect a "*Foetor Judaicus* (Judaic odor)" attached to views he thought descended from Judaism, helped to support the anti-Semitism of **Richard Wagner** and Adolph Hitler. Within a discussion of what Schopenhauer regarded as the worst side of religions, that their believers regard themselves as justified in treating others with the greatest wickedness and cruelty, he attempted to account for the historical basis of Exodus by appealing to the Roman historians Tacitus and Justine. Thus, in a footnote to section 174 of the second volume of *Parerga and Paralipomena*, he wrote that these Roman writers show how much the Jews were despised and loathed by all nations, which "may be due partly to the fact that they were the only people on earth who did not credit humans with any existence beyond this life and were, therefore, regarded as cattle, as the dregs of humanity—but great masters of lies." Hitler quoted the line that the Jews were the "great masters of lies" twice in *Mein Kampf*, conveniently forgetting that this remark made by Schopenhauer was in fact denouncing fanatical cruelty, such as that of "Christians against the Hindus, Mohammedans, American natives, Negroes, Jews, heretics, and others." Still, he said that he knew this functional cruelty as only stemming from monotheistic religions, "thus Judaism and its branches, Christianity and Islam," suggesting, of course, that Jewish monotheism was its source.

JUSTICE (*GERECHTIGKEIT*). Philanthropy and justice were Schopenhauer's two cardinal virtues, the virtues from which all other virtues are derived. *Neminem laede*, the injunction to harm no one, summarized the virtue of justice, and he viewed the virtue of justice to be a person's disposition to refrain from harming or injuring another. In a world populated by willful beings, all of whom are motivated to preserve their lives and to satisfy their desires, conflict is inevitable, according to Schopenhauer. A just individual, he argued, is disposed not to act in ways that would cause others' suffering, because of his or her **compassion** for another's suffering. That is, the prospects of causing another misery would lead a just individual to refrain from doing as she or he had originally planned. Because

Schopenhauer identified justice with not causing another misery or harm, as checking an individual's natural **egoism** and **malice**, he saw it as the first degree of compassion, as a checking of egoistic or malicious motivations. Justice as the first degree of compassion is merely negative; it prevents a person from causing another suffering, something that does not yet exist. *See also* ETERNAL JUSTICE; TEMPORAL JUSTICE.

– K –

KANT, IMMANUEL (1724–1804). Schopenhauer esteemed Kant more than he did any other philosopher. He thought that Kant and **Johann Wolfgang von Goethe** were the greatest minds ever produced in Germany, and he once remarked that Kant might have had the most original mind that nature brought forth. He venerated Kant's distinctions between **appearances** and **things in themselves**, and between the empirical and intelligible **characters**, and he said that these distinctions represent some of the greatest of all ideas. Schopenhauer took great pride in calling himself a Kantian, and since he believed that only the pseudo-philosophies of **Johann Gottlieb Fichte**, **Friedrich Wilhelm Joseph von Schelling**, and **Georg Wilhelm Friedrich Hegel**, each of which failed to appreciate Kant's great insights, stood between himself and Kant, he claimed that he was Kant's only legitimate philosophical heir. He also blamed these "three sophists" for contributing to the neglect of Kant during the first part of the 19th century. Unlike these sophists, he claimed that his **philosophy** was based on Kant's, and that it was simply Kant's philosophy taken to its proper conclusion.

Although Schopenhauer had the highest respect for Kant's philosophical achievements, and while he retained and employed much of his philosophical vocabulary, he was also highly critical of Kant. His first book, *On the Fourfold Root of the Principle of Sufficient Reason*, while highlighting the significance of **Plato** and Kant, he also wrote it as if he were a post-Kantian philosopher. The first edition of *The World as Will and Representation* contained a lengthy appendix, "Criticism of the Kantian Philosophy," which he prefaced with a quote from Voltaire, "It is the privilege of true genius, and especially of the genius who opens up a new path, to make great mistakes with impunity." This quote certainly sets the tone of Schopenhauer's attitude toward Kant. He was a great genius who made great mistakes. By retaining fidelity to Kant's great insights and avoiding his errors, Schopenhauer viewed himself as continuing Kant's philosophy. This appendix, which he revised significantly in the second edition of his main work, as well as section 13 of his "Fragments for the History of Philosophy," from the first volume of *Parerga and Paralipomena*, are the most sustained loci of his assessment of Kant's philosophy, although all of his philosophical works show his critical engagement with Kant. Over one-third of his *On the Basis of Morality* is devoted to a sustained and harsh critique of Kant's moral philosophy.

Although it is not clear when Schopenhauer first read Kant, a meeting in 1809 with Carl Leonhard Reinhold (1758–1823) at one of his mother's parties in Weimar might have drawn him to Kant. At that time, Reinhold was recognized as one of the foremost interpreters and popularizers of Kant's philosophy and it was not uncommon for people to refer to a Kant-Reinholdian philosophy. While at the University of Göttingen, **G. E. Schulze** recommended to Schopenhauer that he study **Plato** and Kant. In conjunction with this recommendation, as well as Schulze's lectures, Schopenhauer commenced his study of Kant in the winter semester of 1810–1811, and it was in his notebooks from that time that he recorded his first reflections of Kant. After his enrollment at the University of Berlin in the fall of 1811, he initiated a more intense private study of Kant, a study that occupied him during his entire stay at Berlin. This study was certainly motivated by his exposure to Fichte at Berlin. In his notes from Fichte's lectures it is easy to observe the way in which Schopenhauer's increasing understanding of Kant helped motivate his increasing dissatisfaction with Fichte.

Schopenhauer continued to read Kant throughout his entire life, but it appears that he was stimulated to explore Kant's writings in an even more exacting fashion around 1826, after the discovery of the first edition of Kant's *Critique of Pure Reason*. Prior to that time, he had only read later editions of Kant's masterpiece, which received substantial revisions in the second edition. From his discovery of the first edition, Schopenhauer thought Kant had moved away from his original radicalism and **idealism** in the second edition and that it had obscured his original insights by introducing various contradictions into his thoughts. He attributed Kant's alterations in the second edition to his likely succumbing to various external pressures, particularly to his critics' charges that he proposed a form of idealism like **George Berkeley**'s. Kant had also made, he thought, unwarranted concessions to **religion** and naïve ordinary ideas. Later, in 1837, when he discovered that two Königsberg professors were assembling a new edition of Kant's collected works, Schopenhauer managed to convince them that they should include a printing of the first edition of the *Critique of Pure Reason*. The discovery of the first edition, moreover, seems to have been the stimulus for his revision of the appendix to the second edition of *The World as Will and Representation* (1844), a revision that constituted the most significant revision of his original volume. In late 1829 Schopenhauer also attempted to secure a commission from a British publisher to translate into English a number of Kant's philosophical books, including the *Critique of Pure Reason*. Unfortunately, he was not able to do so, and his "great master's doctrines" were not introduced into England by Schopenhauer, who had described himself as longing to be Kant's "apostle in England" in his letter from 21 December 1829, in which he made his proposal "to the author of Damiron's Analysis."

Scholars tend to vary on their assessment of the results of Schopenhauer's fidelity to Kant. Some have suggested that Schopenhauer was not sensitive to his departures from Kant, due to differences of their philosophical methodologies. Others have suggested that Schopenhauer's allegiance to Kant's terminology led to various problems in the expression of his own ideas, since Kant's language was incapable of expressing Schopenhauer's insights. Still others have suggested that Schopenhauer's deep commitment to Kant's ideals, especially the prescription to express a fully immanent philosophy, one that avoids any **transcendent** claims, that is, any talk of things beyond the realm of all possible experiences, is found throughout his philosophy. In any case, Schopenhauer tended to view his **epistemology** and metaphysics as more indebted to Kant than his **aesthetics**, and his aesthetics more than his **ethics**. Indeed, in *On the Basis of Morality*, he remarked that his foundations for ethics were "diametrically opposed to Kant's."

Schopenhauer embraced **transcendental idealism** and the distinction between **appearances** and the thing in itself. While Kant's transcendental idealism can be characterized by the claim that we can know only appearances of things and never the thing in itself, Schopenhauer claimed to have advanced beyond the philosophy of his master by showing that we can know the **will** as thing in itself. He also agreed with Kant that the *a priori* forms of **space**, **time**, and **causality** structure our experiences of things, but Schopenhauer argued for this claim by radically streamlining Kant's complex and sophisticated analysis of human **cognition**. All **perception** is intellectual, Schopenhauer argued, a function of the **understanding**'s automatic reference of bodily sensations to a spatial-temporal cause. His discovery of the will as thing in itself, moreover, also served to further illustrate the differences between Schopenhauer's and Kant's methodologies. He rejected the type of transcendental arguments Kant employed to establish the necessary conditions for the possibility of experience, because he viewed this method as being too abstract, conceptual, and derivative. Instead, his method tends to bear more kinship to that of the British empiricists, and he emphasized the primacy of **intuition**, or the immediately given, over the conceptual. Indeed, all **concepts**, he held, are derived from intuitions. For this reason, he claimed that Kant worked from the secondary and not the primary source of **knowledge**. Moreover, he exploited **self-consciousness** as the means for discovering the will as the essence of inner content of all **representations**, all objects of our **consciousness of other things**. By using the discovery of the will through self-consciousness, he claimed that he had found the key for deciphering all experiences and the means to satisfy the demands of metaphysics, the un-Kantian demand to provide a comprehensive explanation of the totality of experiences. In this way, he claimed that his philosophy was completely immanent and never transcended the bounds of all possible experiences. Whenever Kant had brought the thing in itself closest to the light, he claimed, he also did so as will. He had, he said, completed Kant by showing the will as the thing in itself.

Schopenhauer perceived his aesthetics as less indebted to Kant than he did his theoretical philosophy. Still, he recognized some debts. In his consideration of Kant's aesthetics, he reiterated his general complaint about Kant's method in a more specific form. By analyzing judgments about the **beautiful** rather than the experience of beauty itself, Kant was once again a step removed from the true article of inquiry. He even diagnosed a personal reason lying behind Kant's approach to aesthetics. Schopenhauer suspected that Kant lacked susceptibility to the beautiful and, by never leaving the area around Königsberg during his entire life, Kant had little opportunity to experience great works of **art**. Thus Schopenhauer compared Kant's aesthetics to a theory of **color** developed by a colorblind person. Both had to rely on the accurate statements of others. He also lamented that Kant did not seem to have knowledge of Goethe, his "giant brother." Nevertheless, he held that Kant had performed a lasting service to the philosophy of art by directing attention away from the object called "beautiful," and the search for characteristics or properties of beautiful objects, and by focusing consideration on the subject who made the judgment that something was "beautiful." Although Schopenhauer thought he should have gone deeper in his analysis by considering the subjects' experience of the beautiful, this move was, by itself, in the direction of the right path. And when Schopenhauer turned to consider the aesthetic contemplation or enjoyment of great art, Kant's influence can be detected in his analysis of the beautiful and the **sublime** (which he considered the most significant thing in Kant's *Critique of Judgment*), especially in his analysis of the disinterested nature of these experiences and the general conceptual frameworks by which he explained their dynamics. To be sure, Schopenhauer attributed a higher cognitive value to aesthetic **contemplation** than Kant, since he held that the objects of aesthetic contemplation were **Platonic Ideas**, adequate grades of objectification of will. Unlike Kant, who, in his classification of the arts, attributed the lowest aesthetic worth to music, Schopenhauer found it to possess the highest value, since music presents a copy (*Abbild*) of the will. Moreover, both tragedy and music, he argued, counsel **resignation** and the **denial of the will**.

Schopenhauer viewed his ethics as being more distant from Kant than any other area of his philosophy. Although Schopenhauer recognized connections between Kant's ethics and his own, he also claimed that Kant was ultimately unable to support their shared ideas. Thus he praised Kant for purging **eudaemonism** or happiness from ethics, for divorcing ethics from theology, and for recognizing that the ethical conduct of humans is metaphysically significant. Yet he also argued that Kant's ethics was ultimately eudaemonistic; that it was based on theology; and that he failed to understand the metaphysical significance of morality. He also decried Kant's rational, non-empirical, and prescriptive ethics of **duty**, and he attempted to supercede Kant by his **voluntaristic**, empirical, and descriptive virtue ethics. He argued that Kant's ethics, which rejected **compassion**, sympathy, and **love** as the grounds of moral conduct, is repugnant to any person who possesses genuine moral sensitivity. Compassion, Schopenhauer said, is the basis of morality. Following his general philosophical methodology, he argued that the basis of ethics could only be discovered empirically, and he deplored Kant's claims that pure **reason** discovered the foundation of morality and that reason could practically determine the will. Kant had developed an ethics for "dear little angels," he said, and not one for human beings, whose essence is the will. Instead of his ethics serving as the basis of Kant's moral theology, he contended that theology is presupposed by the very concepts that function centrally in his ethics, especially his concepts of categorical moral laws and absolute, unconditional obligations. Ultimately, Schopenhauer concluded that Kant's conception of practical reason and his supreme principle of morality, the categorical imperative, were unjustified, groundless, and fictitious assumptions. Indeed, he thought that Kant's ethics was an intellectual catastrophe, which resulted from his love for architectonic symmetry, a boldness and rashness based on his philosophical reputation, and the debilitating effects of old age. It is easy to understand why, in explaining his lengthy critique of Kant's ethics in *On the Basis of Morality*, Schopenhauer said that people would be better able to understand his views in light of this critique, since "opposites illuminate each other."

KNOWLEDGE (*WISSEN*). Schopenhauer held that knowledge is propositional and that to know something is to have a **cognition** of a true judgment. Since the faculty of **reason** is responsible for formulating judgments by combining **concepts**, he held that reason is the faculty of knowledge. In his analysis of the **principle of sufficient reason of knowing**, he argued that **truth** is a relational property of judgments, that is, the truth of any judgment is based on something other than itself, upon some external ground or reason. Since he recognized four kinds of reasons that form the ground of truth, he also recognized four kinds of truth, namely, logical, empirical, **transcendental**, and metalogical. In the 17th chapter of the second volume of *The World as Will and Representation*, Schopenhauer described his metaphysics as knowledge (*Wissen*) of the world drawn from **intuition** (*Anschauung*) of the external world and from information drawn from **self-consciousness**, deposited in distinct concepts.

– L –

LIBERUM ARBITRIUM (FREE CHOICE OF THE WILL). *See* ASEITY; FREEDOM, MORAL; PRINCIPLE OF SUFFICIENT REASON OF ACTING; RESPONSIBILITY.

LIBERUM ARBITRIUM INDIFFENTIAE (FREE CHOICE OF INDIFFERENCE). *See* FREEDOM, MORAL.

LINDNER, ERNST OTTO (1820–1867). Lindner was an assistant editor of the *Vossische Zeitung*, a German newspaper. He was drawn to Schopenhauer after reading *Parerga and Paralipomena* in 1852, after which he arranged a personal meeting with Schopenhauer. Lindner also arranged to have a German translation, made by his wife, of John Oxenford's "Iconoclasm in German Philosophy" appear in the *Vossische Zeitung* in June 1853, an event that contributed significantly to the growth of Schopenhauer's popularity among the educated public in Germany. In addition, Lindner played an active role in promoting Schopenhauer's **philosophy** and in popularizing his philosophy of **music**. Together with **Julius Frauenstädt**, he published a book about Schopenhauer, *Arthur Schopenhauer: Of Him; On Him* (*Arthur Schopenhauer. Von ihm, Über ihm*. Berlin 1863).

LOCKE, JOHN (1632–1704). Schopenhauer tended to think highly of the classical British empiricists, Locke, **George Berkeley**, and **David Hume**. Yet of the three, Locke appears to be the one he esteemed the most. Indeed, he referred to Locke within his **philosophy** more than he did to Berkeley and Hume counted together. While he decried Locke's **realism** and criticized his assumption that material objects cause our experiences or ideas of them, a claim he viewed as empirically unjustified, he regarded Locke as a *summus philosophus*, a distinguished philosopher. Indeed, he even took **Johann Gottlieb Fichte**'s remark that Locke was the worst of all philosophers as speaking to Locke's credit. Unlike Berkeley and Hume, Schopenhauer argued that his philosophy, Kant's, and Locke's presented the gradual development of a coherently consistent train of thought. Indeed, he claimed that he stood to **Immanuel Kant** as Kant stood to Locke. Just as Kant transcended Locke's philosophy while retaining Lockean insights, he maintained that he transcended Kant while retaining Kantian insights. In this way, he stated, his philosophy was related to Locke's through mediation by Kant. The intimate connection that he perceived between himself, Locke, and Kant resided in their shared epistemic commitments, however. He used Locke as an ally to argue against Kant's **ethics**. In section four of *On the Basis of Morality*, where he used Locke's assertion that any conception of the law entailed some reward or **punishment** connected to the law, Schopenhauer argued that Kant's idea of unconditional moral laws was a *contradictio in adjecto*, since his moral laws were conditioned by a threat of punishment or a promise of reward.

It appears that Schopenhauer's first reading of Locke was in a self-directed study of Locke's *An Essay Concerning Human Understanding* (12th edition—his library at his death would include its 14th edition, as well as Locke's *On the Conduct of the Understanding* and *Two Treatises of Government*). This study of Locke was in the summer of 1812, while he was a student at the University of Berlin. He embarked on a second study of Locke in January 1816, when he was living in Dresden and working on *The World as Will and Representation*. Schopenhauer's notes to these studies of Locke can be found in the second volume of *Manuscript Remains*. Already in these studies one can detect the roots of his view concerning Kant's relationship to Locke: Kant's philosophy advanced beyond Locke's, but Lockean insights were retained by Kant. Although his second reading of Locke occurred as he was writing his chief work, Schopenhauer only referred to Locke once in the first edition of *The World as Will and Representation*, when he reiterated an observation he made in his notes, namely, that Locke had stated the true difference between nonhuman **animals** and humans. Humans alone have the capacity to develop abstract and universal **concepts**. Schopenhauer regarded this capacity to be the sole function of the faculty of **reason**, and some of his commentators have argued that his account of concepts as being abstracted from **intuitions** or **perceptions** follows Locke's view. Schopenhauer's notes from the 1820s, found in the third volume of *Manuscript Remains*, also show his continued reflection on Kant's relationship to Locke and, thereby, the significance of Locke for his own philosophy. These reflections were articulated in the second edition of his chief work (1844), especially in his reworked appendix "Criticism of the Kantian Philosophy," and later in the first two essays of the first volume of *Parerga and Paralipomena* (1851).

Schopenhauer praised Locke for investigating the origin of concepts and for rejecting the rationalists' notion of innate ideas. He viewed Locke, therefore, as rejecting pure **reason** as a source of **knowledge**, and he claimed that Locke focused on intuition and experience to discover the origin of concepts. This was the same method that he attributed to both Kant and himself, namely, each takes what is given to **consciousness** and, on this basis, each presents the mechanisms by which the world exhibits itself. Thus he credited Locke as the originator of the method used by both Kant and himself. Kant, he argued, brought Locke's method toward a higher state of perfection, while his philosophy brought it to perfection. It is by virtue of Schopenhauer's perception of this methodological kinship between Locke, Kant, and himself, as well as his belief that Kant had improved Locke and he Kant, that Schopenhauer claimed that their philosophies represented the gradual development of a coherently consistent train of thought.

Schopenhauer viewed Locke's distinction between primary and secondary qualities as prefiguring Kant's distinction between **appearances** and **things in themselves**. He read Locke as claiming that our ideas of things are caused by material objects, and while we experience primary qualities: extension, place, and impenetrability, and secondary qualities: **colors**, sounds, temperature, and taste, only the former are qualities of material objects and the latter are only creations of the action of material objects on our senses, and bear no resemblance to features of these objects. Kant, he argued, correctly went deeper than Locke, and he demonstrated that his primary qualities are the *a priori* forms of **cognition** and are of subjective origin. In this way, he believed that Kant had shown that Locke's primary qualities were also only features of our experiences of things and not of things in themselves. Yet, he also believed that Kant retained a notion central to Locke's realism, that our experiences of things are caused by some object, of which we have no experience. Following the lead of **G. E. Schulze**, but diagnosing the problem residing in Kant's fidelity to Locke, Schopenhauer claimed that the "Achilles' heel" of Kant's philosophy was that he applied the principle of **causality** beyond the limits of possible experience by viewing things in themselves as the cause of sensuous **representations**. Reaching back to Locke, who recognized sensation and reflection as the sources of all experience, Schopenhauer exploited reflection (**self-consciousness**) as the means for discovering the **will** as the **thing in itself**. Thus Schopenhauer claimed that he had completed a line of thought originated by Locke and improved by Kant.

LOVE (*LIEBE*). In the 66th section of the first volume of *The World as Will and Representation*, Schopenhauer advanced the claim that all love is **compassion**, as well as the seemingly paradoxical claim that love leads to **salvation**. By reducing love to compassion, Schopenhauer viewed love as both displacing a person's inclination to **egoism** and as also disposing the agent to treat another's **weal** just like his or her own. By linking love to salvation, however, he did not literally mean that love was salvation. Rather, since he held that compassion involves seeing oneself in another, it expresses the same kind of **cognition** as that which functions in salvation. Seeing oneself in another involves seeing through the ***principium individuationis***, but he said, the degree to which this occurs is more metaphysically revealing and deeper in salvation. *See also* PHILANTHROPY; LOVE, SEXUAL.

LOVE, SEXUAL (*GESCHLECHTSLIEBE*). Next to the love of life, that is, our striving for our continued existence and well-being, Schopenhauer viewed sexual love as our strongest and most active motive. Its satisfaction is the goal of almost all human effort, he said, and it claims half the powers and thoughts of the young. It perplexes even the greatest minds, and it interrupts our most serious occupations, interfering in the negotiations of statesmen and the investigations of the learned. Under the sway of sexual love, we engage in quarrels with our friends and family, and it breaks the bonds of our strongest and most valuable relations. **Love** leads to the fall of the upright and honorable, and it makes traitors of those who were once loyal and faithful. For its satisfaction we sacrifice our wealth, health, and social position, sometimes even our lives. Sexual love is also the principal theme in poetry, drama, tragedy, and comedy, and it is a theme accepted by humankind with an abiding interest. Due to the central role of sexual love in human life and our deep interest in it, Schopenhauer found it odd that philosophers, who were keenly interested in **death**, the end of our lives, paid so little attention to that which brings us into existence. Even Schopenhauer himself was slow to consider the topic of sexual love, and he waited until the second edition of *The World as Will and Representation*, the second volume, (1844) to consider this topic. In the infamous 44th essay, "The Metaphysics of Sexual Love," Schopenhauer lamented the fact that he lacked philosophical predecessors to either use or refute through his analysis of sexual love. In this essay Schopenhauer recognized, long before **Sigmund Freud**, the omnipresence of sexuality in human life, and he argued that it is more than a trifle, more than a question of "every Jack finding a Jill." He found its significance deeper than a simple quest for sexual pleasure. His work on sexuality would prepare the grounds for **Friedrich Nietzsche**, Karl Jung, Freud, and others to also seriously consider the topic.

Schopenhauer warned his readers, especially those under the spell of this powerful passion, that they were likely to find his account of sexual love to be too physical, material, metaphysical, and (here he used a term he seldom applied to his own **philosophy**) **transcendent**. He averred, however, that the topic requires the same profound seriousness in philosophy as sexual love plays in human life. The ultimate aim of all love affairs, he claimed, is more important than all other affairs in human life, and instinct holds the reigns in sexual love. It creates illusions in those who express it, and thus it hides its true ends. Consequently, by stripping its delusions, his explanation of sexual love would seem too physical and materialistic to some, and since he found sexual love deep within human nature, he had to also articulate its deeply metaphysical basis. Partially from his own personal inclination to speculate beyond his formal argumentation, and partially because of the connections he drew between sexual love and the **will** as **thing in itself**, he recognized that his explanation of sexual love bordered, at times, on the transcendent.

Schopenhauer argued that sexual love is the means by which the human species seeks its own ends through its ephemeral individual members. Thus he claimed that what is at stake is the composition of the next generation, the *dramatis personae* of all love affairs. If one were to consider the collected love affairs of the present generation, one would find that this represents the human race's meditation on the composition of the future generation, the generation on which in their turn all future generations depend. Therefore it is not the **weal** and **woe** of individuals, their personal and subjective interests and desires, that are significant in love affairs, Schopenhauer reasoned; rather, it is the continued existence of the human species itself. He said it is as if sexual love expresses the interests and aims of the species, and the great importance on which all the pathetic and **sublime** elements of love affairs rest, the "transcendent element" of all of love's ecstasies and pains.

All amorousness is rooted in the sexual impulse, Schopenhauer argued, and considered in itself it is the **will to life**. As objectified in individuals, this impulse is always directed toward another, and it expresses itself as a need to physically enjoy the other, a necessary condition for bringing forth new life, the craving of the will to life, which always wills life. Thus he claimed when a man and woman begin to love one another, "to fancy each other," as he said, using this English expression, it is to be regarded as the very first formulation of a new individual, the *punctum saliens* of life. It is as if the longing glances of lovers connote a potential new being, a new individual or new **Platonic Idea**, which like all Ideas strives to objectify itself. Consequently, even if this child does not come into being, the true end of all love stories is that the lovers produce a particular child, even though both parties are unaware of this end. Lovers possess the need to physically enjoy each other, he claimed, and this need for physical union and sexual satisfaction is often masked from the consciousness of the lovers by the many ethereal ways they pledge devotion and ultimate concern for each other's well-being. Behind the union of souls, however, is the drive for the union of bodies for the

production of new life. The sexual impulse, this drive to copulate and
achieve sexual satisfaction, is egoistic, and thus he claimed that egoistic aims drive lovers. But at a deeper level, the sexual impulse is an
instinct, and like most instincts, it represents the will of the species,
which creates the delusion in individuals that they are seeking their
own good when in fact they are seeking the good of the species (the
continued existences of individuals of its kind). To lovers, however,
it appears as if the good things of life are attached to their love, and
they are ready to undertake any sacrifice for its sake. It is not uncommon, Schopenhauer noted, to hear of the common **suicide** of two
lovers thwarted by external circumstances.

Schopenhauer thought he could account for the ubiquity and significance of sex in human life by emphasizing that what is at stake in
sexual love is the continuation of the human species. Yet he found the
metaphysical aim of sexual love highly problematic. So he closed his
discussion of the metaphysics of sexual love by noting that lovers are
the traitors who perpetuate the wretchedness of life, since they produce new individuals to suffer and die. Sex is the means by which the
will continuously affirms itself, and although it promises delight, it
brings despair. Consequently, it is easy to understand why Schopenhauer claimed that voluntary chastity is the first step to
asceticism and the **denial of the will**. *See also* GENITALS;
PEDERASTY; WOMEN.

– M –

MALICE (*BOSHEIT*). This is one of Schopenhauer's four basic or ultimate **incentives** for human action. He characterized malice as the desire for another's **woe**, and he argued that it is the source of **morally
reprehensible** behavior. Although he believed that everyone is susceptible to malice to some degree, he considered people who are regularly
disposed to malice as possessing a morally **evil** character. When malice is the *leitmotif* of a person's **character**, he thought, you have the
very worst sort of person. In section 14 of *On the Basis of Morality*,
Schopenhauer summarized the line of conduct exhibited by malicious
characters by the maxim *omnes, quantum potes, laede* (injure all people as much as you can), and he identified envy, disaffection, ill-will,

Schadenfreude, prying curiosity, slander, insolence, petulance, hatred, treachery, perfidy, thirst for revenge, and cruelty as vices based on malice.

Schopenhauer reserved his strongest condemnation for people disposed to malice, and he viewed extremely malicious characters as expressing a devilish attitude toward others. Although he believed that **egoism** leads to all sorts of terrible **wrongs**, and he held that extremely egoistic people are strongly inclined to do horrible things, he believed they act as if there were no other people, thereby practically expressing **theoretical egoism**. Consequently, he held that egoists simply pursue their own self-interests and that the harm they do to others is secondary and only contingently connected to their conduct. The malicious characters, however, have to recognize that others exist, since it is their misery that they desire, and the misery of others is necessarily connected to their behavior. This desire for another's woe, moreover, expresses an attitude directly opposed to **compassion**, which he viewed as the incentive for all actions possessing **moral worth**. Instead of seeking to relieve another's suffering, which is the aim of compassion, malice seeks to cause suffering.

Schopenhauer argued that extremely malicious characters suffer from an excessive **will to life**, something that leads them to experience an excessive inner torment and an incurable pain. In these rare individuals, those who exhibit malice to its highest degree, he suggested that they share a realization with the most enlightened person, namely, that the pursuit of their own self-interests is empty, that the satisfaction of their desires promises a false reward. In section 65 of *The World as Will and Representation*, he argued that the recognition of the failure to ever secure one's well-being intensifies a malicious person's hatred of others and makes them seek the misery of others, something that makes them strongly attached to life and the **affirmation of the will**, a stance toward the world opposite to that of a person on the path to **salvation**.

MARQUET, CAROLINE LOUISE (1771–1842). It is common among Schopenhauer's Anglophone commentators to note that people often know more about the details of his life than his **philosophy**. The Marquet case seems to be one of these details. Marquet was a friend of his landlady, the widow Becker, and she lived in the same

Berlin lodgings as Schopenhauer. On 12 August 1821, there was an incident between Marquet and the philosopher. According to Schopenhauer, two weeks earlier he had complained to his landlady that some strange women were using the *Entrée* to his rooms as a meeting place, a state of affairs that upset him. He claimed that his landlady promised this would not happen again, but it did. Schopenhauer claimed he demanded that Marquet and her two friends vacate the room, offering his arm to escort Marquet out. She, however, refused to leave, telling Schopenhauer she was a "respectable person." More forcefully, he said, he demanded they leave, and he returned to his rooms. After a short period of time, Schopenhauer returned to the *Entrée*, observing that the women still remained. Schopenhauer became angry, calling Marquet an "old wench," and demanded that the women leave immediately.

What exactly happened next is a matter of dispute. It is clear that Schopenhauer physically removed Marquet from the room twice. The first time, he alleged, he had to grab her around her torso and drag her out, since she struggled with all her might to stay. After he removed her, he claimed, she began screaming, threatening to sue him and demanding her things that remained in the room. Schopenhauer promptly tossed them out, but under what he claimed to be a pretext to retrieve some trinket, she reentered the room, whereupon he seized her again, and as she struggled against him, he forced her out of the room. At that point, he said that she fell on purpose. Marquet, however, claimed that Schopenhauer ripped the bonnet from her head, kicked her, beat her with his fists, and that she fainted from the assault.

True to her word, however, Marquet sued Schopenhauer. Through a series of hearings and appeals of the judgment by both parties, the Marquet trial lasted five years. Ultimately Marquet claimed, after discovering that Schopenhauer was a man of means, that her injuries prevented her from earning her livelihood as a seamstress. The final verdict was issued on 4 May 1827. It required Schopenhauer to pay 60 talers a year, that is, 15 talers per quarter, for as long as Marquet's injuries persisted. Unfortunately, said injuries lasted until she died. He did, however, get in the last word on the case. When Marquet died, Schopenhauer wrote on her death certificate, "*Obit anus, abit onus* [the old woman dies, the burden departs]."

MATERIALISM (*MATERIALISMUS*). Schopenhauer argued that **realism** necessarily leads to materialism, the view that everything that exists is a modification of **matter**. In particular, he claimed that materialism focuses on the **subject of cognition**, maintaining that the subject is material. By doing so, he ironically described materialism as a philosophy of the subject that has forgotten itself, and as a philosophy that prompts an equally unsatisfactory form of realism, **spiritualism**, as a rear-guard attempt to salvage the subject by viewing it as an immaterial substance. Schopenhauer credited **Immanuel Kant** with undermining materialism by demonstrating that matter is an *a priori* form of cognition. Consequently, he viewed anyone subscribing to materialism as being philosophically uninformed. *See also* IDEALISM.

MATTER (*MATERIE*). Schopenhauer thought that by thinking of something perceived as an object in the natural world, or the world as **representation**, without its formal properties (its special spatial location at a particular time) and its specific properties (say, being round, red, and hot), what remains is the concept of matter, some property-less "residue." The matter of any particular object is identical to that of any other, he held, because the formal and specific properties of objects are the bases for distinguishing between different things and none of these properties belong to matter. Since he also claimed that the specific properties of things constitute their specific modes of operation or activity, he concluded that the concept of pure matter is the idea of activity in general or "pure activity." This idea is the same, he said, as the idea of pure **causality**, the idea of causality itself—in contrast to that of some specific causal relationship. (By calling matter and causality "pure," Schopenhauer emphasized that neither were objects of **perception**.) The difference between pure matter and pure causality is that the idea of "pure activity" denoted by pure matter is conceived objectively, as a feature of the world. Thus, he held that matter is just causality objectively conceived as a necessary feature of the world, while pure matter is this idea of pure activity, subjectively conceived as a function of the faculty of the **understanding**. But since he ultimately held that the natural world is produced by the understanding, matter is simply causality projected beyond the subject, and he also stated that matter is the objective correlate of the pure understanding; it is causality in general and nothing else, just as the understanding is immediate cognition of cause and effect in general and nothing else. Ultimately, the ideas of pure matter and pure causality become for him the necessary features for the **cognition** of the world as representation, a point he dramatized in a dialogue between matter and the subject at the close of the first chapter of the second volume of *The World as Will and Representation*. He also accounted for the permanency of matter by claiming that all coming to be and passing away occurs by virtue of causality and that the law of causality does not apply to itself. This entails, he thought, that the idea of coming to be and perishing does not apply to the objective correlate of causality, matter.

MĀYĀ, VEIL OF (*SCHLEIER DER MAJA*). Already by late 1818 and the first edition of *The World as Will and Representation*, Schopenhauer had drawn an equivalence between his idea of the *principium individuationis*, **space** and **time**, and the idea of the veil of *mā yā* found in **Hinduism**. Space and time are the necessary conditions for the possibility of plurality and, as such, are features of the world as **representation** and ordinary experience, and not the world as will. Schopenhauer understood the Hindu idea of *māyā* as illusion and the idea of the veil of *māyā* to refer to our ordinary **perception** and behavior in the world of illusion. Schopenhauer argued that the source of virtuous conduct and nobility of character, as well as the **denial of the will**, is a cognition that sees through the *principium individuationis* and abolishes the distinctions between a person's own individuality and that of others. This cognition, he said, reveals the identity of the **will** in all **appearances** and the illusory status of individuation. Schopenhauer wrote that for a person who has had this cognition, the veil of *māyā* has become transparent and he or she recognizes his or her self in all things. *See also* HINDUISM; TAT TVAM ASI.

MOTIVE (*MOTIV*). Since Schopenhauer believed that all changes in the world as **representation** follow from a sufficient **cause**, and since he also thought that all **animal** behavior occurs in the world as representation, he concluded that all changes in animal behavior follow from a sufficient cause. The causal relationship he saw in animal behavior is that of a motive, which he defined as **causality** passing through **cognition**, and the effect, which is a willed action. Although he recognized some changes in animal bodies as proceeding from a **cause** or **stimulus**, Schopenhauer argued that an animal is any entity susceptible to motives, such that its external movements and changes, which are peculiar and appropriate to its nature, always result as a consequence of a cognized or represented object, a motive, to which its **will** reacts. While Schopenhauer recognized a finely shaded and varied hierarchy expressed in animal life, which ranges from animals barely distinguishable from plants, through humans, he held that all animals have the capacity to have representations; that is, to have some degree of **consciousness of other things**.

Schopenhauer also held that there are two different types of motives, each of which constitutes a different kind of cognition. Nonhuman animals are moved by intuitive representations, their cognitions of the immediately present in **intuition**. Although this type of cognition can motivate humans, they are also susceptible to abstract representations or thoughts as motives. In other words, nonhuman or nonrational animals are susceptible only to intuitive representations, whereas, humans or rational animals, due to their ability to formulate **concepts**, can transcend the immediately given by entertaining various possible alternative courses of action in any situation. This ability to deliberate, Schopenhauer claimed, gives humans a **freedom** of sorts when compared to nonhuman animals, who are always motivated by the actually present, but this freedom from causal determination of their actions is only relative, since human action is always determined by a sufficient motive.

MUSIC (*MUSIK*). Schopenhauer attributed a deep significance to the **arts**, and of all the arts, he assigned the greatest significance to music. The other arts communicate **Platonic Ideas**, the adequate objectivity of the **will**. Music, however, presents a copy (*Abbild*) of the will. Consequently, he viewed music as more metaphysically revealing than all of the other arts. These other arts, he said, present shadows while music bestows reality. Due to its revelatory power, he emphasized a direct kinship between **philosophy** and music, and he argued that if you would express in tones what is stated in philosophy, you would have music. Both communicate the nature of the world, philosophy through **concepts** and music through sounds. Just as he argued that the world as **representation** is objectified will, he argued that the world as representation could be viewed as objectified music. For this reason, he concluded that music makes every picture or scene from real life and the world more significant.

MYSTICISM (*MYSTICISMUS*). Schopenhauer defined mysticism as the **consciousness** of the identity of one's own inner being or essence with that of all things, or with the essence of the world. Like traditional religious accounts of mysticism, he viewed mysticism as the apprehension of something beyond the spatiotemporal world; he held that it brings serenity and tranquility to the mystic; and he claimed that this consciousness is beyond description. He also found a close connection between mysticism, **asceticism**, and **quietism**. Each expresses the **denial of the will**, brings **resignation**, and signifies **salvation**. Although he eschewed trying to describe the mystical experience, he recommended to his readers that they become familiar with the writings of mystics found in all the great **religious** traditions of the world, since he believed that the conduct of mystics expresses the mystical experience. But he also warned that they try to say what cannot be said and they clothe their common insight according to the doctrinal and ritualistic contexts of their particular religious traditions.

– N –

NATURAL SCIENCES, THE (*DIE NATURWISSENSCHAFTEN*). Schopenhauer had a keen interest in the natural sciences. His interest in science probably predates his enrollment as a student of medicine at the University of Göttingen in 1809. At his death, his library contained approximately 200 titles on scientific topics, ranging from botany, chemistry, comparative anatomy, geology, optics, physics, physiology, to zoology. Moreover, his philosophical writings and notebooks include references to scientific works that were not found in his library, something that further illustrates the breadth of his reading of scientific literature. He considered his second publication, ***On Vision and Colors***, as broadly scientific in nature, and it includes descriptions of a variety of **color** experiments, some of which he conducted with **Johann Wolfgang von Goethe**, that had been employed to substantiate his

color theory. Because this work was more "scientific" than philosophical, he claimed that it was not required reading for understanding his **philosophy**. In the second volume of *Parerga and Paralipomena*, in his essay "On Philosophy and Natural Science," Schopenhauer displayed his broad knowledge of the natural sciences as well as his tendency to assemble data drawn from science to express his metaphysics and his inclination to formulate scientific hypotheses of his own.

While it might be true that Schopenhauer did not have a thorough and profound understanding of scientific investigations of the world, it should also be observed that, compared to most of his philosophical contemporaries, he was more scientifically informed. Indeed, he chided the *bête noire* of his philosophy, **Georg Wilhelm Friedrich Hegel**, for his ignorance of science, and **Friedrich Wilhelm Joseph von Schelling**, for whose philosophy of nature he had some respect, he accused of secretly abstracting a metaphysics from science and pretending to find *a priori* what he had learned *a posteriori*. Philosophers, he thought, need both to keep track of the best findings of science and to develop a philosophy that accommodates these findings. But if the philosopher needs to be scientifically literate, the scientist also needs to be philosophically literate. Many of his scientific contemporaries failed this requirement, he argued, and due to their ignorance of philosophy (especially of **Immanuel Kant**'s), they tended to express either a shallow and crude form of **materialism** or views derived from their catechism, either of which intruded in ways that distorted the soundness of their views.

The work that probably best illustrates Schopenhauer's interest in science and the relationship he perceived between philosophy and science is *On the Will in Nature*. Its subtitle, "A Discussion of the Corroborations from the Empirical Sciences That the Author's Philosophy Has Received since Its First Appearance," highlights his belief that anything worthy of calling itself philosophy must be consistent with the best results of science. But this subtitle is misleading, if one infers that he was simply using science to confirm the **truth** of his philosophy. While this is part of what he attempted to do, he also had a greater goal, that of providing a metaphysical grounding or explanation for scientific explanations of the world. Thus he claimed that physics, in the broadest sense of the term, requires the support of a system of metaphysics. Both metaphysics and science are empirical, Schopenhauer argued, and both must ultimately appeal to experience to justify and meaningfully express their claims. Metaphysics, however, aims both to provide a comprehensive explanation of the totality of experience as well as to express this totality's meaning. Science, he asserted, is concerned with particular experiences.

In the second book of the first volume of *The World as Will and Representation*, he divided the natural sciences into two branches. The morphological sciences, such as "natural history," botany and zoology, develop classification schemes by uniting particular things into recurring natural kinds. The etiological sciences, such as physiology, chemistry, and physics, extrapolate **causal laws** by observing regularities within the changing natural world. Ultimately, both morphological and etiological accounts of the world require the use of terms that are scientifically unexplainable. To account for natural kinds, such as granite or tiger, so that they do not seem as "hieroglyphics that are not understood," and natural forces, such as gravity and electricity, which Schopenhauer said, are treated by science as "occult qualities," he appealed to his doctrine of **Platonic Ideas** as philosophical or metaphysical analogs to natural kinds and natural forces. Thereby, he thought, he had given a philosophical explanation of necessary and scientifically unexplainable elements of the scientific worldview. In *On the Will in Nature*, he took a more direct approach. He attempted to show that particular natural kinds are particular instantiations of willing and natural forces are identical to our **self-conscious** experience of our **will**. In particular, he claimed that the chapter "Physical Astronomy" discussed with greater distinctness than anywhere else the fundamental truth of his philosophy, that the world is will, and that he brought it down to the empirical knowledge of nature.

Lastly, Schopenhauer's attitude toward science is also reflected in the way that he saw science related to other ways of viewing the world. Like our ordinary **cognitions** of the world, science operates within the scope of the **principle of sufficient reason**. It is, however, superior to our ordinary and everyday cognition of things, which is colored by the will, that is, is "interested," viewing natural things as potential means for sating or frustrating our desires. Thus, he claimed, ordinary cognition of the world focuses on particular things at a specific time and place and within definite causal relationships, especially their particular effects on one's own **weal** and **woe**. While science is concerned with spatial, temporal objects standing in causal relationships, it connotes for him a more "objective" form of cognition compared to ordinary cognition, because it seeks to understand the world as **representation** by subsuming numerous particular things within classification schemes (morphology) or by formulating causal laws or universal rules describing necessary changes of **matter** (etiology). Still, he believed that science involves interested cognition, since scientific knowledge is ultimately practical; it provides more efficient means than ordinary cognition for reshaping and manipulating the world to better serve human needs. **Art**, however, has a higher cognitive value than science, Schopenhauer argued, since it depicts Platonic Ideas, and **aesthetic contemplation** of great works of art transcends the principle of sufficient reason and interested cognition. **Tragedy** and **music**, however, can express the nature of the will, the essence of the world, better than the other arts, plus they can counsel **resignation**. Thus, unlike science, art is metaphysically revelatory, expressing the nature of reality and its meaning, neither of which can be done by science. The pinnacle of **knowledge** for Schopenhauer is philosophy (of course!), which duplicates in **concepts** that which music expresses in tones.

NIETZSCHE, FRIEDRICH (1844–1900). Nietzsche's philosophy was greatly influenced by Schopenhauer's, and he may be the philosopher Nietzsche knew best. He quoted extensively from the full range of Schopenhauer's *oeuvre*, including his *Nachlass*, and there are numerous allusions to Schopenhauer within his writings that do not mention Schopenhauer specifically.

Nietzsche reported that he discovered in a bookstore, quite by accident, Schopenhauer's *The World as Will and Representation* in October 1865, but it is likely that he had been exposed to Schopenhauer that same year during his summer at the University of Bonn. Nietzsche was captivated by Schopenhauer's honest recognition of the ubiquity of suffering and **death** and the means by which he used this recognition to raise questions about the meaning and the value of existence. He was also attracted to Schopenhauer's atheism, his brilliant writing style, his commitment to speak his **truth** even when it did not please the world, and his high estimation of the value of **art**, especially his high estimation of the cognitive value of **music**. Nietzsche's enthusiasm for Schopenhauer's **philosophy** was also enhanced by the ascendancy of the latter's philosophy in the intellectual world and by the admiration of his friends and colleagues for Schopenhauer. The Swiss cultural historian, **Jakob Burckhardt**, Nietzsche's colleague at the University of Basel, and Nietzsche's friend, **Paul Deussen**, a German philologist, philosopher and Indologist, were also devotees of Schopenhauer, with Deussen becoming so through Nietzsche's endorsements. **Richard Wagner**'s love for Schopenhauer also helped create the grounds for his friendship with Nietzsche.

In 1874, Nietzsche published *Schopenhauer as Educator* as one of his "untimely meditations." In that work Nietzsche presented Schopenhauer as a knight in the service of the truth who heroically spoke his "truths" to a world too timid to hear them. Nietzsche claimed that he presented a "philosophy to live by." Yet Nietzsche's attitudes toward Schopenhauer's philosophy were ambivalent, and as his thought matured, he radically distanced himself from his "only educator, the *great* Arthur Schopenhauer," and he came to view Schopenhauer (and Wagner) as his antipodes. He diagnosed Schopenhauer's philosophy as nihilistic and as an expression of the decadence and sickness of its author, whom he saw as too weak to affirm the **will to life**. Consequently he wrote openly and directly against Schopenhauer's morality of **compassion**, his view of the moral significance of life and the world, and his promotion of the **denial of the will**. Against Schopenhauer, Nietzsche condemned compassion, argued that the world and life have no intrinsic moral significance, and promoted the **affirmation of the will** as the ultimate human accomplishment. Yet, despite Nietzsche's reversals and oppositions to many of Schopenhauer's fundamental ideas, his confrontation with Schopenhauer's philosophy aided him significantly in the development of his own views, and elements of Schopenhauer's thought, such as his voluntarism, hard determinism, and his conception of the will, as well as some of his methodological strategies remained viable within Nietzsche's thought. *See also* WITTGENSTEIN, LUDWIG.

NOUMENON. Schopenhauer censured what he saw as **Immanuel Kant**'s conflation of the terms "noumenon" and **"thing in itself,"** just has he did with Kant's use of the terms **"phenomenon"** and "**appearance**." By "noumenon," he referred to that which is merely thought or is conceivable, and he did not use this term to refer to either the thing in itself or the **will**.

– O –

OBJECT. *See* SUBJECT AND OBJECT.

ON THE BASIS OF MORALITY. *See* BASIS OF MORALITY, ON THE.

ON THE FOURFOLD ROOT OF THE PRINCIPLE OF SUFFICIENT REASON. *See* FOURFOLD ROOT OF THE PRINCIPLE OF SUFFICIENT REASON, ON THE.

ON THE FREEDOM OF THE HUMAN WILL. *See* FREEDOM OF THE HUMAN WILL, ON THE.

ON VISION AND COLORS. *See* VISION AND COLORS: AN ESSAY ON.

ON THE WILL IN NATURE. *See* WILL IN NATURE, ON THE.

OPTIMISM (*OPTIMISMUS*). Like the term "**pessimism**," Schopenhauer used this term infrequently in his philosophy. All of his references to it are, however, derisive. Optimism, he said, is a wicked way of thinking in light of the unspeakable suffering expressed in the world; it is a false and pernicious way of thinking. Schopenhauer understood each of the following claims, and any of their conjunctions, as expressing optimism: the Leibnizian claim that this is the best of all possible worlds; that **history** reveals a general progress to some desirable state of human existence; that the world is **God (pantheism)**; or that a human life can be happy. In contrast to each of these claims, Schopenhauer argued that he had demonstrated the following: this is the worst of all possible worlds that are capable of sustained existence; **history** only reveals the same—the wretchedness of existence, suffering and **death** clothed in new dress; the world is better conceived as an expression of **evil** than an expression of the divine; and lastly, a happy life is impossible. He also argued that the fundamental difference between **religions** is whether they are optimistic or pessimistic. Optimistic religions, he claimed, present the world as justified by itself and, on this basis, they praise and commend the world. Naturally, he favored pessimistic religions, ones that view the world as a consequence of guilt and which, due to the recognition of the wretchedness of existence, conclude that the world ought not to be. Indeed, he thought that any of the claims of optimism are contradicted by the wretchedness and vanity of existence. *See also* BUDDHISM; CHRISTIANITY; HINDUISM; JUDAISM; SPINOZA, BARUCH.

OUGHT (*SOLLEN*). Following **John Locke**, Schopenhauer held that every ought derives all meaning and sense solely in reference to another who threatens **punishment** or promises reward. Although he saw a close connection between the concepts of **duties** and obligations, unlike an obligation, duties were viewed by him as voluntarily assumed liabilities for which the duty-holder obtains a right, but an obligation rests on pure compulsion. That is, an employee has a duty to provide labor for his or her employer in exchange for a wage, but a slave has no duties, since a slave has no rights and the slave's labor is compelled by a master. Because Schopenhauer viewed obligations as based on the **will** of another capable of punishing or rewarding, he saw all obligations as conditional and connately affective due to fear of punishment or the desire for a reward. He rejected **Immanuel Kant**'s ethics of duty, which stated categorical or unconditional moral obligations. He argued that the idea of an unconditional or absolute obligation is logically contradictory, like the concept of "wooden iron," and that all actions performed out of duty are self-interested, and done to avoid punishment or to obtain a reward.

– P –

PANTHEISM (*PANTHEISMUS*). Although Schopenhauer viewed his philosophy as sharing an insight expressed in pantheism, namely, that the inner essence of everything in the world is one, he radically distanced himself from pantheism. He found pantheism to have committed at least four grave mistakes. First, by claiming everything is **God**, or that God is everything, he argued that pantheists attempt to explain the world, which we know, by something that is unknown. Consequently, he claimed that the pantheists' God is simply an unknown X and, because of this, calling the world "God" does nothing to explain it. In contrast, he claimed, his **will** is something intimately cognized or known, and as such, serves as the key for explaining what is not known. Second, and this was probably his greatest objection to pantheism, the deification of the world, that is, its **optimism**, is incompatible with the wretchedness of existence, he argued, since it implies that the world is justified as it is and that the world is as it **ought** to be. In this regard, he claimed, the pantheist has to sophisticate away the **evils** of the world and has no basis for an **ethics**. Conversely, he averred that his **philosophy** shows both that the evils of this world are due to its being the objectification of the will and that the world ought not to be. Third, by claiming that everything is God, pantheists cannot recognize the possibility he held open within his doctrine of the **denial of the will**. Fourth, he alleged that the pantheist is unable to account for the appearance of things revealed in **perception**, or how this one appears as many, whereas he claimed that his philosophy solves this problem by showing how the **intellect** accounts for the appearance of plurality and how the intellect is simply the servant of the will. *See also* PESSIMISM; SPINOZA, BARUCH; and THEISM.

PARERGA AND PARALIPOMENA (*PARERGA UND PAR-ALIPOMENA*). This two volume work accomplished something that no other of Schopenhauer's books provided. It drew a readership to his writings, and it helped to usher in the fame for which Schopenhauer had longed so desperately. After the failure of the second edition of *The World as Will and Representation* (1844), Schopenhauer feared the loss of his intellectual capacities, and he sensed his own mortality. Consequently, he adopted a new strategy to draw a readership to his **philosophy**. In 1850 he approached his publisher **F. A. Brockhaus** with the manuscript for *Parerga and Paralipomena*, telling him he had written a "philosophy for the world" that would draw a readership for his other works and break through the silent opposition to his thought by the "guild of professors of philosophy." He also reminded Brockhaus that he was not the only person who believed that his work was the best produced in the century. Although Schopenhauer offered the work to Brockhaus *gratis*, Brockhaus was not moved by Schopenhauer's arguments and declined the manuscript. Schopenhauer sought other publishers, and largely through the efforts of one of his early followers, **Julius Frauenstädt**, the Berlin publisher A. W. Hayn accepted the book, and he published an edition of 750 copies in 1851, for which Schopenhauer accepted 10 copies as the author's honorarium.

Parerga and Paralipomena managed to draw a readership when it first appeared, and two of its readers would play an active role in bringing Schopenhauer's philosophy to the popular consciousness. In April 1852, John Oxenford wrote a favorable review of *Parerga and Paralipomena* for the British *The Westminster Review*, when George Eliot was responsible for most of the German reviews published in the journal. One year later, Oxenford would publish a general review of Schopenhauer's philosophy, "Iconoclasm in German Philosophy," in the same journal. In May 1853, **E. O. Lindner**, who became well disposed to Schopenhauer's philosophy after reading *Parerga and Paralipomena*, published his British wife's German translation of Oxenford's essay in the German *Vossischen Zeitung*. Schopenhauer's philosophy caught fire, and the general demand for his work enabled him to publish new editions of all his earlier books during the next few years. Although he had originally planned a second edition of *Parerga and Paralipomena*, he did not live long enough to do it. Frauenstädt, however, published a second edition in 1862, in which he incorporated materials from Schopenhauer's notes.

Schopenhauer justified the pedantic title of *Parerga and Paralipomena* by claiming that a Latin title was required for work written for scholars. The title literally means, "subordinate work and things left out" of his philosophy proper. In the preface, Schopenhauer wrote that some of his essays would have found their way into his earlier philosophical works had they not come so late. Others, he said, would not find a place within his more systematic works, due to their subject matter. In either case, Schopenhauer asserted that all of the essays would be interesting and intelligible to readers unfamiliar with his more comprehensive works (except for "a few passages"). For readers acquainted with his philosophy proper, Schopenhauer claimed, the essays "left out" of his systematic works would furnish additional explanations for his ideas, and the "subordinate" essays would illuminate his philosophy, since everything that emanated from his mind helped to elucidate his philosophy.

The first volume, the "*Parerga*," contains six essays. The first two, "Sketch of a History of the Doctrine of the Ideal and Real," and "Fragments for the History of Philosophy," serve as glosses on modern philosophy and the history of Western philosophy. The former details Schopenhauer's analysis of what he saw as the major problem in modern philosophy, the philosophy from **René Descartes** through **Immanuel Kant**, the relationship of the ideal to the real, the relationship between our **perception** of things and things that exist independently from perception. In the essay he surveyed Descartes, Nicolas de Malebranche, **Baruch Spinoza**, Gottfried Leibniz, **John Locke**, **George Berkeley**, **David Hume**, and Kant on this issue, and he concluded that his philosophy alone solved this problem by showing that the ideal or the **representation**, and the real or the represented thing, are the **will**. Schopenhauer also showed his contempt for his contemporaries, **Johann Gottlieb Fichte**, **Friedrich Wilhelm Joseph von Schelling**, and **Georg Wilhelm Friedrich Hegel**, by relegating their views on this issue to a hypercritical and harsh appendix to this essay. In the latter essay, Schopenhauer surveyed the history of Western philosophy from the pre-Socratics through his own philosophy. The 13st section, "Some further elucidations of the Kantian philosophy," while reiterating ideas found in his other writings, provides a useful summary of his views on Kant, and it details the relationship he saw between Locke's, Kant's, and his own philosophy. The 14th section, "Some observations of my own philosophy," recounts the Kantian basis of his philosophy and highlights its "consistency," and it endeavors to account for the reason why his philosophy might appear to have some kinship to Fichte's and Schelling's philosophies due to its Kantian basis. Both of the historical essays that begin *Parerga and Paralipomena* can be read as Schopenhauer's attempt to show that his philosophy belongs intimately within the main philosophical traditions of the West and that it also represents its highest development.

The third essay, "On Philosophy at the University," is a harsh polemic against academic philosophy, where Schopenhauer decried the state of philosophy within German universities. He recommended that only logic and a one-semester, descriptive course on the history of philosophy should be given at the university. This course of study should be sufficient, he thought, to serve as a student's guide for his or her own future course of study, which should consist of original works by genuine philosophers.

The fourth and fifth essays, "**Transcendent** Speculations on the Apparent Deliberateness in the Fate of Individuals," and "Essay on Spirit Seeing and Everything Connected Therewith," are very curious writings. The former, Schopenhauer said, could be termed a "metaphysical fantasy," in which one gropes around in the dark for an explanation of that which seems to appear as a form of supernatural guidance of the events within an individual's life. Schopenhauer, who prided himself with maintaining a fully **immanent** philosophy, one that did not transcend the bounds of possible experience, cautiously and circumspectly advanced a transcendent claim by concluding that this invisible guidance that seems to direct individuals' lives suggests that each individual has a life that expresses the will's turning away from life. The latter essay expresses his deep interest in occult phenomena and in it he offers an idealistic account of such phenomena as spirit seeing, clairvoyance, animal magnetism, sympathetic cures, table-rapping, and telekinesis, by suggesting that the basis of these phenomena connotes a *nexus metaphysicus* underlying the physical order of things.

While Schopenhauer used the last two essays to speculate and opine in ways he would not have used in his philosophical writings proper, in the sixth and concluding essay of the first volume of *Parerga and Paralipomena*, "Aphorisms on the Wisdom of Life," he formally suspended "the higher metaphysical-ethical standpoint of his real philosophy," which concludes that nonexistence is preferable to existence, to write an **eudaemonism**, which details a life whose existence is more preferable than its nonexistence. This is Schopenhauer's "philosophy for the world," and it was the most popular of all his essays. He argued that a relatively happy and pleasant life is derived from three sources: what a person is, what a person has, and what a person represents, that is, how a person is regarded by others. Ultimately, Schopenhauer concludes that central to living well is what a person is, and he recommends that one needs to know oneself, one's own deepest tendencies and character, and to mold a life most suitable for one's own personality.

The second volume of this work, the so-called "*Paralipomena*," consists of 31 chapters and concludes with a set of poems drawn primarily from Schopenhauer's early years. The first 16 chapters are supplements to his philosophical writings and cover topics as diverse as philosophy and its method, observations on the antithesis of the **thing in itself** and appearances, **ethics**, philosophy and **science**, **color** theory, remarks on the vanity of existence, **suicide**, and **religion**. The remaining 15 chapters are more obliquely related to his philosophy, containing his observations on Sanskrit literature, archaeology, mythology, **aesthetics**, literary criticism, physiognomy, among other subjects. The 27th chapter contains his infamously misogynistic essay, "On **Women**." Although Schopenhauer recognized that he was a philosopher and not a poet, he concluded the work with a set of poems. He did so, he said, because poetry communicates more freely and openly than prose one's feelings in a personal and human way, and those who may desire a more personal acquaintance with the author of his philosophy would benefit from his poetry.

PAYNE, ERIC F. J. (1895–1983). Payne was a professional soldier who retired as a lieutenant colonel in the British Army. He became the foremost translator of Schopenhauer, having translated into English all of Schopenhauer's books and most of his *Nachlass*. Payne first read Schopenhauer in 1930, when he returned from England after a 10-year tour of duty in India. At that time, his father, Francis, gave him a collection of essays from *Parerga and Paralipomena*, which had been translated by Bailey Saunders. Payne continued to read Schopenhauer, drawn by the deep affinities of Schopenhauer's thought and **Buddhism**, to which he had been exposed at home, since his father had been the secretary of the Buddhist Society of Great Britain and Ireland and the editor of the *Buddhist Review*. Payne decided to learn German to read Schopenhauer in the original, and he soon became dissatisfied with the quality of existing translations. (His assessment of early English translations can be found in his "Schopenhauer in English: A Critical Survey of Existing Translations," *Schopenhauer-Jahrbuch*, 1949–1950.)

Payne began translating Schopenhauer when he served a second tour of duty in India, during World War II. In 1942, his translation, *On Vision and Colours*, appeared through an obscure Indian publisher. After the war, he was posted in northern Germany, and in 1947 he became personally acquainted with the great Schopenhauer scholar, **Arthur Hübscher**. The two men became fast friends, and Hübscher encouraged Payne to continue his translating. (After Payne's death, Hübscher wrote that Payne was the best, most loyal friend a person could have.)

Yet Payne found it almost as difficult to have his translations of Schopenhauer published as Schopenhauer had with the originals. His translations were published by various publishers and some appeared only after his death. *The World as Will and Representation* appeared in 1958, through an obscure publisher in the United States, Falcon's Wing Press (Indian Hills, Colorado). Its present publisher, Dover (New York), obtained its rights in 1966. In 1965 Payne's translation of *On the Basis of Morality* was published by Bobbs-Merrill (Indianapolis, revised edition by Berghahn [Oxford], 1995). Both *On the Fourfold Root of the Principle of Sufficient Reason* (La Salle, Illinois., Open Court) and *Parerga and Paralipomena* (Oxford, Clarendon Press) appeared in 1974. After Payne's death, and through the efforts of his daughter, Valerie Egret-Payne, Angelika Hübscher, Bryan Magee, and others, Berg (Oxford, New York) issued his translation of Schopenhauer's *Nachlass, Manuscript Remains* (4 volumes, 1988), *On the Will in Nature* (1992), and *On Vision and Colors* (1994). Cambridge University Press published *Prize Essay on the Freedom of the Will* in 1999, thereby making all of Schopenhauer's philosophical writings available through the hands of a single translator.

Due to his important and tireless work on Schopenhauer, Payne was elected an honorary member, then an honorary vice president, and ultimately an honorary president of the Schopenhauer-Gesellschaft (1980). Payne's papers are located in the Special Collections Department, University of Iowa Libraries, Iowa City, Iowa.

PEDERASTY (*PÄDERASTIE*). In the third edition to *The World as Will and Representation* (1859), Schopenhauer added an untitled appendix to chapter 44 of the second volume, "The Metaphysics of **Sexual Love**." In that essay he had briefly remarked that pederasty was a "misguided instinct," since it was contrary to the natural end of human sexual impulse, which is reproduction. After further reflection on it, Schopenhauer claimed that pederasty presents a paradox. The tendency to pederasty appears at all times and in all cultures, and it is ineradicable even in societies that condemn and punish it. For this reason, he concluded that the tendency to pederasty must arise from human nature itself even though it is contrary to nature's strongest interest, the reproduction of new life. To resolve this paradox, Schopenhauer claimed to have discovered the secret that lies at the roots of pederasty. The secret of this "unnatural," natural tendency, he argued, is that it appears in individuals in a decided proportion to the decline in the ability to beget strong and healthy children. Thus he argued that a tendency to pederasty appears in two stages of life, in adolescence and old age, when individuals are either two young or too old to produce healthy children. By directing the sexual impulse away from the procreation of children, the species itself is benefited by not having individuals produce weak, deformed, and short-lived offspring. In this way, Schopenhauer concluded that pederasty only appears to work against the ends of nature; in reality it serves nature's ends indirectly. It prevents the production of miserable and unfit children who would threaten the viability of the species.

Schopenhauer knew that his treatment of pederasty would likely shock his readers. But pederasty was a fact, he argued, and as it was his aim to investigate **truth** everywhere and to get to the bottom of things, he felt bound to acknowledge the phenomenon and to draw the inevitable conclusions. He claimed that his explanation of pederasty cast new light on the inner essence of nature and that the only metaphysical objection to pederasty is that it prevents the creation of new individuals who might **deny the will** and obtain **salvation**. He closed his discussion by chiding his contemporaries. Because he discussed pederasty, professors of philosophy could slander him by claiming that he defended and commended it.

PERCEPTION. *See* INTUITION.

PESSIMISM (*PESSIMISMUS*). This is the most frequently used term to refer to Schopenhauer's **philosophy**, and he is typically cited as the greatest pessimist in the Western philosophical tradition. Given the strong association between his philosophy and pessimism, it is somewhat ironic to note that both the terms "pessimism" or "pessimistic" occur infrequently in his writings and that he never used them to describe his philosophy in any of the books that he prepared for publication. The word "pessimism" only became part of Schopenhauer's philosophical vocabulary after 1827, and the only time he used it to describe his philosophy was in a note from 1828, where he wrote that "my doctrine is pessimism," (*Manuscript Remains*, vol. III, "*Adversaria*," para. 66). He made this remark within a comparison and contrast between his philosophy and **pantheism**, which he said was "essentially **optimism**." He would use many of the claims made in this note later in the second volume of *The World as Will and Representation* (1844) to distinguish between his philosophy and pantheism. While he continued to identify pantheism with optimism, he did not repeat the claim that his philosophy was pessimism, although he claimed that the optimism of pantheism was expressed in the view that the world is divine and excellent, that the world is, therefore, praiseworthy and commendable. In contrast to this, he argued, his philosophy honestly recognized the wretchedness of this world; that it is **evil**; that it is something that ought not to be; and that it is, therefore, something we need to overcome. This cluster of claims, moreover, were the same type as those he used in his 1828 note to describe his "doctrine" as pessimism.

It is odd that Schopenhauer did not contrast the optimism of pantheism with the pessimism of his philosophy in his main work. The reason for this may be that his most robust use of the term "pessimism" in *The World as Will and Representation* was within the discussion of **religion**. In the 18th chapter of the second volume of his main work, "On the Metaphysical Need of Humans," he argued that the fundamental difference between religions is not whether they are monotheistic, polytheistic, pantheistic, or atheistic, but whether they are optimistic or pessimistic. Optimistic religions, he said, present the existence of the world as justified by itself and they, therefore, praise or commend the world. Conversely, he identified pessimistic religions as advancing the claims that the world is a consequence of guilt and that it is something that really ought not to be, basing these claims on the observation that pain and **death**, intrinsic features of the world, cannot exist in the eternal, original, and immutable order of things or in that which "in every respect **ought** to be." Of course, Schopenhauer favored "pessimistic" religions, and he claimed that genuine **Christianity**, **Hinduism**, and **Buddhism** are pessimistic.

Indeed, he claimed that he demonstrated the **truth** of that which is allegorically expressed by these religions. Thus it is not a surprise to find that when his friends would refer to his philosophy as "pessimistic" in letters to Schopenhauer, he said nothing to dissuade them from this view.

PHENOMENON. Schopenhauer criticized what he viewed as **Immanuel Kant**'s tendency to refer to **appearances** as "phenomena," just as he did Kant's use of the term **"noumenon"** to denote the **thing in itself**. Schopenhauer understood "phenomenon" to refer to that which is perceivable, in contrast to that which is conceivable (noumenon). There is a tendency common to the Anglophone literature on Schopenhauer to use the contrasts noumenon/phenomenon to do duty for his distinction between the thing in itself and appearance, which is something Schopenhauer did not do. The basis of this confusion is likely due to **E. F. J. Payne**'s translation of "*Erscheinung /Erscheinungen*" as "phenomenon/phenomena," whereas it should have been "appearance/appearances." Since the term "*Erscheinung*" is a major term of craft in Schopenhauer's philosophy, the term "phenomenon" appears frequently in Payne's translations. This seems to have led many of Schopenhauer's Anglophone commentators to use the Kantian contrast between phenomenon and noumenon to characterize Schopenhauer's distinctions between appearance and the thing in itself, as well as Schopenhauer's distinction between **representation** and the **will**.

PHILANTHROPY (*MENSCHENLIEBE*). **Justice** and philanthropy are Schopenhauer's two cardinal virtues, the virtues from which all other virtues are derived. *Omnes, quantum potes, juva*, the injunction to help everyone as much as you can, summarizes the disposition of individuals who expressed the virtue of philanthropy. He attributed the virtue of philanthropy to individuals who were highly susceptible to **compassion**. While he also claimed that the virtue of justice followed from compassion, he argued that philanthropic individuals were more compassionate than just individuals. Compassion is always a response to another's suffering or **woe**, and when it is expressed in just individuals, he called it negative and the first degree of compassion, since in this regard compassion simply prevents a person from doing something which would harm another. Compassion as expressed in philanthropy, however, he referred to as positive and the second degree of compassion. In other words, compassion moves a philanthropic person to help or aid another.

PHILOSOPHY (*PHILOSOPHIE*). Schopenhauer called humans the *animal metaphysicum*, a designation that reflects both a kinship and difference between humans and other **animals**. Unlike other animals, humans possess the faculty of **reason** and, therefore, have the capacity to formulate **concepts**, and thereby, the ability to reflect on their past and present, and to anticipate their future. Other animals, he said, lack this capacity and their **cognitions** are confined to the immediately present. The result of this, he claimed, is that animals simply flow with the course of life. Because humans can reflect on their existence, they can marvel at what they do, and more deeply, at what they are. Thus Schopenhauer came to agree with both **Plato** and **Aristotle**. Philosophy begins with wonder or astonishment, and he found the disposition to philosophize connected to the human capacity to wonder at ordinary events and the daily occurrences in life, but in a manner that seeks to understand the totality of things, the universal. The philosophical disposition is different, he argued, than that expressed by investigators in the **natural sciences**, who marvel at only select and rare phenomena and who attempt to relate these specific phenomena to those already known better. Philosophy, he argued, has the peculiarity of presupposing absolutely nothing as known, and it views everything as equally strange and problematic. While he claimed that the basis of both science and philosophy is experience, he also held that the natural sciences are confined to experiences of the external world and that science ultimately employs explanations of natural phenomena that are both necessary and scientifically unexplainable. Philosophy begins, he asserted, when science ends, and provides a deeper explanation of the totality of experience by explaining that which science cannot.

Schopenhauer also held that the form of wonder that drives philosophical inquiry has to be conditioned by a higher development of the **intellect** than that found in the majority of people. The intellect of most people is directly tied to their **will**s, and so most people view things subjectively, that is, as possible means to either satisfy or frustrate their desires. The philosopher, he held, has an overabundance of intellect and therefore, is capable of looking at things objectively, a hallmark of the **genius**. Even more deeply, he argued, the disposition to philosophize is tied to the recognition of the wretchedness of life and the ubiquity of **death**. This recognition provides the strongest impulse for philosophical reflection and metaphysical explanations of the world, he argued, so that in the absence of death and misery, he hypothesized that it would not possibly occur to anyone to ask why the world exists as it does, and humans would be much like other animals; they would just take life as a matter of course. But of course, the world is not free from pain and human life is not eternal, and therefore, he claimed that the deep human need for metaphysics is ultimately tied to the recognition of the miserable state of existence itself. By emphasizing the vital role played by death and suffering in philosophical speculation, Schopenhauer would claim that philosophy seeks to solve the ever-disquieting puzzle of existence and seeks to understand both why the world is as it is and what this means. **Religion**, he held, shares this program with philosophy, but with one important difference. Religion employs myths and allegories to solve this problem, whereas philosophy requires the demonstrable **truth**. The objective stance of the philosopher, he held, seeks nothing less than the truth.

The faculty of reason not only makes philosophical speculation possible, Schopenhauer viewed it as being the faculty of philosophy. He compared philosophy to **art**, moreover, since both of them simply seek to reproduce the world. The difference, he said, concerns their respective media. **Music**, for example, does so in tone and philosophy in concepts. Thus while often using the terms metaphysics and philosophy as synonyms, he defined metaphysics as **knowledge** (*Wissen*) drawn from our **consciousness of other things** and the facts of **self-consciousness**, which is deposited in concepts. Since consciousness of other things and self-consciousness represent the sources of all possible experiences, he viewed philosophy as ultimately the complete recapitulation of the totality of experience presented in abstract concepts. By tying philosophy to experience, Schopenhauer saw himself as remaining faithful to **Immanuel Kant**'s requirements that philosophy must remain **immanent**, that is, it must remain within the bounds of all possible experiences, and it must never become **transcendent**, that is, it must never appeal to things outside the scope of all possible experience. Although Schopenhauer retained his allegiance to Kant, he redefined metaphysics as the correct explanation of experience as a whole, and he rejected Kant's claim that metaphysics seeks knowledge that goes beyond the realm of all possible experiences. Since he held that the bounds of meaningful philosophical discourse is also the bounds of experience, Schopenhauer also recognized that his philosophy left many questions unanswered, questions such as, "Why is that which is proven as a fact as it is and is not otherwise?" or "How far do the roots individually go in the being-in-itself of the world?" Questions of this type require an answer that transcends the bounds of experience. His philosophy, he said, ranges only from the **affirmation of the will** through its denial. He could not say anything about what the will was prior to its appearance or after its denial.

Because Schopenhauer believed that philosophy must begin with experience, that which is given to consciousness, he held that philosophy must always be a form of **idealism**. When one is able to explain the connection between our experiences of other things and self-consciousness, he claimed, that one can give the correct explanation of the totality of experiences. The key for drawing the connection between these experiences is provided, he argued, by our self-conscious experience of our will. By appealing to this experience, Schopenhauer claimed that he could provide a uniform and unified explanation of the totality of experiences, which previously had appeared like a cryptograph. His philosophy, as one would expect him to claim, allows the correct deciphering of this cryptograph; it casts a uniform interpretation of all experiences without remainder. Unlike other philosophies, he argued that his enables its reader to recognize the agreement and consistency in what was hitherto a confusing and apparently inconsistent set of experiences. Since he held that his philosophy simply duplicates the world, he also stressed that it bears the same unity and consistency of its object. So unlike the **optimism** of Gottfried Wilhelm Leibniz, which is contradicted by the wretchedness of existence, and unlike **Baruch Spinoza**'s view of the world as the expression of an absolutely necessary substance, which is incompatible with our astonishment about the world's existence, Schopenhauer held that his philosophy is consistent with the world itself. More deeply, however, Schopenhauer also believed that his philosophy shows what it means to live in a world that is the expression of the will. It shows that it is best not to be, an observation that he called the most important of all truths and something allegorically expressed by genuine **Christianity** and **Buddhism**.

Schopenhauer also discussed the various divisions or areas of philosophy. In order to present the correct explanation of the nature and significance of the totality of experiences, one has to investigate the faculty of **cognition** itself, since it is there that experience, the material of philosophy, is given. Consequently, it is necessary, he argued, to understand the nature of cognition, the laws of its application, and the validity and limits of cognition. This sort of investigation, his **epistemology**, leads to the metaphysics of nature, which reveals that the external world expresses an essence distinct from appearances, and which discovers the will as the **thing in itself**. This leads, he noted, to the metaphysics of the **beautiful**, a consideration of the experience of the purest and most perfect representations, **Platonic Ideas**. Lastly, philosophy proceeds to the metaphysics of morals (*Sitten*), which is the manifestation of the will in human conduct, and which shows, again, that the ultimate inner essence of all representations is our own will.

Schopenhauer's discussion of the divisions of philosophy follows the very structure and sequence of the four books of the first volume and first edition of *The World as Will and Representation*. In the preface to that work, however, he also said that the form of that work was not essential to the communication of the **single thought** that his chief work expresses. His philosophy, he once claimed, is like Thebes with a hundred doors, each one of which opens a path to its center. This simile refers to his claim that a thorough investigation of anything in the world leads to the center of his philosophy, his metaphysics of the will.

Although Schopenhauer made numerous reflections about the nature of philosophy generally, and about his philosophy specifically, his most extensive reflections can be found in section 15 of the first volume of *The World as Will and Representation*, and in chapter 17, "On Man's Need for Metaphysics," and chapter 50, "Epiphilosophy," from its second volume; and in *Parerga and Paralipomena* in section 14, "Some Observations on my Philosophy," from the essay "Fragments for the History of Philosophy," and in the essay, "On Philosophy at the Universities," from the first volume; and in the second volume, the first essay, "Philosophy and its Method."

PLATO (427–347 B.C.E.). While Schopenhauer was a student at the University of Göttingen, his first philosophy professor, **G. E. Schulze**, recommended the study of Plato and **Immanuel Kant**. Schulze's advice brought him to the two philosophers whom he considered the greatest in the Western philosophical tradition. It might appear paradoxical that Schopenhauer would passionately embrace both Plato, the metaphysician *par excellence*, and Kant, the "all-crushing" (*Alleszermalmer*) critic of **metaphysics**, to use Moses Mendelssohn's pregnant designation, one that Schopenhauer also used to describe Kant. Yet Schopenhauer viewed both philosophers as simply taking separate paths to the same destination. Consequently, Schopenhauer reconciled their two "most paradoxical doctrines," Plato's theory of Ideas and Kant's **thing in itself**, by claiming that both philosophers recognized that the world revealed by the senses is merely a world of **appearances** and not true reality. Plato's Ideas and Kant's things in themselves are analogous, Schopenhauer argued, and his **philosophy** demonstrates the true relationship between **Platonic Ideas** and the thing in itself. His philosophy would elucidate the significant difference between the two by showing that Platonic Ideas are adequate grades of the objectification of the **will** as thing in itself. Each Idea, he claimed, is fully the will, but some Ideas express the nature of the will more clearly than others.

Schopenhauer's early study of Plato at Göttingen immediately made a deep and lasting impression. Already in his notes from that period (1810), he referred to "Plato the divine," a title he would later use in the preface to the first edition of *The World as Will and Representation* (1819). After telling his readers that a thorough acquaintance with Kant's philosophy was assumed by his own, he told them that they would be even better prepared to understand and be susceptible to what he had to say, had they also dwelt for a time "in the school of the divine Plato." At first blush, his recommendation appears strange because of the many ways Plato's philosophy was antithetical to Schopenhauer's. Plato emphasized the ultimately rational and divine nature of reality and Schopenhauer its irrational and demonic form. Plato exalted pure **reason** and degraded experience as the source of **knowledge**, and Schopenhauer adopted the reverse epistemological stance. Politics and the State assumed a central role in Plato's philosophy, and these themes were treated almost as an afterthought by Schopenhauer. Then there was the significance of **art**. Always suspicious about the affect of art on the masses, Plato was willing to censure art in his ideal State, insisting that it play a didactic role. He viewed art as imitating deceptive reality and as distancing its consumer from true reality, suggesting that it was twice removed from the Ideas. Schopenhauer called art the "flower of existence," and he claimed that it moved us away from our selfish yearnings and the stinging pressures of our desires. The contemplation of great works of art, Schopenhauer held, leads to objectivity and reveals metaphysical truth. It expresses Platonic Ideas, a claim that would have shocked his "divine Plato."

In his early reading of Plato, Schopenhauer sensed Plato's greatness in his drive to find unity among the diversity of things in the world, and to view the myriad of transitory particular items revealed by the sensory experience as the letters by which he read "the divine Ideas." These claims would later guide Schopenhauer's thought, and they would be reiterated in his account of **genius**, whose special gift, he said, was to cognize Platonic Ideas expressed by particular things, and in his description of his philosophy as a reading of experience as a panel of hieroglyphics, for which he discovered the key for a unified account in his metaphysics of the will. Throughout his entire life, Schopenhauer would also remain faithful to Plato's claim that philosophy began in wonder or astonishment about the world, and he would argue that pseudo-philosophers like **Johann Gottlieb Fichte** were moved to philosophy by perplexity about other philosophical systems. In particular, he found Socrates' claim in the *Phaedo* that philosophy was a preparation for **death** to mean that reflection on death motivated philosophical astonishment, a central claim of his own philosophy.

It is probably true to claim, however, that Schopenhauer admired Plato more than he did any of Plato's philosophical doctrines. Although he never subjected Plato's thought to the same robust criticism as he did Kant's, he never referred to himself as a "Platonist," but he did call himself a "Kantian." In particular, he decried Plato's censureship of art, especially poetry, and he rejected his view that we have an immortal and immaterial soul, whose exercise of pure reason is the source of knowledge, and a material body, whose sensory experiences are deceptive and an obstacle to knowledge. Indeed, in the fourth section of his "Fragments for the History of Philosophy," in the first volume of *Parerga and Paralipomena*, he credited Kant for crushing this nonsense, and he called his own philosophy the corrected analogue to Plato's withdrawing knowledge from all connection to the **body** and sensory perception. Even Schopenhauer's doctrine of Platonic Ideas was developed in a way to separate it from the view of its namesake. Thus Schopenhauer charged that because Plato had failed to distinguish between **concepts** and Ideas, his world of Ideas was overpopulated. For Schopenhauer, there are no Ideas of bodies, numbers, relationships, **colors**, and values; he recognized Ideas only for natural species and **forces of nature**. For him, Ideas are objectifications of the will, the will cognized in the most basic representational form, as an object for a subject, although they are contemplated outside the scope of the **principle of sufficient reason**. He also claimed that Kant's critique of rational psychology had exposed the errors behind Plato's views on the soul. Lastly, the ultimate status Plato attributed to the Idea of the **Good** or the **Beautiful** is reversed in Schopenhauer's recognition that the will is **evil**.

Still, despite the distance between Schopenhauer's and Plato's philosophies, Plato always remained Schopenhauer's philosophical hero. He credited Plato for his un-Platonic view of Platonic Ideas, and he always agreed with Plato that wonder prompts genuine philosophical speculation about the world. Plato, he said, lived for and not by philosophy. Consequently, he viewed Plato to be radically distinct from his *bête noire*, the professor of philosophy. Plato's mode of philosophy represented for him that of the genius who serenely and objectively contemplates Ideas, and who always seeks the universal and shuns the particular and transitory. Thus he cited Plato against his contemporaries, especially **Georg Wilhelm Friedrich Hegel**, and their attempt to base philosophy on **history**. The goal of philosophy is Platonic, he maintained; it is the search for that which appears in all things and is the same at all times.

PLATONIC IDEAS (*PLATONISCHE IDEEN*). The doctrine of Platonic Ideas plays a number of significant functions in Schopenhauer's

philosophy. It serves to provide an explanation of natural forces and natural species. In this regard, Ideas provide a philosophical explanation for necessary but scientifically unexplainable elements in the account of the world given by the **natural sciences**. The most extensive discussion of Platonic Ideas occurs, however, within Schopenhauer's **aesthetics**. Ideas function centrally within his discussion of the goal of **art**, his analysis of aesthetic **contemplation**, his explanation of **genius**, and his classification of the various visual and verbal arts.

Schopenhauer introduced the concept of Platonic Ideas in the 25th section of the first volume of *The World as Will and Representation*, where he defined an Idea as a definite and fixed grade of the **will**'s objectification, insofar as it is the **thing in itself** and foreign to plurality. He called these fixed grades of the will's objectification "Platonic Ideas," because they were what **Plato** called "Ideas." They are eternal forms or patterns that are imperfectly expressed in innumerable, transitory particulars or individuals. Ideas are, he said, the archetypes for a plurality of individual copies that arise and pass away through **causality**. Ideas are not cognized through the **principle of sufficient reason**. Thus he said Ideas are atemporal, aspatial, and not subject to change; an Idea always was, is, and will be. Like everything, Ideas are the will, according to Schopenhauer, but unlike Plato, they do not constitute ultimate reality, because they are objectifications of the will. Ideas are objects of **cognition**, and thus they are within the most elementary form of **representations**, the **subject and object** distinction. As such, they are not the will as thing in itself, but like the will, an Idea is nonplural. Our world, he said, is nothing but the **appearance** of Ideas in plurality, the Idea's entrance within the *principium individuationis*. To obtain insight into the nature of the world, Schopenhauer argued that it is necessary to learn to distinguish between the will as thing in itself, Ideas, and the appearance of Ideas, which comprise the world of changing, spatial-temporal particulars.

Schopenhauer's most robust discussion of Platonic Ideas occurs in the third book of *The World as Will and Representation*, which presents his **aesthetics**, or philosophy of art. In this book, he tells us that he will consider the representation independent of the principle of sufficient reason: "The Platonic Idea: The Object of Art." He prefaced this book with a quote from Plato's *Timeaus*: "What is that which eternally is, and which has no origin? And what is that which passes away, but in truth never is?" His answers to these Platonic queries are straightforward. The former are Platonic Ideas, the objects of aesthetic contemplation, and the latter are all the objects found in ordinary perception of the world, the cognition of changing, spatial and temporal objects.

Schopenhauer held that great art depicts Platonic Ideas. The only exception is **music**, which Schopenhauer claimed is a copy of the will. Aesthetic contemplation or the experience of a great work of art is a truly transforming experience. Normally, individuals experience particular objects standing in spatial and temporal relations to other objects and these objects are viewed either as the direct or indirect means for satisfying or thwarting their desires. Consequently, our ordinary experience is structured by the principle of sufficient reason and by cognition colored by the will. Aesthetic contemplation, which Schopenhauer claimed comes suddenly, entails the loss of will-colored perception and the perception of an individual thing. It is as if the cognizer becomes one with the object, and Schopenhauer claimed that the **subject of cognition** becomes the clear mirror of an Idea. Although it seems that **consciousness** becomes one with the object, Schopenhauer argued that this experience still has the form of **subject and object**. But unlike ordinary experience, the object of cognition is an Idea and the subject of cognition is a pure, will-less, painless, timeless subject of cognition. Thus, the loss of will-colored or interested perception constitutes a deliverance of cognition from the service of the will. The pleasure found in aesthetic contemplation, Schopenhauer argued, is delight in the mere cognition of the **object** and release from the will. He distinguished between the feeling or the experience of the **beautiful** and the **sublime** by the means in which the subject of cognition becomes a pure subject. In the experience of the beautiful, this transformation occurs smoothly due to the type of Idea cognized. With the sublime, there is a struggle involved in this transformation, since the contemplated Idea connotes something in opposition to the will.

Schopenhauer classified the visual and verbal arts on the basis of the type of Idea an art expresses. He argued that there is a higher objectification of the will in the plant than in the stone and a higher degree in the **animal** than in the plant. The highest objectification of the will is the human, where the nature of the will is given in its greatest clarity. Consequently, the lower arts express Ideas of the **forces of nature** and the higher arts express Ideas of humanity. On this basis, he classified architecture as the lowest art on his scale of the hierarchy of the arts, since it expresses the Ideas of natural forces like gravity and rigidity, and he designated **tragedy** as the highest art, since it depicts the wretchedness and misery of human existence and the antagonism of the will itself. The experience of tragedy is sublime, Schopenhauer wrote, since it presents to its audience the world as the battleground of the will, and thereby, it counsels resignation from the world.

POODLES (*PUDEL*). Schopenhauer owned a series of poodles from his student days at Göttingen through his death in Frankfurt am Main. It is not surprising to discover that a person who found his relationships with other people generally disappointing, and who viewed most human conduct as self-serving, would prefer the company of his dogs, his only live-in companions. There is a well-known anecdote told about Schopenhauer concerning his dogs. He was said to take them to task by scolding them, saying, "You are not a dog. You are a human. A human, a human!" Once, when he related this practice to a fellow diner, this man asked Schopenhauer whether he would take it as an honor to be addressed as "you dog." Schopenhauer was said to have replied that he would have nothing to say against that.

Schopenhauer called all of his dogs, Atma (the Hindu name for the supreme and universal soul from which all individual souls arise), and affectionately, they were all "Butz." This odd practice of giving each of his individual dogs the same name seems to have been done because of his theory of individuality, which maintained that in lower animals there was little individuality, with each instance of a particular type of animal expressing closely the **Platonic Idea** of its species.

He was especially fond of a white poodle he owned in the 1840s and a brown poodle he owned up to his death, and for which he made provision for its care in his will. It has been said that the children of Frankfurt used to call his dog "Young Schopenhauer," and his dogs always accompanied him on his daily, afternoon walks. Once Schopenhauer became well-known, many of his fellow Frankfurters purchased poodles.

Given his love of his dogs, it would only have been expected that references to them would occur in his philosophical writings. In *On the Fourfold Root of the Principle of Sufficient Reason*, section 21, he used the example of his "very intelligent poodle" to help motivate his claim that all **perception** is intellectual by noting his poodle's re-action to a new bedroom curtain of the type that is drawn open in the middle when a cord is pulled. The dog, he said, looked for a cause that he knew *a priori* must have previously taken place. In his moral philosophy, Schopenhauer held that **animals** possess moral standing, and he found fault with **Baruch Spinoza**'s view on animals, remark-ing that he appeared not to know dogs at all, and he quoted the Span-ish proverb that "whoever has never kept dogs does not know what it is to love and be loved." If this is true, Schopenhauer knew love.

PRINCIPIUM INDIVIDUATIONIS. Schopenhauer held that **space** and **time** are the necessary conditions for the possibility of plurality and numerical diversity. Consequently, he referred to space and time as the principle of individuation, the *principium individuationis*, a Latin term he adopted from scholastic philosophy. Since he viewed space and time as *a priori* forms of **sensibility**, they function as nec-essary features of the **cognition** of the world as **representation** or **appearance**. The **will**, he argued, is beyond the conditions for the possibility of plurality. Thus he concluded that the will was nonplural or "one."

The ability to "see through" (*durchschauen*) the *principium indi-viduationis* plays a central role in Schopenhauer's analysis of moral goodness and the **denial of the will**. He argued that moral goodness and denial of the will arise from seeing through or penetrating the *principium individuationis*. Using terms he borrowed from **Hin-duism**, he claimed that morally good persons glance behind the "**veil of *māyā***" (delusion), to realize *tat tvam asi* ("That thou art"). This form of cognition is expressed by good persons' **compassion** for an-other's suffering, which leads them to treat others as themselves. Con-versely, he described the behavior of morally **evil** people, those in-clined to extreme **egoism** and **malice**, as treating others as absolute others or non-egos. These individuals act, he argued, as if the *princip-ium individuationis* expresses the true order of things. Schopenhauer thought that those who overcome the will, those who have denied the will, recognize more clearly the identity of the will in all appearances, and he claimed that this involves their seeing through the *principium individuationis* with greater distinctness than good persons. They see that this will is that which is expressed in all the suffering and destruction found in the world, and this cognition becomes the quieter of all their willing. Conversely, those who recognize only particular things in relations to their own persons, have renewed motives for willing, for the affirmation of the world, and are involved in the *principium individuationis*.

PRINCIPLE OF SUFFICIENT REASON (*SATZ VOM ZURE-ICHENDEN GRUND*). This principle was the topic of Schopenhauer's doctoral dissertation, ***On the Fourfold Root of the Principle of Sufficient Reason***. He expressed this principle in its most general form by using a statement from the German philosopher, Christian Wolff: "Nothing is without a reason why it is rather than is not." He made it clear in his dissertation, however, that his formula is an abstraction that unifies different laws of our cognitive faculties. In this regard, he was following the law of **homogeneity**, which seeks unity in diversity, and he said that this statement of the principle summarized four "roots" or specifications of the principle of sufficient reason. Indeed, part of his argument in his dissertation was to expose the errors and confusions found in the work of earlier philosophers who had neglected to recognize the different implications resulting from the principle's application to four distinct classes of possible objects of **cognition**.

Since Schopenhauer held that the principle of sufficient reason is basic and intrinsic to our **intellect**, he viewed it as *a priori* applicable to all possible objects of cognition. This entails for him that it is only applicable to **appearances** and not to the **thing in itself**. For this reason, he rejected the cosmological proof for the existence of **God**, which reasons from a premise that applies the principle beyond its proper scope, namely, the premise that "the world and all things therein exist by virtue of something else," to claim that this "something else" is God.

Schopenhauer also held that the principle of sufficient reason is the basis of all **science** and that it is the ultimate principle of explanation. It is that, moreover, he argued, that entitles us to ask "why?" about anything. Since he viewed the principle as the basis or presupposition of all demonstration and proof, he claimed that it is not capable of proof. It would be absurd to ask why the principle is true, he averred, because the very questioning of the principle presupposes it, and anyone foolish enough to challenge the principle would be caught in the vicious cycle of demanding a proof for the right to demand a proof. *See also* PRINCIPLE OF SUFFICIENT REASON OF ACTING; PRINCIPLE OF SUFFICIENT REASON OF BECOMING; PRINCIPLE OF SUFFICIENT REASON OF BEING; PRINCIPLE OF SUFFICIENT REASON OF KNOWING.

PRINCIPLE OF SUFFICIENT REASON OF ACTING (*SATZ VOM ZUREICHENDEN GRUNDE DES HANDELNS*). This principle is the specific application of the **principle of sufficient reason** to a class of objects that has for any person only one object, his or her **will**. More concisely, Schopenhauer referred to this principle as the law of motivation. This law holds that for any action a person performs, there is a sufficient reason or **motive** for the action. The designation of this principle as both the principle of sufficient reason of acting and the law of motivation was prepared by Schopenhauer's analysis of the experience each person has of his or her **body** as both **representation**, as a spatial-temporal object standing in causal relationships with other representations, and as **will**. This identity of one's body as both representation and will allows Schopenhauer to identify acting with willing, which he claimed, is always motivated. Indeed, he claimed that without a motive, an action is just as inconceivable as the motion of an inanimate body without a push or shove. The experience of our body as will, the inner experience of our body as representation is, he said, the cornerstone of his metaphysics, and it serves as the basis of his extension of the concept of the will to all other representations. He also said that motives are **causes** seen from "within," just as wills are bodies seen from "within." This claim enables him to argue that our experience of the one member of this class of objects, the will, is the key for understanding the class of objects covered by the **principle of sufficient reason of becoming**, since the relationship between motives and actions is identical to that between causes and effects in natural objects. He called the type of necessity that prevails in this form "moral necessity," using the term, moral, in the sense that contrasts with "physical," that is, the mental in contrast to the physical, and not in the sense of the ethical or moral quality of something. He also associated this instance of the principle of sufficient reason with **self-consciousness**. *See also* PRINCIPLE OF SUFFICIENT REASON OF BEING; PRINCIPLE OF SUFFICIENT REASON OF KNOWING.

PRINCIPLE OF SUFFICIENT REASON OF BECOMING (*SATZ VOM ZUREICHENDEN GRUNDE DES WERDENS*). This principle is the specific iteration of the **principle of sufficient reason** relating to intuitive **representations**, that is, empirical objects in **space** and **time**, whose changes are governed by the **law of causality**. He stated this law as the claim that if a new state of one or more real or empirical objects appears, another state must have preceded it upon which the new state follows regularly, namely, after the first state appears. This following, he said, is called "ensuing" and "resulting," and he called the first state the "**cause**" and the second the "effect." For example, if an object ignites, this ignition must have been preceded by a particular state in which oxygen, fuel, and heat existed, and as soon as this state occurs, the ignition has to follow immediately. This state could not have always existed, he claimed, but only at the moment of ignition. The appearance of this state is a change, and he concluded that the law of causality is related only to changes. Thus, when every effect appears, it is a change, and since this change did not appear earlier, he also said that it follows that there was another change that preceded the earlier change. This meant, he claimed, that there is a chain of causality necessarily without a beginning. In other words, for any effect there is a cause, and that cause is the effect of an earlier cause, *ad infinitum*. On this basis, Schopenhauer rejected cosmological arguments for the existence of **God**, which views God as the uncaused First Cause of all events. The law of causality, he playfully remarked, was not like a cab that one can dismiss after reaching one's destination. (He also found the notion that God is *causa sui*, or self-causing, absurd and he viewed **Georg Wilhelm Friedrich Hegel**'s entire philosophy to be an elaborate cosmological argument.)

Like all expressions of the principle of sufficient reason, Schopenhauer held that the law of causality is an *a priori* and necessary **truth**. He attributed both its origin and existence to the **subject** and he held that it is constitutive of our **intuition** of empirical objects. More specifically, he viewed this principle as a function of the **understanding**. He referred to the type of necessity expressed by the principle of sufficient reason of becoming as "physical necessity," which connotes the inevitability of an effect from a cause. *See also* PRINCIPLE OF SUFFICIENT REASON OF ACTING; PRINCIPLE OF SUFFICIENT REASON OF BEING; and PRINCIPLE OF SUFFICIENT REASON OF KNOWING.

PRINCIPLE OF SUFFICIENT REASON OF BEING (*SATZ VOM ZUREICHENDEN GRUNDE DES SEINS*). When the class of objects, to which the **principle of sufficient reason** is applied is the pure or non-empirical **intuitions** of **space** and **time**, you have what Schopenhauer called the principle of sufficient reason of being. Space and time are the *a priori* forms of our **sensibility** and, as such, they are imposed on sensory data to help create the experience of natural objects. Schopenhauer also held that space and time could be the objects of non-empirical intuitions that enable us to grasp the nature of space and time better than the consideration provided by either the **understanding** or **reason**. To support this, he cited **Immanuel Kant**'s claim that the difference between right and left gloves cannot be made intelligible except by means of **intuition**, that is, seeing the difference. Schopenhauer argued also that space and time are constituted such that every part determines and is determined by every other part. This relationship, he said, is called "position" in space and "succession" in time. The principle of sufficient reason of being states, therefore, that the parts of space and time mutually condition each other. Arithmetic is based on counting in time and thereby it provides an intuitive grasp of temporal relations. Twelve, for example, is determined by and determines a sum, such as seven plus five. Geometry deals with the non-empirical intuition of space, he said, and as such, every part of space determines and is determined by every other part. Thus the proposition that "a triangle with two equal angles have equal subtending sides" is something that can be grasped by intuition. Although this proposition could be demonstrated by Euclidean geometry, he viewed geometry as a formal system in which its constituent theorems are deduced from other theorems and its axioms. For this reason, he saw Euclidean geometry as relating judgments to other judgments, as articulating logical truths, and as expressing the **principle of sufficient reason of knowing**. Like all products of reason, he argued, Euclidean geometry is less capable than intuition for apprehending the world. The type of necessity he attributes to this form of the principle of sufficient reason is what he termed "mathematical," and he assigned the principle to pure sensibility. *See also* PRINCIPLE OF SUFFICIENT REASON OF ACTING; PRINCIPLE OF SUFFICIENT REASON OF BECOMING.

PRINCIPLE OF SUFFICIENT REASON OF KNOWING (*SATZ VOM ZUREICHENDEN GRUNDE DES ERKENNENS*). This principle is the expression of the **principle of sufficient reason** when its object is abstract **representations** or **concepts**. More specifically, it governs judgments, which Schopenhauer viewed as combinations of concepts and as that which express **knowledge**. Schopenhauer thought that no judgment by itself is intrinsically true; the **truth** of any judgment necessarily depends on something other than itself. Thus the principle of sufficient reason of knowing states that every true judgment has a sufficient ground or **reason** for its truth. In this way, Schopenhauer restricted the concept of "true" only to judgments or propositions, and he viewed truth as the relationship between a judgment and something other than or "external" to the judgment. In his account of this principle, Schopenhauer recognized four kinds of truths. A logical truth is a judgment. For example, the conclusion, "no **poodles** are insects" is a logical truth based on the premise, "no insects are poodles." A transcendental truth is a judgment whose truth is based on the *a priori* forms of **sensibility** and **understanding**. For example, "Nothing can happen without a cause," is based on the **law of causality**. An empirical truth is a judgment based on an **intuition**. For example, "My very intelligent poodle was looking for the cause of the curtains moving," whose truth is based on having experiences of the relevant sort. A metalogical truth is a judgment whose truth is based on the formal conditions of thought. For example, the principle of sufficient reason of knowing is itself a metalogical truth, Schopenhauer claimed, because of the impossibility of our thinking in ways opposed to it, something we discover, he said, inductively. The type of necessity he attributed to this principle is "logical necessity," and he associated it with the faculty of reason. *See also* PRIN-

CIPLE OF SUFFICIENT REASON OF ACTING; PRINCIPLE OF
SUFFICIENT REASON OF BECOMING; PRINCIPLE OF SUFFI-
CIENT REASON OF BEING.

PUNISHMENT (*STRAFE*). The principal object of the state,
Schopenhauer thought, was to provide public security for its citizens.
It does so primarily through its laws, which aim at preventing the various **wrongs** or harms that individuals inflict upon one another. There
is no right to punish separate from the state, Schopenhauer argued.
This right is only established by positive law, which must determine
prior to an offense its punishment, and punishments are justified only
on the grounds that they deter wrongdoing. To punish is always to inflict an **evil** on another, and Schopenhauer held that inflicting an evil
could never be justified simply on the basis that a person committed
an evil. Therefore, he rejected **Immanuel Kant**'s justification of punishment, which is based on *jus talionis*, the idea of reciprocal punishment in kind. This, he claimed, is simply revenge and an act of
cruelty. The proper aim of punishment is to prevent wrongs in the future by offering to potential wrongdoers counter-motives that over-
ride egoistic inclinations to wrong others. In other words, legal punishment is justified only because it induces citizens to refrain from
wrongful conduct out of a fear of punishment.

– Q –

QUIETISM (*QUIETISMUS*). This term generally refers to a form of
spirituality that minimizes human initiative and activity, leaving everything to the will of **God**. Schopenhauer philosophically redefined it as
the abandonment or giving up of all willing. Therefore, he viewed it as
a form of the **denial of the will**. He also found it to be intimately related to **asceticism** and **mysticism**, since each of these phenomena
arise from an inner, direct and intuitive knowledge (*intuitive Erkenntnis*), that is, a non-conceptual, not abstract, and non-discursive apprehension of the essence of the world, of the **will**. This insight becomes,
he said, the quieter of the will, and it brings **resignation** and **salvation**.

He held that, like asceticism and mysticism, quietism is expressed by
the lives of the saints and great souls recognized by all world **religions**.

To understand quietism, he encouraged his readers to become acquainted with the writings of Johannes Eckhart, Johann Tauler, John Bunyan, Miguel de Molinos, and others. In particular, he felt deep reverence for the French quietist and mystic Madam Jeanne-Marie Bouvier de la Motte-Guyon (1647–1717), and he strongly recommended her *Autobiography* and *Torrens* to his readers.

– R –

REALISM (*REALISMUS*). Schopenhauer understood realism as the view that the objects of our normal **intuitions** have an existence apart form their being perceived. To state this in different terms, he identified realism with the thesis that the world exists as we know it independently from our **consciousness** of it. Schopenhauer rejected realism, which he accused of forgetting the **subject**, and for that reason, it presents a thesis that is impossible to conceive, i.e., think of something existing without thinking of it existing. *See also* IDEALISM; MATERIALISM; SPIRITUALISM.

REASON (*VERNUNFT*). Schopenhauer characterized reason as one of three cognitive faculties or capacities possessed by humans, along with **understanding** and **sensibility**. He argued that reason is a uniquely human cognitive capacity, one possessed by, and only by, humans. The single function of reason, he claimed, is the formulation of a unique class of **representations**, which are representations of representations or **concepts**. The ability to develop concepts and to combine concepts to formulate judgments is the basis by which Schopenhauer distinguished between humans and nonhuman **animals**. Although Schopenhauer's position concerning reason as the distinguishing characteristic between humans and nonhumans continued a tradition central to Western philosophical thought, he deviated from this tradition by claiming that reason is not the essence of humans, as this is the **will**, and he did not believe that the possession of reason solely by humans entails that humans alone are morally considerable and that nonhumans, lacking reason, are not.

The possession of reason is a mixed blessing, according to Schopenhauer. While it enables humans to develop and express everything that distinguishes human life from animal life, it also makes humans susceptible to torments and forms of suffering from which animals are free. Although reason and discursive thought enables humans to have **knowledge** (*Wissen*), it also leads to doubt, error, and confusion. By denoting concepts with words, humans possess language and speech, and thereby humans have the ability to communicate in more complex and significant ways than animals, but the substance of this communication often misleads more than it enlightens. He also thought that reason enables humans to escape the narrow confines of the immediately present, to which animals are confined. The ability to entertain the past and to anticipate the future makes humans susceptible to forms of suffering to which the animal is immune. Thus he claimed that humans could be haunted by the past and by feelings of remorse and regret, and that humans could suffer from anxiety and concern about the future. More deeply, humans are aware that their **deaths** hover in the future. Reason also enables humans to deliberate and plan future actions and thereby have a greater choice than is possible for animal behavior, which he thought is motivated by the immediately present circumstances. This freedom of choice is only apparent, he argued, since human behavior that is motivated by abstract thought is equally caused and necessary.

RELIGION. Schopenhauer did not subscribe to a religion, and he was an atheist. Still, he took a lively interest in the religions of the world. That he would do so is not surprising, since he saw a strong kinship between **philosophy** and religion, and also a natural antagonism. He held that both philosophical and religious systems attempt to address a deep human need for metaphysics. He attributed this need to a sense of wonder or astonishment, one that arises from the recognition of the ubiquity of suffering and **death** within the world. To address this need, both religion and philosophy provide metaphysical explanations for these troubling aspects of existence, as well as accounts of the significance of living in a world permeated by these "**evils**." In particular, he thought that religion and philosophy are concerned with the problem of death and so have as their strongest and essential point of interest some dogma about a future existence after death. Thus he thought that it only appears that the existence of some **god** or gods is the main point of religion. Rather, he argued that if the existence of a god or gods excluded the possibility of immortality, then religion would abandon the gods in favor of immortality.

Religion provides a "metaphysics for the people," according to Schopenhauer, thereby providing consolation for the deep sorrows of life. This "metaphysics" is expressed in a form suitable to the level of comprehension possessed by the majority of people, who he claimed are unable to perceive the naked **truth**. The metaphysics of religion, he argued, is capable of expressing the truth, but it does so only through myths and allegories and solely in a *sensu allegorico*. Yet religion does not recognize the figurative sense of its truths, and it tends to maintain that it expresses the truth *per se*. This is the reason why he thought religion is naturally antagonistic to **science** and **philosophy**, both of which strive to present the truth *sensu proprio*, that is, in a strict and proper sense, in which good reasons and evidence are offered to support their claims. These truths, however, expose the mythic dimensions of religion and challenge the status of religion, and Schopenhauer was particularly sensitive to the many ways in which religion actively and sometimes brutally represses the development of science and philosophy. Due to this tendency, Schopenhauer also saw religion as being antagonistic to culture.

In his review of the differences between religions, Schopenhauer argued that the fundamental difference between religions is not whether they are monotheistic, polytheistic, pantheistic, or atheistic. Instead, he found the major difference between types of religion to be whether they are **optimistic** or **pessimistic**. "Optimistic" religions are those that view the existence of the world as justified by itself, that see the world as it is as praiseworthy and commendable. Conversely, "pessimistic" religions view the world as something that ought not to be. On these bases, Schopenhauer classified the polytheism of the Greeks and Romans, **Judaism**, **Islam**, and any **pantheistic** religion as "optimistic," whereas, **Hinduism**, **Buddhism**, and "genuine" **Christianity** are "pessimistic." Since Schopenhauer viewed optimism as a pernicious perspective, a mockery of the suffering and perishing world, he tended to condemn optimistic religions. The religions he regarded as pessimistic, however, were religions that express the truth, and he held that Buddhism expresses the truth under the lightest veil of allegory. Since Schopenhauer sought confirmation of his own philosophical views, his hermeneutics of religion quested to understand the doctrines of Hinduism, Buddhism, and "genuine" Christianity as figuratively expressing the same truths as his philosophy.

REPREHENSIBLE, MORALLY (*MORALISCH VERWERFLICH*). Morally reprehensible actions constitute one of three classes of actions evaluated from a moral point of view. The hallmark of morally reprehensible actions is, Schopenhauer argued, that they aim at another's **woe**, and he attributes **malice**, the desire for another's woe, as the motive for actions of this kind. The main translator of Schopenhauer into English, **E. F. J. Payne**, has rendered "*moralish verwerflich*" as "morally bad," which accords with Schopenhauer's metaethics, where "bad" connoted something contrary to a person's will, but Payne missed Schopenhauer's point. Judgments of the moral value of an action are a function of the affective responses to the action by the actor and an impartial witness. The former experiences the sting of conscience, and the latter a feeling of disapprobation towards the action. Schopenhauer's point was that actions motivated by malice are reprehensible, repulsive, and off-putting to both the actor and the uninvolved observer. *See also* INDIFFERENT, MORALLY; WORTH, MORAL.

REPRESENTATION (*VORSTELLUNG*). Representation is a central term of craft in Schopenhauer's philosophy, and it is one, like many, he adopted from **Immanuel Kant**. The German noun "*Vorstellung*," which literally refers to "something put before," is difficult to translate with a simple English equivalent. Schopenhauer used "idea" as a translation of Kant's use of the term "*Vorstellung*," and there is much to be said in favor of this translation. In particular, it harkens back to **René Descartes**, **John Locke**, and **George Berkeley**, each of whom used "idea" to refer to any item of which we are aware, and this seems to capture Schopenhauer's claim that any object for a subject is a *Vorstellung*. Moreover, the infamous opening line of *The World as Will and Representation*, "The world is my *Vorstellung*," is a truth, he said, already found in the skeptical reflections of Descartes and, in a positive form, was articulated by Berkeley. Contemporary translators of both Kant and Schopenhauer tend to use the term "representation" for *Vorstellung*, and to avoid confusion, Schopenhauer's translators have used "idea" to translate "*Idee*," a term that has a special significance for Schopenhauer's conception of **Platonic Ideas**.

Although in its broadest sense a representation is any object for a subject, Schopenhauer distinguishes between intuitive and abstract representations. Intuitive representations constitute our entire experience of the external world. Abstract representations, which he also called "representations of representations," are **concepts**, which are formulated by our faculty of **reason**, which constructs them from intuitive representations. Since Schopenhauer believed that nonhuman **animals** lack this faculty, he argued that humans have a class of representations not possessed by nonhumans.

RESIGNATION (*RESIGNATION*). Schopenhauer viewed resignation as the attitude expressed by a person who has withdrawn from the world, and he identified complete or perfect resignation as the **denial of the will**. The person who has overcome the **will** has also overcome the world, he argued, since the world is the will. This overcoming of the world is based on the self-knowledge of the will, and the resigned person becomes indifferent to the world. So he wrote that nothing promises any charm; nothing moves this person to engage in life, since this person has severed the thousands of threads of willing that bind people to the world and that are the source of constant craving, fear, envy, anger, and despair that drag others here and there in constant pain. A resigned person, he said, looks calmly and with a smile on the phantasmagoria of this world, and life floats before this person as a light morning dream of one half awake, but through which reality shines, so that this person is no longer deceived. Resignation, he said, is like an inherited estate; it frees its owner from all worry and care forever. The bliss of the resigned person, Schopenhauer held, is akin to that of the experience of the **beautiful**, but unlike this temporary reprieve from the will, for the resigned person this state is more enduring. *See also* ASCETICISM; QUIETISM; SALVATION; TRAGEDY.

RESPONSIBILITY (*VERANTWORTLICHKEIT*). Schopenhauer argued that everything in nature operates in accordance with its nature or essence, and all changes in the world follow from **causes** that express this nature. He argued that the same is true of human behavior. All humans act according to their essence and all human actions follow from causes that express their essence. Consequently, he held that our actions are strictly determined like everything in nature. Still, he also argued that we are responsible for what we do, since what we do follows from what we are, an idea he captured by the Latin slogan, "*operari sequiter esse* [acting follows being]." Our being or essence, he held, is our intelligible **character** or the **will** as **thing in itself**, and this essence is expressed by our empirical character, which is the set of our deeds. Since the intelligible character is outside the scope of the **principle of sufficient reason**, the basis of all necessity, our essence is free, that is, it is not determined by causes. In this way, he claimed, our actions are necessary and our essence is free. Therefore, he arrived at the view that **freedom** is compatible with necessity, a view he found in **Immanuel Kant** and which, he said, is one of the greatest creations of the human mind. But unlike Kant, Schopenhauer rejected the view that freedom is some type of **causality** different from the type of causality found in the natural world. Our essence is involved in all of our actions, but it is itself neither caused nor causing. In this way, he conceived of our character as one of the **forces of nature**, something involved in all causality, but neither caused nor causing. Freedom, he said, is **transcendental**; it applies to our essence and not to the world as **representation**, the world cognized under the forms of **space**, **time**, and causality.

The transcendental nature of freedom is revealed by two "facts of **consciousness**," according to Schopenhauer. These facts point to the intelligible character or the will as that which is expressed by our deeds. We have, he noted, a deep feeling of responsibility or accountability for our actions. We are also conscious of the spontaneity and originality of our actions, which makes them feel like they are *our* actions, a consciousness of an "I will" that accompanies all of our deeds. Both of these point to our character, he argued, which is, along with **motives**, the second necessary factor for any specific type of action. Our character underlies the efficacy of motives, and it is that which makes a motive the sufficient motive for a specific act. This character, however, is neither motivating nor motivated, but it is that which is expressed by our actions, and that which exhibits the moral tendency of our character. Our actions, he argued, are used by our **conscience** to become aware of the moral quality of our character, and he argued, other people also use our actions as evidence for judging the moral value of our character. Since our deeds are the means by which the moral quality of a person's character is judged, Schopenhauer concluded that we are ultimately responsible for our character, something that is also reflected by our sense that had we been a different person, our actions could have been different, but given who we are, they follow necessarily. *See also* PRINCIPLE OF SUFFICIENT REASON OF ACTING.

RIGHT (*RECHT*). Schopenhauer viewed the concept of **wrong** to be original and positive and the concept of right to be derivative and negative. A wrong entails the affirmation of an individual's will that requires the denial of another's will. His concept of a right is the negation of the concept of a wrong, and it includes every action that is not the denial of another's will for the affirmation of one's own will. Consequently, Schopenhauer held that all possible actions are either right or wrong, and that all non-wrong actions are right. For example, if I refuse to give food to a starving person and that person dies, I have not committed a wrong. Conversely, if I steal food from a starving person to sate my own hunger, I have wronged the other.

Schopenhauer also argued that the warding off of a wrong is not a wrong, and consequently, it is right. Thus he argued that a person has a right to deny a wrong with whatever force is necessary to prevent it, including the use of physical force and deception. Thus he claimed that if a person is held in captivity by pirates, that person has a right to kill them in order to gain freedom, or if a person gambles with a thief to regain stolen money, that person has a right to use false dice. *See also* JUSTICE.

RUNGE, JOHANN HEINRICH CHRISTIAN (1768–1811). After his two-year stay in France (1797–1799), Schopenhauer attended Dr. Runge's private school in Hamburg from 1799 until 1803, when he joined his parents on a tour of England and Europe. Runge was educated at the Johanneum and the Akademisches Gymnasium, both in Hamburg, and he received his doctorate in theology from the University of Halle, which was a center for Pietistic ideas. Runge opened his school in 1797 and it soon came to enjoy the reputation as the finest educational institute in Hamburg, especially for the education of boys who would become merchants.

Runge was an enlightened and progressive educator. For Runge, education was based on reason and persuasion. He sought to develop his students into well-educated and morally responsible men. He freely interacted both with his students and their parents, encouraging the latter to treat their children firmly, but fairly, and to shun inconsistency and mindless authoritarianism as guides to their treatment of the children. Runge's educational philosophy and the general spirit that permeated his school were most likely a result of Runge's education at Halle, where he studied under August Hermann Niemeyer (1754–1828), who professed a more enlightened and humane form of Pietism, which was reflected in Runge's religious instructions. Although four hours a week were scheduled for instruction in "religion," it was primarily instruction in **ethics** that emphasized the significance of tolerance of others, charity, and service to others. Undergirding this instruction was an emphasis on the awareness of the suffering of others, which may have helped play a formative influence on Schopenhauer's deep sensitivity to human misery, especially noted in his reflections on his experiences during his tour of England and Europe in 1803–1804. Later, Schopenhauer would argue that it is the recognition of the omnipresence of **death** and suffering that prompts both religious and philosophical reflections on the nature of the world.

Schopenhauer thought very highly of Runge personally and of the education he received in his school. He said that he learned from Runge everything useful for a merchant, but he also lamented that the instruction he received in Latin was simply prefatory.

– S –

SALVATION (*ERLÖSUNG*). Schopenhauer conceived of salvation as the redemption or the liberation from all desire and, thus, as the freedom from all willing. It entails the abandonment of all individual need, want, wish, desire, and all striving or craving in general. Since he held that willing is the basis of living, and that willing is suffering, he held that life is suffering. Perfect salvation, therefore, is deliverance from life and suffering for Schopenhauer, and this is the result of the **denial of the will**. Suffering itself, all the misery, privation, despair, and pain

found in life, has a potentially sanctifying dimension, he argued, and
he found that it opens two paths to salvation, although he also held that
very few people are saved. The purifying force of suffering is found
either in extreme personal suffering or through the knowledge of the
inner conflict and essential vanity of life, which is due to the world being the objectification of the **will**. Most of those who achieve **resignation** and salvation are led to this through extreme personal suffering, he
thought, but no matter the course, salvation is the same, denial of the
will. Those who obtain salvation are purified and sanctified, he
claimed, and they obtain inviolable peace, bliss, and sublimity. They
also gladly welcome **death**, he said, and overcome the fear of death,
which is deeply rooted in the **will to life**. By calling the denial of the
will "salvation," Schopenhauer claimed he had expressed philosophically one of the great **truths** allegorically stated in **Christianity**, just as
he did its other great truth, "original sin," by his conception of the **affirmation of the will**. According to Schopenhauer, since the world is
will, to a person who is saved, the world is nothing, since the will is denied. With this theory of salvation, Schopenhauer's **philosophy**, which
he said ranges from the affirmation through the denial of the will, ends.
See also ASCETICISM; MYSTICISM; QUIETISM; SUICIDE.

SCHADENFREUDE. This is a German term for which it is difficult
to find a simple English equivalent. It literally connotes a joy in another's misfortune. Schopenhauer called *Schadenfreude* fiendish and
diabolical, and he viewed it, along with envy, as one of the sources
behind the ill will expressed in **malice**. Since *Schadenfreude* is a response to another's **woe**, he contrasted it to **compassion**. Unlike
compassion, which is a response to another's suffering that moves a
person to seek another's well-being, a *schadenfreudig* individual de-
lights in the other's misery. For this reason, he argued that it expresses the worst trait in human nature and there is no more infallible
sign of a thoroughly bad heart and the **moral reprehensibility** of a
person's character than having a disposition to have *Schadenfreude*.

**SCHELLING, FRIEDRICH WILHELM JOSEPH VON
(1775–1854).** Along with **Johann Gottlieb Fichte** and **Georg Wilhelm Friedrich Hegel**, Schopenhauer counted Schelling as one of
the three sophists whose pseudo-philosophies ruined **Immanuel**

Kant's insights and helped to corrupt the German mind. Schopenhauer's disdain for Schelling, however, was not as deep as his disgust for Fichte and his seething hatred of Hegel. He viewed Schelling as the most gifted of the three sophists, but given his low regard for the other two, this was slight praise. Thus he begrudgingly attributed some merit to Schelling's **philosophy** of nature. It also irritated him when several reviewers of *The World as Will and Representation* claimed that Schelling's philosophy stimulated his thought.

Schopenhauer started to read Schelling in 1810 during his second semester of philosophy at the University of Göttingen, roughly about the same time he started to read **Plato**. Schelling's thought is notorious for its Protean nature, and Schopenhauer appeared to have concentrated on Schelling's works that were published prior to 1809, especially *On Ideas to a Philosophy of Nature* (*Ideen zu einer Philosophie der Natur*, 1797, second edition 1803), *On the World Soul* (*Von der Weltseele*, 1798), and *System of Transcendental Idealism* (*System des transzendentalen Idealismus*, 1800). During his third semester at Göttingen (1810–1811), Schopenhauer attended lectures on metaphysics and psychology given by **G. E. Schulze**, whose critical treatment of Schelling found resonance in Schopenhauer, and he stopped reading him, until he enrolled at the University of Berlin in 1811. As he attended Fichte's lectures at Berlin, he was once again stimulated to read Schelling. His notes to these readings are instructive. They show some sympathy for some of his ideas. Still, this sympathy is counter-balanced by many disagreements with Schelling's views and the recognition of various "absurdities," by the young Schopenhauer. Yet it would be unreasonable to believe, as Schopenhauer would have it, that his critical engagement with Schelling had no formative influence on the development of his philosophy. Schelling's metaphysical aspiration to overcome the **subject and object** distinction through the recognition of some more basic unity that expresses itself dynamically and non-rationally as **will** suggests a deep affinity between both philosophers. Both Schelling and Schopenhauer, moreover, seem to have shared an appreciation for the value of **art** that was greater than those of their philosophical contemporaries.

But if there are affinities between Schelling and Schopenhauer, there are also deep differences between the form and content of their philosophies. The various phases of Schelling's philosophical career, the incompatibility between the phases of development of his thought, his Protean nature itself, stand in stark contrast to Schopenhauer's life-long fidelity to the basic ideas of his thought, those that were expressed in its first appearance. Schelling's writings, moreover, exhibit extraordinary obscurity and grandiose modes of expression which, compared to Schopenhauer, make him appear unusually direct and clear. Schopenhauer himself took the chameleon-like form of Schelling's philosophy as signifying that his philosophy lacked any sustained core of thought and that Schelling was somewhat of a philosophical dabbler, a sampler of current and changing ideas. The obscurity of his philosophical discourse, Schopenhauer argued, serves to ultimately mask the poverty of his thought. Had he been honest and had he been a genuine philosopher, Schopenhauer claimed, he might have been able to produce some temporarily useful ideas, instead of humbug.

Schopenhauer did attribute some merit to Schelling's philosophy of nature, but it also included claims that he categorically rejected. In particular, he claimed that Schelling had simply asserted the identity of the real and the ideal, the object and the subject. For Schopenhauer, the subject and the object were correlates, a relationship that entails that they are inseparable and distinct. At a deeper level, Schelling's identification of the absolute with **God** knifed against Schopenhauer's atheism and his sense of the wretchedness of existence, which he took as a fact that spoke against the divine nature of the world. It is better, he thought, to see it as demonic. Lastly, Schelling's prized intellectual **intuition**, the means to cognize the **absolute**, was a fairy tale, Schopenhauer wrote, something akin to the sixth sense of bats.

SCHOPENHAUER, HEINRICH FLORIS (1747–1805). Schopenhauer's father was a successful merchant, banker, and broker, although he is frequently described as a grain merchant. He was known for his cosmopolitan sensibilities and fierce desire for independence. He was partially educated in England and France, and he was an unabashed Anglophile who also had a deep appreciation for Voltaire. These traits he seemed to pass on to his son. Heinrich Floris planned to have his son head the family business, and he sought to have Schopenhauer schooled by both experiences of the world, through travel, and by training designed to create a successful merchant. On 20 April 1805, Schopenhauer's father was found dead beneath a warehouse loft on the family residence. His death was likely a **suicide**, at least this is what Schopenhauer believed. The death of Schopenhauer's father would enable him to become a philosopher. It freed him from a career that he dreaded, and the estate that he inherited enabled him to live for **philosophy**, by freeing him from the demands of an income earning occupation. Schopenhauer would describe his inheritance as a consecrated treasure that was entrusted to him to fulfill his task of solving the puzzle of existence. Schopenhauer tended to glorify the memory of his father, in part, to denigrate the character of his mother.

SCHOPENHAUER, JOHANNA HENRIETTE (1766–1838). Schopenhauer's mother, born Trosiener, was one of four daughters of Christian Heinrich and Elisabeth (Lehmann) Trosiener. Her father was a Danzig merchant, like her husband, **Heinrich Floris Schopenhauer**, whom she married on 16 May 1785 at the age of 18. Her husband was 38. She would later write that her marriage was not based on an ardent love, something neither expected from the other. It appears that Schopenhauer's father was looking for an heir to the family business and that his mother desired a well-positioned and secure life. Husband and wife did share, however, a love of travel, literature, and most things British, dispositions they passed on to their son.

Upon the death of her husband in 1805, Johanna sold the family business and, in 1806, moved to Weimar with her daughter **Adele**. Arthur remained in his apprenticeship in Hamburg. Johanna was attracted to the rich cultural life available in Weimar, where she felt able to pursue "the desires of her heart." She established a lively literary salon that attracted numerous luminaries. Both she and Adele became very good friends with **Johann Wolfgang von Goethe**. Her interactions with members of Weimar's literary scene inspired her to become a writer. Johanna wrote travel diaries, collections of short stories, and novels. She became a well-respected author, and for many years, much to his dislike, Schopenhauer was known as the son of "the authoress Johanna Schopenhauer." In 1831 her collected works, in 24 volumes, were issued by **F. A. Brockhaus**, the major publisher of her son.

Johanna never seemed to be strongly attached to Arthur, something that can be detected from her extant letters to her young son, which appear cool and detached. In 1814, after a particularly nasty argument, mother and son became so alienated that they never saw one another again. She viewed her son as overbearing, hypercritical of others, arrogant, and depressing in attitude. He found her to be egocentric, superficial, and a bad mother and wife. Curiously, Schopenhauer did think she was a good novelist. She was working on her memoirs in Jena, where she moved in 1837, after having lived in Bonn since 1828, when she died on 16 April 1838. Ironically, she had gotten no further in her life's story than the birth of her son.

SCHOPENHAUER, LOUISE ADELAIDE (1797–1849). Schopenhauer's only sibling, his sister "Adele," lived an emotionally difficult life, caught between the strong and willful personalities of her quarrelsome mother and brother. She lived most of her life with her mother, and in the later years of her mother's life, she took care of her. **Johanna Schopenhauer** seemed not to reciprocate with the same degree of concern for her daughter, since she had spent most of Adele's inheritance from her father's estate. After her mother's death, Adele survived through her own small means and through the help of her friend, Sybille Mertens, with whom she lived in Bonn and Italy.

Adele seems to have been a sensitive, intelligent woman, and artistically talented. **Johann Wolfgang von Goethe** favored her, and complemented her on her acting ability and her readings. She wrote poems, short stories, fairy tales, besides her best-known novel, *Anna*, which met with little success. Her beauty appeared to lie in her personality, however, since she was a very plain, if not homely, woman. She desired love, but felt unloved most of her life. Adele died from cancer on 25 August 1849, never having married.

SCHULZE, GOTTLOB ERNST (1761–1833). Schulze was a German philosopher, skeptic, and critic of **Immanuel Kant**, and a professor of **philosophy** at Wittenberg, Helmstadt, and Göttingen, where Schopenhauer first studied philosophy under his direction in 1810. Schopenhauer's exposure to Schulze helped move him to switch his field of study from medicine to philosophy. His encouragement of the study of **Plato** and Kant brought Schopenhauer to consider more deeply the philosophers he would esteem the most. Schulze's main work, *Aenesidemus*, appeared anonymously in 1792, and it did not even bear the place of its publication. In this work, Schulze argued against Kant's philosophy and Carl Leonhard Reinold's attempt to vindicate it from its critics. Schulze argued that Kant had failed to answer **David Hume**'s skepticism and that Kant's philosophy was contradictory. There is little doubt that Schulze's interpretation of Kant influenced Schopenhauer, especially Schulze's charge that Kant had made illicit use of the category of **causality** by viewing **things in themselves** as the cause of our experiences of things. Schopenhauer accepted this criticism, accusing Kant of employing the category of causality transcendentally, extending the principle of causality beyond the scope of all possible experiences.

SCIENCE. *See* NATURAL SCIENCES, THE.

SELF-CONSCIOUSNESS (*SELBSTBEWUβTSEIN*). Schopenhauer distinguished between two types of consciousness, differentiated by their objects: **consciousness of other things** and self-consciousness. Self-consciousness is not consciousness of some object referred to as a "self"; rather, it is the immediate consciousness or awareness of one's willing. In his essay "**On the Freedom of the Human Will**," Schopenhauer characterized the self-consciousness of the **will** to include, in addition to volitional activities, the entire scope of an individual's affective dispositions and feelings of pleasure and displeasure. Consequently, he recognized all willing, desiring, striving, wishing, longing, yearning, hoping, loving, rejoicing, exulting, as well as the feelings of unwillingness, repugnance, detesting, fleeing, fearing, being angry, hating, mourning, suffering, and all affects and passions, each of which exist in a great variety of degrees and kinds, as the content of self-consciousness. Ultimately, Schopenhauer emphasized that the object of self-consciousness is the constant passage of pleasurable or displeasurable affections. Schopenhauer used the self-conscious experience of the will to discover the key for explaining all experiences. *See also* I.

SENSIBILITY (*SINNLICHKEIT*). Schopenhauer viewed sensibility as a faculty or capacity possessed by humans and nonhuman **animals**. He understood the capacity to have sensations to be a subjective phenomenon, an event within the organism, and as something "beneath the skin." Sensations can be pleasant or unpleasant, and thus they can have a reference to a being's **will**, but in themselves they are not objective. Sensibility, therefore, provides only the raw material upon which the **understanding** applies its sole function, the **law of causality**, to transform sensation into the objective **intuition** of an external world, a world of spatial-temporal objects standing in causal relationships.

SINGLE THOUGHT, THE (*DER EINE GEDANKE*). In the preface to the first edition of *The World as Will and Representation*, Schopenhauer claimed that this book imparted a single thought. This tantalizing assertion has led some scholars to attempt to express it in a single proposition. Some scholars point to the title of the book itself as a clue to this thought, and they claim that it is "the world is both **will** and **representation**." Other scholars have proposed that it is found in his notes, in the claim that "My entire **philosophy** can be summarized in the one expression: the world is self-knowledge of the will" (1817). Yet, if the general content of *The World as Will and Representation* serves to express this thought, both of these formulations appear too brief. John E. Atwell has proposed that the following proposition expresses this thought: "The double-sided world [as both will and representation] is the striving of the will to become conscious of itself so that, recoiling in horror of its inner, self-divisive nature, it may annul itself and thereby its self-affirmation, and then reach **salvation**," (*Schopenhauer on the Character of the World: The Metaphysics of Will*). Atwell's formulation has the virtues of including the meaning of the two earlier statements—namely, the world is will and representation, and the world is self-knowledge of the will; it captures the teleological and soteriological dimensions of Schopenhauer's **philosophy**, which become increasingly emphasized in the third and fourth books of Schopenhauer's main work; and it delineates the scope of Schopenhauer's philosophy, which he said ranged from the **affirmation** to the **denial of the will**.

SOCRATES (470–399 B.C.E.). Schopenhauer had an ambivalent attitude toward Socrates. He admired Socrates' honesty and his willingness to speak the truth in ways that did not please his contemporaries. His death at the hands of his fellow Athenians symbolized, for

Schopenhauer, Socrates' ultimate commitment to the **truth**. He also drew parallels between his beloved **Immanuel Kant** and Socrates. Both philosophers claimed ignorance in metaphysical matters, and both were clearly aware of their ignorance. They rejected all dogmatism, Schopenhauer wrote, and they suffered the same fate by having their allegedly declared immediate disciples produce metaphysics through dogmatic systems of thought—a reference to **Johann Gottlieb Fichte**, in the case of Kant, and perhaps **Plato**, in the case of Socrates.

Yet Schopenhauer was skeptical about Socrates' alleged wisdom. He viewed Plato's Socrates as a poetic ideal who voiced Plato's own thoughts, and he claimed that the Socrates presented by Xenophon displayed no wisdom at all. If Socrates had a fat belly, as some reported, then Socrates possessed a characteristic not associated with **genius**, Schopenhauer thought. But what called into question more than anything else the quality of Socrates' mind was the fact that he did not write. Every profound thinker, Schopenhauer argued, necessarily has the drive to express his or her thoughts with the greatest clarity and precision. This could only be done to perfection by writing. In this way, the thinker functions as the educator of the human race and speaks to all other great thinkers through time. By working only orally, Schopenhauer suspected that Socrates failed the requirements of a great mind, and that he probably affected more by the force of his personality than by his brains.

SPACE (*RAUM*). Because Schopenhauer viewed space as an *a priori* form of human **sensibility**, he held that all of our normal **perceptions** of individual, natural objects are structured spatially. In other words, he claimed that space is a necessary feature of our **consciousness of other things**, as are **time** and **causality**, and that all of our **cognitions** of natural objects are spatial. Since space is an *a priori* form of cognition, Schopenhauer referred to it as something "subjective" and as not applicable to the **will** as **thing in itself**. In his analysis of the **principle of sufficient reason of being**, which deals with the *a priori* or pure **intuitions** of space and time, Schopenhauer argued that space provides the basis of geometry. *See also* MATTER; PRINCIPIUM INDIVIDUATIONIS.

SPECIFICATION, THE LAW OF (*DAS GESETZ DER SPECI-FIKATION*). Citing the authority of **Plato** and **Immanuel Kant**, Schopenhauer opened the introduction to *On the Fourfold Root of the Principle of Sufficient Reason* by claiming that the laws of **homogeneity** and specification govern the method of all philosophizing and of all **knowledge** in general. Whereas the former seeks to find unity in diversity, the law of specification seeks to distinguish for each other the species subsumed under a wider genus, and to distinguish from each other the things falling within a species. Thus this law counter-balances the law of homogeneity by instructing us to keep in mind the diversity within a unity, the many in a one. He also claimed that this law is **transcendental**, as taught by Kant, and that it is essential to our faculty of **reason**, so that nature must conform to it. This law is found, he claimed, in Kant's remark that "the varieties of entities must not be diminished unnecessarily." Schopenhauer chided earlier philosophers for not following this law in their treatments of the **principle of sufficient reason** because they failed to apply it to this fundamental principle of all knowledge. This led earlier philosophers to fail to distinguish between its different applications, in each of which it acquires another meaning, and which also indicates different powers of the mind. Schopenhauer ultimately recognized four forms or "roots" of the principle of sufficient reason as it applies to different classes of objects.

SPINOZA, BARUCH (or BENEDICT) (1632–1677). While he was a student at the University of Göttingen, Schopenhauer was advised by **G. E. Schulze** against reading **Aristotle** or Baruch Spinoza until he had read **Plato** and **Immanuel Kant**. He followed Schulze's recommendation, and he did not read Spinoza until 1811, when he was attending the University of Berlin. He ultimately came to respect Spinoza as a man and to reject his **philosophy**. He praised, therefore, Spinoza's intellectual integrity and his living for and not by philosophy. In doing so, Schopenhauer likely had in mind Spinoza's decision to grind lenses for a living instead of accepting an academic appointment, since he feared that an academic position would cost him his **intellectual freedom**, and his expulsion from the synagogue because of his philosophical views. To reconcile the separation he drew between Spinoza, the philosopher, and his philosophy, Schopenhauer noted that he had only Giordano Bruno, **René Descartes**, Thomas Hobbes, and Nicholas de Malebranche to stimulate him philosophically. Thus he said that Spinoza suffered a philosophical disadvantage compared to himself, since many important philosophical concepts had not been developed, nor had many significant philosophical problems been clearly recognized when Spinoza developed his thought. Most importantly, of course, Schopenhauer meant that Spinoza could not have benefited by the work of Kant. He also claimed, however, that Jewish theology unconsciously intruded into Spinoza's philosophy, much to his philosophy's detriment. In particular, he argued that his decision to call his single substance "**God**," his unenlightened view of **animals**, and his **optimism** issued from this source. Schopenhauer succinctly stated his view on Spinoza by saying he was a great man and a bad philosopher.

Schopenhauer noted that his philosophy agreed with Spinoza's by recognizing that the world is the expression of a single thing and that the world is sustained by its own power, and although he also praised Spinoza for rejecting the view that the world was created out of nothing by a God that was distinct from creation, but he also categorically rejected the main contours of Spinoza's thought. He decried Spinoza's rationalism, his belief that substantive knowledge of the world could be obtained by *a priori* demonstrations. While he viewed Spinoza's *Ethics* as expressing some **truths**, he also said that it included many falsehoods, and so he said it was both admirable and bad. In particular, he claimed that its geometrical mode of development failed to obtain the certainty of geometry and that Spinoza had stripped the ideas of demonstration, scholia, and corollaries of their original significance. Yet, what troubled him the most was his belief that Spinoza's **pantheism** was a form of optimism. By calling nature itself "God," Spinoza deified the world, Schopenhauer argued, and this made his philosophy incapable of supporting an **ethics**, since this deification entails that everything has to be conceived as it ought to be. This is immediately contradicted by the obvious wretchedness of the world, Schopenhauer claimed. By recognizing that the world is something that ought not to be, and by admitting that the many **evils** of the world follow from its essence, Schopenhauer claimed in "Reference to Ethics," from *On the Will in Nature*, that he had a greater right than Spinoza to call his metaphysics "ethics."

SPIRITUALISM (*SPIRITUALISMUS*). Schopenhauer viewed spiritualism as a form of **realism** that maintains that the **subject** of **cognition** is an immaterial substance, whereas the objects of cognition are material substances. Consequently, he viewed spiritualism to entail a metaphysical dualism, claiming that there are two types of basic substances, material and immaterial. By rejecting realism, Schopenhauer rejected both **materialism** and spiritualism. Schopenhauer also chided his contemporaries for confusing **idealism** and spiritualism. Realism and idealism, he argued, concern the status of the object of cognition, and he found the debate here to be centered on whether what is cognized exists independently from cognition. He saw the debate between materialism and spiritualism as centered on the status of the subject of cognition and whether the subject is material or immaterial.

STERNE, LAURENCE (1713–1768). Schopenhauer developed an abiding fondness for this satirical Irish novelist early in his life, and it is likely that his mother introduced him to the writings of Sterne. In a letter to his publisher **F. A. Brockhaus** (26 January 1825), he said that Sterne's multi-volume novel, *The Life and Opinions of Tristram Shandy, Gentleman* (1759–1769), was an immortal book and "one of the books that I always read again," and he proposed translating it into German, an offer that Brockhaus declined. Later, in the second volume of *Parerga and Paralipomena*, in the essay "On the Metaphysics of the Beautiful and Aesthetics," he called *Tristram Shandy* one of "four novels at the top of their class," along with **Johann Wolfgang von Goethe**'s *Wilhelm Meister*, Jean Jacques Rousseau's *La Nouvelle Héloise*, and Miguel de Cervantes' *Don Quixote*.

Although the English novel appeared in the mid-18th century, *Tristram Shandy* already challenged its conventions by telling its story backward, by a narrator who was born halfway into the story. It is full of wildly eccentric characters and contains lengthy, nonsensical philosophical digressions on arcane subjects. It is also replete with jokes and puns, something that Schopenhauer appreciated to such a degree that, in a letter dated 21 December 1829, which he wrote in English to the "Author of Damiron's Analysis," he quoted from *Tristram Shandy* to help sell his proposal to translate **Immanuel Kant** into English. He explained that he would also have to write an introduction to his translation that concentrated on the elucidation of Kant's terminology, since Kant was often obscure and used terms "in some rather uncommon signification." He then noted a "prophetical pun" found in *Tristram Shandy*, "of all the cants that are canted in this canting world the cant of criticism . . . is the most tormenting." He then informed his reader that "criticism" is the common name for Kant's philosophy in Germany and that "Kant chang'd the original C of his name in a K."

While Schopenhauer delighted in Sterne's humor, *Tristram Shandy* had other features that he appreciated. In a note from his Berlin period in 1813, Schopenhauer quoted Sterne's observation, "There is no passion so serious as lust," and he observed that all the tender charms and playfulness between two lovers disappears "at the beginning of the *actus*," during which they display a profound seriousness, the seriousness of animals and mechanical nature. This observation would be repeated later in his analysis of **sexual love**, which he said served the species and not individual lovers. Likewise, he probably was also attracted by Sterne's promotion of tolerance in *Tristram Shandy*, as well as his critique of the bigotry of the Anglican clergy, something Schopenhauer experienced during his stay in 1803 at Wimbledon School, an English boarding school about which he complained bitterly. Although Sterne was inclined to sentimentality in *Tristram Shandy*, Schopenhauer overlooked this fault, but he later found this to be a highly problematic feature of Sterne's *Sentimental Journey* (1768).

STIMULUS (*REIZ*). One of the central claims in Schopenhauer's philosophy is that every change in the world as **representation** follows from a sufficient reason or **cause**. He referred to the specific type of cause that prevails uniquely in plants as a "stimulus" and its specific effect as a "response." By identifying stimulus/response as the causal relationship prevailing uniquely in changes in plants, he did not suggest that a plant is not subjected to chemical, mechanical, or physical causes, nor did he deny that stimulus/response operates in **animal** bodies. Rather, he highlighted stimulus/response as the type of causal relationship appropriate to the nature of plant life. Unlike causes in the inorganic realm, Schopenhauer argued that the hallmarks of a stimulus was that its object neither undergoes a reaction proportionate to its action, nor is there a uniformity between the intensity of the stimulus and that of the response. For example, the stimuli of heat, light, and nutrition lead to the response of growth, such that a small increase in each can lead to extraordinarily rapid growth, but a smaller incremental increase in one can also lead to the death of a plant. *See also* MOTIVE.

SUBJECT AND OBJECT (*SUBJEKT UND OBJEKT*). Schopenhauer regarded the subject and object division as the first, universal, and essential form of all **cognition**. In this sense, it is more basic than any of the distinctions that followed from the **principle of sufficient reason**, which always governs objects of cognition. Since he held that there is no object without a subject, this means that each of the fourfold roots of the principle of sufficient reason presupposes the subject and object correlation. Moreover, he claimed that the correlation between the subject and object entails that having an object means being cognized by a subject and being a subject means having an object. Schopenhauer did not propose a theory of the relationship between the subject and the object, because he thought that it was impossible to do so. To propose a theory requires the employment of the principle of sufficient reason, he argued, and the principle of sufficient reason does not apply to the subject and object.

Schopenhauer claimed that his **philosophy** differs from all other philosophies, since his starts from that which is given to **consciousness**, the **representation**, which presupposes the subject and object correlation. Thus he argued that to be an object for a subject and to be a representation are one and the same. All other systems, he said, start from either the subject or the object and proceed to employ the principle of sufficient reason to derive the one from the other. Thus he chided **Johann Gottlieb Fichte** for making the subject the ground of the object, for claiming that the absolute ego posits the non-ego. The subject or absolute ego, he claimed, cannot be thought without the object, and he accused Fichte of treating the principle of sufficient reason as a *veritas aeterna*, applicable to anything. Thus he failed, Schopenhauer thought, to appreciate the limitations of this principle, its application only to the object. In contrast to Fichte, whose philosophy was interesting, he said, because it was the system most consistently starting from the subject, he mentioned **materialism** as the most consistent system that starts from the object. Materialism, of course, displays the same problem that he saw in Fichte, only in reverse. Moreover, he contended that both Fichte's **idealism** and materialism treat the beginning points of their systems as the **thing in itself**, something to which the subject and object distinction does not apply. By recognizing the **will** as the thing in itself, he also held that this distinction does not apply to the will.

Schopenhauer's account of aesthetic **contemplation** provides an account of the subject and object correlation independent of the principle of sufficient reason. The objects of such cognitions are **Platonic Ideas** and the subject is a pure **subject of cognition**. More specifically, a pure, timeless, will-less, painless, subject of cognition, and he emphasized that the contemplator and the contemplated become disentangled from the will-colored cognition of individual things as the possible means for satisfying or frustrating the subjects' desires. In this regard, Schopenhauer emphasized the subject of cognition's temporary liberation from the **subject of willing** and a sense of individuality. Thus he claimed that the aesthetic contemplator experiences no difference or separation from the object of cognition. The subject becomes, he wrote, a pure eye that simply mirrors the object.

Schopenhauer did contend, however, that for those who have **denied the will**, only cognition itself remains. He could not, however, say anything about such a condition, one that entails the transcendence of the subject and object correlation and a negation of the will, representation and the world. *See also* I.

SUBJECT OF COGNITION (*SUBJEKT DES ERKENNENS*). That which knows all things, that is, that which is aware of all things but is never aware of itself, Schopenhauer called the subject of cognition. He said that it is the supporter (*Träger*) of the world, the universal condition of all that appears. Consequently, he argued that all that exists does so only for a subject. All beings capable of **cognition** are subjects of cognition, including nonhuman **animals**. *See also* SUBJECT AND OBJECT.

SUBJECT OF KNOWLEDGE. *See* SUBJECT OF COGNITION.

SUBJECT OF WILLING (*SUBJEKT DES WOLLENS*). We experience ourselves as the willer or the willing subject through introspection or as an object of the inner sense. Since Schopenhauer held that will-ing is given immediately, he argued that it is impossible to provide definition or description to the nature of willing, something given in the mildest wish through the most passionate desire. *See also* I; SELF-CONSCIOUSNESS.

SUBLIME, THE (*DAS ERHABENE*). Schopenhauer viewed the sub-lime as almost identical to the **beautiful**. Both entail the **cognition** of a **Platonic Idea** by a pure, will-less, timeless **subject of cognition**. He also attributed an aesthetic pleasure or enjoyment to the feeling of the sublime and a deliverance from cognition in service of the **will**. The difference between the feelings of the beautiful and the sublime concern the types of objects that prompt a person's becoming a pure subject of cognition. The objects that affect the feeling of the sub-lime, Schopenhauer claimed, are threatening to the person, hostile to a person's will, and due to their threatening nature, the transforma-tion from ordinary cognition to that of pure cognition involves some violent turning away from these objects, which involves an exaltation of the subject beyond the hostile relation of the object to the will. Schopenhauer regarded **Immanuel Kant**'s discussion of the sublime to be the most excellent thing in his *Critique of Judgment*, and he fol-lowed Kant in distinguishing between the dynamically and mathe-matically sublime. The former involves natural objects that threaten the annihilation of the individual, such as a raging storm at sea, and the latter involves the perception of the innumerable worlds revealed in the heavens at night, which makes the individual seem insignifi-cant. In both instances, the exalted state of the feeling of the sublime results from a sense of the dependency of the world on the **subject of cognition**.

SUICIDE (*SELBSTMORT*). Schopenhauer's most significant analy-ses of suicide are located in section 69 of the first volume of *The World as Will and Representation*, sections five and seven of *On the Basis of Morality*, and the essay "On Suicide" from the second vol-ume of *Parerga and Paralipomena*. These writings reflect his am-bivalent attitude toward suicide. Although he harshly criticized the ways by which it is socially stigmatized, the criminalization of sui-cide, and the condemnation it received from Western religions and

European moral philosophers, he also held that there is a valid moral reason against suicide. Still, he recognized a type of suicide, a voluntarily chosen death by starvation, which is immune to his moral reason against suicide. Schopenhauer's ambivalence toward suicide may be a function of his view on the **death** of his father, **Heinrich Floris Schopenhauer**, which he believed was a suicide, and the difficulty he found in distinguishing between suicide and the **denial of the will**.

Suicide is often popularly criticized as an act of cowardice or madness, but Schopenhauer thought that it need not be either. The fear of death is generally so strong that it is this fear that inhibits most people from taking their lives. Moreover, he thought that when the terrors of life become overwhelming, it is not unreasonable to end one's life. Unlike nonhuman **animals**, whom he believed only suffer physically and strive to live as long as they can, humans possess the faculty of **reason** and therefore only humans suffer psychologically and more greatly than animals. It is as if, he wrote, nature compensates humans for this greater burden by giving them the ability to live only as long as they choose.

Schopenhauer was also scornful toward the criminalization of suicide. In particular, he condemned the "vulgar bigoted England" for treating it as a crime. Since he believed the only legitimate function of the state is to prevent "**wrong**" or harm to others, and that the only valid reason for criminal sanctions is to deter the commission of wrongful acts, he found laws against suicide unfounded. Every person has, he held, "an indisputable right to his own person and life," and he thought that nothing will deter a person who seeks death. Indeed, as a matter of fact, since the law can only punish a person who is unsuccessful, all the law punishes a person for is a lack of skill. But to consider even more deeply whether suicide is a crime, Schopenhauer invited his readers to think of true crimes, such as murder, fraud, and theft, and then to think of suicide. Moral feelings should decide the matter, he thought, and he believed that we would discover that true crimes arouse indignation and a demand for **punishment**, whereas with the suicide, we feel sorrow and **compassion**, and sometimes also the mingling of admiration for the courage of the person. In other words, we do not find the same affective response to reports of suicide that we experience with reports of "**bad** actions." Also, perhaps Schopenhauer was thinking about his father when he recommends challenging anyone who would stigmatize as a crime an act "committed by many who were honored and beloved by us."

Moreover, Schopenhauer argued that neither Western religion nor Western moral philosophy have sound arguments against suicide. He claimed that there is no basis in the Bible that supports the condemnation of suicide, and that **David Hume**, in his essay "On Suicide" had exposed the "sophisms" behind religious proscriptions against suicide. He diagnosed "**optimism**" as the hidden foundation behind the extraordinary zeal by which the clergy condemned suicide. It is only by viewing creation as "**good**" that one could view suicide as an affront to **God** and as a rejection of his gift of life. For Schopenhauer, however, the miserable world is **evil** and there is no creator distinct from creation. Optimism, moreover, is only inherent in **Judaism**. It is foreign to the spirit of genuine **Christianity**, he thought, which teaches the overcoming of this wretched world. Most "European moral philosophers" simply let religious biases slide into their ethics, or worse, they consciously followed popular religious sentiments to maintain their professorships, according to Schopenhauer. Even **Immanuel Kant**, he argued, advanced such weak arguments against suicide that they could be refuted by a laugh. To classify the duty against suicide as a **duty to ourselves**, he argued, showed the poverty of Kant's thought, since it is impossible to have duties to ourselves.

The only moral reason against suicide, Schopenhauer argued, is based on a moral perspective higher than that expressed in European moral philosophy. Suicide opposes the highest moral goal and substitutes apparent for real **salvation**. It represents what Schopenhauer called "the strongest **affirmation of the will**," instead of its denial. In reality, the suicide does not reject life, he thought, but only the form in which one lives. He or she rejects the suffering and misery of his or her life, but not the **will to life** itself. This is shown, he thought, with ordinary cases of suicide, where the person would be willing to continue to live if the causes of his or her misery were absent. By killing him or herself, all that is lost is life and not the will to life itself. Certainly, in suicide the person dies, that individual appearance of the **will** perishes as an individual, but this is exactly the same as any death. Everyday, countless people die, and each day numerous individuals kill others, and the result of this is no different in the case of suicide. Indeed, Schopenhauer contended that suicide itself is a willful act, and thus an affirmation of the will. The problem with suicide, moreover, is that it precludes the possibility of true salvation, the realization of the type of **knowledge** that prompts **resignation** and not willing. Salvation, he argued, can only spring from insight itself into the essence of the will, the essence of life, and never from force in any form, even the violence associated with suicide.

Schopenhauer still was prepared, however, to recognize a type of suicide to which his moral reason against suicide did not apply. A voluntarily chosen death by starvation, a type of suicide that he said had not been adequately verified, represented for him the most extreme form of **asceticism**, and as such, is the denial and not the affirmation of the will. This agonizing type of death does not connote a fleeing from suffering and misery like ordinary suicide, but represents the acceptance of suffering and a rejection of the "good" things in life. In this regard, voluntary death by starvation signifies for him the denial of the will to life.

At the end of section 69 of the first volume of *The World as Will and Representation*, Schopenhauer remarked that there were many intermediate stages and combinations between the voluntarily chosen death from extreme asceticism and the ordinary suicide based on despair. These stages ranging between the two are difficult to explain, he confessed, since human nature has depths, obscurities, and intricacies that are difficult to elucidate.

– T –

TAT TVAM ASI. This is one of the great sayings in *Mahāvākya* from the *Chāndogya Upanishad*. Translated from Sanskrit, it means "That thou art," and it connotes that ultimate reality (*Brahman*) is **immanent** in the self (*ātman*) of all beings. Schopenhauer claimed that this phrase expresses the **cognition** that the plurality and diversity of individuals in the world is only apparent and that one's inner being or essence is the same in all individuals. This cognition is that which is expressed through **compassion**, the basis on which all virtue depends, and in which the suffering of another is treated just as one's own. By recognizing themselves in all others, Schopenhauer claimed that morally **good** persons live in an external world that is homogeneous to their own true being and that others are not treated as non-egos, but as an "I once more."

TEMPORAL JUSTICE (*ZEITLICHE GERECHTIGKEIT*). Temporal **justice** is a function of the state and its criminal laws. The only justification for **punishment**, Schopenhauer argued, is to deter people from future wrongful conduct. Since he viewed **just** or **right** conduct as being conduct that does not harm or wrong others, punishment has as its aim the prevention of wrong by providing individuals with a self-interested motive, fear of punishment, for not wronging others. Temporal justice, as its name implies, entails **time**. A crime is committed at one time, and its punishment at another, and the goal of temporal justice is to deter future crimes. Because it requires human institutions, Schopenhauer thought that it is always imperfect and uncertain. Some wrongdoers escape punishment, and others are punished too lightly, while still others are punished too harshly. *See also* ETERNAL JUSTICE.

THEISM (*THEISMUS*). Schopenhauer identified theism with the view that there is a single, all-perfect **God** who freely created the world out of nothing and who is distinct from creation. Consequently, he viewed theism as the stance expressed by the monotheistic religions of the West, **Judaism**, **Christianity**, and **Islam**. Schopenhauer categorically rejected theism, and he was a self-professed atheist. He found theism untenable for at least three reasons. First, he argued that the creation of something out of nothing is logically impossible. Second, he claimed that the existence of **evil**, that is, the ubiquity of suffering and **death**, entails that the world could not be the work of an all-perfect being, an omniscient, omnipotent, and all-good being. Indeed, in a note from 1832, he observed that because of the wretchedness of existence, it makes more sense to conceive of this world as the creation of a devil who summoned into existence creatures in order to gloat over their agony, than it does to see the world as the work of an infinitely good being (*Manuscript Remains*, Vol. IV, "Cholera-Buch," para. 36). Thus he thought that no one with a hint of moral sensitivity could embrace theism. He poignantly observed this idea in a note from 1822, where he wrote, "If a God has made this world, then I would not like to be the God; its misery would break my heart," (*Manuscript Remains*, Vol. III,

"Reisebuch," para. 138). Third, by making humans the creations of a God, he contended that theism could not account for the truth of our deep feelings of moral **responsibility**, since our **will** would be the work of God, which would make God responsible for our conduct.

THING IN ITSELF (*DING AN SICH*). Schopenhauer adopted this term, as well as its contrast, **appearance**, from **Immanuel Kant**. This, however, is not surprising, since he thought that the distinction between appearance and the thing in itself is one of the most important distinctions ever introduced into **philosophy**. In the appendix to *The World as Will and Representation*, he called this distinction "Kant's greatest merit," and he condemned post-Kantians like **Johann Gottlieb Fichte**, **Friedrich Wilhelm Joseph von Schelling**, and **Georg Wilhelm Friedrich Hegel** for abandoning this profound Kantian insight. Schopenhauer, of course, retained this distinction, and it served as one of the deep bases upon which he claimed to have remained faithful to Kant. Moreover, he also claimed that by showing that the **will** is the thing in itself, he had completed the Kantian philosophy. Indeed, he also argued that whenever Kant brought the thing in itself closest to the light, he had also done so by showing it as will.

Kant argued that we could only have experience of the appearance of things and not things in themselves. He, however, appeared to be ambivalent about the status of things in themselves, as scholars have recognized that, at times, he presented the distinction between appearances and the thing in itself conceptually, as an epistemic distinction, and at other times, ontologically, as a distinction between existents. On the epistemic reading, Kant presented the thing in itself as one of two aspects under which objects of experience can be viewed. In this presentation, we can only have knowledge of things as they appear in experience and we cannot have knowledge of them apart from the *a priori* forms of **cognition**, which structure and make possible our experiences of things. In other words, we cannot have knowledge of things independent of the conditions of our experiences of them. We can, he argued, think of things in themselves, the items of our experiences without these forms. On the ontological presentation, however, Kant held that there are objects other than those of our experiences, things in themselves, and that they are impossible to know.

Schopenhauer read Kant's distinction between appearance and the thing in itself, whose roots he saw in **John Locke**'s philosophy, as an ontological distinction. Following the lead of his first philosophy professor, **G. E. Schulze**, he claimed that Kant viewed things in themselves as the cause of our experiences of things. This is a **transcendent** use of the category of **causality**, he continued, a category that Kant himself recognized as valid only within our experiences of things and never applicable to the thing in itself. Instead of viewing the thing in itself as the **cause** of our experiences, Schopenhauer contended that it is the inner content and essence of all appearances; that everything in nature is simultaneously appearance and thing in itself, and that his metaphysics demonstrated that the **will** is what Kant called the thing in itself. *See also* CONSCIOUSNESS OF OTHER THINGS; SELF-CONSCIOUSNESS.

TIME (*ZEIT*). Schopenhauer regarded time as the simplest *a priori* form of the **cognition** of any object. Consequently, he held that all of our normal cognitions of particular, natural objects, as well as all objects of introspection, are necessarily structured by time. In other words, he viewed time as a necessary feature of our **consciousness of other things** and of **self-consciousness**. Since he also argued that a person's self-consciousness of his or her **will** is an item of self-consciousness, he claimed that we only experience our will as acts of will, which are in time. Because time is simply an *a priori* form of cognition, he referred to time as "subjective" and as not attributable to the will as **thing in itself**. In his analysis of the **principle of sufficient reason of being**, he argued that the pure cognition of time was the basis of arithmetic. *See also* MATTER; PRINCIPIUM INDIVIDUATIONIS.

TRAGEDY (*TRAUERSPIEL*). Tragedy represents the pinnacle of the visual and verbal **arts**, the summit, as Schopenhauer said, of the arts that present **Platonic Ideals**. It depicts human life and thereby presents the highest and clearest level of the objectification of the **will**. Tragedy displays, Schopenhauer argued, the terrible side of human existence, the prevalence of misery and death, the triumph of wickedness, the scornful play of chance, and the irretrievable fall of the innocent, just and good. Thus it presents more clearly than the other fine arts the antagonism of the will with itself. In great tragedy, the struggles and ultimate fall of the tragic hero shows the dreadful nature of the will, and Schopenhauer claimed that the hero's atonement for "sin" signifies atonement for the guilt of existence itself, for the **affirmation of the will**. By showing the essential misery of life, Schopenhauer held that tragedy urges a turning away from life, and thereby it counsels the **denial of the will** and **resignation**. The best tragedies present the spirit of resignation in their heroes, such as Gretchen in **Johann Wolfgang von Goethe**'s *Faust* and the steadfast prince in **Pedro Calderón de la Barca's** *El príncipe constante*, Schopenhauer claimed, but even when a tragedy fails to show this, it still teaches resignation. In fact, it is largely on this point that Schopenhauer claimed that the tragedies of the ancient Greeks were inferior to those of the moderns: the tragic heroes of the Greeks displayed little of the spirit of resignation, but the horrors depicted on stage allow the spectator to recognize that it is better to turn away from life than to love the world and life. Thus he argued that William Shakespeare was greater than Sophocles and that Goethe's *Iphigenia* was better than Euripides'.

The pleasure spectators take in tragedy belongs to the feeling of the **sublime**, Schopenhauer argued, and it expresses the highest degree of this feeling. Tragedy's effect is akin to that of the dynamically sublime, and it raises the spectators above the will and its interests, leading to a pleasure in the sight of that which directly opposes the will. This experience leads spectators to become aware of something that they recognize only negatively—there is something about them that does *not* will life.

TRANSCENDENT (*TRANSZENDENT*). Schopenhauer took this term from **Immanuel Kant** to refer to anything beyond all possible experience. Like Kant, Schopenhauer viewed any transcendent claim as meaningless. *See also* IMMANENT; TRANSCENDENTAL.

TRANSCENDENTAL (*TRANSZENDENTAL*). This is another technical term that Schopenhauer adapted from **Immanuel Kant**. It refers to anything that is a necessary condition of possible experience. *See also* TRANSCENDENT.

TRANSCENDENTAL IDEALISM (*TRANSZENDENTALE IDEALISMUS*). This is **Immanuel Kant**'s theory that we only experience or have knowledge of the **appearances** of things and not **things in themselves**. Schopenhauer ascribed to Kant's distinction between appearances and things in themselves, and he agreed with Kant, but for different reasons. Our experiences of empirical reality are conditioned by the *a priori* forms of **space**, **time**, and **causality**, but he maintained that the essence expressed in all appearances, the thing in itself, is **will**.

TRUTH (*WAHRHEIT*). Schopenhauer frequently, and with great passion, declared that the sole goal and only object for a genuine philosopher is nothing but the truth. He constantly chided his contemporaries for lacking this solemn commitment, and he claimed that they put their own self-serving interests before the truth. In particular, he held that this was a stance all-too-common among professors of philosophy, "gentlemen of the philosophical trade," as he would derisively refer to them, since their academic positions, and hence their livelihoods, required them to formulate their thought to please religion and the state. In making this point, Schopenhauer was reiterating an underlying presupposition of his view of the truth, namely, that its recognition requires the suspension of any personal stake in an issue and that one has to subject to critical scrutiny even the ideas that one holds deeply in heart. He prided himself in speaking his truths with no regard for pleasing anyone. **Friedrich Nietzsche**, who rejected many of Schopenhauer's "truths," praised this as his "honesty," his willingness to say uncensored what he found true.

From a technical point of view, "truth" is a property of judgments or propositions, according to Schopenhauer, and he argued that the truth of any proposition necessarily depends on something other than the proposition itself. He captured this idea in his analysis of the **principle of sufficient reason of knowing**, which states that every true judgment has a sufficient reason or ground for its truth. In his account of this root of the **principle of sufficient reason**, he recognized four separate grounds for the truth for four types of judgments. Consequently, he recognized four types of truth, namely, logical, transcendental, empirical, and metalogical. *See also* KNOWLEDGE; PHILOSOPHY; REASON.

TWO FUNDAMENTAL PROBLEMS OF ETHICS, THE (*DIE BEIDEN GRUNDPROBLEME DER ETHIK*). This book appeared in 1841, through the Frankfurt publishing firm of Johann Christian Hermann'sche Buchhandlung, F. E. Suchsland. It consists of two essays that Schopenhauer wrote for prize essay contests, **"On the Freedom of the Human Will,"** and **"On the Basis of Morality."** It includes a lengthy preface in which Schopenhauer related these essays to the fourth book of *The World as Will and Representation*; criticized the decision of the Royal Danish Society for Scientific Studies not to "crown" his "On the Basis of Morality" with its prize; and heaped abuse on **Johann Gottlieb Fichte** and **Georg Wilhelm Friedrich Hegel**. The book went virtually ignored, receiving reviews in two popular magazines and two lukewarm reviews in scholarly journals. A second edition, published in Leipzig by **F. A. Brockhaus**, appeared in 1860, shortly before Schopenhauer's death. In the preface to this second edition, Schopenhauer continues to rant against the Royal Danish Society's verdict on his "uncrowned essay," and he mentions that both essays are also relevant to chapter 47 of the second volume of *The World as Will and Representation* and chapter eight of the second volume of *Parerga and Paralipomena*.

– U –

UNDERSTANDING, THE (*DER VERSTAND*). The understanding is one of the three cognitive faculties or capacities Schopenhauer attributed to humans, and it is one that, along with **sensibility**, is shared with nonhuman **animals**. Schopenhauer viewed the understanding as having one function: the immediate, non-reflective and non-conceptual **cognition** of the relation of **cause** to effect. He argued that our cognition of the external world, of intuitive **representations**, is the production of the unconscious and immediate application of the **law of causality** to **sensations**, which are things "beneath the skin." The understanding attributes a cause for these sensations, with the cause being referred to a location in space. In other words, Schopenhauer held that the understanding takes raw material from sensations and transforms them into the representations composing an outer world cognized as distinct from the **subject of cognition**. Schopenhauer rejected

Immanuel Kant's view of the understanding as a faculty of judgment that applies **concepts** or categories to sensuous **intuitions** to have a **perception** of an external object. Schopenhauer contended that intuitions are already a **consciousness** of things.

– V –

VISION AND COLORS: AN ESSAY, ON (*ÜBER DAS SEHN UND DIE FARBEN: EINE ABHANDLUNG*). This essay appeared in May 1816, through the Leipzig publisher Johann Friedrich Hartnoch. A second edition appeared in 1854, and a third edition, incorporating Schopenhauer's marginal notes to his copy of the second edition, was published by the Leipzig publisher **F. A. Brockhaus**, edited by **Julius Frauenstädt**. A Latin revision of this essay appeared in 1830 as "*Commentatio undecima exponens Theoriam Colorum Physiologicam eandemque primariam*," in the third volume of *Scriptores Ophthalmologici minores*, edited by Justis Radius.

Schopenhauer was induced by **Johann Wolfgang von Goethe** to work on **color** theory. In the fall of 1813, Goethe approached Schopenhauer at one of **Johanna Schopenhauer**'s parties in Weimar, and he thanked the young philosopher for sending him a dedicated copy of his dissertation. He also congratulated Schopenhauer for receiving his doctorate in philosophy. Goethe's attraction to Schopenhauer seems due to his sense of an affinity in their thought, since Schopenhauer had argued in his dissertation that geometrical proofs require a visual **representation**, a requirement Goethe had set for optical proofs within his massive *On the Theory of Colors* (1810). In addition to this shared suspicion of the purely conceptual and the favoring of the perceptual, Goethe also perceived in Schopenhauer a "proselyte" for his color theory. Goethe viewed his color theory as a significant accomplishment, despite the fact that the learned world ignored it. In the winter of 1813–1814, Goethe and Schopenhauer met frequently, discussing philosophy generally, color theory specifically, and conducting experiments. Afterward, they continued to correspond, until a few months after the appearance of Schopenhauer's essay.

Although *On Vision and Colors* spoke favorably about Goethe's color theory, attacked Isaac Newton's view, and chided the public for

not recognizing the merits of Goethe's accomplishments, Goethe ultimately viewed Schopenhauer's stance as opposed to his own. Their
correspondence during this time reveals an increasing distancing of
their views on colors as well as dimensions of Schopenhauer's personality that had to be viewed by Goethe as disconcerting. In his letters to Goethe, Schopenhauer claimed he had assembled Goethe's
impressive set of data into the first true theory of colors in the history
of science, and he had done this as a secondary concern when measured against the other and more important theories that he had in
mind. (Schopenhauer had been working on *The World as Will and
Representation* during this time.) When Schopenhauer completed the
manuscript for *On Vision and Colors*, he sent it to Goethe, hoping
that he would help arrange for its publication and that he would bless
his theory. Of course, Goethe did neither. It is odd that Schopenhauer
thought Goethe would do either, but the fact that he would expect
Goethe's endorsement of his theory shows the degree to which
Schopenhauer could be oblivious to the ways in which his behavior
could alienate other people.

The first chapter of this essay, "On Vision," had an initial significance in regard to Schopenhauer's **philosophy**. In the preface to the
first edition of *The World as Will and Representation*, Schopenhauer
referred his readers to this work, claiming that it would have appeared "word for word" in *The World as Will and Representation* had
he not been disinclined to either quote himself or say, for a second
time, something he had stated well once. The significance of "On
Vision" was that it contained Schopenhauer's first clear and extended
account of the intellectual nature of **intuition** and his physiological
arguments for the *a priori* nature of **causality**. (It is likely that his interest in perception also helped to motivate Schopenhauer to explore
color theory.) However, when he revised his dissertation in 1847,
Schopenhauer used an expanded version of his physiological arguments in section 21. This led him to view the arguments from "On
Vision" as simply precursors for his later thought.

Schopenhauer developed his color theory in the second chapter, "On
Colors." Building on the work from the first chapter, it clearly dis-
tances itself from Goethe's views. In *On the Theory of Colors*, Goethe
rejected the Newtonian view that white light contains the spectrum. He
argued that light and darkness are basic and primary phenomena

(*Urphänomene*), phenomena capable of no further analysis or reduction into other phenomena. Color, he argued, is produced by the interplay of the polarities of lightness and darkness, and thus he viewed colors as having a shadowlike nature. Schopenhauer thought that Goethe was basically correct, but only to a point. He argued that all earlier theories of color concentrated mistakenly on the cause of color sensations, thereby neglecting something even more basic, the effect of the physiological phenomenon of color. Color sensation, Schopenhauer argued, is not passive; rather, it is a reaction to a **stimulus**. With this in mind, Schopenhauer claimed that Goethe's lightness and darkness were not primary phenomena. Lightness or white constituted the full activity of the retina, and darkness or black constituted the inactivity of the retina. Colors became, for Schopenhauer, the qualitatively divided activity of the retina. Consequently, Schopenhauer's primary phenomenon is the capacity of the retina to cause its nervous activity to separate and successfully appear in two qualitatively opposite halves, which are sometimes equal and other times unequal. Much to Goethe's chagrin, Schopenhauer argued that color phenomena resulted from a divisional process, as Newton had held, but contrary to Newton, this is found in the eye rather than in light. Schopenhauer then continued to argue that each color is comprehended as a portion of the retina's activity, which can be expressed by a fraction. Since Schopenhauer viewed lightness, darkness, and colors as states or modifications of the eye, his theory emphasized the subjective nature of colors instead of the objective account found in the work of Goethe (and Newton), where colors emerge from the interplay of light and dark.

On Vision and Colors occupies an odd position in Schopenhauer's *oeuvre*. He often claimed that it was necessary to read everything he wrote to obtain a fundamental understanding of his philosophy. Yet his attitude toward this essay was ambivalent. He once wrote to one of his followers that it was not a required reading, but it was still worth reading along with his other books. However, when he drafted a plan for his collected works, he included *On Vision and Colors* as its last entry. And still later, Schopenhauer wrote in his notes that his theory of colors should be seen as being separate from his other writings. Despite this ambivalence, it is worth noting that he did prepare a second edition of *On Vision and Colors* in 1854 and that he continued to write notes in his own copy of the second edition. Consequently, Schopenhauer's interest in color theory was expressed throughout his philosophical career.

VOLUNTARISM. The word "voluntarism" is derived from the Latin *voluntas*, "will," and it generally refers to any philosophical position that views **reason** and the **intellect** as subservient or secondary to the **will**. It is common within the secondary literature, especially the English-language literature, to use this term to describe Schopenhauer's **philosophy**. The will is metaphysically primary for Schopenhauer: it is the essence of everything in the world, and everything is the objectification of the will, which is a goalless and nonrational striving. This also entails for him that the essence of human beings is not reason but the will. Consequently, he argued that it is the will or desire, passion, and appetite that determine the ends or goals of human behavior and that the intellect functions instrumentally, that is, it serves to present the means to satisfying the will by providing various possible courses of action. The will determines the actual action, which follows necessarily from a sufficient **motive**, with a bodily action itself being an act of will.

At a deeper level, he argued that our sensuous perceptions of things are colored by the will because we normally view things as direct or indirect means for satisfying or thwarting our desires. In this way, Schopenhauer emphasizes the interested or subjective nature of our ordinary **cognitions**, things that are only transcended in aesthetic **contemplation**, which he viewed as a disinterested and objective cognition in which the subject loses a sense of self. In his **ethics**, voluntarism is found in his claim that desires of particular types determine the moral quality of an action and the moral value of a persons' **character**.

– W –

WAGNER, RICHARD (1813–1883). In addition to being a composer of the first rank, Wagner was a polymath, publishing on topics in literature, politics, **aesthetics**, **history**, and **philosophy**. He was introduced to Schopenhauer by the poet Jörg Herwegh, and he read *The World as Will and Representation* in 1854. This experience transformed Wagner, and he continued a lively interest in Schopenhauer's philosophy for the remainder of his life. He made his friends read Schopenhauer, and he sent Schopenhauer's writings to a number of his correspondents. **Friedrich Nietzsche** was drawn to Wagner, in part, by their mutual devotion to Schopenhauer. Nietzsche captured, perhaps, the effect Schopenhauer had on Wagner when he said that Schopenhauer gave Wagner to himself. (When he said this, however, Schopenhauer had become for Nietzsche the "philosopher of decadence" and Wagner its artist.) In any case, there may not be a better example of the work of a great artist being influenced by that of a great philosopher than Wagner and Schopenhauer.

Wagner and Schopenhauer never met, although they had mutual acquaintances and Wagner even stayed for a time in 1860 in Frankfurt. Wagner's deep respect for Schopenhauer was not reciprocated, however. Wagner had 50 copies of the libretto for *The Ring of the Nibelung* privately published and in December 1854, he sent a dedicated copy "out of reverence and gratitude" to Schopenhauer. Wagner was too demure, moreover, to include a letter. Schopenhauer never directly thanked Wagner, but in the summer of 1855 he sent, through an acquaintance, his belated thanks for the libretto. He also included the advice that Wagner stop writing music, since his genius was poetry. For himself, Schopenhauer also said, he remained faithful to Rossini and Mozart. In the meanwhile, Schopenhauer annotated his copy of the libretto with a number of sarcastic comments. Schopenhauer did not respond at all in 1858, when Wagner sent him the libretto for *Tristan and Isolde*. Despite his treatment by Schopenhauer, Wagner's enthusiasm for his philosophy never abated, and unknown to Schopenhauer, Wagner's promotion of his philosophy was an important force for enhancing Schopenhauer's popularity.

WEAL (WOHL). **Woe** and weal are the ultimate aims of all actions. Schopenhauer understood weal as anything in agreement with the **will**, and since he claimed that anything in conformity with the will is **good**, anything that produces an individual's weal was called "good." Since someone's weal is an ultimate end of an action, the idea of "weal" plays a vital role in Schopenhauer's explanation of basic or fundamental human **incentives** or **motives**. Consequently, he argued that **egoism**, the desire for one's own weal, is the incentive for **morally indifferent** actions, and **compassion**, the desire for another's weal, is the incentive for actions possessing **moral worth**.

WILL (*WILLE*). The concept of the will is the most significant one in Schopenhauer's philosophy. The title of his main work, ***The World as Will and Representation***, highlights a double aspect view of the world as both will and **representation**. More deeply, however, the world is ultimately the will, since Schopenhauer viewed the will as the essence of the world, the ultimate substrate, the agent in unconscious functions of organisms, the common stuff of all being, and as that which is known empirically or *a posteriori*. The will is, he said, a true *ens realissimum*, the most real being. The world in all of its parts and plurality is will, and he argued that existence itself, the kind of existence of the whole and each part of the world, is from the will. The world as representation is simply the mirror of the will, and he viewed all the finiteness, suffering, and misery in the world as following from the will. He viewed the will as the **thing in itself**.

Thus everything is the will, according to Schopenhauer. It exists whole and undivided in every being. It has been everything that was; it is everything that is; and will be everything that will be. It is also all of this taken together, he believed. The will in its most expanded sense, in its most cosmological sense, is a goalless striving that exemplifies itself everywhere in nature, from the most universally expressed phenomena, the **forces of nature**, such as gravity, through the deliberate conduct of humans. The only difference between the two, he claimed, was the degree to which the will is objectified and not the inner nature of what is manifest. The objectification of the will has endless graduations analogous to that found between the feeblest to the brightest sunray or as that between the loudest tone and its softest echo.

Schopenhauer also argued that the will is one. Yet it is one not as an object is one, occupying a particular place at a specific time, nor is it one as a **concept** might be viewed as one, since a concept is abstracted from a plurality of things or particulars. The will is one, he claimed, as that which is outside the scope of the *principium individuationis*, **space**, and **time**, thus it is beyond the possibility of plurality and individuation. This suggests that the "oneness" of the will is best described as a form of non-plurality. Schopenhauer also argued that the will is not within the scope of the **principle of sufficient reason**, which applies only to the world as representation, and as such, it is outside the scope of all necessity. The **freedom** of the will is therefore a freedom from all necessity, according to Schopenhauer. This freedom, he said, is **transcendental**, not found in the world as representation. The will has **aesity**, he claimed, an independence from anything else, and the will is as it expresses itself. Thus he also attributed **responsibility** to the will. Because of the aesity of the will, Schopenhauer argued that his metaphysics of the will is also ethical. For that reason, he claimed more right than **Baruch Spinoza** to call his metaphysics "**ethics**," and unlike other philosophical systems, he could account for all of the monstrous, heartrending miseries from the will. In this way he said that his metaphysics of the will showed that the world had a moral significance; it is something that ought not to be; and he claimed that the **denial of the will**, the basis of the misery of existence, constitutes **salvation**. *See also* BODY.

WILL, AFFIRMATION OF THE (*DIE BEJAHUNG DES WILLENS*). Schopenhauer held that the world is the affirmation of the **will** or the **will to life**. (He used these two terms interchangeably.) The world is because the will affirms or objectifies itself, he claimed, and the nature of the world is as it is because the "will so wills." By viewing everything in the world as an objectification of the will, he also viewed everything within the world as the affirmation of the will. Still, although nature is the affirmation of the world, some natural objects express the nature of the will more completely or clearly than others. Thus he saw the conflict between struggle and conflicting chemical forces as affirmations of the will, but he held that these phenomena express the nature of the will less completely than the behavior of humans. Indeed, humans represent for him the most complete expression of the will and the affirmation of the will is the drive to maintain the body, to seek health, and to satisfy desire. The affirmation of the will, he said, is expressed most vehemently in the drive to procreate. Consequently, he found the sexual impulse to be the strongest affirmation of the will to life. *See also* LOVE, SEXUAL; WILL, DENIAL OF THE.

WILL, DENIAL OF THE (*DIE VERNEINUNG DES WILLENS*). Schopenhauer identified the denial of the **will** or the denial of the **will to life** (he used these terms interchangeably) with complete **resignation** or holiness. It proceeds, he said, from the quieter of the will, which is **cognition** (*Erkenntnis*) of the inner conflict and essential vanity of life, something that is expressed by everything that lives. This cognition can be the result of extreme personal suffering, he wrote, or by seeing through (*Durchschauen*) the ***principium individuationis***. The denial of the will represents true **salvation** for Schopenhauer, a deliverance from life, and since he viewed life as suffering, he claimed that it is a deliverance from suffering.

The denial of the will connotes the ultimate triumph of the **intellect** or **cognition** over the will. Instead of the intellect proving **motives** for the will, he claimed that possible motives for actions fade in the background, as it were, as the will itself is solely mirrored by the intellect. The denial of the will is not caused, he claimed, nor is it reached forcibly by intention or design. It comes suddenly, he argued, as if it flew from without. The denial of the will is the one and only point where the freedom of the will enters directly into the world as **representation**. It constitutes, he said, the "transcendental change" in the subject, using the words of Asmus (Matthias Claudius [1740–1815], German poet and publisher of the *Wandsbecker Boten*), and a radical transformation of a person's nature. In this regard, Schopenhauer saw equivalence between denial of the will and the Christian idea of new or rebirth.

Schopenhauer intimated that the denial of the will suggests that behind our existence lies something accessible to us only by shaking off the world. In this sense, he called the denier of the will the overcomer of the world, and he wrote that for this person, there is no will, no representation, no world. As such, he argued in the final section of the first volume of *The World as Will and Representation* that the state of the denier is not an absolute but a relative nothing, since it is the negation of everything that appears real to those full of will. In **religious** terms, this state is referred to as ecstasy, rapture, illumination, and union with **God**. Technically, he said, this is not a state of knowledge, since it lacks the **subject and object** correlation. It is also something that cannot be communicated; it is something we are unable to think. The state of the denier of the will is, he said at the end of the 41st chapter of the second volume of his main work, what **Buddhism** calls *nirvāna* or extinction. *See also* ASCETICISM; SINGLE THOUGHT; WILL, AFFIRMATION OF THE.

WILL IN NATURE, ON THE (*ÜBER DEN WILLEN IN DER NATUR*). Schopenhauer wrote this book with the hope and ardent desire that it would cultivate an audience sufficient to justify a second edition of *The World as Will and Representation*. It appeared in 1836 through the Frankfurt publisher Siegmund Schmerber. However, Schopenhauer's hope was not realized and his desire was not sated. The book attracted even less attention than his main work. It initially received one negative review in which the author correctly predicted that the book would not draw a readership for his earlier work. Five years after its publication, it received a second, negative review. In the fall of 1854, *On the Will in Nature* appeared as a second, improved edition, in which its vitriolic preface first appeared. Schopenhauer expected to publish a third edition, but this task was left to his literary executor, **Julius Frauenstädt**, who used Schopenhauer's notes and corrections from his interleaved copy of the book to publish the third edition in 1867, seven years after Schopenhauer's death.

The somewhat clumsy subtitle of *On the Will in Nature*, "A Discussion of the Corroborations from the Empirical Sciences That the Author's Philosophy Has Received since Its First Appearance," may suggest that Schopenhauer was doing no more than confirming in new forms that which he had already established in his main work through different means. While Schopenhauer attempted to show how "unprejudiced empiricists" articulated, from *a posteriori* sources, scientific theories that supported his thesis that what we recognize in ourselves as **will** is that which is expressed in all natural phenomena, his argument goes deeper than this. He analyzed the **natural sciences** to show how they lead to his metaphysics, and he argued that his metaphysics completes the scientific image of the world by providing an explanation of that which is presupposed and unexplainable by science. Consequently, he thought his metaphysics of the will provides a comprehensive explanation of the totality of experiences.

In the preface, Schopenhauer chided scientists and professors of philosophy for their ignorance of **Immanuel Kant**, and he took to task scientists who maintained a crude form of **realism** and "stupid **materialism**," and he chastised philosophy professors for serving the state, church, their own self-interests, and not the **truth**. Schopenhauer used the introduction to describe his project, *On the Will in Nature*, to promote Kant, and to condemn **Johann Gottlieb Fichte** and **Georg Wilhelm Friedrich Hegel**.

In addition to chiding some of his contemporaries for plagiarizing his work, Schopenhauer attempted to show in the first chapter, "Physiology and Pathology," that the will is the agent in both voluntary and involuntary bodily functions. The second chapter, "Comparative Anatomy," moved to consider the physical structures of **animal** life as spatial-temporal expression of their wills. He also drew on teleologically suggestive features of animal life and its adaptation to its environment to conclude that a **will**, unguided by **intellect**, was operative in nature. The third chapter, "Physiology of Plants," continued this theme, and Schopenhauer argued that what sprouts forth in vegetative nature is the will. This chapter contains one of his clearest discussions of the varieties of **causality** prevailing in animal life, plant life, and inorganic nature, namely, **motivation**, **stimulation**, and brute causality.

Schopenhauer attributed an especial significance to the fourth chapter, "Physical Astronomy," since he claimed in the supplementary essays to the second book of *The World as Will and Representation*, chapter 18, volume 2, that it states the fundamental truth of his philosophy with greater distinctness and clarity than anywhere else in his writings, namely, the transition from **appearance** to the **thing in itself**. Thus he claimed that anyone who wants to seriously investigate his philosophy has to carefully consider this chapter. Schopenhauer's goal in this chapter was to show that the will is the agent in all fundamental **forces of nature**. His argument, however, tends to rub against his claim that he corroborates his view by appeal to the sciences. The only corroborator of his view, the British astronomer John Herschel (1792–1871), was cited as holding that gravity is an expression of will. But Schopenhauer was forced to argue that Herschel's confirmation was only partial, since Herschel viewed the will as a function of the intellect. Consequently, Schopenhauer was left to his own devices, and instead of using science to vault to his metaphysics, he proceeded to mount his argument that the will is that which is expressed or objectified in everything in nature, by presenting an account in which the will is said to be all that is known empirically and *a posteriori* in nature. He attempted to show this by denying a venerable philosophical tradition in which the motion of bodies are attributed to two different sources, an internal source, attributed to a soul or will, and external source, attributed to an external **cause**. Schopenhauer collapsed this distinction, and he argued that all movements arising from a will presuppose a cause and those brought forth from an external source are a manifestation of a **body's** will. After surveying the hierarchical scale of nature, beginning with gravity and ending with human beings, Schopenhauer argued that his metaphysics of will enables us to develop a comprehensive explanation of nature from the insight that the will expressed in our bodily movements is the same force manifest in all of nature.

"Physical Astronomy," concludes Schopenhauer's survey of the natural sciences. The next three chapters draw on other "empirical" sources that support his metaphysics. The fifth chapter, "Linguistics," explores the ways in which various languages imply or suggest that a will or willing is expressed in organic and inorganic nature. Curiously, the sixth chapter, "Animal Magnetism and Magic," is the lengthiest chapter of the book. It provides the reader with Schopenhauer's deep interest in occult phenomena. Here, Schopenhauer attempts to show how his metaphysics provides an explanation for hypnotism, sympathetic cures, clairvoyance, table-rapping, and the like. The seventh chapter, "Sinology," discusses the affinities Schopenhauer saw between his metaphysics and Taoism, Confucianism, **Buddhism**, and **Hinduism**. This chapter would be of interest to those studying the formative influences on Schopenhauer's thought, and it includes a footnote in which he lists the European literature on Buddhism with which he was familiar.

The eighth chapter, "Reference to **Ethics**," may seem out of place in a work in which Schopenhauer said that he would not deal with any area of his **philosophy** other than metaphysics. Yet Schopenhauer claims here that he had more entitlement than **Baruch Spinoza** to call his metaphysics "ethics." His metaphysics connects the physical world order to the moral world order, he argued, since it demonstrates that the metaphysical will satisfies the requirements of any moral attribution, namely, it is both free and responsible for the nature of the world. In particular, Schopenhauer claimed that his metaphysics challenges the **optimism** found in Western philosophy and it explains why wickedness and **evil** follow from the very essence of the world. He also used the chapter to reprimand European readers of his work by claiming that what they perceived as the paradox of the **ascetic** results of his **philosophy** would not be viewed as paradoxical to the Eastern mind.

Schopenhauer's brief "Conclusion" does not summarize his work. Rather, he used his concluding remarks to, once again, berate his contemporaries for living from and not for philosophy, and he reiterates that living for philosophy requires an uncompromising pursuit of the **truth**.

WITTGENSTEIN, LUDWIG (1889–1951) • 187

WILL TO LIFE (*WILLE ZUM LEBEN*). In the 54th chapter of the first volume of his main work, *The World as Will and Representation*, Schopenhauer said that it is a mere pleonasm or redundancy to call the **will** the will to life, since "what the will wills is always life [*Was der Wille will immer das Lebens ist*]." There are a number of ways to understand this claim. He held that the world as **representation** is the mirror of the will whereby the will expresses itself in increasing degrees of distinctness and completeness, the highest objectification of which is the human being. Once the will objectifies itself, he argued also that its development is necessary, culminating in the human being. The lowest level of this development, the least complete expression, constitutes the inorganic world, which necessarily leads to the organic, and thus to life. But in the lower expressions of the will, inorganic and vegetative nature, the will is a blind, irresistible urge to be. With cognitive beings, nonrational or nonhuman **animals** and rational animals or human beings, the will is expressed as an urge to reproduce, to produce life, to continue the species. So in a sense, the will is the will to life, an impulse not simply for the self-preservation of individuals, but as he claimed in the 45th chapter of the second volume of his main work, "the will wills life absolutely and for all times," exhibiting itself as the sexual impulse, which has endless generations of living beings as its end. Humans, as the most distinct and complete manifestation of the will, express the will most distinctly, and this is shown by the dominance of sexuality in human life, which he thought only appears to serve the individual, but in reality furthers the continuation of life, or the **affirmation of the will**. *See also* LOVE, SEXUAL.

WITTGENSTEIN, LUDWIG (1889–1951). It has often been noted that, along with **Friedrich Nietzsche**, Wittgenstein was the most significant and influential philosopher affected by Schopenhauer. Like in the case of Nietzsche, there is little doubt that Wittgenstein derived some inspiration from Schopenhauer, but the specifics and enduring effects of Schopenhauer on his philosophy are far less clear with Wittgenstein than with Nietzsche. Scholars tend to recognize two phases to Wittgenstein's philosophical career, the "early" and "later" Wittgenstein. In his two major works representing these two phases, the early Wittgenstein of the *Tractatus Logicos-Philosophicus* (1922) and the later Wittgenstein of the *Philosophical Investigations* (1953), there are no direct references to Schopenhauer and there are numerous views radically distinct from Schopenhauer's. Nietzsche, however, did not share Wittgenstein's indifference toward his philosophical ancestors, and he referred to Schopenhauer in almost all of his books. Moreover, many of Nietzsche's antipodal views were self-consciously presented in opposition to Schopenhauer's, and even when Nietzsche presented particular ideas antithetical to those of his "only educator, the *great* Arthur Schopenhauer," his educator's imprimatur can be detected in some of the means through which he arrived at these oppositions. It is clear that Schopenhauer was a more important figure for Nietzsche than he was for Wittgenstein, and it is also the case that Nietzsche read more intensely and knew Schopenhauer better than Wittgenstein. Moreover, when scholars detect affinities between Wittgenstein and Schopenhauer, the question of Schopenhauer's direct influence on Wittgenstein is further complicated by the fact that he read others who were influenced by Schopenhauer, such as Oswald Spengler, Leo Tolstoy, and Otto Weininger. Through these sources, Schopenhauerian ideas could have found resonance in Wittgenstein's work, but in a form mediated and altered by others. Nevertheless, in *Culture and Value* (1980, written largely in 1931), Wittgenstein named Schopenhauer as an influence on his thought, along with Ludwig Boltzmann, Gottlob Frege, Heinrich Hertz, Karl Kraus, Adolph Loos, Bertrand Russell, Oswald Spengler, Piero Sraffu, and Otto Weininger. Later in the same book, however, he also called Schopenhauer a "crude mind" in the sense that when real depth begins, his thought comes to an end.

It has been widely reported that Wittgenstein said that he read **The World as Will and Representation** in his youth; that his first philosophy was a Schopenhauerian epistemological idealism; and that he was impressed by Schopenhauer's world as **representation**, but not his account of the world as **will**. In addition to his youthful encounter with Schopenhauer when he was around the age of 16, it appears he reread Schopenhauer during his service as an Austrian soldier in the World War I. His *Notebooks 1914–1916*, especially the entries from 21 July through 19 November 1916, appear to represent Wittgenstein's rethinking of a cluster of Schopenhauer's ideas, although Schopenhauer is mentioned only once. In the entry from 8 August

1916, Wittgenstein wrote, "One could say (like Schopenhauer [*Schopenhauerisch*]): The world of representation is neither good nor evil, but the willing subject." It has also been claimed that Wittgenstein was deeply affected by Schopenhauer's views on **suicide**. (Wittgenstein appeared suicidal at various points in his life and three of his brothers committed suicide.) He also was influenced by Schopenhauer's views on **music**. In addition, he was fond of quoting from the "Aphorisms on the Wisdom of Life," from the first volume of *Parerga and Paralipomena*. Wittgenstein's familiarity with the "Aphorisms" might explain his remarks on happiness and unhappiness found in both the *Notebooks 1914–1916* and the *Tractatus*.

To explain how Schopenhauer "influenced" Wittgenstein's thoughts, the secondary literature focuses primarily on the early Wittgenstein. Scholars tend to sense the spurs of Schopenhauer lingering in remarks made towards the end of the *Tractatus*, which concern solipsism, the I, **ethics**, **aesthetics**, the connection between ethics and aesthetics, death, wishing, willing, acting, **God**, the riddle of existence, and **mysticism**. To this list some also attribute to Schopenhauer the metaphors of the eye (*Tractatus* 5.6331) and the ladder (*Tractatus* 6.54). Wittgenstein's treatments of these remarks are cryptic, and they seem not to have been prepared well by what he had earlier asserted. This has led scholars to turn to the discussion of these topics in the *Notebooks 1914–1916*, where Schopenhauer's spirit is more visible. By turning to Schopenhauer, many scholars find a broader context in which Wittgenstein's enigmatic remarks receive greater articulation. Within this context, scholars find that, while Schopenhauer prompted some of Wittgenstein's reflections, he used Schopenhauer's insights to also undermine his metaphysics of the **will**. Some scholars have also heard a faint echo of Schopenhauer in the "later" Wittgenstein's concepts of "forms of life," "family resemblance," "seeing as," and Wittgenstein's argument against a private language.

WOE (*WEHE*). Schopenhauer argued that the ultimate aim of all actions is some being's **weal** or woe. By "woe" he meant something contrary to the **will**, and since he regarded things contrary to the will as either **bad** or **evil**, he claimed that whatever brings about someone's woe is either bad or evil. As an ultimate aim of human actions, the concept of "woe" plays a central explanatory role in Schopenhauer's account of the basic and fundamental **incentives** for human behavior. He described **malice** as the desire for another's woe, and he concluded that malice is the motive for **morally reprehensible** actions. In a footnote within chapter 48 of the second volume of *The World as Will and Representation*, Schopenhauer wrote that the desire for one's own woe is the motive for **asceticism**.

WOMEN (*FRAUEN*). Women were a problem for Schopenhauer. This was true in both his personal and philosophical lives. He had a horrible relationship with his mother, **Johanna Schopenhauer**, and his relationship with his sister, **Adele Schopenhauer**, caused her considerable distress. As a young man, he engaged in a number of meaningless sexual affairs, and he fathered a daughter out of wedlock. He was much taken by the actress Karoline Jagemann, later the Countess of Heygendorff, but his love was not reciprocated. He contemplated marriage seriously several times, most seriously with an actress and chorus girl, Caroline Richter, later "Medon," but suspicions about her motives and health prevented a union. Later, he would write in his notes that all genuine philosophers have remained unmarried, a reflection **Friedrich Nietzsche** would use—unattributed—in his *On the Genealogy of Morality*. Then, in 1821, there was a notorious incident with **Caroline Marquet**. She accused Schopenhauer of beating her and she eventually won a series of lawsuits against him. Her reward was 60 talers a year for the last 20 years of her life.

Schopenhauer is well known for his misogyny, and a number of commentators attribute this to his unhappy relationship with his mother and his inability to establish a healthy sexual relationship with a woman. He was reported to have once remarked that he was very fond of women, but they were not fond of him. In his private journal, "About Myself," which is included in the fourth volume of *Schopenhauer: Manuscript Remains*, he approvingly quoted Byron: "The more I see of men, the less I like them; if I could say so of women too, all would be well." Thus, for some of his commentators, Schopenhauer's misogyny was a case of "sour grapes." While this may be true, it is also important to note that this cultural milieu was steeped in sexism and that he supported many of his observations by drawing on religious and philosophical traditions of both the East and

West. Indeed, the two philosophers he esteemed most, **Plato** and **Immanuel Kant**, were also hardly known for their enlightened views concerning women. In many ways, his **philosophy** said little about women that had not been said before, and its uniqueness is probably found in the ways in which he integrated traditional views concerning women within his philosophy.

In addition to the Marquet affair, which is highlighted in almost all biographical sketches of Schopenhauer's life, his essay "On Women," from the second volume of the *Parerga and Paralipomena*, established Schopenhauer's reputation as an arch-misogynist. Not only was this book highly successful, compared to his other books, but more importantly, collections of essays from it were published under separate titles in German and in translation. This was especially true of his essay "On Women." Consequently, Schopenhauer's views on women became well known and better known among the general populace than those of other philosophers. Due to this, his misogyny became more apparent than that of other philosophers.

Schopenhauer viewed women as the *sexus sequoir*, the inferior sex that takes second place in every respect. The female form itself shows that a woman is not destined for great work intellectually or physically, he argued, and the female sex is better called the "unaesthetic," rather than the "fairer sex." It is only the male **intellect** clouded by the sexual impulse that would find this "undersized, narrow-shouldered, broad-hipped, and short-legged sex" the fairer sex, he wrote. Yet nature endows women with beauty and charm during their childbearing years in order to play with male sexual desire, he argued, and this enables them to attract a man who will care for them and their children. Women prefer young, strong, and handsome men, he said, because they desire to produce strong children. Women are especially qualified to raise children, he said, because they are really just grown-up children themselves and not real human beings like men. Because women exist solely for the propagation of the race, they live generally more in the species than in individuals, he also argued, and their "unconscious and innate morality" is tied to the continuation of the species. This broader interest in the species gives rise to discord and disharmony in marriages, he claimed, since women identify with their children and place their children's well-being above that of their husbands, who often are regarded simply as a means of support. Women should be housewives or girls who hope to become so, he argued, and they should not be allowed to inherit property, he said, because they are inclined to extravagance and are likely to squander wealth in a short time.

He also claimed that women possess a weaker faculty of **reason** than men. Consequently, they are more focused on the immediately present and intuitively present, rather than on the past and future. This also entails that women are less capable of abstract thought, fixed resolve, and principle governed behavior. Since principles and abstract rules are central to **justice**, he held that injustice is a major failing of women. This, coupled with their being weaker than males, means that women cannot do their will through force. Thus they have to rely on cunning, and Schopenhauer said that women posses an instinctive tendency to lie, something nature gave them for their defense and protection, just as it gave bulls their horns. Because women are incapable of taking a purely objective interest in anything, Schopenhauer claimed that they have no bent or receptivity for **art** and that the most eminent minds of the whole sex had never produced a genuinely great work of art or any work of permanent value.

Schopenhauer's bleak view of women does contain some elements of praise, but as is often the case, these elements of praise can also reflect more subtle elements of his misogyny. Because women are more matter-of-fact than men, he said, they do not see in things more than actually exists, whereas men are inclined to abstraction and can easily magnify what is present and add something imaginary. Consequently, he thought it not to be a bad thing to consult women, since men tend to overlook what "lies under their noses" and women's different way of apprehending things can allow men to regain a sense of reality. Women are also more expressive of **compassion** and outdo men in the virtue of **philanthropy**, which is the highest virtue, Schopenhauer argued, but they are inferior in justice, honesty, and conscientiousness. This, of course, is due to women's lesser rational capacity and heightened susceptibility to feelings. Since he thought we inherit our **will** from our fathers and our **intellect** from our mothers, he suggested that the source of human greatness and **salvation** comes from our mothers, whereas that which we need to overcome and deny—our will—is from our fathers. (I will leave it up to you, my reader, to think about the Freudian implications of this.) *See also* LOVE, SEXUAL.

WORLD AS WILL AND REPRESENTATION, THE (*DIE WELT ALS WILLE UND VORSTELLUNG*). This is Schopenhauer's *magnum opus*, his main philosophical book. He regarded virtually all of his other books as supporting, clarifying, augmenting, and extending to new topics of inquiry the central ideas and discussions found in its first edition. As early as 1813, Schopenhauer envisioned developing a **philosophy** that would be metaphysics and **ethics** in one, and he labored on this philosophy from 1814 through 1818 in Dresden. The book appeared in December 1818, although it bore a publication date of 1819. It was published by the Leipzig publishing firm of **F. A. Brockhaus**, a firm that would also publish its second and third editions in 1844 and 1859, respectively. Brockhaus would later publish the first collected edition of Schopenhauer's works in 1873.

Schopenhauer had great expectations concerning the reception of his book. In its preface, he claimed that he had provided that which had been long sought under the name of philosophy, and he believed that he had solved the great problem of existence, that is, he had explained the ubiquity of suffering and **death** and that he had shown the meaning of the wretchedness of life. Yet what he thought philosophy sought, or at least what he had provided, was not what the public was buying. Certainly, it drew no resonance among professors of philosophy. *The World as Will and Representation* did draw a few reviews, but the best were lukewarm. He was viewed by some of his reviewers as an epigone of **idealism** and some said that what was worthwhile in his book could be found already in **Johann Gottlieb Fichte** and **Friedrich Wilhelm Joseph von Schelling**. In any case, he was not viewed as making a substantial contribution to philosophy. Later, Schopenhauer would view the lack of reception of his philosophy as a conspiracy of silence among professors of philosophy, something due to the prevailing "Hegel*gloria*" of his times.

Still, in 1821, Schopenhauer imagined that by 1828 there would be a public demand for a second edition of his masterpiece. When he wrote his publisher in 1828 about bringing out a new edition, Brockhaus told him that he still had 150 copies of the original 750 and that he could not even say how many had actually sold, since he had many of the copies converted to scrap. It was not until 1844 that Schopenhauer convinced Brockhaus to bring out a second edition, but this was only done after he waived the author's honorarium and told his publisher that the first edition was a sketch to which the second added detail and color. So, once again, Brockhaus printed 750 examples, but this new edition was also virtually ignored. The third edition finally appeared in 1859, roughly a year before Schopenhauer's death, and after he had obtained the fame he so desperately desired. Now there was a demand for his philosophy, and Brockhaus responded to the demand by publishing a run of 2,230 copies.

The second edition of *The World as Will and Representation* put it in the form in which it is read today. Schopenhauer added a second volume of 50 essays that were organized to supplement the four main divisions of the first edition, which now became the first volume. To this volume, he had a second preface, where, among other observations, he claimed that he had not changed his mind about any of his fundamental ideas during the 25 years between editions. He also numbered, for the first time, the sections in the first edition, included references to Eastern thought to articulate his doctrines, and revised and expanded its appendix, "Criticism of Kantian Philosophy."

Schopenhauer provided instructions for reading his book in the preface to its first edition. He asserted that it imparted a **single thought**, rather than articulating a system of thoughts. In the latter, he claimed, there is an architectonic connection between thoughts, such that an earlier one supports and is not supported by a later one. A single thought, however, represents an organic unity which, when split into parts for the purpose of being communicated, has a very different relationship between its parts than that expressed in a system of thoughts. Every part supports the whole, he said, just as much as the part is supported by the whole. One comes gradually to understand this whole as one comes to understand every part, and every part, even the smallest, cannot be fully understood until the whole has first been understood. Due to this, he warned his readers that the form of his book contradicts its matter. A book has a first and last line, but a single thought has no first and last part. So he advised his readers not to lose sight of his single thought as they worked through all the details found in the book.

In order to grasp his single thought, Schopenhauer specified that *The World as Will and Representation* should be read twice. One should be very patient during the first reading, he said, and bear in mind that the beginning material of his book presupposes the end almost as much as the end the beginning, and that the earlier parts pre-

suppose the later almost as much as the later the earlier. He emphasized, moreover, that he said "almost," since the book gave priority
to material that would lead to the greatest possible comprehensibility
and clearness. So as one reads the work, he stated, do not merely
think of what is being said, but also think of its possible conse-
quences. Moreover, he also warned his readers that his philosophy
contradicts many current philosophical opinions and that it is likely
to do so with their own opinions. The result of this conflict is that one
may feel a lively disapproval about some topic, but this is just a misunderstanding, he claimed, and if one has patience, and works
through the book, a second reading will dispel one's qualms, since
the second reading will cast everything in a new light. In this way, he
suggested that the whole of his single thought emerges by understanding all the details of his work and that once one has this thought
in mind, the second reading leads to an understanding of even the
smallest details of his thought.

In the same preface Schopenhauer also specified the background
required to understand his philosophy. Since his philosophy started
from **Immanuel Kant**'s, he said a thorough acquaintance with the
"great Kant" was necessary. Yet, because Kant's philosophy contained grave errors as well as profound insights, he directed his readers to study the appendix, "Criticism of the Kantian Philosophy" before reading the first book. To be even better prepared both to hear
him and be more susceptible to what he had to say, his reader should
have dwelt for a while with the "divine **Plato**," he said. Even better,
he continued, if his reader has assimilated the ancient Indian wisdom
expressed in the *Upanishads*, then it would not appear that he is
speaking in a hostile and foreign tongue.

Schopenhauer realized that the demands he placed on his readers
were presumptuous and immodest. But he thought that they should
show gratitude rather than reproach him. After all, if they were unable
to meet his reading requirements, they would not understand his philosophy. Thus, he said, his warnings should keep them from wasting
even an hour on a book they would not understand. Still, he anticipated that his readers would be in a dilemma, since they had bought a
book that they could not read. So he reminded them that they knew
how to use a book without reading it. Bind it handsomely and use it to
fill a gap in your library, or place it on the dressing table of a "learned

lady friend." But the course of action that he especially advised was to write a review of it. Given the dismal sales of *The World as Will and Representation*, it is unlikely that many people found themselves in the dilemma of finding a use for an unread book, but it is likely that he thought that its reviewers followed his advice.

Schopenhauer asserted on numerous occasions that a fundamental understanding of his philosophy requires reading every line he wrote (although he was ambivalent about the significance of *On Vision and Colors* by the time the second edition of his main work appeared). The final structure of *The World as Will and Representation* reinforces this assertion, and it also shows the centrality of this book in Schopenhauer's *oeuvre*. Before reading the book, he assigned its "introduction," that is, his dissertation, *On the Fourfold Root of the Principle of Sufficient Reason*. With the second edition, he dropped the requirement to read the book twice, and recommended reading the first volume and then the supplementing essays in the second volume. In the second volume he claimed that *On the Will in Nature* was the essential supplement for the second book of the first volume and that the essays in the second volume presupposed its knowledge. He also said the same about *The Two Fundamental Problems of Ethics* in regard to the fourth book of the first volume and its supplementing essays in the second. Lastly, in the preface to the third edition, he mentions that the essays in the second volume of *Parerga and Paralipomena* belong to the systematic presentation of his philosophy, and they were not integrated in his main work because in 1851 he had doubted that there would be a third edition of his main work. Through these statements he thereby related all of his books directly back to his philosophical masterpiece, and back specifically to the four books or divisions of its first edition.

The first four divisions, or what Schopenhauer referred to as "books" in his table of contents, present different aspects or points of view on his single thought. The books alternate from a beginning reflection on the world as **representation** to a reflection on the world as **will**, returning once again to the world as representation and then moving to a final reflection on the world as will. Thus the first and third books treat of the world as representation, and the second and fourth treat of the world as will.

In the first book, Schopenhauer presented the general contours of his **epistemology**. Among other subjects, he stressed the **subject and**

object correlation, the **principle of sufficient reason** and the *a priori* form of **cognition**, on laying the grounds for his **idealism**. The third book, which still considers the world as representation, focuses on his **aesthetics**. In it, he emphasized representations that were outside the scope of the principle of sufficient reason. There he considered and analyzed aesthetic **contemplation** and the objects of such contemplation, which are **Platonic Ideas**; he presented his views on the **beautiful** and the **sublime**; he classified the **arts**; he presented his view on **genius**; and he connected his ideas of **resignation** and **denial of the will** to the experience of **tragedy** and great **music**.

The second book of *The World as Will and Representation* presents his metaphysics or philosophy of nature. He argued that the will as **thing in itself** is the essence of all representations and that it is that which is objectified in all of nature. Among other subjects, he discussed the limits of scientific explanations of nature and the relationship between **science** and his philosophy. He introduced, for the first time, his doctrine of Platonic Ideas in this book. The fourth book, his "ethical book," deals with the most serious subject, human behavior, which, he said, expresses the highest or most adequate objectification of the will. In it he presents his philosophy of **right**, his ethics, and he describes the connections between virtue and **salvation**. It culminates in his theory of salvation as **denial of the will**.

The work ends with the remark that to those who have denied the will, "this very real world of ours with all its suns and galaxies, is— nothing." This naturally complements the very first line of his masterpiece, "The world is my representation." Together they represent what Schopenhauer regarded as the entire range of his philosophy, which he said went from the affirmation to the denial of the will. What came before this affirmation or what comes after this denial, he claimed could not be said. Both were **transcendent**.

WORLD, KNOT OF THE (*WELTKNOTEN*). *See* I.

WORTH, MORAL (*MORALISHER WERT*). The concept of moral worth played such a central role in Schopenhauer's **ethics** that in the key statement of his method of ethics in section 13 of *On the Basis of Morality*, he claimed that the discovery of the **motive** for actions possessing moral worth was the discovery of the ultimate ground or

explanation of morality and that the knowledge of human susceptibility to this motive was the knowledge of the foundation of morals.
He employed as paradigm cases of actions possessing moral worth,
actions expressing voluntary **justice**, pure **philanthropy**, and real
magnanimity. What these sorts of actions had in common, he argued,
was that they solicited the actor's feeling of self-satisfaction and the
feeling of approbation by an impartial or disinterested witness. Fur-
thermore, he viewed all actions possessing moral worth as expressing an agent's desire for another's **weal**. Consequently, he argued
that **compassion**, the desire for another's weal, was the motive for
all actions possessing moral worth and that human susceptibility to
compassion, to be moved to seek another's well-being, was due to
the **cognition** that others are ourselves once more. *See also* TAT
TVAM ASI.

WRONG (*UNRECHT*). Schopenhauer viewed a wrong as an action
by which one individual compels another to serve the wrongdoer's
interests instead of his or her own. In a more technical sense, he
claimed that when one individual acts to affirm his or her **will** in a
manner that requires the denial of another person's will, you have a
wrong. He also argued that wrongdoing is inevitable, since the will
manifests itself in the self-affirmation of one's own body in innumerable individuals, each one of which seeks their continued existence and **weal**, that is, each person is driven to act egoistically to
some degree. The many wrongs individuals inflict on one another
also illustrates what Schopenhauer saw as the great conflict of the
will with itself, as expressed in the world as **representation**.

The most graphic illustration of a wrong is cannibalism, where one
individual literally eats the body of another. Here, the self-affirmation of
a person's own body is literally the denial of another's self-affirmation
of his or her body. (He did say that the will is a hungry will!) Murder,
mutilation, assault, slavery, and theft constitute wrongs, according to
Schopenhauer. Wrongs are committed, he said, by either violence,
where one physically forces another to serve one's will, or by cunning,
where one employs some form of deception to mislead another to pursue one's interests. A lie, he argued, is like all acts of violence, since it
has as its purpose the extension of the authority of the liar's will over
another, of affirming one's will by denying another's.

Appendix: Chronology of the First Appearances of Schopenhauer's Philosophical Books in English Translation

1877

The Will in Nature: An Account of the Corroboration Received by the Author's Philosophy. Trans. Unknown. New York: Eckler.

1883

The World as Will and Idea. Trans. R. B. Haldane and J. Kemp. London: Trüber. 3 vols.

1889

Two Essays: On the Fourfold Root of the Principle of Sufficient Reason and On the Will in Nature. Trans. Mme. Karl Hillebrand (Jessie Taylor). London: G. Bell.

1903

The Basis of Morality. Trans. Arthur Brodrick Bullock. London: Swan Sonnenschein; New York: Macmillan.

1942

On Vision and Colours. Trans. E. F. J. Payne. Karachi: The Federation Book-Stall.

1960

Essay on the Freedom of the Will. Trans. Konstantin Kolenda. Indianapolis: Bobbs-Merrill.

1974

Parerga and Paralipomena. Short Philosophical Essays. Trans. E. F. J. Payne. Oxford: Clarendon Press. 2 vols.

* * *

There has not been a translation of Schopenhauer's *Die beiden Grundprobleme der Ethik* under a single cover. Kolenda (1960) is a translation of its first essay, "*Über die Freiheit des menschlichen Willens*," and Bullock (1903) is a translation of its second essay, "*Über das Fundament der Moral.*" Payne's translation, *On the Basis of Morality* (Indianapolis: Bobbs-Merrill, 1965) includes prefaces to the first and second editions of *Die beiden Grundprobleme der Ethik.* Payne (1974) was the first complete English translation of *Parerga and Paralipomena.* From 1881 to 1974, all of these essays, in various combinations, were published under separate titles and covers by different translators.

Bibliography

CONTENTS

READER'S NOTE

The aims of this first part of the bibliography, "Writings of Schopenhauer," are fourfold: to provide a listing of the most frequently cited
German collected editions of Schopenhauer's works; to list additional
significant German primary source materials; to provide a comprehensive listing of English translations of Schopenhauer's books; and to

provide a selected listing of English-language collections of essays drawn from Schopenhauer's *Oeuvre*.

The single, most comprehensive bibliography for Schopenhauer's primary and secondary literature is Arthur Hübscher's *Schopenhauer-Bibliographie* (Stuttgart-Bad Cannstatt: Frommann-Holzboog, 1981). It includes a comprehensive listing of Schopenhauer's writings in German and in translation through 1981. A more updated bibliography, through 1995, is Joachim Aul's *Schopenhauer Bibliogaphie* (Englesbach: Hänsel-Hohenhausen, 1996). The *Schopenhauer-Jahrbuch* publishes an annual bibliography of the recent primary and secondary literature in each of its volumes. A comprehensive chronological listing of Schopenhauer's writings from 1813–1988, compiled by David E. Cartwright and Eric von der Luft, can be found in *Schopenhauer: New Essays in Honor of his 200th Birthday*, edited by Eric von der Luft (Lewiston, New York: The Edwin Mellen Press, 1988).

The goal of the second part of the bibliography, "Writings on Schopenhauer," is to provide a comprehensive listing of the Anglophone literature on Schopenhauer. To make this bibliography more useful for the reader, I have subsumed entries under nine major categories: Biographical Works; General Works; Aesthetics; Epistemology and Metaphysics; Moral Philosophy; Religion; Other Philosophers; Other Significant People; and Electronic Sources, Journals, and Societies.

Some of the principles that guided the listing of entries under the general categories are straightforward, and others are not. Those that are straightforward involve the categories of Biographical Works, General Works, and Electronic Sources, Journals, and Societies. Entries under the first category focus on Schopenhauer's life or events in his life; those listed under the second discuss Schopenhauer's philosophy as a whole; and those listed under the third concern web-based resources, journals specializing in Schopenhauer's philosophy, and philosophical societies.

Entries listed under Aesthetics, Epistemology and Metaphysics, and Moral Philosophy have been guided by principles less straightforward. While these categories include writings on topics and issues traditional to these areas of philosophy, I have followed Schopenhauer's placement of topics and issues within the four books of the first volume of *The World as Will and Representation*, and the supplementary essays to these four books in its second volume. For that reason, writings that discuss Schopenhauer's view of history are listed under Aesthetics, since that is the theme of the third book of *The World as Will and Representation* and the primary location of his reflections on history. I have combined the themes of the first two books, epistemology and metaphysics, into one general category, since many of the entries listed in this category deal with topics common to both of these areas. Schopenhauer referred to the fourth book of his chief work as the "ethical book." I have used the broader rubric of "moral philosophy" to capture Schopenhauer's very broad sense of morality, whose topic, he held, is the actions of humans. In addition to topics traditional to ethics, entries listed under this category involve discussions of Schopenhauer's views on the moral significance and value of the world, death, pessimism, sexual love, denial of the will, asceticism, and salvation. To gain a robust sense of topics for these categories, the reader is advised to consult the listings under "see also" that are found after the dictionary entries for Aesthetics, Epistemology, Metaphysics, and Ethics. Under the category "Religion," I have listed writings that discuss Schopenhauer's view of religion and those that discuss his relationships to figures and topics found in Western and Eastern religious thought.

Since many readers will want to find the literature on Schopenhauer's relationships to other Western philosophers, I have developed the general category of Other Philosophers. In this category I have included entries whose focus was Schopenhauer and one or more other philosophers, regardless of the specific area of philosophy under discussion. Entries listed under Other Significant People discuss Schopenhauer's relationship to important figures in science, art, literature, psychology, sociology, and music.

WRITINGS OF SCHOPENHAUER

Schopenhauer in German

Faksimilenachdruck der 1. Auflage der Welt als Wille und Vorstellung. Edited by Rudolf Malter. Frankfurt am Main: Insel, 1987.
Gesammelte Briefe. Edited by Arthur Hübscher. Bonn: Bouvier, 1987.
Der handschriftliche Nachlass. 5 volumes. Edited by Arthur Hübscher. Frankfurt am Main: Kramer, 1970.

1. *Frühe Manuskripte* (1804–1818).
2. *Kritische Auseinandersetzungen* (1809–1818)

3. *Berliner Manuskripte* (1818–1830)
4. I. *Die Manuskriptbücher der Jahre* (1830–1852)
5. II. *Letzte Manuskripte* / Gracians Handorakel
6. *Randschriften zu Büchern*

Philosophische Vorlesungen aus dem handschriftlichen Nachlass. 4 volumes. Edited by Volker Spierling. Munich: R. Piper, 1984–1986.

1. *Theorie des gesammten Vorstellens, Denkens und Erkennens*
2. *Metaphysik der Natur*
3. *Metaphysik des Schönen*
4. *Metaphysik der Sitten*

Die Reisetagbücher. Edited by Ludger Lütkehaus. Zurich: Hoffmans, 1988.
Schopenhauer: Sämtliche Werke. 7 volumes. Edited by Arthur Hübscher. Mannheim: F. A. Brockhaus, 4th edition, 1988.

1. *Schriften zur Erkenntnislehre*
   Ueber die vierfache Wurzel des Sutzes vom zureichenden Grunde
   Ueber das Sehn und die Farben
2. *Die Welt als Wille und Vorstellung*, volume 1
3. *Die Welt als Wille und Vorstellung*, volume 2
4. *Schriften zur Naturphilosophie und zur Ethik*
   Ueber den Willen in der Natur
   Die beiden Grundprobleme der Ethik
5. *Parerga und Paralipomena*, volume 1
6. *Parerga und Paralipomena*, volume 2
7. *Ueber die vierfache Wurzel des Satzes vom zureichenden Grunde* (1st edition, 1813)

Sämtliche Werke. 5 volumes. Edited by Wolfgang Frhr. von Löhneysen. Darmstadt: Wissenschaftliche Buchgesellschaft, 2nd edition, 1968.

1. *Die Welt als Wille und Vorstellung*
2. *Die Welt als Wille und Vorstellung*
3. *Kleinere Schriften*
4. *Parerga und Paralipomena*
5. *Parerga und Paralipomena*

Werke in fünf Bänden: Nach den Ausgaben letzter Hand. 5 volumes. Edited by Ludger Lütkehaus. Zurich: Hoffmans Verlag, 1988.

Werke in zehn Bänden [Zürcher Ausgabe]. 10 volumes. Edited by Arthur Hübscher. Zurich: Diogenes, 1977.

1. *Die Welt als Wille und Vorstellung*
2. *Die Welt als Wille und Vorstellung*
3. *Die Welt als Wille und Vorstellung*
4. *Die Welt als Wille und Vorstellung*
5. *Über die vierfache Wurzel des Satzes vom zureichenden Grunde*
   Über den Willen in der Natur
6. *Die beiden Grundprobleme der Ethik*
7. *Parerga und Paralipomena*
8. *Parerga und Paralipomena*
9. *Parerga und Paralipomena*
10. *Parerga und Paralipomena*

Schopenhauer in English Translation

Books

Die beiden Grundprobleme der Ethik

There is no English translation of this book under separate cover. The two essays that compose this work have appeared under separate covers:

1. *Über die Freiheit des menschlichen Willens*
   Essay on the Freedom of the Will. Translated, with an introduction by Konstantin Kolenda. Indianapolis: Bobbs-Merrill, 1960; reprint, Oxford: Basil Blackwell, 1985.
   Prize Essay on the Freedom of the Will. Translated by E. F. J. Payne. Edited with an introduction by Günter Zöllner. Cambridge: Cambridge University Press, 1999.
2. *Über das Fundament der Moral*
   The Basis of Morality. Translated, with an introduction by Arthur Broderick Bollock. London: Swan Sonnenschein, 1903; 2nd edn., London: Allen & Unwin, 1915.
   On the Basis of Morality. Translated by E. F. J. Payne. With an introduction by Richard Taylor. Indianapolis: Bobbs-Merrill, 1965; revised edition, Oxford: Berghan Books, 1995 (edited, with an introduction by David E. Cartwright); reprint, Indianapolis: Hacklett, 1997.

Parerga und Paralipomena: Kleine philosophische Schriften

Parerga and Paralipomena. 2 volumes. Translated by E. F. J. Payne. Oxford: Clarendon Press, 1974; reprint, 2001.

Über die vierfache Wurzel des Satzes vom zureichenden Grunde. Eine philosophische Abhandlung

On the Fourfold Root of the Principle of Sufficient Reason. Translated by Mme. Karl Hillebrand. London: G. Bell, 1889; reprint, London: G. Bell, 1986. Published as *Two Essays* with Hillebrand's translations of *On the Will in Nature*.
On the Fourfold Root of the Principle of Sufficient Reason. Translated by E. F. J. Payne. With an introduction by Richard Taylor. La Salle, Ill.: Open Court Press, 1974; reprint, 2003.
Schopenhauer's Early Fourfold Root. Translated by F. C. White. Aldershot: Avebury, 1997. This is a translation of the 1st edition (1813).

Über den Willen in der Natur

On the Will in Nature. Translated by E. F. J. Payne. Edited, with an introduction by David E. Cartwright. New York: Berg, 1994.
On the Will in Nature. Translated by Mme. Karl Hillebrand. London: George Bell & Sons, 1889; reprint, London: G. Bell, 1986. Published as *Two Essays* with Hillebrand's translation of *On the Fourfold Root of the Principle of Sufficient Reason*.
The Will in Nature, an Account of the Corroborations Received by the Author's Philosophy from the Empirical Sciences. Translator not given. New York: P. Eckler, 1877; new edition, 1899.

Die Welt als Wille und Vorstellung

The World as Will and Idea. 3 volumes. Translated by A. B. Haldane and J. Kemp. London: Trübner, 1883; 11th edn., London: Routledge and Kegan Paul, 1964.
The World as Will and Idea: Abridged as One Volume. Translated by J. Berman. Edited by D. Berman. London: Everyman, 1995.
The World as Will and Representation. 2 volumes. Translated by E. F. J. Payne. Indian Hills, Co.: The Falcon's Wing Press, 1958; reprint, with minor corrections, New York: Dover Publications, 1966; reprint 1969.

Nachlass

Manuscript Remains in Four Volumes. Translated by E. F. J. Payne. Edited by Arthur Hübscher. Oxford: Berg, 1988.

1. *Early Manuscripts (1804–1818)*
2. *Critical Debates (1809–1818)*

3. *Berlin Manuscripts (1818–1830)*
4. *The Manuscript Books of 1830–1852; Last Manuscripts*

Selections

The Complete Essays. Translated by T. Bailey Saunders. New York: Willey Book Company, 1942.
Essays and Aphorisms. Translated, with an introduction by R. J. Hollingdale. Middlesex: Penguin Books, 1976.
The Living Thoughts of Schopenhauer. Translated by R. B. Haldane and J. Kemp. [Presented by Thomas Mann]. New York: Longmans Green, 1939.
The Pessimist's Handbook: A Collection of Popular Essays. Translated by T. B. Saunders. Edited by Hanzel Barnes. Lincoln, Neb.: University Press, 1974; reprint 1988.
Philosophical Writings. Translated by E. F. J. Payne. Edited with an introduction by Wolfgang Schirmacher. New York: Continuum, 1994.
Selections. Translated by R. B. Haldane and J. Kemp. Edited with an introduction by DeWitt H. Parker. New York: Charles Scribner's Sons, 1928; reprint, 1956.
"Some Observations on the Antithesis of the Thing-in-Itself and the Phenomenon." *The Philosophical Forum*, 22 (1964–1965): 25–32.
"Transcendent Speculation on the Apparent Deliberation in the Fate of the Individual." Translated by E. F. J. Payne. *The Philosophical Forum*, 22 (1964–1965): 3–24.
The Will to Live. Selected Writings. Translated by R. B. Haldane and J. Kemp. Edited with an introduction by Richard Taylor. New York: Doubleday, 1962; 2nd edn., New York: Frederick Ungar, 1967.
The Wisdom of Life and Counsels and Maxims. Translated by T. Bailey Saunders. Buffalo, N.Y.: Prometheus Books, 1995.
The Wisdom of Schopenhauer as Revealed in Some of his Principal Writings. Translated by Walter Jekyll. London: Watts, 1911.
The Works of Schopenhauer, Abridged. Translated by R. B. Haldane and J. Kemp. Edited by Will Durant. With an introduction by Thomas Mann. Garden City, N.Y.: Ungar, 1955.

WRITINGS ON SCHOPENHAUER

Biographical Works

Bridgwater, Patrick. *Arthur Schopenhauer's English Schooling*. New York: Routledge, 1988.

Brink, Louise. Abstract of Edward Hitschmann, "Schopenhauer: An Attempted Psychoanalysis of the Philosopher" (*Imago*, II, Nor. 2), *Psychoanalytic Review* IV (1917): 110–15.

Hübscher, Arthur. *The Philosophy of Schopenhauer in Its Intellectual Context: Thinker Against the Tide*, trans. Joachim T. Baer and David E. Cartwright. Lewiston, N.Y.: Edwin Mellen Press, 1989.

Mockrauer, Franz. "Unknown Schopenhauer Documents." *Time Literary Supplement* (27 June 1936).

Safranski, Rudiger. *Schopenhauer and the Wild Years of Philosophy*, trans. Ewald Osers. Cambridge: Harvard University Press, 1990.

Wallace, William. *Life of Arthur Schopenhauer*. London: W. Scott, 1890; reprinted St. Clair Shores, Mich.: Scholarly Press, 1970.

Wisdom, J. O. "The Unconscious Origin of Schopenhauer's Philosophy." *International Journal of Psychoanalysis* 26 (1945): 44–52.

General Works

Barua, Arati. *The Philosophy of Arthur Schopenhauer*. New Delhi: Intellectual Publishing House, 1992.

Beer, Margrieta. *Schopenhauer*. London: T. C. & E. C. Jack, 1914.

Bykhovsky, Bernard. *Schopenhauer and the Ground of Existence*, trans. Philip Moran. Amsterdam: B. R. Gründer Publishing, 1984.

Caldwell, William. *Schopenhauer's System in Its Philosophical Significance*. Edinburgh & London: Blackwood & Sons, 1896.

Carroll, Noël. "Arthur Schopenhauer." In *The Blackwell Guide to Continental Philosophy*, ed. Robert C. Solomon. Malden, Mass.: Blackwell Publishing, 2003.

Copleston, Frederick J. *A History of Western Philosophy, Vol. 7, Part II: Modern Philosophy, Schopenhauer to Nietzsche*. Garden City, N.Y.: Doubleday Image Books, 1965 Chaps. 13 & 14.

———. *Arthur Schopenhauer: Philosopher of Pessimism*. London: Barnes & Noble, 1975.

———. "Schopenhauer." In *Great Philosophers: An Introduction to Western Philosophy*, ed. Bryan Magee. New York: Oxford University Press, 1987.

Deussen, Paul. *The Elements of Metaphysics*, trans. C. M. Duff. London: Macmillan, 1984.

Eichenwald, I. I. "A Note on Schopenhauer (1910)," trans. Nina J. Katz. In *Schopenhauer: New Essays in Honor of His 200th Birthday*, ed. Eric Von Der Luft. Lewiston, N.Y.: Edwin Mellen Press, 1988.

Fox, Michael, ed. *Schopenhauer: His Philosophical Achievement*. Totowa, N.J.: Barnes & Noble Books, 1980.

Gardiner, Patrick. *Schopenhauer*. Harmondsworth, Middlesex: Penguin, 1963.
———. "Schopenhauer." In *The Encyclopedia of Philosophy*, ed. Paul Edwards. New York: Macmillan & the Free Press, 1967.
Hamlyn, D. W. *Schopenhauer*. London: Routledge & Kegan Paul, 1980.
Hueffer, Francis. "Literary Aspects of the Work of Schopenhauer." *New Quarterly Magazine* 8 (1874): 352–78.
Janaway, Christopher. "Arthur Schopenhauer." In *The Blackwell Guide to the Modern Philosophers from Descartes to Nietzsche*, ed. Steven Emmanuel. Cambridge: Blackwell, 2001.
———. *Schopenhauer: A Very Short Introduction*. Oxford: Oxford University Press, 2002.
Janaway, Christopher, ed. *The Cambridge Companion to Schopenhauer*. Cambridge: Cambridge University Press, 1999.
Kimpel, B. F. *The Philosophy of Schopenhauer. An Analysis of the World as Will and Idea*. Boston: Student Outlines, 1964.
Lauxtermann, P. F. H. *Schopenhauer's Broken World-View: Colours and Ethics Between Kant and Goethe*. Dordrecht: Kluwer Academic Publishers, 2000.
Magee, Bryan. *Great Philosophers: An Introduction to Western Philosophy*. New York: Oxford University Press, 1987; reprinted New York: Oxford University Press, 2000.
———. *Misunderstanding Schopenhauer*. London: Institute of Germanic Studies, University of London, 1990.
———. *The Philosophy of Schopenhauer*. New York: Oxford University Press, 1997.
Mann, Thomas. "Presenting Schopenhauer." In *Schopenhauer: His Philosophical Achievement*, ed. Michael Fox. Totowa, N.J.: Barnes & Noble, 1980.
McGill, Vivian J. *Schopenhauer: Pessimist and Pagan*. New York: Haskell House, 1977.
Miller, Bruce R. *The Philosophy of Schopenhauer in Dramatic Representational Expression*. Albuquerque, N. M.: American Classical College Press, 1981.
Neeley, G. Steven. *Schopenhauer: A Consistent Reading*. Lewiston, N.Y.: Edwin Mellen Press, 2003.
Nietzsche, Friedrich. "On Schopenhauer (1868)." In *Willing and Nothingness: Schopenhauer as Nietzsche's Educator*, ed. Christopher Janaway. Oxford: Clarendon Press, 1999.
———. "Schopenhauer as Educator," trans. James W. Hillesheim. In *Untimely Meditations*, trans. R. J. Hollingdale. Cambridge: Cambridge University Press, 1983.
Odell, S. Jack. *On Schopenhauer*. Australia: Wadsworth/Thomson Learning, 2001.

Oxenford, John. "Iconoclasm in German Philosophy." *The Westminster Review* New Series III (1853): 388–407.

Payne, E. F. J. "Arthur Schopenhauer." *The Philosopher* 5 (1953).

——. "Schopenhauer in English: A Critical Survey of Existing Translations." *Schopenhauer-Jahrbuch* 23 (1949–1950): 95–102.

Radakrishnan, Sarvepalli. *History of Philosophy Eastern and Western* II. London: Allen & Unwin, 1953, 285–96.

Rethy, Robert. "Schopenhauer." In *A Companion to Continental Philosophy*, ed. Simon Critchley and William R. Schroeder. Oxford: Blackwell Publishers, 1998.

Roberts, Julian. *German Philosophy: An Introduction*. Atlantic Heights, N. J.: Humanities Press, 1988, Chap. 4.

Royce, Josiah. "Schopenhauer." In *The Spirit of Modern Philosophy*. New York: George Braziller, 1955.

Russell, Bertrand. "Schopenhauer." In *History of Western Philosophy*, 2nd edn. London: George Allen & Unwin, 1961.

Sallis, John. *Crossings: Nietzsche and the Space of Tragedy*. Chicago: University of Chicago Press, 1991.

Salter, William Mackintire. "Schopenhauer's Contact with Pragmatism." *Philosophical Review* 19 (1910): 137–53.

Santayana, George. *Egoism in German Philosophy*. New York, 1915.

Saunders, T. B. *Schopenhauer: A Lecture*. London, 1901.

Schnädelbach, Herbert. *Philosophy in Germany 1831–1833*. Cambridge: Cambridge University Press, 1984, Chap. 5.

Snow, James. "Schopenhauer's Style." *International Philosophical Quarterly* 33, no. 4 (December 1993): 401–12.

Stone, Mark. *The Giants of Philosophy: Arthur Schopenhauer*, nar. Charlton Heston. Nashville: Knowledge Products, 1991.

Strathern, Paul. *Schopenhauer in 90 Minutes*. Chicago: Ivan R Dee, Inc., 1999.

Tanner, Michael. *Schopenhauer: The Great Philosophers*. New York: Routledge, 1999.

Tarachand, Kaikushru J. "Stray Observations on Schopenhauer's Philosophy." *Schopenhauer-Jahrbuch* 32 (1945/48): 140–48.

Taylor, Richard. "Arthur Schopenhauer." In *Nineteenth Century Religious Thought*. Cambridge: Cambridge University Press, 1984.

——. "Schopenhauer." In *A Critical History of Western Philosophy*, ed. D. J. O'Connor. New York: The Free Press, 1964.

Von Der Luft, Eric, ed. *Schopenhauer: New Essays in Honor of His 200th Birthday*. Lewiston, N.Y.: Edwin Mellen Press, 1988.

Whittaker, T. *Schopenhauer*. London: Constable, 1909.

Young, Julian. *Willing and Unwilling: A Study in the Philosophy of Arthur Schopenhauer*. Dordrecht: Nijhoff, 1987.

Zimmern, Helen. *Schopenhauer: His Life and Philosophy*. London: Longmans Green, 1876.

Aesthetics

Alperson, Philip. "Schopenhauer and Musical Revelation." *The Journal of Aesthetics and Art Criticism* 40 (Winter 1981): 155–66.

Atwell, John E. "Art as Liberation: A Central Theme of Schopenhauer's Philosophy." In *Schopenhauer, Philosophy, and the Arts*, ed. Dale Jacquette. Cambridge: Cambridge University Press, 1996.

Bakst, James. "A Comparative Study of Philosophies of Music in the Works of Schopenhauer, Nietzsche, and Tolstoi." Ph.D. diss., New York University, 1942.

Budd, Malcolm. *Music and the Emotions*. London: Routledge, 1985 Chap 5.

Collinson, Diané. "Ethics and Aesthetics Are One." *The British Journal of Aesthetics* 25 (Summer 1985): 266–72.

De Mul, Jos. "The Art of Forgetfulness, Schopenhauer and Contemporary Repetitive Music." In *XIth International Congress in Aesthetics, Nottingham 1988*, ed. Richard Woodfield. Nottingham: Nottingham Polytech, 1990.

Desmond, William. "Schopenhauer, Art, and the Dark Origin." In *Schopenhauer: New Essays in Honor of His 200th Birthday*, ed. Eric Von Der Luft. Lewiston, N.Y.: Edwin Mellen Press, 1988.

Dickie, George. "Taste and Attitude: The Origin of the Aesthetic." *Theoria* 39 (1973): 153–70.

Diffey, T. J. "Schopenhauer's Account of Aesthetic Experience." *The British Journal of Aesthetics* 30, no. 2 (April 1990): 132–42.

Ferrara, Lawrence. "Schopenhauer on Music as the Embodiment of Will." In *Schopenhauer, Philosophy, and the Arts*, ed. Dale Jacquette. Cambridge: Cambridge University Press, 1996.

Foster, Cheryl. "Ideas of Imagination: Schopenhauer on the Proper Foundation of Art." In *The Cambridge Companion to Schopenhauer*, ed. Christopher Janaway. Cambridge: Cambridge University Press, 1999.

———. "Schopenhauer and Aesthetic Recognition." In *Schopenhauer, Philosophy, and the Arts*, ed. Dale Jacquette. Cambridge: Cambridge University Press, 1996.

———. "Schopenhauer's Subtext on Natural Beauty." *The British Journal of Aesthetics* 32, no. 1 (January 1992): 21–32.

Goehr, Lydia. "Schopenhauer and the Musicians: An Inquiry into the Sounds of Silence and the Limits of Philosophizing about Music." In *Schopenhauer, Philosophy, and the Arts*, ed. Dale Jacquette. Cambridge: Cambridge University Press, 1996.

Gottfried, Paul. "Schopenhauer as Critic of History." *Journal of the History of Ideas* 36 (1975): 331–38.

Gupta, R. K. Das. "Schopenhauer on Literature and Art." *Schopenhauer-Jahrbuch* 62 (1981): 156–69.

Guyer, Paul. "Pleasure and Knowledge in Schopenhauer's Aesthetics." In *Schopenhauer, Philosophy, and the Arts*, ed. Dale Jacquette. Cambridge: Cambridge University Press, 1996.

Jacquette, Dale. "Schopenhauer on the Antipathy of Aesthetic Genius and the Charming." *History of European Ideas* 18, no. 3 (May 1994): 373–85.

Jacquette, Dale, ed. *Schopenhauer, Philosophy, and the Arts*. Cambridge: Cambridge University Press, 1996.

Janaway, Christopher. "Knowledge and Tranquility: Schopenhauer on the Value of Art." In *Schopenhauer, Philosophy, and the Arts*, ed. Dale Jacquette. Cambridge: Cambridge University Press, 1996.

Johnson, Kenneth M. "Beautiful Truths: Schopenhauer's Philosophy of Art." *Dialogue: Journal of Phi Sigma Tau* 35, no. 1 (October 1992): 14–8.

Jones, K. "Schopenhauer on Animals." *Schopenhauer-Jahrbuch* 72 (1991): 131–42.

Knox, Israel. *The Aesthetic Theories of Kant, Hegel and Schopenhauer*. New York: Columbia University Press, 1936; reprinted New York: Humanities Press, 1958.

———. "Schopenhauer's Aesthetic Theory." In *Schopenhauer: His Philosophical Achievement*, ed. Michael Fox. Totowa, N.J.: Barnes & Noble, 1980.

Koestbaum, P. "The Logic of Schopenhauer's Aesthetics." *Revue Internationale de Philosophie* 18 (1960): 85–95.

Krueger, Steven. "Arthur Schopenhauer on Aesthetics, History and Tragedy." Masters thesis, Dalhousie University (Canada), 1996.

———. "On the Aesthetic and Non-Aesthetic Forms of the Sublime in Schopenhauer's Theory of Tragedy." *Schopenhauer-Jahrbuch* 81 (2000): 45–58.

———. "Schopenhauer on the Pleasures of Tragedy." *Schopenhauer-Jahrbuch* 82 (2001): 113–20.

Krukowski, Lucian. *Aesthetic Legacies*. Philadelphia: Temple University Press, 1992.

———. "Schopenhauer and the Aesthetics of Creativity." In *Schopenhauer, Philosophy, and the Arts*, ed. Dale Jacquette. Cambridge: Cambridge University Press, 1996.

Kuderowicz, Zbigiew. "Suffering and the Meaning of History." *Dialectics and Humanism* 8 (Spring 1981): 133–44.

Masing-Delic, J. "Schopenhauer's Metaphysics of Music and Turgenev's *dvorjanskoe gnezdo.*" *Die Welt der Slawen* 31 (1986): 183–96.

Neill, Alex. "Schopenhauer on Tragedy and Value." In *Art and Morality*, ed. José Luis Bermúdez. London: Routledge & Kegan Paul, 2003.

Nelson, Byron. "Wagner, Schopenhauer, and Nietzsche: On the Value of Human Action." *The Opera Quarterly* 6 (1989): 29–32.

Neureiter, Paul R. "Schopenhauer's 'Will' as Aesthetic Criterion." *The Journal of Value Inquiry* 20 (1986): 41–50.

Nitzberg, Howard. "Schopenhauer, Cendrars, and the Sense of the Sublime." *Feuille de Route* 16 (April): 6–20.

Rotenstreich, Nathan. "Schopenhauer on Beauty and Ontology." In *Schopenhauer, Philosophy, and the Arts*, ed. Dale Jacquette. Cambridge: Cambridge University Press, 1996.

Schwarzer, Mitchell. "Schopenhauer's Philosophy of Architecture." In *Schopenhauer, Philosophy, and the Arts*, ed. Dale Jacquette. Cambridge: Cambridge University Press, 1996.

Scruton, Roger, and Peter Jones. "Laughter, Part I." *The Aristotelean Society Supplementary Volume* 56 (1982): 197–212.

Stern, J. P. "The Aesthetic Re-Interpretation: Schopenhauer." In *Re-Interpretations: Seven Studies in Nineteenth-Century German Literature*. London: Thames and Hudson, 1964.

Stolnitz, Jerome. "The Aesthetic Attitude in the Rise of Modern Aesthetics." *The Journal of Aesthetics and Art Criticism* 36 (Summer 1978): 409–22.

Taylor, Terri Graves. "Platonic Ideas, Aesthetic Experience, and the Resolution of Schopenhauer's 'Great Contradiction'." *International Studies in Philosophy* 19 (Fall 1987): 43–53.

van Niekerk, Anton A. "Death, Meaning, and Tragedy." *South African Journal of Philosophy* 18, no. 4 (1999): 408–27.

Vandenabelle, Bart. "Schopenhauer on the Beautiful and the Sublime: A Qualitative or Gradual Distinction?" *Schopenhauer-Jahrbuch* 82 (2001): 99–112.

Walker, Alan. "Schopenhauer and Music." *The Times Literary Supplement* (3 January 1975): 11–12.

Willey, T. E. "Schopenhauer, Modernism, and the Rejection of History." In *Schopenhauer: New Essays in Honor of His 200th Birthday*, ed. Eric Von Der Luft. Lewiston, N.Y.: Edwin Mellen Press, 1988.

Young, Julian. "The Standpoint of Eternity: Schopenhauer on Art." *Kantstudien* 78 (1987): 424–41.

Epistemology and Metaphysics

Angus, Ian. "A Historical Entry Into the Problem of Time: Hegel and Schopenhauer." *Kinesis* 6 (1973): 3–14.

Aquila, Richard E. "On the 'Subjects' of Knowing and Willing and the 'I' in Schopenhauer." *History of Philosophy Quarterly* 10, no. 3 (July 1993): 241–60.

Atwell, John E. "Doers and their Deeds: Schopenhauer on Human Agency." In *Schopenhauer: New Essays in Honor of His 200th Birthday*, ed. Eric Von Der Luft. Lewiston, N.Y.: Edwin Mellen Press, 1988.

———. *Schopenhauer on the Character of the World: The Metaphysics of Will*. Berkeley: University of California Press, 1995.

Barth, Hans. "Schopenhauer's 'True Critique of Reason'," trans. Frederick Lilge. In *Truth and Ideology*. Berkeley: University of California Press, 1976.

Barua, Arati. "Schopenhauer and Krausz on Objects of Interpretation." *Philosophy in the Contemporary World*. Forthcoming.

———. "Schopenhauer on Will: A Critique." *Indian Philosophical Quarterly* 6 (January 1989): 43–60.

———. "Schopenhauer's Concept of Causality." *Review of Darshan* 12, no. 2 (October 1988): 7–18.

———. "Sensation and Perception: A Schopenhaurian View." *Viswabharati Journal of Philosophy* (August 1990): 19–24.

Beasley, Stephen Michael. "The Mind-Body Problem in Selected Explanations of Mental Illness." Ph.D. diss., University of Maryland College Park, 1987.

Botton, Alainde. "The Schopenhauer Method." *New York Times Magazine* 149, no. 51297 (2000): 58–64.

Brann, Henry W. "The Role of Parapsychology in Schopenhauer's Philosophy." *International Journal of Parapsychology* (1966): 397–415.

Cartwright, David E. "Schopenhauer on Suffering, Death, Guilt, and the Consolation of Metaphysics." In *Schopenhauer: New Essays in Honor of His 200th Birthday*, ed. Eric Von Der Luft. Lewiston, N.Y.: Edwin Mellen Press, 1988.

———. "Two Senses of 'Thing-in-Itself' in Schopenhauer's Philosophy." *Idealistic Studies* 31, no. 1 (Winter 2001): 31–54.

Chansky, James. "Schopenhauer and Platonic Ideas: A Groundwork for an Aesthetic Metaphysics." In *Schopenhauer: New Essays in Honor of His 200th Birthday*, ed. Eric Von Der Luft. Lewiston, N.Y.: Edwin Mellen Press, 1988.

———. "Schopenhauer's Aesthetic Metaphysics." Ph.D. diss., Boston College, 1985.

Colvin, Stephen S. *Schopenhauer's Doctrine of the Thing-In-Itself and his Attempt to Relate it to the World of Phenomena*. Providence: The Franklin Press, 1897.

Crone, R. A. "Schopenhauer on Vision and the Colors." *Documenta Ophthalmologica* 93, no. 1–2 (1997): 61–71.

Davis, Bret W. "On the Way to Gelassenheit: The Problem of the Will and the Possibility of Non-Willing in Heidegger's Thought." Ph.D. diss., Vanderbilt University, 2001.

De Cian, Nicoletta, and Segala Marco. "What is Will?" *Schopenhauer-Jahrbuch* 83 (2002): 13–42.

Fox, Michael. "Schopenhauer on the Need of Metaphysics." In *Schopenhauer: New Essays in Honor of His 200th Birthday*, ed. Eric Von Der Luft. Lewiston, N.Y.: Edwin Mellen Press, 1988.

Gardiner, Patrick. "The Possibility of Metaphysics." In *Schopenhauer: His Philosophical Achievement*, ed. Michael Fox. Totowa, N.J.: Barnes & Noble Books, 1980.

Gardner, Sebastian. "Schopenhauer, Will, and the Unconscious." In *The Cambridge Companion to Schopenhauer*, ed. Christopher Janaway. Cambridge: Cambridge University Press, 1999.

Gram, Moltke S. "Things in Themselves: The Historical Lessons." *Journal of the History of Philosophy* 18 (1980): 407–31.

Hall, Roland. "The Nature of the Will and Its Place in Schopenhauer's Philosophy." *Schopenhauer-Jahrbuch* 76 (1995): 73–90.

Hamlyn, D. W. "Schopenhauer and Knowledge." In *The Cambridge Companion to Schopenhauer*, ed. Christopher Janaway. Cambridge: Cambridge University Press, 1999.

——. "Schopenhauer on Action and Will." In *Idealism: Past and Present, Royal Institute of Philosophy Lectures, Vol. 13, 1978–9*, ed. Godfrey Vesey. Brighton, Sussex: Harvester Press, 1981.

——. "Schopenhauer on the Principle of Sufficient Reason." In *Schopenhauer: His Philosophical Achievement*, ed. Michael Fox. Totowa, N.J.: Barnes & Noble Books, 1980.

——. "Schopenhauer on the Will in Nature." *Midwest Studies in Philosophy* 8 (1983): 457–67.

——. "Why Are There Phenomena?" In *Zeit der Ernte: Studien zum Stand der Schopenhauer-Forschung, Festschrift für Arthur Hübscher zum 85. Geburtstag*, ed. Wolfgang Schirmacher. Stuttgart-Bad Cannstatt: Frommann-Holzboog, 1982.

Hein, Hilde. "Schopenhauer and Platonic Ideas." *Journal of the History of Philosophy* 4 (1966): 133–44.

Henle, R. J. "Schopenhauer and Direct Realism." *The Review of Metaphysics* 46, no. 1 (September 1992): 125–40.

Hill, William Patton. "Schopenhauer's Metaphysics of the Will." Ph.D. diss., Wesleyan University, 1941.

Howard, Don. "A Peck behind the Veil of Maya: Einstein, Schopenhauer, and the Historical Background of the Conception of Space as a Ground for the Individuation of Physical Systems." In *The Cosmos of Science: Essays of Exploration*, ed. John Earman and John Norton. Kronstranz: Universitätsverlag, 1997.

Jacquette, Dale. "Schopenhauer's Circle and the Principle of Sufficient Reason." *Metaphilosophy* 23, no. 3 (July 1992): 279–87.

——. "Schopenhauer's Metaphysics of Appearance and Will in the Philosophy of Art." In *Schopenhauer, Philosophy, and the Arts*, ed. Dale Jacquette. Cambridge: Cambridge University Press, 1996.

Janaway, Christopher. "Nietzsche, the Self, and Schopenhauer." In *Nietzsche and Modern German Thought*, ed. Keith Ansell-Pearson. New York: Routledge, 1991.

———. *Self and World in Schopenhauer's Philosophy.* Oxford: Oxford University Press, 1997.

———. "Will and Nature." In *The Cambridge Companion to Schopenhauer*, ed. Christopher Janaway. Cambridge: Cambridge University Press, 1999.

Kuhlenbeck, Hartwig. *Brain and Consciousness: Some Prolegomena to an Approach of the Problem.* Basel, N.Y.: S. Karger, 1957.

———. "The Meaning of 'Postulational Psychophysical Parallelism'." *Confinia Neurologica* 18 (1958): 588–603.

Larson, Duane Jason. "Critical Tensions Between Schopenhauer's Metaphysics and His Veneration of Asceticism." Masters thesis, California State University, Long Beach, 2002.

Lauxtermann, P. F. H. "Five Decisive Years: Schopenhauer's Epistemology as Reflected in His Theory of Color." *Studies in History and Philosophy of Science* 18 (September 1987): 271–91.

———. "Hegel and Schopenhauer as Partisans of Goethe's Theory of Color." *Journal of the History of Ideas* 51, no. 4 (October-December 1990): 599–624.

Legutko, Ryszard. "The Problem of Substantiality in Arthur Schopenhauer's Philosophy." *Reports on Philosophy* (1972): 23–31.

Logan, Carrie Elizabeth. "The Psychology of Schopenhauer in Its Relation to His System of Metaphysics." Ph.D. diss., New York University, 1902.

Long, B. M. "Schopenhauer and Individuality." *Mind* XXVI (1917): 171–87.

Lukács, Georg. "The Bourgeois Irrationalism of Schopenhauer's Metaphysics." In *Schopenhauer: His Philosophical Achievement*, ed. Michael Fox. Totowa, N.J.: Barnes & Noble Books, 1980.

———. *The Destruction of Reason*, trans. Peter Palmer. Atlantic Highlands, N. J.: Humanities Press, 1980, Chap. 4.

Mandelbaum, Maurice. "Schopenhauer: The Will and the Intellect." In *History, Man and Reason: A Study in Nineteenth Century Thought*, ed. Maurice Mandelbaum. Baltimore and London: John Hospers University Press, 1971. Reprinted in Fox (ed.).

McDermid, Douglas James. "Schopenhauer as Epistemologist: A Kantian against Kant." *International Philosophical Quarterly* 42, no. 2 (September 2002): 209–30.

Mijuskovic, Ben L. "The Simplicity Argument and Time in Schopenhauer and Bergson." *Schopenhauer-Jahrbuch* 58 (1977): 43–57.

Minnich, John W. "The Antagonism between the Intuitive and Discursive in Schopenhauer." Ph.D. diss., Claremont Graduate School, 1974.

Morgan, Karen Gail. "Intellect and Will in the Nineteenth Century: A Structural Model for Psycho-Theology." Ph.D. diss., Fuller Theological Seminary, School of Psychology, 1991.

Mudragei, N. S. "The Rational and the Irrational: A Philosophical Problem (Reading Arthur Schopenhauer)." *Russian Studies in Philosophy* 34, no. 2 (Fall 1995): 46–65.

——. "The Thing in Itself: From Unknowability to Acquaintance (Kant-Schopenhauer)." *Russian Studies in Philosophy* 38, no. 3 (Winter 1999–2000): 64–89.

Navia, Luis E. "The Problem of the Freedom of the Will in the Philosophy of Schopenhauer." Ph.D. diss., New York University, 1972.

——. "Schopenhauer's Concept of Character." *Journal of Critical Analysis* 5 (1974): 85–91.

Neeley, G. Steven. "A Re-Examination of Schopenhauer's Analysis of Bodily Agency: The Ego as Microcosm." *Idealistic Studies* 22, no. 1 (January 1992): 52–67.

——. "The Knowledge and Nature of Schopenhauer's Will." *Schopenhauer-Jahrbuch* 77 (1996): 85–112.

——. "Schopenhauer and the Limits of Language." *Idealistic Studies* 27 (Winter/Spring 1997): 47–67.

——. "Schopenhauer and the Platonic Ideas: A Reconsideration." *Idealistic Studies* 30, no. 2 (Spring-Summer 2000): 121–48.

Nicholls, Moira. "The Kantian Inheritance and Schopenhauer's Doctrine of Will." *Kantstudien* 85, no. 3 (1994): 257–79.

——. "Schopenhauer, Feeling and the Noumenon." *Schopenhauer-Jahrbuch* 76 (1995): 53–71.

——. "Schopenhauer, Young, and the Will." *Schopenhauer-Jahrbuch* 72 (1991): 143–57.

Nicholls, Roderick. "Schopenhauer's Analysis of Character." In *Schopenhauer: His Philosophical Achievement*, ed. Michael Fox. Totowa, N.J.: Barnes & Noble, 1980.

Nussbaum, Charles. "Schopenhauer's Rejection of Kant's Analysis of Cause and Effect." *Auslegung* 12 (Winter 1985): 33–44.

Orenstein, A. "Schopenhauer's Challenge to Self Determinism." In *Rationality and Science*, ed. Eugene T. Gadol. Vienna: Springer, 1982.

Parrhysius, Kurt. "A Physician on Schopenhauer's Philosophy of the Will-to-Live." *Schopenhauer-Jahrbuch* 53 (1972): 427–29.

Rethy, Robert. "The Metaphysics of Nullity." *Philosophy Research Archives* 12 (1986–1987): 357–86.

Richey, Lance Byron. "The Metaphysics of Human Freedom in Schopenhauer and Saint Augustine." Ph.D. diss., Marquette University, 1995.

Rotenstreich, Nathan. "Self-Knowledge of the World." *Schopenhauer-Jahrbuch* 70 (1989): 66–74.

——. "The Thing in Itself and Will." *Schopenhauer-Jahrbuch* 69 (1988): 127–37.

Salter, William Mackintire. "Schopenhauer's Type of Idealism." *The Monist* 21 (1911): 1–18.

Schroeder, Gale Young. "Arthur Schopenhauer: Iconoclasm for a Contemporary Communication Philosophy." Ph.D. diss., University of California, Los Angeles, 1978.

Sheeks, Wayne. "Intellect and Will in the Philosophy of Schopenhauer." Ph.D. diss., Southern Illinois University at Carbondale, 1967.

——. "Intellect and Will in the Philosophy of Schopenhauer." *American Rationalist* 1 (February 1972).

——. "Schopenhauer's Solution of the Intellect-Will Problem." *Midwestern Journal of Philosophy* (Winter 1974): 39–47. Reprinted in Fox (ed.).

Shepard, Gilbert L. "Schopenhauer's Metaphysics of the Will." Ph.D. diss., University of Wisconsin–Madison, 1999.

Snow, Dale, and James Snow. "Was Schopenhauer an Idealist?" *Journal of the History of Philosophy* 29, no. 4 (October 1991): 633–55.

Steinhauser, H. "A Concrete Interpretation of Schopenhauer's Notion of Will." *The Monist* 39 (1929): 161–69.

Stewart, Jon. "Schopenhauer's Charge and Modern Academic Philosophy: Some Problems Facing Philosophical Pedagogy." *Metaphilosophy* 26, no. 3 (July 1995): 270–78.

Taylor, Richard. "The Fourfold Root of the Principle of Sufficient Reason." Introduction to Schopenhauer's *The Fourfold Root of the Principle of Sufficient Reason*, trans. E. F. J. Payne. La Salle, Ill.: Open Court Publishing Co., 1974.

Trautmann, Frederick. "Communication in the Philosophy of Arthur Schopenhauer." *Southern Speech Communication Journal* 40 (Winter 1975): 142–57.

White, F. C. *On Schopenhauer's 'Fourfold Root of the Principle of Sufficient Reason'*. Leiden: Brill Academic Publishers, 1992.

——. "The Fourfold Root." In *The Cambridge Companion to Schopenhauer*, ed. Christopher Janaway. Cambridge: Cambridge University Press, 1999.

Young, Julian. "Is Schopenhauer an Irrationalist?" *Schopenhauer-Jahrbuch* 69 (1988): 85–100.

Zöller, Günter. "Schopenhauer and the Problem of Metaphysics: Critical Reflections on Rudolf Malter's Interpretation." *Man World* 28, no. 1 (January 1995): 1–10.

——. "Schopenhauer on the Self." In *The Cambridge Companion to Schopenhauer*, ed. Christopher Janaway. Cambridge: Cambridge University Press, 1999.

Moral Philosophy

Alexander, A. "Pessimism of Schopenhauer and German Thought." *Princeton Review* (March 1978): 492–504.

Alexander, W. M. "Philosophers Have Avoided Sex." *Diogenes* 72 (Winter 1970): 56–74.

Atwell, John E. "Schopenhauer on Women, Men, and Sexual Love." *Midwest Quarterly* 38, no. 2 (1997): 143–58.

——. *Schopenhauer: The Human Character*. Philadelphia: Temple University Press, 1990.

——. "Schopenhauer's Account of Moral Responsibility." *Pacific Philosophical Quarterly* 61 (1980): 396–410.

Basinski, Paul A. "Nihilism and the Impossibility of Political Philosophy." *The Journal of Value Inquiry* 24, no. 4 (October 1990): 269–84.

Blum, Lawrence A. "Altruism and Women's Oppression." *Philosophical Forum (Boston)* 8 (Fall-Winter 1973): 222–47.

——. *Friendship, Altruism, and Morality*. London: Routledge & Kegan Paul, 1980.

Cartwright, David E. "Compassion." In *Zeit der Ernte: Studien zum Stand der Schopenhauer-Forschung, Festschrift für Arthur Hübscher zum 85. Geburtstag*, ed. Wolfgang Schirmacher. Stuttgart-Bad Cannstatt: Frommann-Holzboog, 1982.

——. "The Ethical Significance of Sympathy, Compassion, and Pity." Ph.D. diss., University of Wisconsin–Madison, 1981.

——. "Schopenhauer as Moral Philosopher—Towards the Actuality of his Ethics." *Schopenhauer-Jahrbuch* 70 (1989): 54–65.

——. "Schopenhauer on Human and Canine Friendship." *The Siberian Quarterly* (Spring 1982): 32–4, 42.

——. "Schopenhauerian Optimism and an Alternative to Resignation?" *Schopenhauer-Jahrbuch* 66 (1985): 114–23.

——. "Schopenhauer's Axiological Analysis of Character." *Revue Internationale de Philisophie* 42 (1988): 18–36.

——. "Schopenhauer's Narrower Sense of Morality." In *The Cambridge Companion to Schopenhauer*, ed. Christopher Janaway. Cambridge: Cambridge University Press, 1999.

——. "Varner's Challenge to Environmental Ethics." *Environmental Ethics* 9 (Summer 1987): 189–90.

Choron, Jacques. *Death and Western Thought*. New York: Collier Books, 1963, Chap. 20.

——. "Death as Motive and Motif of Philosophical Thought with Special Consideration of Schopenhauer." Ph.D. diss., New School for Social Research, 1960.

Ci, Jiwei. "Schopenhauer on Voluntary Justice." *History of Philosophy Quarterly* 15, no. 2 (April 1998): 227–44.

Cyzyk, Mark. "Conscience, Sympathy, and Love: Ethical Strategies toward Confirmation of Metaphysical Assertions in Schopenhauer." *Dialogue: Journal of Phi Sigma Tau* 32, no. 1 (October 1989): 24–31.

220 • BIBLIOGRAPHY

Dienstag, Joshua Foa. "The Pessimistic Spirit." *Philosophy & Social Criticism* 25, no. 1 (1999): 71–95.

Ettun, Moti. "Was Schopenhauer a Pessimist?" *Iyyun: The Jerusalem Philosophical Quarterly* 48 (October 1999): 401–19.

Fox, Michael. "Schopenhauer on Death, Suicide and Self-Renunciation." In *Schopenhauer: His Philosophical Achievement*, ed. Michael Fox. Totowa, N.J.: Barnes & Noble Books, 1980.

Giles, Donald Alexander. "Schopenhauer, Suffering and Salvation: On the Relation between Reality and Happiness." Ph.D. diss., University of Kentucky, 1995.

Godart-van der Kroon, Annette. "Schopenhauer's Theory of Justice and Its Implication to Natural Law." *Schopenhauer-Jahrbuch* 84 (2003): 121–45.

Haber, Honi. "Schopenhauer as the Embodiment of the Socratic and Postmodern Man: An Examination of Character." *Journal of the History of Ideas* 56, no. 3 (July 1995): 483–99.

Hamlyn, D. W. "Eternal Justice." *Schopenhauer-Jahrbuch* 69 (1988): 281–88.

Heller, Erich. "The Glory of Pessimism." *Times Literary Supplement* 10 (October 1975): 1167–8.

Hoffding, Harald. "The Philosophy of Romanticism as a Pessimistic Conception of Life: Arthur Schopenhauer," trans. B. E. Meyer. In *A History of Modern Philosophy* II. New York: Dover Publications, 1955.

Horkheimer, Max. "Schopenhauer Today." In *The Critical Spirit: Essays in Honor of Herbert Marcuse*, eds. Kurt H. Wolff and Barrington Moore, Jr. Boston: Beacon Press, 1967. Reprinted in Fox (ed.).

Jacquette, Dale. "Schopenhauer on Death." In *The Cambridge Companion to Schopenhauer*, ed. Christopher Janaway. Cambridge: Cambridge University Press, 1999.

———. "Schopenhauer on the Ethics of Suicide." *Continental Philosophy Review* 33, no. 1 (January 2000): 43–58.

Janaway, Christopher. "Schopenhauer's Pessimism." *Philosophy* 74, no. 288 (1999): 47–64.

———. "Schopenhauer's Pessimism." In *The Cambridge Companion to Schopenhauer*, ed. Christopher Janaway. Cambridge: Cambridge University Press, 1999.

Katwan, Ron Benedict. "The Primacy of the Will: Schopenhauer's Critique of the Conception of Practical Reason." Ph.D. diss., Yale University, 1996.

Kolenda, Konstantin. "Schopenhauer's Ethics: A View from Nowhere." In *Schopenhauer: New Essays in Honor of His 200th Birthday*, ed. Eric Von Der Luft. Lewiston, N.Y.: Edwin Mellen Press, 1988.

Koontz, Mark Lehman. "Schopenhauer's Critique of Kant's Foundation for Morals." Ph.D. diss., University of Pennsylvania, 1993.

Lacroix, J. P. "Schopenhauer and his Pessimism." *Methodist Quarterly* 58 (1876): 487–510.

Libell, Monica. "Compassion in Schopenhauer's View of Animals." *Schopenhauer-Jahrbuch* 79 (1998): 113–25.

Madigan, Timothy J. "Legor et Legar: Schopenhauer's Atheistic Morality." *Philo* 1, no. 2 (Fall-Winter 1998): 36–48.

Maidan, Michael. "Schopenhauer on Altruism and Morality." *Schopenhauer-Jahrbuch* 69 (1988): 265–72.

Mannion, Gerard. "Mitleid, Metaphysics and Morality: Understanding Schopenhauer's Ethics." *Schopenhauer-Jahrbuch* 83 (2002): 87–117.

———. *Schopenhauer, Religion and Morality: The Humble Path to Ethics.* Burlington, Vt.: Ashgate Publishing, 2003.

Migotti, Mark. "Schopenhauer's Pessimism and the Unconditioned Good." *Journal of the History of Philosophy* 33, no. 4 (October 1995): 643–60.

Navia, Luis E. "Reflections on Schopenhauer's Pessimism." *Journal of Critical Analysis* 3 (October 1971): 136–47. Reprinted in Fox (ed.).

Neeley, G. Steven. "A Critical Note on Schopenhauer's Concept of Human Salvation." *Schopenhauer-Jahrbuch* 75 (1994): 97–127.

———. "Schopenhauer and the Morality of Compassion: The Culmination of the 'One Single Thought'." *Contemporary Philosophy* 22 (January-February & March-April 2000): 52–62.

Raschke, Carl A. "Schopenhauer on the Delusion of Progress." *Schopenhauer-Jahrbuch* 58 (1977): 73–85.

Rotenstreich, Nathan. "Prophecy of Reason." In *Zeit der Ernte: Studien zum Stand der Schopenhauer-Forschung, Festschrift für Arthur Hübscher zum 85. Geburtstag,* ed. Wolfgang Schirmacher. Stuttgart-Bad Cannstatt: Frommann-Holzboog, 1982.

Siwek, P. "Pessimism." In *The Philosophy of Evil.* New York: Ronald Press, 1951.

Smith, Joseph W. "Philosophy and the Meaning of Life." *Cogito* 2 (June 1984): 27–44.

Soll, Ivan. "On Desire and Its Discontents." *Ratio: An International Journal of Analytic Philosophy* 2, no. 2 (December 1989): 159–84.

Sprigge, T. L. S. "Is Pity the Basis of Ethics? Nietzsche versus Schopenhauer." In *The Bases of Ethics,* ed. William Sweet. Milwaukee: Marquette University Press, 2000.

Stock, Georg. "Arthur Schopenhauer's Concepts of Salvation." In *Kreise um Schopenhauer. Arthur Hübscher zum 65. Geburtstag,* ed. Carl August Emge. Wiesbaden, 1962.

Sully, James. *Pessimism, a History and a Criticism.* London: H. S. King, 1877: 74–105.

Taylor, Richard. "Introduction." In Schopenhauer's *On the Basis of Morality*, trans. E. F. J. Payne. Indianapolis: Bobbs-Merrill Co., Inc., 1965. Reprinted as "On the Basis of Morality" in Fox (ed.).

Van Eura, James W. "On Death as a Limit." *Analysis* 31 (April 1971): 170–76.

Varner, G. E. "The Schopenhauerian Challenge in Environmental Ethics." *Environmental Ethics* 7 (Fall 1985): 209–30.

Wynne-Tyson, Esmé. *The Philosophy of Compassion: The Return of the Goddess*. London: Vincent Stuart, 1962.

Young, Julian. "A Schopenhauerian Solution to Schopenhauerian Pessimism." *Schopenhauer-Jahrbuch* 68 (1987): 53–67.

Religion

Abelsen, Peter. "Schopenhauer and Buddhism." *Philosophy East and West* 43, no. 2 (April 1993): 255–78.

App, Urs. "Notes and Excerpts by Schopenhauer Related to Volumes 1–9 of the *Asiatick Researches*." *Schopenhauer-Jahrbuch* 79 (1998): 11–33.

Berger, Douglas Leo. "The Veil of Maya: Schopenhauer's Theory of Falsification: The Key to Schopenhauer's Appropriation of Pre-Systematic Indian Philosophical Thought." Ph.D. diss., Temple University, 2000.

Bhatt, Chetan. "Primordial Being: Enlightenment, Schopenhauer and the Indian Subject of Postcolonial Theory." *Radical Philosophy: A Journal of Socialist and Feminist Philosophy* 100 (March-April 2000): 28–41.

Bonner, Joey. "The World as Will: Wang Kuowei and the Philosophy of Metaphysical Pessimism." *Philosophy East and West* 29 (October, 1979): 443–66.

Dauer, Dorothea W. *Schopenhauer as Transmitter of Buddhist Ideas*. Berne: Herbert Lang, 1969.

Dharmasiri, Gunapala. "Principles and Justification: The Buddha and Schopenhauer." *Schopenhauer-Jahrbuch* 53 (1972): 88–92.

Dumoulin, Henrich. "Buddhism and Nineteenth-Century German Philosophy." *Journal of the History of Ideas* 42 (1981): 457–70.

Garfield, Jay L. "Western Idealism through Indian Eyes: A Cittamatra Reading of Berkeley, Kant and Schopenhauer." *Sophia: International Journal for Philosophy of Religion, Metaphysical Theology and Ethics* 37, no. 1 (March-April 1998): 10–41.

Gesteerning, Johann J. *German Pessimism and Indian Religion: A Hermeneutic Reading*. New Delhi: Ajanta, 1986.

Glasenapp, Helmuth von. "The Influence of Indian Thought on German Philosophy and Literature." *Calcutta Review* 29 (1928): 189–219.

Gonzales, Robert A. "The Ambiguity of the Sacred in the Philosophy of Schopenhauer." *Auslegung* 19, no. 2 (Summer 1993): 143–66.

——. *An Approach to the Sacred in the Thought of Schopenhauer.* Lewiston, N.Y.: Edwin Mellen Press, 1992.

——. "The Back Door to God in the Philosophy of Schopenhauer." Ph.D. diss., Pontificia Universitas Gregoriana (Vatican), 1990.

——. "Schopenhauer's Demythologization of Christian Asceticism." *Auslegung* 9 (1982): 5–49.

Gupta, R. K. Das. "Schopenhauer and Indian Thought." *East and West* New Series XIII, no. 1 (March 1962): 32–40.

Hegstrom, Victor Harald. "Schopenhauer and Ancient Hindu Philosophy: A Comparative Study in Pessimism." Ph.D. diss., Yale University, 1894.

Irvine, David. *Philosophy and Christianity. An Introduction to the Works of Schopenhauer.* London: Watts, 1905.

Kishan, B. V. "Arthur Schopenhauer and Indian Philosophy." *Schopenhauer-Jahrbuch* 48 (1967): 167–69.

——. "Schopenhauer and Buddhism." *Schopenhauer-Jahrbuch* 53 (1972): 185–90. Reprinted in Fox (ed.).

Muses, Charles. *East-West Fire: Schopenhauer's Optimism and the Lanhavatara Sutra.* Indian Hills, Colo.: Falcon's Wing Press, 1955.

Nanajivako, Bhikkhu. *Schopenhauer and Buddhism.* Kandy, Ceylon: Buddhist Publication Society, 1970.

Nicholls, Moira. "The Influence of Eastern Thought on Schopenhauer's Doctrine of the Thing-In-Itself." In *The Cambridge Companion to Schopenhauer,* ed. Christopher Janaway. Cambridge: Cambridge University Press, 1999.

Pandey, K. Ch. "Interest in Schopenhauer's Philosophy in India." *Schopenhauer-Jahrbuch* 48 (1967): 167–69.

——. "Svatantryavâda and Voluntarism of Schopenhauer." *Schopenhauer-Jahrbuch* 48 (1967): 159–66.

Rollmans, Hans. "Deussen, Nietzsche, and Vedanta." *Journal of the History of Ideas* 39 (January-March 1978): 125–32.

Salter, William MacKintire. "Schopenhauer's Contact with Theology." *The Harvard Theological Review* 4 (1911): 271–310.

Sedlar, Jean W. *India in the Mind of Germany: Schelling, Schopenhauer and Their Times.* Washington: University Press of America, 1982.

——. "India in the Philosophies of Schelling and Schopenhauer: A Study in Cross-Cultural Influence." Ph.D. diss., University of Chicago, 1971.

Stoltzfus, Philip Edward. "Theology as Performance: The Theological Use of Musical Aesthetics in Friedrich Schleiermacher, Karl Barth, and Ludwig Wittgenstein." Ph.D. diss., Harvard University, 2000.

Thomas, D. J. "Schopenhauer and Vedanta." *Vedanta for East and West* (July-August 1971): 8–14.

Tietge, Katherine Leigh. "Ontology and Genuine Moral Action: Jnana (Intuitive Perception), Ethics, and Karma-Yoga in Sankara's 'Advaita Vedanta' and Schopenhauer's 'On the Basis of Morality'." Ph.D. diss., Southern Illinois University at Carbondale, 1997.
Welborn, Guy Richard. "Arthur Schopenhauer." In *The Buddhist Nirvāna and Its Western Interpreters*. Chicago: University of Chicago Press, 1968.

Other Philosophers

Alles, Adam. "Appetition in Leibniz and Will in Schopenhauer." Ph.D. diss., Yale University, 1926.
Atwell, John E. "Nietzsche's Perspectivism." *Southern Journal of Philosophy* 19 (1981): 157–70.
Ausmus, Harry J. *A Schopenhauerian Critique of Nietzsche's Thought: Toward a Restoration of Metaphysics*. Lewiston, N.Y.: Edwin Mellen Press, 1996.
Baig, Mirza Ahmad Ali. "Nietzsche's Schopenhauer: The Peak of Modernity and the Problem of Affirmation." Ph.D. diss., University of Chicago, 1994.
Berman, David. "Schopenhauer and Nietzsche: Honest Atheism, Dishonest Pessimism." In *Willing and Nothingness: Schopenhauer as Nietzsche's Educator*, ed. Christopher Janaway. Oxford: Clarendon Press, 1999.
———. "Spinoza's Spiders, Schopenhauer's Dogs." *Philosophical Studies (Ireland)* 29 (Winter 1982–83): 202–9.
Bernet, Rudolf. "The Unconscious between Representation and Drive. Freud, Husserl, and Schopenhauer," trans. Michael Brockmann. In *The Truthful and the Good*, ed. John J. Drummond, et al. Dordrecht: Kluwer, 1996.
Bonner, Joey. "The Cult of the Irrational: Schopenhauer: Nietzsche." In *Politics and Opinions in the Nineteenth Century: An Historical Introduction*. London: Jonathan Cape, 1954.
Bozickovic, Vojislav. "Schopenhauer on Kant and Objectivity." *International Studies in Philosophy* 28, no. 2 (1996): 35–42.
Brann, Henry W. "Schopenhauer and Spinoza." *Journal of the History of Philosophy* (1972): 181–96.
Breazeale, Daniel. "Becoming Who One Is: Notes on Schopenhauer as Educator." *New Nietzsche Studies* 2 (Summer 1998): 1–25.
Brockhaus, Richard R. *Pulling up the Ladder: The Metaphysical Roots of Wittgenstein's Tractatus*. Lasalle, Ill.: Open Court, 1991.
Buchanan, Brett Charles. "Who Is Nietzsche's Philosophy: Psychological Remainders of Post-Kantian Anthropology." Master's thesis, University of Western Ontario (Canada), 1999.
Burlingame, Charles E. "Wittgenstein: His Logic and His Promethean Mission." *Philosophy Research Archives* 12 (1986–1987): 195–218.

Caldwell, William. "Schopenhauer's Criticisms of Kant." *Mind* 16 (1891): 355 ff.

Cartwright, David E. "Kant, Schopenhauer, and Nietzsche on the Morality of Pity." *Journal of the History of Ideas* XLU, no. 1 (1984): 83–98.

———. "The Last Temptation of Zarathustra." *Journal of the History of Philosophy* 31 (1993): 49–69.

———. "Locke as Schopenhauer's (Kantian) Ancestor." *Schopenhauer-Jahrbuch* 84 (2003): 147–56.

———. "Nietzsche's Use and Abuse of Schopenhauer's Philosophy for Life." In *Willing and Nothingness: Schopenhauer as Nietzsche's Educator*, ed. Christopher Janaway. Oxford: Clarendon Press, 1999.

———. "Reversing Silenus' Wisdom." *Nietzsche-Studien* 20 (1991): 309–13.

———. "Scheler's Criticisms of Schopenhauer's Theory of 'Mitleid'." *Schopenhauer-Jahrbuch* 62 (1981): 144–52.

———. "Schopenhauer's Compassion and Nietzsche's Pity." *Schopenhauer-Jahrbuch* 69 (1988): 557–67.

Chansky, James. "The Conscious Body: Schopenhauer's Difference from Fichte in Relation to Kant." *International Studies in Philosophy* 24, no. 3 (1992): 25–44.

Churchill, John. "Wittgenstein's Adaptation of Schopenhauer." *Southern Journal of Philosophy* 21 (Winter 1983): 489–502.

Clark, Maudemarie. "Learning to Read Nietzsche." *International Studies in Philosophy* 33, no. 3 (2001): 53–64.

———. "On Knowledge, Truth, and Value: Nietzsche's Debt to Schopenhauer and the Development of His Empiricism." In *Willing and Nothingness: Schopenhauer as Nietzsche's Educator*, ed. Christopher Janaway. Oxford: Clarendon Press, 1999.

Clegg, Jerry S. "Logical Mysticism and the Cultural Setting of Wittgenstein's Tractatus." *Schopenhauer-Jahrbuch* 59 (1978): 29–46.

———. *On Genius: Affirmation and Denial from Schopenhauer to Wittgenstein.* New York: Lang, 1994.

———. "Schopenhauer and Wittgenstein on Lonely Languages and Criterialess Claims." In *Schopenhauer: New Essays in Honor of His 200th Birthday*, ed. Eric Von Der Luft. Lewiston, N.Y.: Edwin Mellen Press, 1988.

Cooper, David E. "Self and Morality in Schopenhauer and Nietzsche." In *Willing and Nothingness: Schopenhauer as Nietzsche's Educator*, ed. Christopher Janaway. Oxford: Clarendon Press, 1999.

Copleston, Frederick. "Schopenhauer and Nietzsche." In *Schopenhauer: His Philosophical Achievement*, ed. Michael Fox. Totowa, N.J.: Barnes & Noble, 1980.

Delaere, Mark. "Classification of Art as Primary Source for Musical Aesthetics: Kant, Hegel, Kierkegaard, and Schopenhauer." *Sonus* 18, no. 2 (1998): 19–37.

Dolson, Grace Neal. "The Influence of Schopenhauer upon Friedrich Nietzsche." *Philosophical Review* 10 (1901): 241–50.

Duvall, Trumbull. "Life as a Task to be Done—Not Understood: Schopenhauer and Nietzsche." In *Great Thinkers.* New York: Oxford University Press, 1937.

Edwards, Jane Elizabeth. "A Genealogy of the Will: A Comparison of the Works of Kant, Schopenhauer, and Nietzsche." Master's thesis, University of Richmond, 1986.

Engel, S. Morris. "Schopenhauer's Impact on Wittgenstein." *Journal of the History of Ideas* 7 (1969): 285–302. Reprinted in Fox (ed.).

Engeman, Thomas Sledge. "Nietzsche and the Natural Man: An Interpretation of 'Schopenhauer as Educator'." Ph.D. diss., Claremont Graduate School, 1973.

Flamm, Matthew Caleb. "Santayana and Schopenhauer." *Transactions of the Charles S. Peirce Society: A Quarterly Journal in American Philosophy* 38, no. 3 (Summer 2002): 413–31.

Force, James E. "The Changing Nature of Nietzsche's God and the Architect's Conquest of Gravity." *Journal of the History of Philosophy* 20 (1982): 179–95.

Foster, George Burman. "Nietzsche and Schopenhauer." In *Friedrich Nietzsche.* New York: Macmillan, 1931.

Glock, Hans-Johann. "Schopenhauer and Wittgenstein: Representation as Language and Will." In *The Cambridge Companion to Schopenhauer*, ed. Christopher Janaway. Cambridge: Cambridge University Press, 1999.

Gomez, Michael A. "The Philosophy of Struggle, the Struggle of Philosophy: Unamuno, Schopenhauer, Kierkegaard, Nietzsche and the Relation to Modernism." Ph.D. diss., Boston University, 2002.

Goodman, Russell. "Schopenhauer and Wittgenstein on Ethics." *Journal of the History of Philosophy* 17 (1979): 437–47.

Gorevan, Patrick. "Scheler's Response to Schopenhauer." *Schopenhauer-Jahrbuch* 77 (1996): 167–79.

Griffiths, A. Phillips. "Wittgenstein and the Fourfold Root of the Principle of Sufficient Reason." *Proceedings of the Aristotelian Society* Supplementary Volume L (1976): 1–20.

———. "Wittgenstein, Schopenhauer, and Ethics." In *Understanding Wittgenstein, Royal Institute of Philosophy Lectures, Vol. 7, 1972–3*, ed. Godfrey Vesey. London: Macmillan, 1974.

Guyer, Paul. "Schopenhauer, Kant, and the Methods of Philosophy." In *The Cambridge Companion to Schopenhauer*, ed. Christopher Janaway. Cambridge: Cambridge University Press, 1999.

Hartman, Richard Otis. "Aspects of Personality as Key Analogical Factors in the Metaphysics of Leibniz and Schopenhauer." Ph.D. diss., Boston University, 1963.

Heidegger, Martin. "Kant's Doctrine of the Beautiful: Its Misinterpretation by Schopenhauer and Nietzsche." In *Nietzsche: A Critical Reader*, ed. Peter R. Sedgwick. Cambridge: Blackwell, 1995.

Higgins, Kathleen Marie. "Schopenhauer and Nietzsche: Temperament and Temporality." In *Willing and Nothingness: Schopenhauer as Nietzsche's Educator*, ed. Christopher Janaway. Oxford: Clarendon Press, 1999.

Holbo, John Christian. "Prolegomena to Wittgenstein's 'Tractatus'." Ph.D. diss., University of California, Berkeley, 1999.

Horton, Robert C. "Overcoming Kant's Legacy: Schopenhauer's Theories of Action, Will and Reason." Ph.D. diss., University of Wisconsin–Madison, 1996.

Horwitz, L. P, and Ari Belenkiy. "Relativistic Notion of Mass and a Resolution of a Conflict between Schopenhauer and Hegel." *Foundations of Physics* 32, no. 6 (2002): 963–79.

Hübscher, Arthur. "Hegel and Schopenhauer: Aftermath and Present," trans. Paul P. Gubbins. In *Schopenhauer: His Philosophical Achievement*, ed. Michael Fox. Totowa, N.J.: Barnes & Noble Books, 1980.

Humphrey, Ted. "Schopenhauer and the Cartesian Tradition." *Journal of the History of Philosophy* 19 (1981): 191–212.

Jacob, Alexander. "From the World-Soul to the Will. The Natural Philosophy of Schelling, Eschenmayer, and Schopenhauer." *Schopenhauer-Jahrbuch* 73 (1992): 19–36.

Jacoby, Gunther. "Schopenhauer, Bergson and Pragmatism." *The Monist* 22 (1912): 593–611.

Janaway, Christopher. "Schopenhauer as Nietzsche's Educator." In *Willing and Nothingness: Schopenhauer as Nietzsche's Educator*, ed. Christopher Janaway. Oxford: Clarendon Press, 1999.

———, ed. *Willing and Nothingness: Schopenhauer as Nietzsche's Educator*. Oxford: Clarendon Press, 1999.

Janik, Allan S. *Essays on Wittgenstein and Weininger*. Atlantic Highlands, N. J.: Humanities Press, 1985.

———. "On Wittgenstein's Relationship to Schopenhauer." In *Zeit der Ernte: Studien zum Stand der Schopenhauer-Forschung, Festschrift für Arthur Hübscher zum 85. Geburtstag*, ed. Wolfgang Schirmacher. Stuttgart-Bad Cannstatt: Frommann-Holzboog, 1982.

———. "Schopenhauer and the Early Wittgenstein." *Philosophical Studies (Ireland)* XV (1966): 76–95.

Kanovitch, Abraham. *The Will to Beauty: Being a Continuation of the Philosophies of Arthur Schopenhauer and Friedrich Nietzsche*. New York: Gold Rose Printing Co., 1923.

Kelly, Michael. *Kant's Ethics and Schopenhauer's Criticism.* London: Swan Sonnenschein, 1910.

———. *Kant's Philosophy as Rectified by Schopenhauer.* London: Sonnenschein, 1909.

Korab-Karpowicz, W. J. "A Point of Reconciliation between Schopenhauer and Hegel." *The Owl of Minerva* 21, no. 2 (Spring 1990): 167–75.

Leinfeller, Warner. "The Development of Transcendentalism–Kant, Schopenhauer, and Wittgenstein." In *Wittgenstein–Ästhetick und transzendentale Philosophie. Akten eines symposiums in Bergen,* ed. Johannessen S. Kjell and Tore Nordenstram. Vienna, 1981.

Leiter, Brian. "The Paradox of Fatalism and Self-Creation in Nietzsche." In *Willing and Nothingness: Schopenhauer as Nietzsche's Educator,* ed. Christopher Janaway. Oxford: Clarendon Press, 1999.

Madison, Timothy J. "Nietzsche and Schopenhauer on Compassion." *Philosophy Now* 29 (October-November 2000).

Magee, Bryan. "Schopenhauer and Professor Hamlyn." *Philosophy* 60 (July 1985): 389–91.

Maidan, Michael. "Max Scheler's Criticism of Schopenhauer's Account of Morality and Compassion." *The Journal of the British Society for Phenomenology* 20, no. 3 (May-August 1989): 225–35.

Marshall, James D. "A Critical Theory of the Self: Wittgenstein, Nietzsche, Foucault." *Studies in Philosophy and Education* 20, no. 1 (2001): 75–91.

Mellor, Stanley Alfred. "Individualism in German Thought, with Special Reference to Nietzsche and Schopenhauer." Ph.D. diss., Harvard University, 1909.

Miller, Louis William. "The Revelation of Genius: Toward an Interpretation of Nietzsche's Early Development." Ph.D. diss., Princeton University, 1994.

Miller, Marjorie C. "Essence and Identity: Santayana and the Category 'Women'." *Transactions of the Charles S. Peirce Society: A Quarterly Journal in American Philosophy* 30, no. 1 (Winter 1994): 33–50.

Molner, D. "The Influence of Montaigne on Nietzsche: A Raison d'Etre in the Sun." *Nietzsche-Studien* 22 (1993): 80–93.

Nanajivako, Bhikkhu. "The Philosophy of Disgust: Buddha and Nietzsche." *Schopenhauer-Jahrbuch* 58 (1977): 112–32.

Nussbaum, Martha C. "Nietzsche, Schopenhauer, Dionysus." In *The Cambridge Companion to Schopenhauer,* ed. Christopher Janaway. Cambridge: Cambridge University Press, 1999.

———. "The Transfigurations of Intoxication: Nietzsche, Schopenhauer, and Dionysus." *Arion* 1, no. 2 (Spring 1991): 75–111. Reprinted in *Nietzsche, Philosophy and the Arts,* ed. Salim Kemal. New York: Cambridge University Press, 1988.

Nutt, Kathleen Ann Craig. "Reason and Its Discontents: Schopenhauer's Critique of Kant as the Foundation of the Philosophy of Nietzsche." Ph.D. diss., Queen's University of Belfast (Northern Ireland), 1991.

Perry, Christopher James. "Flexible Meliorism: A Pragmatic Critique of Leibniz, Schopenhauer, and James." Ph.D. diss., Vanderbilt University, 1998.

Q Fiasco, Flash. "The Subject of Wittgenstein's Tractatus." *The Southern Journal of Philosophy* 26 (Winter 1988): 573–86.

Raulet, Gerard. "What Good is Schopenhauer? Remarks on Horkheimer's Pessimism." *Telos* 42 (Winter 1979–80): 98–106.

Ray, Matthew Alan. "On the Principles and Presuppositions of Atheism and Agnosticism in Kant, Schopenhauer, and Nietzsche." Ph.D. diss., University of Warwick, 2000.

———. *Subjectivity and Irreligion: Atheism and Agnosticism in Kant, Schopenhauer, and Nietzsche*. Burlington, Vt.: Ashgate, 2003.

Ray, Sitansu. "Kant, Hegel, and Schopenhauer on Musical Aesthetics." *Sangeet Natak* 63 (1982): 40–51.

Samuel, Adrian. "The Essential Questions: Heidegger, Schopenhauer and Nietzsche." Ph.D. diss., University of Essex (United Kingdom), 2003.

Santayana, George. "Schopenhauer and Nietzsche." In *The German Mind: A Philosophical Diagnosis*. New York: Thomas Y. Crowell, 1968.

Schuman, Daniel Benton. "Essence and Illusion: Schopenhauer, Nietzsche and the Problem of the Thing-In-Itself." Ph.D. diss., University of Kentucky, 2002.

Schweitzer, Albert. "Schopenhauer and Nietzsche," trans. C. T. Campion. In *Civilization and Ethics (The Philosophy of Civilization, Part II)*, 2nd edn. London: A & C Black, 1929.

Shapshay, Sandra Lynne. "Aesthetic and Moral Deliberation: A Kantian-Schopenhauerian Approach to an Understanding of the Relations between Art and Morality." Ph.D. diss., Columbia University, 2001.

Simmel, Georg. *Schopenhauer and Nietzsche*, trans. Helmut Loiskandl et al. Urbana: University of Illinois Press, 1991.

Snow, Dale, et al. "The Limits of Idealism: Schopenhauer and the Early Schelling on the Nature of Reality." *Ultimate Reality and Meaning* 2 (1991): 84–96.

Soll, Ivan. "The Hopelessness of Hedonism and the Will to Power." *International Studies in Philosophy* 18 (Summer 1986): 97–112.

———. "Pessimism and the Tragic View of Life." In *Reading Nietzsche*, ed. Robert C. Solomon. New York: Oxford University Press, 1988.

———. "Schopenhauer, Nietzsche, and the Redemption of Life through Art." In *Willing and Nothingness: Schopenhauer as Nietzsche's Educator*, ed. Christopher Janaway. Oxford: Clarendon Press, 1999.

Stirling, J. H. "Schopenhauer in Relation to Kant." *Journal of Speculative Philosophy* 13 (1879): 1–50.

Sutton, Claud. "The Aftermath of German Idealism (1): Schopenhauer and Nietzsche." In *The German Tradition in Philosophy*. London: Weidenfeld & Nicolson, 1974.

Taminiaux, Jacques. "Art and Truth in Schopenhauer and Nietzsche." *Man and World* 20 (1987): 85–102.

Taylor, Charles Senn. "Nietzsche's Schopenhauerianism." *Nietzsche-Studien* 17 (1988): 45–73.

Tilghman, Benjamin R. *Wittgenstein, Ethics and Aesthetics: The View from Eternity*. Basingstoke: Macmillan, 1991.

Tortura, Giuseppc. "Kierkegaard and Schopenhauer on Hegelianism: Primum Vivere, Deinde Philosopher." *Metalogicon: Rivista Internazionale di Logica Pura e Applicata di Linguistica e di Filosofia* 7, no. 1 (1994): 69–84.

Touey, Daniel. "Schopenhauer and Nietzsche on the Nature and Limits of Philosophy." *The Journal of Value Inquiry* 32, no. 2 (June 1998): 243–52.

Tsanoff, Radoslav A. *Schopenhauer's Critique of Kant's Theory of Experience*. New York: Longmans Green, 1911.

Van Heerden, Gita S. "The Shift from Rationality to Irrationality in German Aesthetic Theory: Kant, Schelling, Schopenhauer." Ph.D. diss., University of Massachusetts, 1992.

Vandenabelle, Bart. "On the Notion of 'Disinterestedness': Kant, Lyotard, and Schopenhauer." *Journal of the History of Ideas* 62, no. 4 (2001): 705–21.

Weiner, David Avraham. *Genius and Talent: Schopenhauer's Influence on Wittgenstein's Early Philosophy*. Madison, N.J.: Fairleigh Dickinson University Press, 1992.

———. "The Ill-Will against Time: Schopenhauer's Influence on Wittgenstein's Early Philosophy." Ph.D. diss., Yale University, 1989.

Welch, Gregory Stephen. "Der Schopenhauer Fall: Schopenhauer as Nietzsche's Educator." Ph.D. diss., Harvard University, 1990.

Wertz, Spencer K. "Notes on Wittgenstein and His Milieu." *Proceedings of New Mexico–West Texas Philosophical Society* (April 1974): 28–31.

———. "On the Philosophical Genesis of the Term 'Form of Life'." *Southwestern Journal of Philosophy* 6 (1981): 1–16.

White, Richard. "Art and the Individual in Nietzsche's Birth of Tragedy." *The British Journal of Aesthetics* 28 (Winter 1988): 59–67.

Wicks, Robert. "Schopenhauer's Naturalization of Kant's A Priori Forms of Empirical Knowledge." *History of Philosophy Quarterly* 10, no. 2 (April 1993): 181–96.

Wilson, Arnold. "Russell and the Idealists." *Telos* 4 (Fall 1969): 83–94.

Woodruff, David Joseph. "Tractarian Mysticism: Moral Transformation through Aesthetic Contemplation in Wittgenstein's Early Philosophy." Ph.D. diss., University of Illinois at Chicago, 1999.

Yates, Robert Cyrus. "Instrumental and Meditative Thinking: A Comparative Inquiry into Schopenhauer and Heidegger." Master's thesis, University of Guelph (Canada), 1995.

Young, Julian. "Immaculate Perception: Nietzsche contra Schopenhauer." *Schopenhauer-Jahrbuch* 74 (1993): 73–85.

———. "Schopenhauer, Heidegger, Art, and the Will." In *Schopenhauer, Philosophy, and the Arts*, ed. Dale Jacquette. Cambridge: Cambridge University Press, 1996.

———. "Schopenhauer's Critique of Kantian Ethics." *Kantstudien* 75 (1984): 191–212.

———. "Wittgenstein, Kant, Schopenhauer, and Critical Philosophy." *Theoria* 50 (1984): 73–105.

Zöller, Günter. "German Realism: The Self-Limitation of Idealist Thinking in Fichte, Schelling, and Schopenhauer." In *The Cambridge Companion to German Idealism*, ed. Ameriks Karl. Cambridge: Cambridge University Press, 2000.

Other Significant People

Argyle, Gisela. "Gissing's *The Whirlpool* and Schopenhauer." *The Gissing Newsletter* 4, no. 17 (1981): 3–21.

Asher, David. "Schopenhauer and Darwinism." *Journal of Anthropology* 1, art. VIII (1866).

Baer, Joachim T. "Arthur Schopenhauer and S. A. Andreyevsky: Affinities of World View." In *Western Philosophical Systems in Russian Literature: A Collection of Critical Studies*, ed. Anthony M. Mlikotin. University of Southern California Press, 1979.

———. "Leopold Staff and Arthur Schopenhauer." *The Polish Review* XXIV (1979): 57–67.

Bailey, J. O. *Thomas Hardy and the Cosmic Mind: A New Reading of the Dynasts*. Chapel Hill: University of North Carolina Press, 1956.

Barker, Olevia Earlene. "The Reigning Influence of Arthur Schopenhauer upon the Major Works of Thomas Mann." Master's thesis, University of Texas at Arlington, 1992.

Bilsker, Richard. "Freud and Schopenhauer: Consciousness, the Unconscious, and the Drive Towards Death." *Idealistic Studies* 27 (Winter-Spring 1997): 79–90.

———. "Schopenhauer on Willing and the Unconscious: Origins and Legacy." Ph.D. diss., Florida State University, 1994.

Bischler, W. "Schopenhauer and Freud: A Comparison." *Psychoanalytic Quarterly* 8 (1939): 88–97.

Caufield, James Walter. "The World as Will and Idea: Dedalean Aesthetics and Influence of Schopenhauer." *James Joyce Quarterly* 35/36, no. 4/1 (1998): 695–715.

Clegg, Jerry S. "Freud and the Issue of Pessimism." *Schopenhauer-Jahrbuch* 61 (1980): 37–50.

———. "Jung's Quarrel with Freud." *Schopenhauer-Jahrbuch* 66 (1985): 165–76.

Crawford, Karin Lorine. "Love, Music, and Politics in Thomas Mann's 'Tristan,' 'Der Zauberberg', and 'Doktor Faustus'." Ph.D. diss., Stanford University, 2000.

Curry, Bryan Timothy. "Philosophical Pessimism and Gothic Convention in the Fiction of Thomas Hardy." Ph.D. diss., Indiana University, 1988.

Dawe, Mary Wanda. "The Philosophy of Pessimism: The Relation of Schopenhauer's Philosophy to Hardy's Art." Master's thesis, Memorial University of Newfoundland (Canada), 1993.

de Monthoux, Pierre Guillet. "Performing the Absolute. Maria Abramovic Organizing the Unfinished Business of Arthur Schopenhauer." *Organization Studies* 21 (1999): 29–52.

Diffey, T. J. "Metaphysics and Aesthetics: A Case Study of Schopenhauer and Thomas Hardy." In *Schopenhauer, Philosophy, and the Arts*, ed. Dale Jacquette. Cambridge: Cambridge University Press, 1996.

Dismukes, Camillus. "The Influence of F. Nietzsche and A. Schopenhauer on Pio Baroja." Master's thesis, University of North Carolina, 1933.

Dooley, Michael Comstock. "Max Beckmann's 'Trapeze'." Master's thesis, Michigan State University, 1996.

Doss-Davezac, Shehira. "Schopenhauer According to the Symbolists: The Philosophical Roots of Late 19th Century French Aesthetic Theory." In *Schopenhauer, Philosophy, and the Arts*, ed. Dale Jacquette. Cambridge: Cambridge University Press, 1996.

Durer, Christopher S. "Moby Dick's Ishmael, Burke, and Schopenhauer." *Midwest Quarterly* 30 (1989): 161–78.

Eddins, Dwight. "Ted Hughes and Schopenhauer: The Poetry of the Will." *Twentieth Century Literature* 45, no. 1 (1999): 94–110.

Fite, Olive L. "Billy Budd, Claggart, and Schopenhauer." *NCF* 23 (1968): 336–43.

Foote, Janet Voth. "Gissing and Schopenhauer: A Study of Literary Influence." Ph.D. diss., Indiana University, 1968.

Forman, Alfred. "Robert Browning and Schopenhauer." *Schopenhauer-Jahrbuch* 3 (1914): 73.

Garwood, Helen. "Thomas Hardy, an Illustration of the Philosophy of Schopenhauer." Ph.D. diss., University of Pennsylvania, 1909.

———. *Thomas Hardy: An Illustration of the Philosophy of Schopenhauer.* Philadelphia: The I. C. Winston, 1911.

Glickman, Susan. "The World as Will and Idea: A Comparative Study of *An American Dream* and *Mr. Summler's Planet.*" *Modern Fiction Studies* 28 (1982): 569–82.

Gray, Ronald. "The German Intellectual Background." In *The Wagner Companion*, ed. Peter Burridge and Richard Sutton. London: Faber & Faber, 1979.

Gupta, R. K. Das. "Billy Budd and Schopenhauer." *Schopenhauer-Jahrbuch* 73 (1992): 91–107.

———. "Freud and Schopenhauer." *Journal of the History of Ideas* 36 (October-December 1975): 721–28. Reprinted in Fox (ed.).

———. "Melville and Schopenhauer." *Schopenhauer-Jahrbuch* 79 (1998): 149–67.

Guthke, Karl S. "The Deaf Musician: Arthur Schopenhauer Reads Richard Wagner." *Harvard Magazine* 99, no. 1 (September-October 1996).

Hamlyn, D. W. "Schopenhauer and Freud." *Revue Internationale de Philisophie* 42 (1988): 5–17.

Hanson, Eric A. "Gustav Mahler and the Will: Tracing a Motive through the Symphonies." Master's thesis, University of Washington, 1986.

Harvey, Lawrence E. *Samuel Beckett: Poet and Critic.* Princeton, N.J.: Princeton University Press, 1970: Schopenhauer 7–80.

Heath, Apryl Lea Denny. "Phelps, Browning, Schopenhauer, and Music." *Comparative Literatures Studies* 22 (1985): 211–17.

Heller, O. "Goethe and the Philosophy of Schopenhauer." *Journal of Germanic Studies* I (1897): 348–410.

Hudson, Jr., Benjamin Franklin. "Zola and Schopenhauer: The Affinity of Some Aspects of Their Thought as Reflected in the 'Rougon-Macquart' Series." Ph.D. diss., University of Michigan, 1959.

Jarrett, James. "Schopenhauer and Jung." *Spring: An Annual of Archetypal Psychology and Jungian Thought* 81 (1981): 193–204.

Jones, K.. "Schopenhauer and Beckett's Proust." *Etudes Irlandaises* 11 (1986): 71–81.

Kaufmann, Fritz. *Thomas Mann: The World as Will and Representation.* Boston: Beacon Press, 1957.

Kelly, Mary Ann. "Hardy's Reading in Schopenhauer: *Tess of the D'urbervilles.*" *Kolby Library Quarterly* 28 (1982): 183–98.

———. "Schopenhauer's Influence on Hardy's *Jude the Obscure.*" In *Schopenhauer: New Essays in Honor of His 200th Birthday*, ed. Eric Von Der Luft. Lewiston, N.Y.: Edwin Mellen Press, 1988.

——. "Thomas Hardy's Reading in Schopenhauer: 'Tess of the D'Urbervilles'." Ph.D. diss., University of Nebraska–Lincoln, 1980.

Kilbourn, R. J. A. "Redemption Revalued in Tristan und Isolde: Schopenhauer, Wagner, Nietzsche." *University of Toronto Quarterly* 67, no. 4 (1998): 781–89.

Kritsch, Erna. "Schopenhauer's Philosophy in the Poetry of Joseph Weinheber." *Modern Languages Quarterly* XXIII, no. 1: 65–74.

Lefew-Blake, Penelope. *Schopenhauer, Women's Literature, and the Legacy of Pessimism in the Novels of George Eliot, Olive Schreiner, Virginia Woolf, and Doris Lessing.* Lewiston, N.Y.: Edwin Mellen Press, 2001.

——. "Schopenhauerian Will and Aesthetics in Novels by George Eliot, Olive Schreiner, Virginia Woolf, and Doris Lessing." Ph.D. diss., Northern Illinois University, 1992.

Levy-Valensi, E. Amado. "Sin and Salvation in the Ontology of D. H. Lawrence." *Human Context* 7 (Summer 1975): 264–92.

Lovejoy, Arthur O. "Schopenhauer as an Evolutionist." *The Monist* 21 (1911): 195–222.

Luepnitz, Deborah Anna. *Schopenhauer's Porcupines: Intimacy and Its Dilemmas.* New York: Basic Books, 2003.

Luft, David S. "Schopenhauer, Austria, and the Generation of 1905." *Central European History* 16 (1983): 53–75.

Maurer, Sigrid Helga. "Schopenhauer in Russia: His Influence on Turgenev, Fet, and Tolstoy." Ph.D. diss., University of California, Berkeley, 1966.

McCobb, E. A. "*Daniel Deronda* as Will and Representation? George Eliot and Schopenhauer." *Modern Language Review* 80 (1985): 533–49.

——. "The Morality of Musical Genius: Schopenhauerian Views in *Daniel Deronda*." *Forum for Modern Language Studies* 19 (1983): 321–30.

McLaughlin, Sigrid. "Tolstoy and Schopenhauer." *California Slavic Studies* V (1970): 187–245.

Medzhibovskaya, Inessa. "Tolstoy's Projects of Transcendence (Reading The Conversion)." Ph.D. diss., Princeton University, 2001.

Minerbi, Treitel. *Schopenhauer's Philosophy in Italo Svevo's La Coscienza di Zeno.* LaFayette, Ind.: *Modern Fiction Studies*, 1972.

O'Hara, J. D. "Beckett's Schopenhauerien Reading of Proust." In *Schopenhauer: New Essays in Honor of His 200th Birthday*, ed. Eric Von Der Luft. Lewiston, N.Y.: Edwin Mellen Press, 1988.

O'Hara, J. E. "Where There's a Will There's a Way Out: Beckett and Schopenhauer." *College Literature* 8 (1981): 249–70.

Panagopoulos, Nic. *The Fiction of Joseph Conrad: The Influence of Schopenhauer and Nietzsche.* New York: Peter Lang, 1998.

Peacock, Ronald. "Novalis and Schopenhauer: A Critical Transition in Romanticism." In *German Studies Presented to Leonard Ashley Willoughby.* Oxford: Basil Blackwell, 1952.

Pearson, Nels C. "The Moment of Modernism: Schopenhauer's 'Unstable Phantom' in Conrad's *Heart of Darkness* and Stevenson's *The Master of Ballantrae*." *Studies in Scottish Literature* 31 (1999): 182–202.

Proctor-Gregg, Nancy. "Schopenhauer and Freud." *Psychoanalytic Quarterly* 25 (1956): 197–214.

Richards, Walter William. "Nature as a Symbolic Element in Richard Wagner's Treatment of Myth." Ph.D. diss., Florida State University, 1997.

Ross, Marion E. "Schopenhauer and Beckett: 'Knights with Death and Devil'." Ph.D. diss., University of Ulster (Northern Ireland), 1987.

Scheick, William J. "Schopenhauer, Maori Symbolism, and Well's Brynhild." *Studies in the Literary Imagination* 13 (1980): 17–29.

Schneider, Daniel J. "Schopenhauer and the Development of D. H. Lawrence's Psychology." *South Atlantic Review* 48 (1983): 1–19.

Stammler, Heinrich A. "Metamorphoses of the Will: Schopenhauer and Fet." *Western Philosophical Systems in Russian Literature, University of Southern California Series in Slavic Humanities* 3 (1979): 35–58.

Walicki, A. "Turgenew and Schopenhauer." *Oxford Slavonic Papers* 10 (1962): 1–17.

Walsh, Harry. "Marginalia: Schopenhauer's *On the Freedom of the Will* and the Epilogue to *War and Peace*." *Slavic and East European Review* no. 4 (October 1979).

——. "The Place of Schopenhauer in the Philosophical Education of Leo Tolstoi." In *Schopenhauer: New Essays in Honor of His 200th Birthday*, ed. Eric Von Der Luft. Lewiston, N.Y.: Edwin Mellen Press, 1988.

Wright, Emily Powers. "Religious Relations: Nature, Sex, and Tragedy in the Novels of Thomas Hardy and the Early Writings of D. H. Lawrence ." Ph.D. diss., Columbia University, 1990.

Wulf, Catherine. *The Imperative of Narration: Beckett, Bernhard, Schopenhauer, Lacan*. Sussex, UK: Sussex Academic Press, 1998.

Yarbrough, Douglas Bond. "Schopenhauer and Freud: Parallel Thinking in the History of Ideas." Master's thesis, University of Louisville, 1979.

Young, Christopher, and Andrew Brook. "Schopenhauer and Freud." *International Journal of Psychoanalysis* 75 (1994): 101–18.

Zoll, Allan R. "Vitalism and the Metaphysics of Love: D. H. Lawrence and Schopenhauer." *D. H. Lawrence Review* 11 (1978): 1–20.

Electronic Sources

Japan Schopenhauer Association. "Arthur Schopenhauer Mailing List." *Arthur Schopenhauer Homepage*. http://www.schopenhauer.org/mailinglist/index .html, [accessed 31 December 2003].

Schopenhauer-Gesellschaft. "Hompage." *Schopenhauer-Gesellschaft e.V.* http://www.schopenhauer-online.de/start.htm, [accessed 31 December 2003].

Schopenhauer Research Centre. "Schopenhauer Forschungsstelle." *Johannes Gutenberg-Universität Mainz.* http://www.schopenhauer.philosophie.uni-mainz.de/indexe.html, [accessed 14 February 2004].

Stollberg, Jochen. "Schopenhaur-Archive." *Stadt- und Universitätsbibliothek Frankfurt am Main.* http://www.stub.uni-frankfurt.de/archive/eschop.htm, 2001 [accessed 31 December 2003].

Journals/Societies

Schopenhauer-Jahrbuch

This is the annual journal of the Schopenhauer-Gesellschaft. It was founded in 1912 by the philosopher, Indologist, and youthful friend of Friedrich Nietzsche, Paul Deussen, and it continues to this day. It publishes articles on all aspects of Schopenhauer's life, philosophy, related themes, and book reviews. It also contains a thorough bibliography of the recently published primary and secondary literature on Schopenhauer (of publications since its last volume) as well as materials missed in earlier volumes of the *Jahrbuch*. German is the language of the majority of articles, but it also publishes many articles in English, and some in French, Italian, and Spanish. It also includes a yearly report from the director of the Schopenhauer-Archiv.

Volumes 1–31 (1912–1944) appeared as the *Jahrbuch der Schopenhauer-Gesellschaft*. Since volume 32 (1945/1948), it has appeared under its present title. A record of the table of contents for volume 1 through 83 (1912–2002) can be found on the web, http://www.schopenhauer.philoso phie.uni-mainz.de/e-yearbook.htm. At the present time the *Jahrbuch* is published by Verlag Königshausen & Neumann, Würzberg, Germany. Its current editor is the president of the Schopenhauer-Gesellschaft, Prof. Dr. Matthias Kossler, Waldstr. 15, D-55124 Mainz, Germany, kossler@mail.uni-mainz.de. The *Schopenhauer-Jahrbuch* remains the best single source for research on Schopenhauer.

Schopenhauer-Studien

This was the journal of the now defunct Internationale Schopenhauer-Vereinigung (Hamburg, Germany, New York, U.S.A.). It was edited by the president of the Vereinigung, Prof. Dr. Wolfgang Schirmacher. This journal tended to emphasize Schopenhauer's relationship to postmodern thought, and German and English were the languages for almost all of its articles, with most appearing in German. It also included book reviews. Its five volumes, which appeared in four books, were published by Passagen Verlag, Vienna, Austria. The titles for *Schopenhauer-Studien* were

Schopenhauer's Aktualität: Ein Philosoph wird neu gelesen (1988). *Schopenhauer-Studien*, 1 and 2.

Schopenhauer in der Postmoderne (1989). *Schopenhauer-Studien*, 3.

Schopenhauer, Nietzsche und die Kunst (1991). *Schopenhauer-Studien*, 4.

Ethik und Vernunft: Schopenhauer in Unserer Zeit (1995). *Schopenhauer-Studien*, 5

Schopenhauer-Gesellschaft

The Schopenhauer-Gesellschaft was founded in 1911 by the philosopher and Indologist Paul Deussen in Kiel, Germany. Presently, it is centered in Frankfurt am Main, Germany. The purpose of the society is to stimulate and advance the study and understanding of Schopenhauer's philosophy. In addition to publishing the annual *Schopenhauer-Jahrbuch*, it sponsors conferences, seminars, and essay contests concerning Schopenhauer's philosophy. Its membership is international in scope, and it remains one of Germany's largest societies devoted to a single philosopher. In addition to maintaining various regional groups, the society also has divisions in India and the United States of America. Inquiries to the society should be addressed to its president, Prof. Dr. Matthias Kossler, whose address can be found above, within the entry on the *Schopenhauer-Jahrbuch*. The contact address for the Indian Division of the Schopenhauer Society is Professor Arati Barua, 157, Uttarakhand, JNU, New Delhi 110067, India, arati_barua@hotmail.com. The contact address for the North American Division of the Schopenhauer Society is Professor David E. Cartwright, Department of Philosophy and Religious Studies, University of Wisconsin–Whitewater, Whitewater, WI 53190, U.S.A., cartwrid@uww.edu.

Schopenhauer-Archive

The Schopenhauer-Archiv is located in the Stadt- und Universitätsbibliothek, Frankfurt am Main, Germany. It contains collections of

Schopenhauer's manuscripts, letters, and other documents, including a copy of the entire set of manuscript holdings of the Staatsbibliothek Stiftung Preußischer Kulturbesitz Berlin (Schopenhauer's Berlin Lecture Manuscripts). It also maintains displays of Schopenhauer's possessions. It also contains roughly 30 percent of Schopenhauer's personal library, as well as oil paintings, graphics, photographs, sculptures of the philosopher and related figures, and Arthur Hübscher's papers. The director of the archives is Mr. Jochen Stollberg, and the contact address is Stadt- und Universitätsbibliothek, Bockheimer Landstrasse 134–138, D60325 Frankfurt am Main, Germany, stollberg@stub.uni-frankfurt.de.

Schopenhauer-Forschungsstelle

The Schopenhauer-Forschungsstelle (Schopenhauer Research Centre) is affiliated with the University of Mainz and was founded and is directed by Prof. Dr. Matthias Kossler, whose address is given above in the entry for the *Schopenhauer-Jahrbuch*. The purpose of the center is to aid in the research of Schopenhauer's philosophy and to serve as a contact point for specialists in Schopenhauer's philosophy.

About the Author

David E. Cartwright (B.S., University of Wisconsin–Stevens Point; M.A. University of Wyoming; M.A. and Ph.D., University of Wisconsin–Madison) studied biology and philosophy at the University of Wisconsin–Stevens Point, philosophy at the University of Wyoming, and philosophy and German at the University of Wisconsin–Madison. Since 1982, he has taught philosophy, including Schopenhauer, at the University of Wisconsin–Whitewater, where he is professor of philosophy and religious studies. He has published numerous articles on German philosophy and ethics, and he edited and wrote introductions to E. F. J. Payne's translations of Schopenhauer's *On Vision and Colors* and *On the Will in Nature*. He also wrote the introduction to Payne's translation of Schopenhauer's *On the Basis of Morality*, and with Joachim T. Baer, he translated Arthur Hübscher's monumental study, *Denker gegen den Strom. Schopenhauer: Gestern-Heute-Morgan*. He is the director of the North American Division of the Schopenhauer Society, a division of the Internationale Schopenhauer-Gesellschaft, on whose Wissenschaftliche Leitung he has served since 1993. In addition to his passion for Schopenhauer, he indulges in landscape gardening, an art that Schopenhauer claimed expresses a lesser artistic accomplishment than any other art. Although his ownership of a standard poodle might be something that Schopenhauer would have endorsed, he also likely would have been displeased that he does not call the dog Atma or Butz. At the present time, he is working on an intellectual biography of Schopenhauer for Cambridge University Press.